THE IMPRINT OF ANOTHER LIFE

THE IMPRINT OF ANOTHER LIFE

Adoption Narratives and Human Possibility

Margaret Homans

The University of Michigan Press
Ann Arbor

First paperback conversion 2015

Published in the United States of America by
The University of Michigan Press
Manufactured in the United States of America
⊗ Printed on acid-free paper

2018 2017 2016 2015 5 4 3 2

A CIP catalog record for this book is available from the British Library.

Library of Congress Cataloging-in-Publication Data

Homans, Margaret, 1952–
The imprint of another life : adoption narratives and human possibility / Margaret Homans.
pages cm
Includes index.
ISBN 978-0-472-11888-5 (cloth : acid-free paper) — ISBN 978-0-472-02931-0 (e-book)
1. American literature—History and criticism. 2. Families in literature. 3. Adoption in literature. 4. Narration (Rhetoric)—Social aspects. I. Title.
PS169.F35H66 2013
810.9'355—dc23 2013006631

ISBN 978-0-472-03634-9 (pbk. : alk. paper)

to
Sylvia

The missing part, the missing past, can be an opening, not a void. It can be an entry as well as an exit. It is the fossil record, the imprint of another life, and although you can never have that life, your fingers trace the space where it might have been . . .

It's why I am a writer.

—Jeanette Winterson, *Why Be Happy When You Could Be Normal?*

Being adopted for me, then, has not been an identification with an unknown lost family; it has not been a marking of myself as scarred or damaged or as having less knowledge than others who are born into their families. Instead, being adopted has been an identity of *possibility*.

—Kimberly Leighton, "Being Adopted and Being a Philosopher"

Acknowledgments

Since the time I began thinking about this book, the study of adoption and culture has become a scholarly field, and I am grateful beyond measure to Marianne Novy, to Emily Hipchen and Carol Singley, and to the other scholars who founded both the field and its professional organization, the Alliance for the Study of Adoption and Culture (ASAC). Its lively biannual conferences starting in 2005, its Modern Language Association sessions, its newsletter, and the journal *Adoption & Culture* have together created an ideal community—both welcoming and challenging—in which to develop ideas and readings. ASAC conferences introduced me to some of the writers and filmmakers discussed here, as well as enabling me to learn from adoption scholars across the disciplines. In addition to those mentioned above, I have especially benefited from conversation with ASAC members Cynthia Callahan, Mark Jerng, the late Betty Jean Lifton, Barbara Yngvesson, and Claudia Nelson, who also generously invited me to give an early version of one chapter as a lecture at Texas A&M University.

Before I knew that adoption would be worth writing about, Holly Laird invited me to contribute to a special adoption issue of *Tulsa Studies in Women's Literature* that appeared in 2002. I am grateful to her and to the other writers in that issue for giving me a place to start.

Parts of this book appeared, in different forms, in the following publications, and I am grateful to the editors for spurring me to write by inviting my contributions: "Adoption Narratives, Trauma, and Origins," *Narrative* 14, no. 1 (January 2006); "Origins, Searches, and Identity: Narratives of Adoption from China," *Contemporary Women's Writing* 1, nos. 1–2 (December 2007); "'The Mother Who Isn't One': New Stories by Birthmothers," *Adoption & Culture* 2 (2009); and "Adoption and Return: Transnational Genealogies, Maternal Legacies," in *Rites of Return: Diaspora Poetics and the Politics of Memory,* edited by Marianne Hirsch and Nancy K. Miller (New York: Columbia University Press, 2011). "'The Mother Who Isn't One'" and "Adoption and Return" are reprinted with permission of their publishers. Great thanks to Jim Phelan, to Susan Stanford Friedman, to Marianne Novy and Emily Hipchen, and to Nancy Miller and Marianne Hirsch for their invitations and encouragement and for their sound editorial advice.

I am particularly grateful to the International Society for the Study of Narrative for giving "Adoption Narratives, Trauma, and Origins" its award for the best essay published in *Narrative* in its year and to audiences at the annual Narrative Conference, who have listened to and asked probing questions of several early versions of work that appears here. Peggy Phelan gave me much-needed encouragement.

I would like to thank Yale University not only for the triennial leaves during which I wrote most of this book but also for the opportunity to teach an undergraduate seminar on adoption narratives several times beginning in 2006. The resourceful, brilliant, generous students in those classes taught me as much as I learned from any other source, helped me to work out readings of many of the literary texts discussed here, and challenged me to defend and revise my ideas about adoption. I have been especially lucky to have had as a student Jenna Cook, whose work on adoption long preceded, and flourishes beyond, my seminar.

Marianne Novy and two anonymous readers for the University of Michigan Press read the entire manuscript with great care and gave me many valuable suggestions for revision; I am grateful to them and to LeAnn Fields and Alexa Ducsay at the press for their thoughtful and generous assistance.

For ongoing conversation about our children as well as their love and support, I thank the members of Spence-Chapin Group 37, who went to China together to adopt our children in 1999 and have stayed close ever since. My dear friends Patricia Klindienst and Julie Rivkin helped me talk through many of the issues raised by my research and to see where I was going when I couldn't see my way myself. Linda Anderson helped in ways too many to count. My older daughter Marian provided precious companionship over the years and technical assistance at the very end. My greatest debt is to my sister and brother-in-law, Katy Homans and Patterson Sims, who led me into the world of adoption and who share my appetite for conversation about it; and to their beloved children from China, and mine—Mardet and Lally, and Sylvia—who, growing up together, have always grounded my thoughts about adoption.

Contents

INTRODUCTION
"Something More and Less than Kinship"

Over the last decade, since becoming an adoptive parent, I have been reading about adoption in an effort to understand how people talk about their experiences of it: the passionately held beliefs that motivate the choices they make and the joys and sorrows that accompany each stage of life with adoption. In the course of my reading—in social science research; in political and historical analysis; in testimony and memoirs; and in fiction, poetry, and drama—I have come to see that adoption raises the most vital questions about human identity and the value and meaning of individual human lives. This book is my attempt to give order both to what I learned about adoption and to what I think adoption reveals.

This book uses readings of literature, documentary films, advice manuals, social science writing, and informal writings by and published interviews with adoptees, parents, and birth parents to address a series of questions about common beliefs about adoption. Underlying these beliefs is the assumption that human qualities are innate and intrinsic, an assumption often held by adoptees and their families, sometimes at great emotional cost. This book explores representations of adoption that reimagine human possibility by questioning this assumption and conceiving of alternatives.

Racial and genetic essentialisms play a large role in adoption. Current popular discourses of adoption assume that even the smallest infant is who she is by birth and that she carries this innate identity wherever she may go in life, even if she knows little or nothing about "who she is." Does an adoptee's identity derive from her DNA, her "blood," her "birth culture," or instead from her upbringing? If identity is innate, and her body is its principal carrier, can an adoptee's social identity livably diverge from the social meaning of her appearance?

Equally striking is the passion with which adoptees demand information about their birth, search for birth families, and invest emotionally in reunions. Does an adoptee's point of origin determine her identity? Can her—can anyone's—origin be known, and what will she accomplish by knowing it? What might alleviate the sorrow of the adoptee who believes her only hope is to be reunited with the birth family she may never find?

Anxiety about money also plays a large role in adoption. Is it never acceptable to exchange money for a child or to instrumentalize a child—to require that she serve the needs of others beside herself? Is human value exclusively intrinsic, never relative or dependent on exchanges? What reply can be offered to the adoptee who believes she was bought on an international market akin to the slave trade?

And finally, why do birthmothers typically occupy positions of abjection and silence in relation to the other two members of the adoption triad? If our biocentric models of family require the birthmother's absence, what other models might ensure her return? What would enable birthmothers to represent themselves and tell their stories?

This book uses literature to think about the early twenty-first-century dilemmas prompted by adoption's challenges to normative, essentializing views of the human. Literature and other cultural forms both delimit what is thinkable and make available new ways of thinking. The romance plot of the special child who is cut off from his origin but is then recognized and restored to his birthright is as old and as compelling as Moses and Christ; does the power of this story make it difficult to imagine other desirable outcomes for a child separated from her first parents? Marianne Novy argues that adoption narratives have historically been limited to a finite set of plots; this book, like hers, tries to see what might lie beyond, or complicate, these options.[1] In order to find out what else we might imagine, I use literary methods to read the kinds of texts that do not usually receive a literary critic's scrutiny, to uncover, for example, the counter-story that a research scholar's metaphors may be telling even as she states what she can logically argue to be true, or to parse a birthmother's silences in an oral history. Alternatives to the stories we now tell ourselves about the limits of human being, identity, and possibility—stories that I believe lead to needless pain—may be with us, not yet recognized.

Adoption has a special relationship to fiction making. Adoption has long been seen as a fictive or "as if" form of family making, fabricated

1. The three main adoption plots she finds in European and American literature are "the disastrous adoption and search for birth parents . . . the happy reunion . . . and the happy adoption": Marianne Novy, *Reading Adoption: Family and Difference in Fiction and Drama* (Ann Arbor: University of Michigan Press, 2005), 7.

or figurative instead of biological or literal. In her pioneering history of adoption in the United States, Judith Modell made the terms "*as-if-begotten*" and "*as-if-genealogical*" indispensable for thinking about adoption.[2] Barbara Katz Rothman opens her sociological study of adoption, *Weaving a Family*, with the idea that adoptive families are made, not born, and must rely on the resources of art—weaving, performing, "mak[ing] a coherent story"—in order to "present" themselves as "ordinary."[3] Memoirist Wayson Choy describes his adoption (discovered late in life) as a form of creation comparable to his own art: "I had been writing fiction about life in Chinatown; Chinatown, all these years, had been writing me."[4] In a less positive tone, an adoptee named Jody, interviewed in Sheila Ganz's documentary *Unlocking the Heart of Adoption*, remarks that despite having had the most loving parents, "I still felt like I was invented, that I invented myself."[5] Or as Jeanette Winterson puts it, "adopted children are self-invented because we have to be; there is an absence, a void, a question mark at the very beginning of our lives." But that "question mark" can be (though it is not always) the prompting for acts of creativity, as Winterson continues: "the missing part, the missing past, can be an opening, not a void. It can be an entry as well as an exit."[6] That orphanhood and adoption are rich resources for fictional narrative has long been recognized. Orphanhood is among the most common ways of producing an interesting hero and plot in the classic English novel, a legacy eloquently extended in J. K. Rowling's Harry Potter novels. In the American tradition, orphanhood and adoption figure significantly in representations of national self-invention: those who "light out for the territory" (in Twain's great phrase) leave their origins behind.

Adoption tends to generate stories rather than uncover bedrock truths. Adoption is lived and represented through an irresolvable tension between essentializing and anti-essentialist apprehensions of human being: between belief in the innate givenness of human traits and

2. Judith S. Modell, *Kinship with Strangers: Adoption and Interpretations of Kinship in American Culture* (Berkeley: University of California Press, 1994), 2.

3. Barbara Katz Rothman, *Weaving a Family: Untangling Race and Adoption* (Boston: Beacon Press, 2005), 4. She maintains the metaphor of weaving throughout the book.

4. Wayson Choy, "The Ten Thousand Things," in *Writing Home: A PEN Canada Anthology*, ed. Constance Rooke (Toronto: McClelland and Stewart, 1997), rpt. in *The Norton Reader*, ed. Linda H. Peterson and John C. Brereton, 11th ed. (New York: W. W. Norton, 2004), 12–17, quotation at 17.

5. Sheila Ganz, prod. and dir., *Unlocking the Heart of Adoption*, DVD (San Francisco: Pandora's Box Productions, 2003).

6. Jeanette Winterson, *Why Be Happy When You Could Be Normal?* (London: Jonathan Cape, and New York: Grove Press, 2011), 5.

belief in their madeness, contingency, and changeability.[7] When Winterson writes that "the missing past" is "the fossil record, the imprint of another life," and that "your fingers trace the space where it might have been," she speaks for adoptees and their parents who, in attempting to recover unrecoverable pasts, of necessity create new stories. Winterson became a writer so as "to tell my own." In the chapters of this book I investigate this tension as it pulls and tugs in the critical areas where controversies about adoption tend to cluster: around value, origins, identity, and self-representation. I structure each set of readings to highlight the anti-essentializing potential of each question, even as I pay heed to the socially normative power and, hence, psychological pull of genetic and other essentialisms. My goal is not to choose one side of a binary opposition over the other, however, but rather to show some of the ways in which literary creation, and a concept of adoption as a form of creativity, manage this tension.

This book is not a historical study or an attempt to cover exhaustively a particular body of literature; it is instead an account of how literature helped me—and could help anyone—to think about adoption. It is therefore a series of meditations on thematic questions, and these questions have directed my eclectic choice of texts for study. Three recent books—by Mark C. Jerng, Carol J. Singley, and Cynthia Callahan—present differing yet compatible historical arguments about adoption in American literature from colonial times to the present.[8] Marianne Novy's *Reading Adoption* constructs a transatlantic adoption canon, defined by her experiences as a reader and ranging from *Oedipus the King* through Shakespeare to late-twentieth-century American fiction, through which she offers a comprehensive cultural history of adoption practices and their representations.[9] I signal my indebtedness and, occasionally, my

---

7. My essay "Adoption and Essentialism," *Tulsa Studies in Women's Literature* 21, no. 2 (Fall 2002): 257–74, includes a semiautobiographical account of my first encounter with adoption's essentialisms and anti-essentialisms.

8. Mark C. Jerng, *Claiming Others: Transracial Adoption and National Belonging* (Minneapolis: University of Minnesota Press, 2010), treats the key role of adoption in changing constructions of American personhood from captivity narratives of the 1820s to the present; Carol J. Singley, *Adopting America: Childhood, Kinship, and National Identity in Literature* (New York: Oxford University Press, 2011), reads American literature from Cotton Mather to Edith Wharton to show how adoption articulates a nation-defining tension between freedom and dependency; and Cynthia Callahan, *Kin of Another Kind: Transracial Adoption in American Literature* (Ann Arbor: University of Michigan Press, 2011), covers the long twentieth century and studies changing attitudes to transracial adoption.

9. In addition to *Reading Adoption,* Novy's pioneering edited collection includes essays

disagreements as they come up, but my aims are different. Most though not all of the literary texts I treat are American, most though not all are twentieth- and twenty-first-century, and there is some overlap between these scholars' canons and mine, but my choices have been determined by their utility for shedding light on contemporary problems and crises in adoption discourse rather than by any claim of mine that they form a comprehensive canon. Disregarding generic boundaries, I also treat some major works of psychological, social, and political analysis of adoption not just as resources for historical context but also as representations of adoption in their own right. I disregard what used to be an impassible conceptual line between transracial and transnational adoption,[10] and I also tend to disregard any line between these two types of adoption and same-race, domestic adoption, because the questions and controversies that interest me cross these lines. Are children beyond price; does love have no economy? Is an adoptee's origin her destiny? Do innate physical traits, including racialized features, determine identity? Must birthmothers remain the mute ground from which adoption's figurative energies spring? Each text I consider has its own historical context, but adoption of all kinds raises these common issues, and different types of adoption can shed fresh light on one another.

Adoption can provide release and relief from the constricting force of what Donna Haraway calls "genetic essentialism," the commonly unquestioned assumption that genetic inheritance precedes and trumps all other sources of identity formation.[11] Toward the close of her ambivalent family memoir about California, Joan Didion finds in adoption just this kind of solace. Watching her five-year-old daughter, dressed in a pinafore and a straw hat and walking down the replica of an 1850 Sacramento street where Didion's forebears once really walked and even kept a saloon, Didion writes,

---

on literary representations of adoption that have also been foundational for this field: Marianne Novy, ed., *Imagining Adoption: Essays on Literature and Culture* (Ann Arbor: University of Michigan Press, 2001).

10. Mary Lyndon Shanley broke ground by crossing this line in *Making Babies, Making Families: What Matters Most in an Age of Reproductive Technologies, Surrogacy, Adoption, and Same-Sex and Unwed Parents* (Boston: Beacon Press, 2001).

11. Donna Haraway, "A Manifesto for Cyborgs," *Socialist Review* 80 (Mar.–Apr. 1985): 65–107; and Haraway, "Universal Donors in a Vampire Culture: It's All in the Family: Biological Kinship Categories in the Twentieth-Century United States," in *Uncommon Ground: Toward Reinventing Nature,* ed. William Cronon (New York: W. W. Norton, 1995), 321–66.

> I was about to explain this to Quintana—the saloon, the wooden sidewalk, the generations of cousins who had walked just as she was walking down just this street on days just this hot—when I stopped. Quintana was adopted. Any ghosts on this wooden sidewalk were not in fact Quintana's responsibility. This wooden sidewalk did not in fact represent anywhere Quintana was from. Quintana's only attachments on this wooden sidewalk were right now, here, me and my mother.
>
> In fact I had no more attachment to this wooden sidewalk than Quintana did: it was no more than a theme, a decorative effect.
>
> It was only Quintana who was real.
>
> Later it seemed to me that this had been the moment when all of it— . . . the entire enchantment under which I had lived my life—began to seem remote.[12]

Identifying with her adopted daughter rescues Didion from the enchantment, which in the book is also the stranglehold, of her genetic heritage. The daughter's story cures the mother's nostalgia and helps her reformulate her own story. At first, the daughter's story seems to produce this effect only by subscribing to the same genetic essentialism from which the mother suffers: the relief Quintana provides depends upon her being "from" somewhere that is not here. But there is a difference: Didion translates genetic essentialism into the terms of location; and the curious and specific formulation "anywhere Quintana was from" (in place of the expected "where she was from") suggests too that Quintana might be from anywhere, which is to say nowhere, and that this kind of origination might be enviable. Then the passage moves beyond even a residual genetic (or locational) essentialism. "It was only Quintana who was real" shifts the speaker from her futile endeavor to travel back to the past to life lived in the present.

Popular representations and much social science literature about adopted children paint a contrasting picture of the effects of adoption on identity formation. Far from a release from constricting genetic essentialism, adoption is commonly viewed and experienced as depriving people of the real and irreplaceable heritage on which their lives depend. Paul, an adoptee interviewed in Ganz's *Unlocking the Heart of Adoption,* describes the urgency behind his search for information about his birth parents:

12. Joan Didion, *Where I Was From* (New York: Knopf, 2003), 219–20.

> The sense of being in time, the sense of being part of the human race, the sense of being part of a continuum that started with Adam and Eve and is going to go on till kingdom come: I don't feel that at all; I feel completely severed from any sense of roots; I feel completely uprooted; I feel like I'm living in this strange separated slice of time. I'm having a hard time joining up my history and what came before . . . and having a sense of moving beyond today into the future.

Being a human being, from this perspective, depends upon having and knowing one's roots. Life without knowledge of one's roots feels like "living without a vital internal organ."[13] Echoing this common simile, a child told adoption therapist Debbie Riley that "trying to develop an identity without information about his past was like 'running without legs. It can't be done.'"[14] And indeed, when Didion returns to her daughter's story in her elegy *Blue Nights,* she writes of the fear of abandonment that shadowed Quintana's short life and of her own egregious failure—perhaps exemplified by the writing of the passage quoted above from *Where I Was From*—to recognize Quintana's losses.[15]

In domestic adoption, the view that adoptees suffer from the loss of their roots has produced groundswells of enthusiasm for searches, reunions, and open adoption and of popular advocacy for the unsealing of legal records (advocacy that has not yet, however, been matched by much legislative change). In domestic transracial adoption, starting with the 1972 statement by the National Association of Black Social Workers (NABSW) that "Black children belong, physically, psychologically and culturally in Black families,"[16] and despite federal legislation in the 1990s aimed at promoting it, this has meant great wariness about the consequences for children of color being raised in households lacking individuals of the same race.[17] In transnational adoption, the oxymoron-

---

13. Adam Pertman, *Adoption Nation: How the Adoption Revolution Is Transforming America* (New York: Basic Books, 2000), 93.
14. "FCC Asks Debbie Riley," interview by Mary Child, *Journal of Families with Children from China* 1, no. 1 (Spring 2009): 20–21, 43–45, quotation at 44.
15. Joan Didion, *Blue Nights* (New York: Knopf, 2011).
16. National Association of Black Social Workers, position paper, Apr. 1972, rpt. in Rita J. Simon and Howard Altstein, *Transracial Adoption* (New York: John Wiley and Sons, 1977), 50–52.
17. Major critiques of transracial adoption include: Sandra Patton, *BirthMarks: Transracial Adoption in Contemporary America* (New York: New York University Press, 2000); Pamela Anne Quiroz, *Adoption in a Color-Blind Society* (Lanham, MD: Rowman and Littlefield, 2007); and Laura Briggs, *Somebody's Children: The Politics of Transracial and Transnational Adoption* (Durham: Duke University Press, 2012).

ic term "birth culture" has been coined to construct an essentialized, identity-generating cultural origin, and new norms of "culture keeping" have arisen that are intended to compensate for the child's displacement from her biological and national origins.[18] A recent essay by Alice Diver lays out the groundwork, in international law, "to conceptualize as a basic human right the hypothetical right to avoid origin deprivation" and attributes to every child an "inherent biogenetic culture."[19] As Toby Alice Volkman puts it in a study of US adoption from China:

> The social pendulum has swung from the virtual denial of adoption and the biological beginnings of the adopted child to an insistent ideology that without an embrace of those beginnings there will forever be a gaping hole, a primal wound, an incomplete self. . . . Searching to repair the wounded self and broken narrative seems almost compulsory. The activism efforts of [domestic] adoptees and birth mothers, changes in adoption law in many states, open adoptions of various sorts, the prevalence of searches and reunions and literature describing them, social work discourse, and recent work in genetics all have created a set of new cultural pressures to find the missing genetic link, what Kaja Finkler calls "the kin in the gene."[20]

Or as Eleana Kim describes this "social pendulum": "The reversal of prior models that advocated secrecy and pathologized adoptees who longed for biogenetic connections as maladjusted has been so complete that adoptees who may not want to find their roots or who are not involved in a search of origins are often viewed as being repressed or in denial."[21]

18. For discussion of the term "birth culture" see Toby Alice Volkman, "Embodying Chinese Culture: Transnational Adoption in North America," *Social Text* 74 (Spring 2003): 29–55, rpt. in *Cultures of Transnational Adoption,* ed. Toby Alice Volkman (Durham: Duke University Press, 2005), 81–113, quotation at 97. For "culture keeping," see Ann Anagnost, "Scenes of Misrecognition: Maternal Citizenship in the Age of Transnational Adoption," *Positions* 8 (2000): 389–421; and Heather Jacobson, *Culture Keeping: White Mothers, International Adoption, and the Negotiation of Family Difference* (Nashville: Vanderbilt University Press, 2008).

19. Alice Diver, "Conceptualizing the 'Right' to Avoid Origin Deprivation: International Law and Domestic Implementation," *Adoption & Culture* 3 (2012): 141–80, quotations at 141, 149.

20. Volkman, "Embodying Chinese Culture," 97–98, citing Kaja Finkler, "The Kin in the Gene: The Medicalization of Family and Kinship in American Society," *Current Anthropology* 42 (2001): 235–63.

21. Eleana J. Kim, *Adopted Territory: Transnational Korean Adoptees and the Politics of Belonging* (Durham: Duke University Press, 2010), 91. She points not only to the "geneticization of identity" but also to the "medicalization of adoptee experience through

In this swing of "the social pendulum," history is understood to inhere in the body, as the repeated use of the organic metaphors of "roots" and of a missing organ or limb help to make clear. The UN Convention on the Rights of the Child (1989) and the 1993 Hague Convention on Intercountry Adoption based on it (signed by the United States in 1998) confer on children rights to the preservation of their "ethnic, religious, cultural and linguistic background,"[22] a "right to origin"—like Diver's hypothetical human right to preserve "inherent biogenetic culture"—the argument for which depends, as Mark C. Jerng points out, upon "conflat[ing] biological processes of reproduction with historical continuities."[23] Adam Pertman emphasizes what he sees as the universal desire of adoptees to know their "background," to find the "people out there . . . with whom they had shared . . . hundreds of years of history,"[24] as if history were embodied in such physical locations as the missing "internal organ" he says adoptees need to find. In this model,

> identity is associated with a root or ground of belonging that is inside the child (as "blood," "primal connectedness," and "identity hunger") (Lifton 1994, 67–71) and is unchanging. But it is also outside the child in the sense that it is assumed to tie him or her to others whom he or she is like (as defined by skin color, hair texture, facial features, and so forth). Alienation from this source of likeness produces "genealogical bewilderment" (Sants 1964, cited in Lifton 1994, 68) and a psychological need for the adopted child to return to where he or she "really" belongs.[25]

---

conditions such as Reactive Attachment Disorder" (88). See also Signe Howell, who holds "psycho-technocrats"—social workers and other state-authorized experts—responsible for establishing "biogenetic connectedness as the mainstay of kinship": "Return Journeys and the Search for Roots: Contradictory Values Concerning Identity," in *International Adoption: Global Inequalities and the Circulation of Children,* ed. Diana Marre and Laura Briggs (New York: New York University Press, 2009), 256–70, quotation at 258.

22. UN Convention on the Rights of the Child (1989), Article 20, www.unicef.org/crc.
23. Jerng, *Claiming Others,* 142; see also Toby Alice Volkman, "Introduction: New Geographies of Kinship," in Volkman, *Cultures of Transnational Adoption,* 1–22; and Barbara Yngvesson, *Belonging in an Adopted World: Race, Identity, and Transnational Adoption* (Chicago: University of Chicago Press, 2010), 19, 49–50.
24. Pertman, *Adoption Nation,* 78.
25. Barbara Yngvesson, "Going 'Home': Adoption, Loss of Bearings, and the Mythology of Roots," *Social Text* 74 (Spring 2003): 7–27, rpt. in Volkman, *Cultures of Transnational Adoption,* 25–48, quotation at 26. She quotes Betty Jean Lifton, *Journey of the Adopted Self: A Quest for Wholeness* (New York: Basic Books, 1994), who cites H. J. Sants, "Genealogical Bewilderment in Children with Substitute Parents," *British Journal of Medical Psychology* 37 (1964): 352–65.

Views and terms such as Lifton's and Pertman's have achieved wide and enduring popular acceptance. From the point of view of the adopted child, loss is almost always troped as biological or organic, a "hole" the filling in of which can "never be complete."[26] And this critique of adoption is made not just on the grounds of individual psychological well-being: the NABSW argued that transracial adoption is bad not only for black children but for the black communities they leave behind, for which it is "a form of genocide."

The friction created by this swing of "the social pendulum" is especially visible in debates over the merits of the overlapping categories of transracial and transnational adoption. Against the view (exemplified by the NABSW) that children are damaged by their removal from their original contexts, Elizabeth Bartholet celebrates transracial and transnational adoptions as expressions of antidiscrimination that promise a salutary mixing of the world's peoples and offer a "model of how we might better learn to live with one another in this society."[27] Claudia Castaneda, among others, critiques this attitude not only for its dependence on the perpetuation of global inequalities that make certain kinds of children available for adoption and not others but also for its dependence on detaching the child from the communities and histories to which her race connects her.[28] For Castaneda, advocacy for transracial and transnational adoption requires a superficial view of race and an "evacuation of history" that "produce[s] a space behind the surface, an empty body, on which to write a story."[29] Castaneda's critique of Bartholet presumes that history inheres in or fills the body, that "race [is] a natural fact, as something that means beneath the skin,"[30] a position hotly contested in recent debates about the history and politics of race. Walter Benn Michaels, for example, points out that the idea that race inheres in the blood and skin has roots in the violent racisms of the Jim Crow era and the xenophobic nativism of the early twentieth-century United States; in *Against Race,* Paul Gilroy similarly traces the modern European concept of race to fascist genocidal anti-Semitism and argues, in the name of cosmopolitanism and "planetary humanism," that "the old, modern idea of 'race' can

26. Yngvesson, "Going 'Home,'" 36.

27. Elizabeth Bartholet, *Family Bonds: Adoption and the Politics of Parenting* (Boston: Houghton Mifflin, 1993), 112.

28. For other critiques of Bartholet see also the works cited in footnote 17, above.

29. Claudia Castaneda, *Figurations: Child, Bodies, Worlds* (Durham: Duke University Press, 2002), 96. Castaneda would likely be just as critical of Didion's description of her daughter as being from "anywhere."

30. Castaneda, *Figurations,* 106.

have no ethically defensible place" in twenty-first-century "multicultural social and political life."[31]

A longstanding American preoccupation with "blood" has become more pronounced with the completion of the Human Genome Project and its promise of ever-growing knowledge of what genes explain. This preoccupation derives in part from our history of race slavery and our historic certainty that blood, even just "one drop" of it, determines human fate. Transracially adopted children, including many transnationally adopted children, need to be equipped for a lifetime of being interpellated, often but not only in racist ways, as belonging to the race(s) of their birth parents, although the assumptions that race is the same as genetic inheritance and that genetic inheritance is the same as cultural heritage are open to question. Over the last three decades, social scientists and other observers have demonstrated the fictitious basis of much that passes for biological fact. Calling for an end to kinship based on blood, Donna Haraway writes:

> The community of race, nation, nature, language, and culture transmitted by blood and kinship never disappeared from popular racialism in the United States; but this bonding has not been meaningfully sustained by the biological sciences for half a century.[32]

In the 1980s, anthropologist David Schneider made the now widely accepted argument, through cross-cultural comparisons, that kinship produces the biological base it appears to derive from, that there are no universal biological relationships "out there in reality" waiting for the social scientist to describe them, and that "biologistic" explanations of character are a European bias.[33] Haraway denounces the fetishization of blood- and gene-based kinship as not only bad science but bad morals:

> I am sick to death of bonding through kinship and "the family"; and I long for models of solidarity and human unity and difference rooted in

31. Walter Benn Michaels, *Our America: Nativism, Modernism, and Pluralism* (Durham: Duke University Press, 1995); Paul Gilroy, *Against Race: Imagining Political Culture Beyond the Color Line* (Cambridge: Harvard University Press, 2000), 6.

32. Haraway, "Universal Donors," 342.

33. Sarah Franklin and Susan McKinnon, "Introduction: Relative Values: Reconfiguring Kinship Studies," in *Relative Values: Reconfiguring Kinship Studies,* ed. Sarah Franklin and Susan McKinnon (Durham: Duke University Press, 2001), 1–25, this topic at 2–3. They draw on David Schneider, *A Critique of the Study of Kinship* (Ann Arbor: University of Michigan Press, 1984).

> friendship, work, partially shared purposes, intractable collective pain, inescapable mortality, and persistent hope. It is time to theorize an "unfamiliar" unconscious, a different primal scene, where everything does not stem from the dramas of identity and reproduction. Ties through blood—including blood recast in the coin of genes and information—have been bloody enough already. I believe that there will be no racial or sexual peace, no livable nature, until we learn to produce humanity through something more and less than kinship.[34]

By Schneider's and Haraway's logic, the past itself in which the adoptee is said to be organically rooted is itself a construct, the product of urgent needs felt in the present. And in a recent critique of the concept of "genealogical bewilderment," Kimberly Leighton argues that the imperative to know one's biogenetic heritage, so widely accepted in the adoption community, is not an essential human need but, rather, a response to social norms that regulate race and reproduction and invalidate family forms not based on biogenetic connection and racial homogeneity.[35]

Indeed, despite mainstream adoption culture's allegiance to biocentric models of kinship, non-genetic and non-blood family forms that owe nothing to biological origins are rapidly emerging, in gay and lesbian families,[36] in the fertility clinic,[37] in cyberspace, and in adoption agencies and the new cultural forms—for example, the "sisterhood" of all the girls adopted from China—that they are cybernetically spawning.[38] Working from Schneider's critique of "blood" as a faulty basis for understanding kinship, anthropologist and adoption scholar Christine Gailey sees all family forms depending not on shared biogenetic substance but on what she calls "substantiation," which she defines as the process by which people enter into "a web of sharing, obligation, reciprocal claiming, and emotional and material support that is considered . . . family."[39] Seeking to emphasize "the absence of naturalness in all kinship," Gailey insists that "shared genetic material may exist, but it is only a ground for

---

34. Haraway, "Universal Donors," 366.
35. Kimberly Leighton, "Addressing the Harms of Not Knowing One's Heredity: Lessons from Genealogical Bewilderment," *Adoption & Culture* 3 (2012): 63–107.
36. Kath Weston, *Families We Choose* (New York: Columbia University Press, 1991).
37. Charis Thompson, "Strategic Naturalizing: Kinship in an Infertility Clinic," in Franklin and McKinnon, *Relative Values*, 175–202.
38. Franklin and McKinnon, "Introduction: Relative Values," 6–11.
39. Christine Gailey, *Blue-Ribbon Babies and Labors of Love: Race, Class, and Gender in U.S. Adoption Practice* (Austin: University of Texas Press, 2010), 117–18 (this quotation and the next).

kinship formation if people think it is." There is no "kin that is not built or believed."

Complementing these ethnographies of new family concepts and forms, and as if in response to Haraway's call for a theory of "an 'unfamiliar' unconscious, a different primal scene," Judith Butler nominates Antigone, "who concludes the Oedipal drama [but] fails to produce heterosexual closure for that drama," as the founding figure of a new psychoanalytic theory, one that would defy heteronormativity and embrace other forms of family romance than those that have been central to Freudian theory and, hence, to normative concepts of identity formation in the United States.[40] In the world of Antigone's family, names for family positions are slippery and interchangeable: brother is also father, mother is also grandmother. On the analogy, too, of "blended families [in which] a child says 'mother' and might expect more than one individual to respond to the call," Butler goes on to suggest positive implications for adoptive families:

> In the case of adoption, a child might say "father" and might mean both the absent phantasm she never knew as well as the one who assumes that place in living memory. The child might mean that at once, or sequentially, or in ways that are not always clearly disarticulated from one another. [In the case of a single mother,] is the father absent, or does this child have no father, no position, and no inhabitant? Is this a loss, which assumes the unfulfilled norm, or is it another configuration of primary attachment whose primary loss is not to have a language in which to articulate its terms?[41]

If "loss . . . assumes the unfulfilled norm," then, as in Leighton's critique of "genealogical bewilderment," the problem lies with the norm, not with the new family form that challenges it. Adoption here has the potential not only to destabilize invidious binaries such as nature and culture, blood and water, but also to put into practice "another configuration of primary attachment" for which there is not yet a common or popular language. The emergence of such a language, however, might help to render recognizable and livable relationships and identities that have not historically counted as such: a daughter's having two mothers or four parents, for example, a situation Deann Borshay Liem struggles

40. Judith Butler, *Antigone's Claim* (New York: Columbia University Press, 2000), 76.
41. Butler, *Antigone's Claim,* 69.

to comprehend and inhabit in her film *First Person Plural;* or a transnational adoptee's belonging to two nations or to none, a situation named and experimentally lived by "KAD Nation," Korean adoptees who "see our KAD culture and identity as stronger than our ties to either the birth or adoptive cultures."[42]

Some recent major works of scholarship on adoption—among others, book-length ethnographies by Sandra Patton, Barbara Yngvesson, and Eleana J. Kim, and Mark C. Jerng's literary study that builds on their work—argue that adoption produces new kinds of personhood that are experienced and understood not, or not only, through biogenetic models of kinship but through discursive constructions of subjectivity. Kim's project, she states, is to investigate how "adoptees articulate a sense of ontological distinctiveness through a process of 'disidentification' with normative categories of personhood and social belonging,"[43] and she cites Sandra Patton's discovery from a decade earlier that the transracial adoptees she interviewed (and among whom Patton includes herself) "feel that we constitute our own race or ethnicity, or even that we belong to a separate ontological category of humans," in which "identities are forged without genealogical patterns" and "through the trope of difference."[44] For the adult Korean adoptees she studied and the "adoptee cultural citizenship" they inhabit both in Korea and internationally, Kim coined the term "contingent essentialism" to describe a form of identity that does not just embrace discursive constructions but defies the boundary between the biogenetic and the discursive. Not relying on national or familial roots or origins to supply a sense of identity, the adoptees identify instead with one another on the basis of shared experiences and "collective personhood," even as they also draw a race-based boundary around their group that "takes on biological associations."

Similarly, Barbara Yngvesson sees in transnational adoptees, who may already experience themselves as having a "complex (and nonidentical) subjectivity," a "shaking" of identity, a "loss of bearings" and discovery of "the precariousness of 'I am'" when they return to their birth countries.[45] Like Kim, she finds new forms of identity in disidentification, as when one Korean adoptee, meeting with her college's Asian American stu-

42. Sunny Jo, "The Making of KAD Nation," in *Outsiders Within: Writing on Transracial Adoption,* ed. Jane Jeong Trenka, Julia Chinyere Oparah, and Sun Yung Shin (Cambridge, MA: South End Press, 2006), 285–90, quotation at 289.

43. All quotations from Kim in this paragraph are from *Adopted Territory,* 86.

44. Patton, *BirthMarks,* 6, 8.

45. Yngvesson, *Belonging,* 153; Yngvesson, "Going 'Home,'" 27, 28, 32.

dents' association, finds that "I'm not like them, but there's no specific name for what I am."[46] Returns locate the adoptee in a "space of non-identity [that] can be excruciating," yet "what emerges in the openings these moments provide is . . . simultaneously disruptive and confirming" for the "subjects who take shape in narratives of return."[47] Although Mark Jerng cautions against the "enthusiasm" of some advocates who celebrate "transracial and transnational adoption as subversive of . . . the essentialisms of biology and race, and as the promise of a new social order," he also notes "the transformative potential of transracial adoption for our notions of kinship" and sees adoption "challeng[ing] fundamental expectations and assumptions about personhood." Contesting norms of family, race, and nation, adoption exposes as illusory the notion that individuals are "preformed [or] prepolitical." All forms of personhood "emerge" instead "in relation to specific arrangements of family, nation, and race relations"; it is adoption that most clearly makes this visible.[48]

Despite such rigorous and eloquent modeling of exemplary ways in which adoptees and adoptive identity may either take up positions on the cultural side of the nature/culture divide or refuse that division altogether, the belief in innate, biogenetic identity remains forcefully real for a large constituency. Witness, for example, a recent semipublic exchange between two adoptees whose voices are influential in the US adoption community. Jean Strauss is a filmmaker whose books and documentaries about searches and reunions complement her legislative activism on behalf of open records. Her 1994 book *Birthright* is a guide to searches and reunions; the ad copy for her 2010 film reads: "What would it be like to never know who you were when you were born? *Adopted: For the Life of Me* follows Dave and Joe as they embark on journeys to find their origins. Their heartwarming sagas, with their unexpected and moving conclusions, illuminate the impact secrets can have over an entire lifetime."[49] Kimberly Leighton is a philosopher whose scholarly essays deconstruct such concepts as "origins" and "knowledge" as she interrogates what it means for adoptees to demand access to birth records. Both are members of the Alliance for the Study of Adoption and Culture (ASAC), an association of adoption scholars, professionals, and activists whose biannual conferences have occasionally flared into arguments over open records.

46. Yngvesson, *Belonging,* 155.
47. Yngvesson, *Belonging,* 176.
48. Jerng, *Claiming Others,* xxxvi, xiii, vii, xxi, xliii.
49. Jean Strauss, website for *Adopted: For the Life of Me* (2010), www.jeanstrauss.com/films/for-the-life-of-me/.

(For example, the 2010 ASAC conference was preceded by the circulation to registrants of a message by two prominent speakers taking another speaker to task for testifying in a Canadian court against the opening of sealed adoption records; during the conference, at a panel entitled "Secrecy and Policy," a heated debate took place on the question of whether the right to open birth records is a fundamental human need and human right.) On May 10, 2011, members of the ASAC address list, among others, received an email from Strauss, under the subject line "New Jersey passes assembly bill—a call to action," urging us to support what she describes as "legislation that will provide the majority of adopted citizens a copy of their original birth certificate."[50] (Her 2006 film *Vital Records: The Debate on Adoptee Access* documents an earlier, failed effort to open records in New Jersey.) She urges the recipients to write or call New Jersey governor Chris Christie and to try to persuade others to do the same.

The next day brought an email from Leighton urging caution and questioning the long-term implications of the bill. Noting that the bill would allow records to be opened not only at the request of the adopted person but also for "a direct descendent . . . of the adopted person if the adopted person is deceased," Leighton observes that this inclusion of "descendents . . . seems . . . to rely upon a normative notion of family" that, she suggests, runs counter to the belief in an adoptee's right to individual privacy that it is the bill's purpose to grant.[51] (Similarly invasive, in Leighton's view, is the requirement that birth parents submit medical information to the state.) This "normative notion of family" is, however, consistent with the biocentric model of family that the bill—like any advocacy for open records—also presumes. Worrying particularly about the bill's use of the term "birthright" in the context of regulating reproduction, Leighton writes: "Such laws and policies as S799/A1406 affect our imaginaries in ways that are neither intended nor foreseen [and can] have regulatory effects on how we live, including on our understandings of identity, on family, and on gender." The norms upheld by the bill have the potential to reinforce, she suggests, among other things, state control of women's reproductive choices and denial of non-heteronormative identities, desires, and family forms.

Leighton's cautions about the bill resonate with her critique of genealogical bewilderment and with her position that the "desire to know"

50. Jean Strauss to mailing list adoptedforthelifeofme@gmail.com, email, May 10, 2011.

51. Kimberly Leighton to mailing lists including asac2010program@mit.edu and asac@mit.edu, May 11, 2011, under the subject heading "Re: NJ's so-called 'Adoptee Birthright Bill' A1406/S799."

about one's origins is not the same as believing that one's identity derives from them. For her, desiring to know constitutes in itself a subject position:

> Being adopted for me, then, has not been an identification with an unknown lost family; it has not been a marking of myself as scarred or damaged or as having less knowledge than others who are born into their families. Instead, being adopted has been an identity of *possibility*. . . . Being an adopted self has encouraged me to imagine the self as both known and unknown, as born as well as produced, in short, as more than *either* natured *or* nurtured.[52]

Like the "contingent essentialism" lived out by the Korean adoptees in Eleana Kim's study, and like the "complex (nonidentical) subjectivity" Yngvesson observes, "'being adopted' opens up a space of non-identity (or non-identicalness) between the self as a subject and the self as an object such that one *cares* about the processes (social, historical, cultural, political, and relational) through which one has come to be." For Leighton, to be adopted is to be positioned as a seeker of knowledge, then, but not to be defined by any particular result of the search.

Compelling as Leighton's view of adoptive identity is, however, positions such as that taken by Strauss, in her tireless and moving advocacy for adoptee rights (and alongside other eloquent defenders of those rights and the identities they presuppose, such as Betty Jean Lifton and Adam Pertman), remain compelling too. "I just want to know who I am before I die," says one of several elderly adoptees in Strauss's *Adopted: For the Life of Me.* Strauss's autobiographical film *The Triumvirate* (2004) documents Strauss's birth grandmother meeting for the first time her birth daughter, with that daughter's children and grandchildren; Strauss films her quietly musing, "It's given me a tremendous sense of freedom to know that I can say to the world . . . see what a family I have." Positions such as those taken by Strauss and Leighton remain for the most part locked in binary opposition.

This tension replicates a tension that has long animated feminist theory, between those who see feminism as advocacy for women, on the one hand, and, on the other, those who see gender norms (including norms

52. Kimberly Leighton, "Being Adopted and Being a Philosopher: Exploring Identity and the 'Desire to Know' Differently," in *Adoption Matters: Philosophical and Feminist Essays,* ed. Sally Haslanger and Charlotte Witt (Ithaca: Cornell University Press, 2005), 146–70, quotations at 147.

defining "women") as the primary object of feminist critique. As Linda Alcoff depicted this tension a generation ago:

> In attempting to speak for women, feminism often seems to presuppose that it knows what women truly are, but such an assumption is foolhardy given that every source of knowledge about women has been contaminated with misogyny and sexism. . . . Our very self-definition is grounded in a concept that we must deconstruct and de-essentialize in all of its aspects.[53]

The paradoxical project Alcoff outlined for feminism, then, was to "ground a feminist politics that deconstructs the female subject."[54] Similarly, thinking about adoption requires simultaneously questioning assumptions of essential—biogenetic, innate—identity and at the same time honoring the urgent social and political claims of those who find their lives' meaning in such forms of identity.

Feminism, in its dividedness, underwrites contradictory positions on adoption: on the one hand advocating for birthmothers as women (often victims of social injustice, traumatized by loss and limited to and silenced as the merely material ground of their children's bodies) and, on the other, endorsing positions such as Haraway's or Butler's by advocating for an "'unfamiliar' unconscious" that takes no gender norms or kinship structures for granted. Laura Briggs's *Somebody's Children* constitutes the most sustained and explicit recent example of the first of these feminist positions, by focusing not so much on outcomes for children and adoptive families (much less on theories of adoptee personhood) as on the US and global political conditions—neoliberalism, "family values," the end of welfare, the anti-communist wars of the late twentieth century—that have impoverished, delegitimized, and disenfranchised entire categories of mothers in the United States and abroad and have made large numbers of children available for adoption. Christine Gailey's equally explicit feminism, by contrast, takes the form of advocacy for non-nuclear, non-biologistic family forms; she sees genetic essentialism as a preoccupation of patriarchy and applauds the single-mother adopters in her sample who bravely assert the legitimacy of their con-

53. Linda Alcoff, "Cultural Feminism versus Post-Structuralism: The Identity Crisis in Feminist Theory," *Signs: Journal of Women in Culture and Society* 13 (1988): 405–36, quotation at 405–6.

54. Alcoff, "Cultural Feminism versus Post-Structuralism," 419.

spicuously nonconforming families.[55] Leighton's defense of adoption, too, includes her feminist defense of non-heteronormative families; she observes that the privileging of "natural biological parents" and "natural biological heritage" by those who oppose both adoption and donor conception amounts to opposition to lesbian and gay family formation.[56]

Nonetheless, it is possible to bridge the divide within feminist approaches to adoption. Gailey advocates for the nonconforming families made possible by adoption, but she also, like Briggs, analyzes the gender hierarchy and the neoliberal policies that produce vulnerable mothers,[57] and she praises the single mothers as feminists who are the most likely of all adopters to empathize with their children's birthmothers. Briggs, too, complicates her passionate advocacy for birthmothers by turning, at the end of her book, to gay and lesbian adopters whose ability to form families—and thus to achieve normative citizenship, conservative as that goal may be—often depends on adoption. She notes the "irony" that gay and lesbian parents have gone "from being a group that often lost their children" to one that claimed "a 'right' to parent [that] seemingly implied a 'right' to take other people's children," and she praises those queer adoptive parents who—like Gailey's single mothers—are, from their own experience of social disenfranchisement, especially alert to the politics of adopted children's so-called availability.[58] Like these parents, Briggs's text reveals divided loyalties. As a feminist scholar, I have long been pulled in these two opposed directions, and in this book I attempt to honor both.

The tensions and oppositions I have been describing animate the study of adoption and the questions it raises about human being; at the same time, they call out for further critical thinking. This book ex-

55. For Gailey's discussion of the feminism of single mothers, see *Blue-Ribbon Babies,* 147–51. Gailey also uses feminist analysis to discuss the high incidence of abuse of young girls in foster and adoption.

56. Leighton, "Addressing the Harms," 83, quoting David Blankenhorn of the Institute for American Values. See also Bruno Perreau, who sees the regulation of adoption in France as the regulation of gender: *Penser l'adoption / Rethinking Adoption: The Pastoral Governance of Gender* (Paris: Presses Universitaires de France, 2012).

57. Gailey addresses the vulnerability of birthmothers in *Blue-Ribbon Babies,* 89–91, 99, 101, 109.

58. Briggs, *Somebody's Children,* 242, 257. David Eng was the first scholar to note the tension between the critique of adoption as a global market in children and the needs of gay and lesbian families; see "Transnational Adoption and Queer Diasporas," *Social Text* 76 (Fall 2003): 1–37, and his more recent development of this problem in *The Feeling of Kinship: Queer Liberalism and the Racialization of Intimacy* (Durham: Duke University Press, 2010), intro. and chap. 3.

plores some of the paradoxes these tensions engender: valued children whose value is both contingent and absolute, origins searches that never reach an origin, identifying marks that cannot identify, impossible speech from the constitutively silent. By investigating adoption's ways of disturbing normative relations between life and value, between origins, appearance, and identity, and between maternity and silence, this book attempts to trouble the binary oppositions through which adoption has been thought. In arguing for the productiveness of these paradoxes, I also argue counterintuitively for the productiveness of suffering and struggle in adoption, the "bliss and bale" of adoption (to borrow Henry James's phrase), what one adoptee terms the "mak[ing] a way out of no way" that adoption makes so arduous for its subjects.[59] As Jeanette Winterson asserts, "the missing part, the missing past, can be an opening, not a void." I argue for the subjectivities that are aided by being priced, for the fiction-generating power of trauma, for the capacity of melancholy to produce identity, and for the speech that silence sometimes compels. "The imprint of another life" is both a haunting absence and an imperative to create.

In chapter 1, "Money and Love," the essentialism I challenge is that of value: the belief that the value of a human life is innate and immeasurable. In the popular yet false binary opposition between natural and adopted, children born into their families are mistakenly seen as priceless while adoption is seen as purchase. Adoptive parents, in the contemporary memoirs and novels I consider in the first section of the chapter, try to claim that their parental love transcends and effaces the economics of adoption: not only whatever specific transactions may have enabled their adoptions but also the geopolitical economic inequities that enable transnational adoption in particular. They call their adoptions "falling in love," the "miracle" that was "meant to be." But adoption makes visible the connection between love and money, as well as the instrumentalization of children that may characterize any situation of family making and child-rearing, adoptive or not; transnational adoption's fiercest critics are mistaken in positing an extra-economic space for natural as opposed to adopted childhood. I close this section by reviewing recent social science research suggesting the merits, in specific contexts, of a parentless child's entering a system of monetary exchange.

---

59. Interviewee Keith J. Bigelow in *In Their Own Voices: Transracial Adoptees Tell Their Stories,* ed. Rita J. Simon and Rhonda M. Roorda (New York: Columbia University Press, 2000), 227.

For the purpose of challenging readers' imaginations to encompass such a possibility, the second and third sections of the chapter turn to two Victorian novels that make explicit (for contemporary readers, startlingly so) the economic value of adopted children: the monetary exchanges in which their lives are embedded and their use value for their parents. *Silas Marner* at first sentimentally effaces this economics, then reveals it; *What Maisie Knew* is frank about Maisie's exchange value from the start, and the novel shows furthermore what the child gains from her knowing participation in the family transactions, even when her "profit" looks like loss. Against the charge that adopted children are singled out to perform uncompensated labor for their parents, I suggest that children in all kinds of families are instrumentalized every day and that Victorian norms and expectations about children's work and value are still with us, if invisibly. Recognizing what adoption can show about nonadoptive as well as adoptive childhoods aids in acknowledging instead of denying the persistence of such norms.

In chapter 2, "Searches and Origins," I question genetic essentialism, the view that an adoptee's origins abide in locatable persons and places and constitute the unique or privileged sources of an adoptee's identity and meaningful life. Although no one can grasp their own origins or sustain an identity that is identical to those origins, many adoptees feel compelled to search for their roots and invest in these searches the belief that they will provide knowledge of who they are and restore them to a condition of authenticity. In the chapter's first section, two bodies of theory provide lenses through which to read narratives of such searches and their outcomes: narrative theory helps to make visible the impossibility of recovering origins, and trauma theory offers a model for reading the fictional origins that adoptees may reconstruct or invent in light of that impossibility. Origins, I argue in a reading of Betty Jean Lifton's memoir *Twice Born,* are created in the present to fulfill present needs and can be neither authentic nor inauthentic. The next section of the chapter explores works of fiction (by Toni Morrison, Barbara Kingsolver, Sherman Alexie, Gish Jen, and Rolin Jones) about searches and returns in order to flesh out the first section's argument about the fictiveness of adoptive origins. The works of fiction, which represent adopted characters' roots searches or their efforts to negotiate some relation to an origin presented as authentic, demonstrate the unimaginability of recovering authentic origins and offer a variety of ways to imagine the rerouting of such searches into works of creative construction that refuse the binary opposition between authentic and inauthentic. The last section of chapter 2 reads ethnographic research and memoirs that confirm that even those reporting on the most heartfelt searches, conducted in real time and space, are apt to find identity not secured but "shaken" and to end up settling for, or even, surprisingly, celebrating, the kinds of created origins that the works of fiction more openly devise. In a cluster of memoirs by adult adoptees who returned to Korea (or in one case, Taiwan) in search of their personal origins, especially their birthmothers, and in search of a sense of home or cultural belonging that the United States does not provide, the writers (and a filmmaker) find jarring dissonances between their imaginings and hopes for their searches and their discovery that their birthmothers cannot be found or, if found, cannot provide the desired sense of home. Instead, these daughter-memoirists recreate their birthmothers as the ground of a new configuration of identity: that of the writer and artist.

In chapter 3, "Marked Bodies and Identity," the essentialism I interrogate is that of embodied identity: I question whether innate biological features (blood, looks) determine or must always be equated with identity. Social norms around not only racial and ethnic but also more narrowly kin-based identities pressure adoptees (by such means as racial interpellation or belief in inherited family traits) to make or find an exact match between their looks and who they are. Paradoxically, however, these biocentric definitions of identity locate identity elsewhere than in or on the adoptee's person, with those whom the adoptee resembles (this is what Mark Jerng terms "claiming others"). Instead of mimicking an impossible ideal of genetic inheritance, identity might alternatively derive from the adoptee's own present situation of being adopted, the identity in difference and "possibility" that Kimberly Leighton affirms. In the first section of the chapter, I read a series of narratives by scholars who are adoptees and by young transnational adoptees about the struggle to reconcile appearance and social and psychological identity and the crises that can ensue when a match is lacking; I read as well some countervailing representations of resistance to these pressures, both from adoption scholarship and from adoptee memoirs. In the next section, I turn to examples of a common wish among adoptees: to be marked in or on the body in such a way as to make birth identity permanently visible, legible to all, and (it follows) fully aligned with the adoptee's sense of self. Such marks often resemble or derive from traces of traumatic injury, and in readings of texts ranging from *Oedipus the King* to *Beloved,* including short adoptee memoirs and ending with a series of representations of marked Chinese children, I turn to the psychoanalytic theory of melancholy loss, and specifically racial melancholy, to argue that the overlap between or condensation of marks of birth identity—sometimes including signs of racial identity—and marks of injury poses difficulties for adoptees who may find themselves cherishing or searching for the very sources of their suffering. Although the dream of locating identity in marks made or passed on by birth parents is as much a fantasy as the impossible searches for origins examined in chapter 2, an adoptee may also use bodily marks to create a new, adopted identity, as I discuss in the final section of chapter 3. Deliberately imprinting the body may serve, like the affirmations of creativity that often compensate for frustrated origins searches, as the basis for an identity affiliated with but not tied to normative biocentric origins.

In chapter 4, "The Mother Who Isn't One," I take issue with an essentialism implied intermittently by the first three chapters: that adoption's critique of innate value, origins, and identity depends upon its negation of and departure from biocentric definitions of family and therefore that it positions the birthmother as the silent, material ground of the adoptee's being. In normative accounts of adoption, adoptive parents are parents only if the metaphoric "as if" is privileged over the literal or material, the position to which the birthmother is relegated. While birthmothers continue to be represented in popular culture as silent, abjected, and closer to nature than to culture, the birthmother-writers I discuss in this chapter find ways to reclaim the speaking subjectivity they are not supposed to possess and to locate themselves as agents of narrative plotting, even while adoption ostensibly negates their agency. Birthmothers resist essentialism by speaking and writing. The book closes with a brief afterword that returns to Winterson's memoir and the special role of writing and invention in the lives of those touched by adoption.

1 / MONEY AND LOVE

FALLING-IN-LOVE AND THE UNSEEN ECONOMY IN RECENT ADOPTION NARRATIVES

"Love" is a costly luxury. It demands time, space, and resources. The authors of the 1834 Poor Law in Britain recognized this when they legislated that husbands, wives, and their children would be housed separately as the price of public support; the poor were not entitled to love. Love was reinvented in Britain with the advent of industrialization, the rise of the middle class, and the invention of separate spheres that divided the middle-class home from the workplace and gave women a special occupation: the disciplined expression of love through child rearing, material consumption, and moral guidance of the family. As Ruskin puts it, "within her gates" the woman is to be "the centre of order, the balm of distress, and the mirror of beauty."[1]

In George Eliot's *The Mill on the Floss,* Maggie Tulliver, starved for beauty as well as affection after her father's financial ruin and death, falls in love only after she has left work and entered her cousin Lucy's upper-middle-class world of leisure and luxury. The characters' frequent drawing-room musical performances both indicate the extent of their leisure and amplify their emotions, which they have the leisure to indulge. When Maggie trembles and thrills to the music, she looks beautiful and desirable to Lucy's suitor Stephen Guest, who offers her "love, wealth, ease, refinement."[2] Stephen addresses Maggie in the language of "love": "What could we care about in the whole world beside, if we belonged to each other?" (*Mill,* 569). Stephen's kind of love claims to be a universal emotion, free from all contingencies of time and place, but the narrator emphasizes that, rather that transcending "the world," it flourishes only

1. John Ruskin, "Of Queens' Gardens," in *Sesame and Lilies* (1864) (London: Dent, 1907), 72.
2. George Eliot, *The Mill on the Floss* (1860) (London: Penguin, 1985), 582 (hereafter cited in the text).

under certain economic conditions. Earlier in the novel when Maggie is poor, lonely, and "panting for happiness," the narrator comments that "good society"—whose members might look down on poor Maggie—"is of very expensive production; requiring nothing less than a wide and arduous national life condensed in unfragrant deafening factories, cramping itself in mines, sweating in furnaces." This "good society, floated on gossamer wings of light irony," enables for its members certain manners and emotions that may not be available to those living in "want," which "spends its heavy years often in a chill, uncarpeted fashion amidst family discord unsoftened by long corridors" (*Mill,* 385). Economic conditions, in other words, determine emotional life, and when Stephen offers Maggie "love," he forgets (but she does not) her obligations to characters altogether differently situated. Stephen, because of his economic position, can imagine a "love" that sweeps aside "the world"; Maggie, by contrast, cannot afford it.

Something akin to this love that is said to be "beside" and not "in" the world can be idealized in the relation between parents and children and within economic constraints that are, as in the case of Maggie and Stephen, more visible to some than to others. In Toni Morrison's *Sula,* Hannah Peace asks her mother Eva a "strange" question: "Mamma, did you ever love us?"[3] Eva, who has struggled up from the deepest poverty, deliberately sacrificing one of her legs (for the insurance money) to support her three children, answers: "No. I don't reckon I did. Not the way you thinkin'." Hannah is prepared to move on, but Eva continues: "You settin' here with your healthy-ass self and ax me did I love you? Them big old eyes in your head would a been two holes full of maggots if I hadn't." When Hannah asks if she ever played with them, Eva recalls how she fought off starvation in the cold winter of 1895. "Don't that count? Ain't that love?" When she sees Hannah burning to death later that day, she throws herself out her upper-story window trying to save her. Hannah's definition of love, that it involves leisure or "play," comes from the relative comfort of her present life, in which there is an abundance of food, time, and sexual love. The narrative links her "strange" questioning of her mother to her fiery death, as if it were retribution for demanding from her mother a "love" that meets the standards of other classes, other economies.

Love is not separable from the economic. Raising children, adopted or not, requires resources, and raising them with that emotional over-

3. Toni Morrison, *Sula* (New York: Knopf, 1974), all quotations at 67–68.

flow called "love" requires additional resources: think of what it would cost to provide even the conditions of possibility for "love"—that is, at the very least, the focused attention of an adult, a lot of the time—for every child in every orphanage in the world. Moreover, middle-class parenthood enmeshes families in daily acts of consumption, from diapers to prom dresses. Responding to a 2004 collection of ethnographic essays about parenting, a collection that opens with her own 1989 expression of hope that motherhood can be disarticulated from the marketplace, Barbara Katz Rothman remarks, "There seems no way to think beyond consumerism. One can consume differently, but almost whatever one does as a mother becomes just one more cog in the consumer wheel."[4] She notes, too, that we still speak of birth as "having" a baby, as if in unintended recognition of the child's status as property.[5] Most of the time, however, middle-class families with children born to them have no reason to see these costs (much less to connect their affectionate acts of consumption with a marketplace in children) and can believe that having and loving their children is merely "natural." All legal adoptions, by contrast, involve fees, and adoption raises the possibility that a child might be exchanged for money or might be valued or devalued in monetary terms. "Americans," writes Igor Kopytoff, "hold on to a sentimental model of kinship affectivities, consecrate it by dubbing it 'traditional,' and worry that the new reproductive technologies risk commoditizing children into designer products."[6] The naturalizing of bio-family love, its rendering invisible of the economic cost of "love," makes the expenses of adoption seem very conspicuous and sets up an apparent binary opposition between adoptive and biological families. Although, as I am arguing, all family life involves expenditure, adoptive parents bear the uncomfortable burden of making visible the connection between love and money, and many adoptive parents seek strategies for evading this burden. Like Stephen Guest and Hannah Peace, adoptive parents would like to think that their "love" transcends "the world" of hunger or "uncarpeted" rooms. This first section of chapter 1 explores writings that define adoptive family-making in this tendentious way.

---

4. Barbara Katz Rothman, "Caught in the Current," in *Consuming Motherhood,* ed. Janelle Taylor, Linda L. Layne, and Danielle F. Wozniak (New Brunswick: Rutgers University Press, 2004), 279–88, quotation at 286–87.
5. Barbara Katz Rothman, "Motherhood under Capitalism" (1989), rpt. in Taylor, Layne, and Wozniak, *Consuming Motherhood,* 19–30, this discussion at 25–28.
6. Igor Kopytoff, "Commoditizing Kinship in America," in Taylor, Layne, and Wozniak, *Consuming Motherhood,* 271–78, quotation at 277.

But first, how does adoption become burdened with its unsavory task of revealing the cost of "love"? Domestically, the economy of adoption is most visible when it involves differentiating among categories of children. In the United States, the Adoption and Safe Families Act (1997) provides tax credits for adoptions, with the greater subsidy going to those who adopt special needs children. By making special needs children cheaper to adopt, this subsidy in effect makes all US adoptions into purchases, even though such adoption costs are—as in one stock response to a question commonly addressed to adoptive parents, "How much did she cost?"—comparable to the price of a C-section birth, a price unlikely to be equated with the purchase of a child.[7] Pamela Anne Quiroz's study of hundreds of US adoption agencies reveals that, despite the federal Multi-Ethnic Placement and Inter-Ethnic Placement Acts (1994 and 1996), which prohibit categorization by race, a large proportion of agencies segregate available children by race, placing African American children in the "special needs" category along with children with disabilities and charging different fees depending on the child's skin color. There are agencies advertising "traditional" and "minority" programs, where "traditional" is clearly a euphemism for "white"; another agency charges more than twice for a Caucasian child what it charges for a "full African American," biracial children falling somewhere in between. Quiroz summarizes: "by law race cannot be factored into placement; yet in private adoption children are categorized, labeled, described, and priced along racial lines."[8] "Priced": to Quiroz it is clear that children are being purchased. The transactions involved in transnational adoption are just as visible and can appear outlandish and frightening to US citizens, with shady lawyers demanding unreasonable fees, envelopes of cash handed over in foreign hotel rooms, incomprehensible bureaucratic procedures, and the lines between legally mandated fees and bribery sometimes hard to discern. Margaret Radin aptly ascribes revulsion toward the exchange

7. Ethnographer Ann Anagnost reports that one of her informants—a user of internet chat groups about adoption—made this analogy when challenged about buying her adopted child; see "Maternal Labor in a Transnational Circuit," in Taylor, Layne, and Wozniak, *Consuming Motherhood*, 139–67, this discussion at 147–48. This essay incorporates and revises Anagnost's earlier, widely cited "Scenes of Misrecognition: Maternal Citizenship in the Age of Transnational Adoption," *Positions* 8 (2000): 389–421. This stock response is also reported by Heather Jacobson, in *Culture Keeping: White Mothers, International Adoption, and the Negotiation of Family Difference* (Nashville: Vanderbilt University Press, 2008), 151–52.

8. Pamela Anne Quiroz, *Adoption in a Color-Blind Society* (Lanham, MD: Rowman and Littlefield, 2007), 62, 72, 50.

of money for children to its proximity to human slavery.[9] Families adopting transnationally often express "unease that the movement of the child across national borders transforms it into a commodity bought and sold as a form of embodied value."[10]

In contemporary adoption practice, a "gray market" makes it possible for adopting parents to spend money on administrative costs, donations to orphanages, and the like: anything but payment for the child.[11] As Rothman puts it, "money is changing hands, but no one is technically selling a baby."[12] As in the internet conversations Anagnost observed, parents' "unease" and "anxiety . . . often [take] the form of a refusal and resignification of the meaning of monetary exchanges."[13] For example, Elizabeth Bartholet, one of the United States' most visible and influential defenders of transnational and transracial adoption, who traveled to Peru to adopt a child with four thousand dollars hidden in her shoes and two thousand dollars in her clothes, acknowledges that there are "some documented instances . . . of improper payments to birth parents" (i.e., "baby-buying") and that transnational adoption can be seen more broadly as "exploitation . . . the taking by the rich and powerful of the children born to the poor and powerless."[14] Yet she downplays these unsavory economies of adoption, explaining "stories of 'child trafficking'" or bribery as misperceptions of routine and proper payments to officials, agencies, or lawyers.

Moreover, she recounts horrific stories about orphanages (e.g., in Romania in the 1980s) to argue that the sale and stealing of children "are by no means the worst things that are happening to children or their birth parents today" (*Family Bonds,* 154–55). She sees adoption largely in terms of individual children, individual parents, and their mutual need for love, arguing, for example, that reluctant "sending countries . . . should stop thinking of . . . their homeless children as 'precious resources'" and instead adhere to the international human rights treaties "that recognize children's rights to a loving, nurturing environment"

---

9. Margaret Jane Radin, *Contested Commodities* (Cambridge: Harvard University Press, 1996), 136–40.
10. Anagnost, "Maternal Labor," 147.
11. Viviana A. Zelizer, *Pricing the Priceless Child: The Changing Social Value of Children* (Princeton: Princeton University Press, 1985), 203–5. For further discussion of the "gray market," see also Christine Ward Gailey, *Blue-Ribbon Babies and Labors of Love: Race, Class, and Gender in U.S. Adoption Practice* (Austin: University of Texas Press, 2010), 88–106.
12. Rothman, "Motherhood under Capitalism," 28.
13. Anagnost, "Maternal Labor," 147.
14. Elizabeth Bartholet, *Family Bonds: Adoption and the Politics of Parenting* (Boston: Houghton Mifflin, 1993), 153, 142 (hereafter cited in the text).

(160). Notice here that she inverts the accusation that adoptive parents are purchasers of children: in this formulation, it is the sending countries that see children as commodified "resources" and adoptive families that remove children from circuits of commerce. This shift of focus onto "rights" is echoed in her book's introduction, when Bartholet, countering the criticism of "adoption's potential for exploitation of the poor and . . . of racial and ethnic minority groups and the Third World," asserts that adoption "can be understood as liberating" and capable of "expand[ing] options for the oppressed" and "as an important part of reproductive autonomy" (xxi). Focusing on women making "choices" is like focusing on children's "rights": both concepts derive from the Enlightenment liberal humanism that both presumes and produces the individual (rather than, say, the state or the global economy) as the central agent of human life.[15] Although Bartholet intends to differentiate a (bad) property-based idea of adoption from (a good) one based on rights, Rothman points out that rights as a concept is so tied to property (to have rights in one's body depends upon ownership of one's body) as to make rights in and to adoption merely a more palatable name for adoption understood as an exchange of property.[16]

In another instance of her turn from the political or economic to the individual, Bartholet acknowledges that the screening system that pairs parents and children and that promises children competent, nurturing parents "operates primarily on the basis of what looks roughly like a market system, one in which ranking produces buying power" (*Family Bonds,* 71). Children and parents are rated according to their degree of desirability, with the most "desirable" or "marketable" children (healthy infants) going to those who most closely resemble normative middle- or upper-class biological parents (young, heterosexual, married couples); money, moreover, can enable parents to circumvent this system through costly private adoptions (71; see also xvi). But what bothers her most seems to be not this "market system's" commodification of children but rather the damage it inflicts on individuals when "'marginally fit' parents are matched with the hardest-to-place children, which means the children with the most extreme parenting needs" (71–72). In Peru she ob-

15. Karen Dubinsky makes a related critique of Bartholet's tendency to individualize adoption: "Bartholet individualizes race, making it a property of individuals, rather than communities"; when she celebrates the positive effects on individuals of racially mixed families, "unequal relations, between races, nations . . . all but disappear"; see *Babies without Borders: Adoption and Migration across the Americas* (New York: New York University Press, 2010), 99.

16. See Rothman, "Motherhood under Capitalism," 21–24.

serves that "gifts" of cash are needed to make the wheels turn smoothly and tells poignant stories of other adopting parents devastated by losing their newly placed children, apparently because their cash outlays are insufficient. Shifting the reader's attention from commodification and trafficking to individual suffering, she consistently changes the subject from the politics and economics of exploitation to "children in need."

Contemporary critics of transnational adoption argue, against Bartholet and the pro-adoption federal policies her advocacy helped to institutionalize in the 1990s, that the practice is a part of the globalization of capital that is often enmeshed in exploitation and illegalities and that adopted children moving from the underdeveloped to the developed world constitute unpaid and unconsenting labor. David Eng, for example, repeatedly asks, "On which side—capital or labor—does the transnational adoptee fall?" and answers that children adopted from Asia perform the unpaid but "crucial ideological labor" of family-making not only for heterosexual but also for gay and lesbian couples.[17] (Again, children born into their families do this kind of work too, but the exchange is invisible.) Citing the costs of transnational adoptions, he compares "the commodification of infant girls as a gendered form of embodied value bought and sold" to mail-order brides and to "military prostitution and the commodification of Third World female bodies for First World male consumption and pleasure."[18] According to Quiroz, "under the pretext of family rights and parental freedom of choice juxtaposed with the benefits to orphans, the market freedoms enjoyed by participants in private adoption negate issues of ethics and social responsibility."[19] Laura Briggs sees transnational adoption as a practice of economically exploitative imperialism, in which "ideologies of 'rescue'" provide cover for US foreign policy aims.[20] On the basis of an extended historical analysis of adoption from Latin America, Briggs argues that transnational adoption is inextricable from the disappearances and kidnappings occurring during the US-backed anti-communist wars of the 1970s and 1980s. She summarizes the consequences sardonically:

> The basic structure through which children came into transnational

17. David Eng, "Transnational Adoption and Queer Diasporas," *Social Text* 76 (Fall 2003): 1–37, quotations at 5, 8, 11.
18. Eng, "Transnational Adoption," 9, 10.
19. Quiroz, *Adoption in a Color-Blind Society*, 9.
20. Laura Briggs, "Mother, Child, Race, Nation: The Visual Iconography of Rescue and the Politics of Transnational and Transracial Adoption," *Gender and History* 15 (2003): 179–99, quotation at 180.

> adoption made it difficult to distinguish between legitimate adoptions—or at least those where the parents had fully and willingly consented, however much that consent may have been conditioned by war's aftermath, community dissolution, refugee status, poverty, violence, or other kinds of desperation—and those that happened as a result of kidnapping, threats, or bribes.[21]

For Tobias Hubinette, commenting on the commodification of children, "contemporary international adoption . . . has parallels to the Atlantic slave trade [and to today's] massive trafficking of women and children for international marriage and sexual exploitation."[22] Reports of global child trafficking continue to this day, with newly disturbing reports coming from China in 2012.[23] These critiques shift the emphasis from individuals back to economic and political systems and from the viewpoint of the adoptive parents and nation to that of the birth parents and their communities.

Like Briggs and Hubinette, Kim Park Nelson sees little difference between legal and illegal procedures in transnational adoption. Nelson's essay "Shopping for Children in the International Marketplace" focuses its critique specifically on the forces that drive consumers to the market in children. Given the "enormous cultural pressure to complete one's life with family," she argues,

> the demand is met with supply from poorer nations around the world, where the potential to procure healthy infants is great and the possibilities for realizing a healthy profit are just as great. Regrettably, the demand is so great that illegal baby markets have developed as child trafficking, and even in many legal transnational adoptions, child procurement and adoption payments border on (or cross the border to) the unethical.[24]

---

21. Laura Briggs, *Somebody's Children: The Politics of Transracial and Transnational Adoption* (Durham: Duke University Press, 2012), 208. Briggs's title is a direct rejoinder to Bartholet's *Nobody's Children*, which advocates transracial adoption.
22. Tobias Hubinette, "From Orphan Trains to Babylifts: Colonial Trafficking, Empire Building, and Social Engineering," in *Outsiders Within: Writing on Transracial Adoption*, ed. Jane Jeong Trenka, Julia Chinyere Oparah, and Sun Yung Shin (Cambridge, MA: South End Press, 2006), 139–49, quotation at 142–43.
23. See "Chinese Police Smash Trafficking Gangs, Frees 181 Children," www.bbc.co.uk/news/world-asia-china-18732817, July 6, 2012; see also David M. Smolin, "The Missing Girls of China: Population, Policy, Culture, Gender, Abortion, Abandonment, and Adoption in East-Asian Perspective," *Cumberland Law Review* 41, no. 1 (2011): 1–65.
24. Kim Park Nelson, "Shopping for Children in the International Marketplace," in Trenka, Oparah, and Shin, *Outsiders Within*, 89–104, quotations at 89–90.

The "cultural pressure to complete one's life with family," on which Nelson blames the global market in children, is a Victorian survival: having a family signifies class status by displaying a parent's capacity to support and nurture dependents who are not economically productive. Among Anagnost's internet informants, "parenting has become a newly intensified domain for the production of middle-class subjectivity for the adult."[25] Christine Gailey's research on adopters of differing social classes reveals that the wealthier the family, the more proprietary its attitudes about the children it may adopt: in contrast to working-class adopters, who typically see themselves as helping "kids . . . to turn out right," upper-class adopters seek children "like us" and lacking ties to their birth communities, children with the greatest potential to reproduce their parents' social status.[26] Borrowing the term "concerted cultivation" from sociologist Annette Lareau, Heather Jacobson sees middle-class adoptive families' "culture keeping" (their often strenuous efforts to "cultivate" their adopted children's connections to the cultures of their birthplaces) as part of maintaining and "expressing social class."[27]

Beyond class maintenance, the imperative to form a family with children also derives from norms of sexuality, personhood, and citizenship. For example, Jane Jeong Trenka's adoption memoir *The Language of Blood* occasionally shifts from narrative to dramatic script to indicate how Jane and her sister perform the perfect family publicly for their parents; Trenka outlines succinctly the small-town social pressures that prompted them to adopt:

> In Harlow men must be husbands and fathers. If they are not, they are eccentric old bachelor cousins or junior high English teachers.
>
> Likewise, women are wives and mothers. They must be mothers, not just wives, and if the children are not born soon, people talk.[28]

Similarly, Eng sees lesbian and gay couples requiring children to turn

25. Anagnost, "Maternal Labor," 141.
26. Gailey, *Blue-Ribbon Babies,* 18, 104; see also her "Ideologies of Motherhood and Kinship in U.S. Adoption," in *Ideologies and Technologies of Motherhood: Race, Class, Sexuality, Nationalism,* ed. Helena Ragone and France Windance Twine (New York: Routledge, 2000), 11–55.
27. H. Jacobson, *Culture Keeping,* 94, 171, citing Annette Lareau, *Unequal Childhoods: Class, Race, and Family Life* (Berkeley: University of California Press, 2003).
28. Jane Jeong Trenka, *The Language of Blood: A Memoir* (St. Paul: Borealis Books, 2003), 18.

them into families so that they may attain "full and robust citizenship,"[29] for as political theorist Carol Pateman has shown, having a family has been a requirement for citizenship starting with Rousseau.[30] Anagnost argues that "the position of parent, for middle-class subjects, has become increasingly marked as a measure of value, worth, and citizenship" and that this linkage of parenthood and citizenship "fuel[s] the desire for adoption as a necessary 'completion' for becoming a fully realized subject in American life."[31] Children still serve the economic functions of reproducing class and securing citizenship, even if adoptive parents and their advocates, such as Bartholet, think of themselves and their children as unique individuals, and even if they call this function by the name of "love."

Far apart though advocates and critics of transnational adoption may be, they share a wish that childrearing might be separable from economic and financial contingencies. Rather than seeking to eliminate the money transactions from transnational adoption, critics such as Nelson and Hubinette would prefer to eliminate transnational adoption itself. But to advocate for that end is to assume—just as much as does Bartholet, if for opposite reasons—that there is a natural state of pre- or extra-economic childrearing that is inherently preferable to transnational adoption; it is to assume that there could be a place for those children apart from economic contingencies. I am arguing, instead, for the importance of facing and addressing the realities of the adoption marketplace; as Anagnost asks, "What would happen if, instead of rituals of decommodification, the specter was confronted head on?"[32]

Bartholet downplays economic exploitation and the danger of trafficking to focus the reader's attention on children's need for love as a way to attack the political, legal, and cultural "barriers" that stand in the way of transnational adoption. In order to make the case for privileging individual feeling, Bartholet opens her book with a gesture echoed by many subsequent adoption narratives written by parents: she establishes not just that the struggle was worth it, that she loves her children, but that she has "fallen in love" with them. After outlining her life narrative up through her adoptions and sketching the daily routines of pleasure and care that make up life with two small children, she writes:

---

29. Eng, "Transnational Adoption," 7–8.
30. Carol Pateman, *The Sexual Contract* (Stanford: Stanford University Press, 1988).
31. Anagnost, "Maternal Labor," 142.
32. Anagnost, "Maternal Labor," 150.

> But I could not have expected these two particular magical children. I could not have predicted the ways in which they would crawl inside my heart and wrap themselves around my soul. I could not have known that I would be so entirely smitten, as a friend described me, so utterly possessed. (*Family Bonds,* xiv)

This "smittenness," the bond that goes beyond merely loving care, enables adoptive parents not to consider the politics and economics of adoption. It allows parents both to justify and to deny or "disavow" the instrumentalization of the child.[33]

With each child, Bartholet describes her discovery that she has "fallen in love" following an episode of dangerous illness that both threatens the success of the adoption and demands of her extraordinary care. For example, after she and the infant Christopher have survived his harrowing case of bronchitis, she recognizes

> that somewhere in these two weeks the falling-in-love process that I now think of as adoption has happened. I am Christopher's mother. It no longer really matters what goes on in the legal process or how long it takes. I won't let him go. (*Family Bonds,* 22)

"Falling-in-love" is here constituted as a process that happens naturally and involuntarily, that renders the parent—who has hitherto been making rational choices—helpless to disobey its dictates. Being "in-love" with the baby also sweeps aside the law and, presumably, all other people: should the birthmother appear, let us imagine, Bartholet would have her answer ready. "I won't let him go" constitutes Bartholet as the mother-in-chief who will defy anyone to stand in her way and for whom the law, including its potential protections for birth parents, is a mere annoyance.

In this passage Bartholet introduces other tropes, too, that will become familiar in later adoption memoirs: the tropes of "meant to be" and of a magical, miraculous, even divinely inspired link between parent and child. Invoking biblical language she writes, "I find myself wondering at the miracle that after all the years of wandering I found my way to this particular child, this one who was meant to be mine" (*Family Bonds,* 22).[34]

---

33. Anagnost, "Maternal Labor," 147.

34. Bartholet's "meant to be" resonates ironically with a phrase common among adoptees, articulated, e.g., in Rolin Jones's adoption play: "These aren't the lives we were supposed to be living": *The Intelligent Design of Jenny Chow: An Instant Message with Excitable Music* (New York: Dramatists' Play Service, 2006), 11. One person's "meant to be" may be another's chronic depression.

The same process occurs with the second adoption. Soon after taking Michael home to her rented Lima apartment, he develops so high a fever she fears he will die; they race to the hospital, where he is treated successfully: "Sometime during that taxi ride, or in that hospital room, I became hopelessly attached. I fell entirely in love during the next few days, as I nursed him back to health" (*Family Bonds,* 40). Again her "bond" with the child precedes its legalization, and again the law is a burden. Briggs points out about this episode that Bartholet reverses its actual power relations: focusing on her own emotional vulnerability, she obscures her economic power and access (as a wealthy white American) compared to the birth parents and birth community.[35] Emotionally at risk, she fears "that this person who already feels like part of me will be taken from me. By law he still belongs to his birth parents, and to the Peruvian adoption system" (*Family Bonds,* 40). Here she is asserting not just the child's need (proven by her extraordinary care) but also her need: the child has become "part of" her, and so her rights to autonomous action now include her rights to him. Despite her rhetoric of helplessness, she exposes her imperial mindset in this idiomatic phrasing: "this person . . . who feels" turns out to refer to her feeling, not his; it means "feels [to me]." "Love" is the name she gives to the ideology of individual rights and entitlements that are above the law and that overwrite the other's feelings with her own. Later she argues for open adoption and the principle that "parenting should not imply that the parent owns the child's affections or has a right to exclude alternative relationships," such as ties to the birth family (61), and yet more frequently in the book she complains "that children *are* treated as property, owned by their biologic parents and their racial, ethnic, and national communities" (50). "I fell entirely in love" suggests both an undeniable emotional bond and the ideology of class entitlement that makes it thinkable. "I fell entirely in love" means that others' relations to this child may be economic, but hers is not.

And yet she cannot completely conceal the connection between this adoption and American consumerism, for indeed she flaunts it: at a hopeful moment in her long process of adopting Michael, she celebrates by buying him "some new clothes of his very own." She "had held off on this symbolic 'claiming' action," fearing that he still might be taken away. But to be able to buy new clothes in a poor country is to assert the class privilege that leads to success before the law (*Family Bonds,* 135). Shopping with and for a newly adopted child is a common trope relabeling ownership as love in parents' adoption narratives; Melissa Fay Greene,

35. Briggs, *Somebody's Children,* 15–17.

for example, takes her newly adopted five-year-old, "Helen, in orphanage clothes and decrepit flip-flops," shopping in Addis Ababa.[36] As both Barbara Rothman and Heather Jacobson point out, consuming on behalf of a child—expressing and exhibiting the child's value to the parent and at the same time enhancing the child's value—confirms the child's place in the marketplace.

The tropes of "falling-in-love," of "meant to be," and of the "miracle" of adoption recur often in writings by adoptive parents from the years since Bartholet's book. Karen Dubinsky, writing in 2010, confirms the prevalence of the discourse of "falling-in-love" when she describes the predictable narrative pattern of transnational adoption stories. Typically they include "the disorienting but intensely joyful moment of meeting one's pre-existing 'kin' in a foreign hotel," and she cites among other sources a newspaper article titled "We Fell in Love with Her."[37] Marianne Novy has shown that adoption search plots sometimes mimic the romance plot, with the adoptee's search for her birth parents plotted like the quest of lover for beloved and reunion taking the structural place of marriage.[38] In the case of adoptive parents, the language of romance—with its distinction between love and "in love" borrowed from the idiom of adult romantic love—plays a different role, that of justifying, naturalizing, and rendering inevitable or fated a relationship whose arbitrary beginnings in an economic transaction are intolerable to think about and must be obscured.

A Love like No Other: Stories from Adoptive Parents, a collection of short memoirs the text of which is graphically punctuated with little hearts, aims to give voice to the experiences of adoptive parents as they overcome various kinds of "struggle" both during the adoption process

---

36. Melissa Fay Greene, *No Biking in the House without a Helmet* (New York: Sarah Crichton Books, 2011), 128.

37. Dubinsky, *Babies without Borders,* 98. See also Anagnost, "Maternal Labor," 148–49.

38. Marianne Novy, *Reading Adoption: Family and Difference in Fiction and Drama* (Ann Arbor: University of Michigan Press, 2005), 28. Claudia Nelson discusses two popular adoption narratives from the early twentieth century in which adoption appears as a pseudo-marriage—*Pollyanna* and *Little Orphan Annie*—although in these cases representing adoption as adult romantic love does not appear intended to obscure the economics of adoption, as in the cases I am discussing; see *Little Strangers: Portrayals of Adoption and Foster Care in America, 1850–1929* (Bloomington: Indiana University Press, 2003), 135, 175. See also Judith Modell, "Natural Bonds, Legal Boundaries: Modes of Persuasion in Adoption Rhetoric," in *Imagining Adoption: Essays on Literature and Culture,* ed. Marianne Novy (Ann Arbor: University of Michigan Press, 2001), 221.

and afterward.[39] The language of romantic love permeates the memoirs about transnational adoption, beginning with a "smitten" father in the introduction (*Love,* 3). (The memoirs about domestic and in-family adoption tend not to use this sentimental language.) Laura Shaine Cunningham writes, "I fell in love with my first daughter" on meeting her, at three days old, in a Romanian hospital (47). Melissa Fay Greene, suffering from "post-adoption depression," fails to experience the "love at first sight," the "falling in love" with which websites, magazine articles, and memoirs "brimmed" (63). Asking herself daily, "Do you love him yet?" she observes, "We don't pursue this line of questioning about the children to whom we give birth" (66). After many ups and downs, the story can have only one outcome: "He gave me a huge sticky smile. Did I love him? I didn't ask" (69).[40] In Amy Rackear's contribution, the obstacle to be overcome is the reluctance of the father, who, however, upon meeting the new baby, "was transfixed and, quite simply, in love" (91). Jill Smolowe, like Bartholet, compares adoption to marriage in terms of the commitment to love and honor that its vows entail (*Love,* 94; *Family Bonds,* 15). Jana Wolff remembers wondering, before the adoption, if she and her husband would love their child, distinguishing (as does Greene) love in adoption from the automatic love for biological children and distinguishing, too (as does Bartholet), between their certain ability to "provide loving care" and the less predictable "loving the child in your care." They "looked," she writes, "for clues about love inside our own wonderful marriage" (*Love,* 105–6), and when their child arrives, and they find themselves "blissed-out parents," her diction borrows again from romantic love. Not only was this match "clearly meant to be"; they feel "the nearly obscene joy of mutual infatuation" (106). On the plane trip home, Bonnie Miller Rubin "fell in love" with the smell of her baby daughter's head. Joe Treen, the reluctant father of the volume's introduction, "fell for the kid" and "was hooked" (197).

In the last contribution (on raising two disabled boys from Cambodia), Jenifer Levin threads the language of adult romantic love throughout by keeping up a running allusion to *Casablanca.* Watching the film prompts a breakthrough in Van's cleft-palate-damaged speech when he struggles to articulate the words "Here's looking at you, kid." Levin comments:

---

39. Pamela Kruger and Jill Smolowe, eds., *A Love like No Other: Stories from Adoptive Parents* (New York: Riverhead Books, 2005), 1 (hereafter cited in the text).

40. See also Greene's book about her family, in which the essay about Jesse reappears, *No Biking in the House without a Helmet.*

> Remember, I tell him, remember those words. And say them, someday, to your own true love. God knows we couldn't afford even one kid, much less two. But I knew we were in trouble—a good kind of trouble—the minute I saw you standing near the orphanage gates with your crooked little legs. And I said to myself, *Of all the gin joints in the world, why'd he have to show up in mine?* (*Love,* 246)

With the *Casablanca* allusions, Levin invokes the central merit for all the volume's adoptive parents of the "falling-in-love" trope: our love was helpless, it disregarded practicalities ("God knows we couldn't afford"), it was an irresistible bolt from the blue ("the minute I saw you") that transcends all contingencies and obstacles.

A Love like No Other opens, however, with a memoir that highlights what such tropes endeavor to obscure. Christina Frank searches for her child's birthmother while in Vietnam, and she wonders and worries about her thereafter. Because the birthmother kept her baby for two months and then left her with an enigmatic note, there is material for Frank to interpret; she speculates on possible reasons why this woman gave up her daughter, arriving finally at "the absolutely worst possibility: Was this woman given money to surrender Lucy?" (*Love,* 15). As she observes, "'baby trafficking' scandals have shut down the international adoption pipeline in Cambodia," and bribery of officials seems normal in Vietnam, "so the grim possibility of a baby-for-cash transaction isn't as comfortingly far-fetched as I'd like it to be" (15–16). Although Frank recognizes as "Hollywoodish" her fantasy of a poor young woman "standing on the side of a dusty road, sobbing as she is forced to sell her baby" (16), she has also been thinking more soberly about the economics of transnational adoption: her child's birthmother is "one among millions of anonymous birth mothers who produce the world's abandoned babies" for parent-consumers in the global north and west (13). And Frank opens the essay with her speculation that Lucy's mother is someone she has seen in Hanoi's markets:

> Was that her—the attenuated woman balancing stacks of sugarcane and chickens over her shoulder? Could this be her, the woman harassing us into buying a conical hat? What about the gracious saleslady at the store where we bought silk scarves and *ao dais*? (*Love,* 11)

Seeing Lucy's mother as a seller, Frank positions herself as a buyer, and a buyer of means, because she prefers silks to the cheap farmer's hat and identifies herself in the next paragraph as a consumer of high-end brand-name goods (her new daughter is "the tiny beauty strapped to my chest in a Baby Bjorn").

Frank is open and self-critical both about the economy of adoption and about her complicit place in it, as someone who gained through someone else's lack of choices. She is offended by the complacency of Americans who profess shock that a mother could bring herself to abandon a child ("How dare you speak that way about a woman in whose shoes you haven't walked?" [*Love,* 19]). And yet she also undermines this brave acknowledgment by deprecating it as her "birth mother obsession," a private foible rather than a public imperative, and she ends the memoir settling for a "spiritual . . . closeness" with Lucy's birthmother when she realizes she will never find her (12, 21), as if a personal connection of one kind or another were the only desirable outcome of such recognitions as hers. No other contribution in the volume echoes Frank's concerns. The rest of the volume is silent on the economics of adoption and noisy, as we have seen, about love. Similarly, in Susan Olding's contribution to *The Lucky Ones: Our Stories of Adopting Children from China*—a volume that, like *A Love like No Other,* comprises parents' celebratory adoption stories—the author thoughtfully worries about her daughter's birthmother, about China's demographics, and about the West's exploitation of China, and yet the essay reaches its emotional climax with a paragraph comparing the baby's skin to "a peony blossom" and answering a Chinese man's question, "Why do you adopt a Chinese baby?" with the resonant and obviously correct answer, "Because we love her."[41]

As Ann Hood's 2010 novel *The Red Thread* is drawing to a close, with the five families the novel has tracked through the adoption process finally about to receive their babies in Hunan, China, the parents ready their hotel rooms by laying out clothes, bath supplies, toys, and books, including copies of Margaret Wise Brown's classic *Goodnight Moon* and Rose Lewis's *I Love You like Crazy Cakes. I Love You like Crazy Cakes* tells the story of an adoption from China from the point of view of the American mother, and its appeal to Bartholet's tropes of "falling-in-love," "meant to be," and the miraculous match is the book's intense focus:

> When you looked at me with those big brown eyes, I knew we belonged together.

---

41. Susan Olding, "At Lingyin Si," in *The Lucky Ones: Our Stories of Adopting Children from China,* ed. Ann Rauhala (Toronto: ECW Press, 2008), 31–51, quotations at 49.

"I love you like crazy cakes," I whispered.

How did someone make this perfect match a world away?

The first night, I laid you down in your crib made up with crisp white linens and new blankets.

I tucked you in and kissed your little hands and tiny feet a hundred times.

I was falling in love.[42]

The mother's falling-in-love with her baby is accompanied by the elision of the birthmother; the story starts with babies in cribs in an orphanage and a lonely woman at home in America and remembers the birthmother only on the last page. Falling in love also leads to the mother's appropriation of the baby's feelings, as when Bartholet turns "[he] feels" into an expression of her own feeling. "I was so happy that I cried the moment I took you in my arms . . . you cried, too" (ellipses in original); the matching tears of mother and child, implying an instantaneous emotional connection, deny that the child's tears are hardly likely to be tears of joy. The book also elides any possible thoughts about the economics of this adoption (of course: it is for very small children) yet emphasizes the material benefits to the child (those new blankets at the hotel, the "new room . . . filled with toys, stuffed animals, and a new crib" that greets the baby in America), as well as repeatedly emphasizing the baby's status as material object among other objects. The mother's first impression is that the baby looks "like a soft, pink doll," and the example she gives of playing with the baby is "I put silly hats on you and took your picture." This book, a classic among families adopting from China, apparently beloved and trusted to express these families' feelings, constructs the adoption as an act of "falling-in-love" that is indistinguishable from self-centered possession and that casts such possession in a rosy light. Like Bartholet, too, it encourages a focus on the needs of individuals (primarily of the mother, secondarily of the child) that transcends circumstances and contingencies.

Although *I Love You like Crazy Cakes* does not construct "this perfect match" through the trope of the red thread, Hood's novel does so, using it to summarize and amplify Bartholet's and Lewis's tropes of "falling-in-love" and miraculous, "meant to be" matching. The red thread is a

42. Rose A. Lewis, *I Love You like Crazy Cakes,* illus. Jane Dyer (New York: Little Brown, 2002), unpaginated.

figure from Asian mythology: invisible, tied around their ankles throughout their lives no matter how far apart they are to start with, it links and inexorably draws together men and women who are destined to become lovers and marry. The culture of adoption from China that has developed in the United States since the early 1990s has appropriated this trope to represent the fate linking children to their new parents. Karin Evans's widely read *The Lost Daughters of China* endorses "the red thread idea [having been] taken up by the Chinese-American adoption community, to include parents and children who are destined to be together."[43] Grace Lin's picture book *The Red Thread: An Adoption Fairy Tale* opens, "There is an ancient Chinese belief that an invisible, unbreakable red thread connects all those who are destined to be together."[44] This image appears not only in book titles but in locations ranging from a line of greeting cards to a film on adoption to the name of a internet chat group for mothers of children from China to a tour company that takes families back to China.[45] Within this culture of adoption, the red thread myth relocates the Western discourse of romantic love to a suitably exotic Asian framework and, at the same time, juvenilizes it. The image is so pervasive that it needs no explication; families with children from China know its meaning even if they do not know it misreads the original Asian story. Although Evans finds merit in its comparing the relation between parents and children to marriage, a few parents and scholars have expressed skepticism both about unintended negative connotations that may carry over from the original story and about what the red thread image is being used to obscure. Toby Alice Volkman quotes a personal communication from Amy Klatzkin: "Given that traditional marriages often brought misery and servitude to women, the fate signified by the red thread was not necessarily a happy one," so that it is all the more peculiar to see the red thread pressed into the service of "an American feel-good,

43. Karin Evans, *The Lost Daughters of China* (New York: Tarcher/Putnam, 2000), 141–50, 218.

44. Grace Lin, *The Red Thread: An Adoption Fairy Tale* (Chicago: Albert Whitman and Co., 2007).

45. Among many examples: "Red Thread Girl Cards" are available through Chinasprout: Chinese Cultural and Educational Products, which markets traditional Chinese clothes, toys, books, and art supplies to adoptive families; a documentary film about adoption from China is titled *The Red String;* "The Red Thread: Motherhood By Adoption" was the name of a discussion group led by Alix Keast on Nov. 30, 2010, in New York City (from FCC-NY newsletter, Nov. 2010); Danling Cali is the president and founder of Red Thread Tours and Services (from FCC-NE newsletter, Nov. 2010).

everything-is-for-the-best ideology of international adoption."[46] Citing Volkman's citation of Klatzkin, Sara Dorow echoes this view when she describes one family's theory that their daughter was "lucky" to have been abandoned.[47] But this kind of skepticism about the common, strenuously positive use of the red thread image is the minority view.

The title of Hood's novel refers to the Red Thread Adoption Agency, founded and run by the protagonist, Maya Lange, who arranges adoptions from China and believes in the myth of the red thread. In a conversation with one of her clients, whom she is carefully shepherding through the anxious waiting period, the following exchange occurs:

> "There is a red thread connecting you to the child you were meant to have," Maya said.
>
> "Do you believe that?" Brooke said. "Really?"
>
> Maya wanted to tell her that she believed it so strongly she sometimes thought she saw them, those thin red threads zigzagging the sky, tethering babies to their mothers.
>
> But she said simply, "I do."
>
> Brooke wiped at her cheeks with the backs of her hands, and nodded. "Thank you."[48]

The agency's brochure insists upon the efficacy of the myth (and the *y* at the end of the agency's logo trails off into a thin red line), as does Maya in her presentations to prospective parents. To a skeptical client who wants to choose her child's characteristics, Maya explains that the matches made in a Chinese government office are at once "random" and "uncanny" and "magical" (*Red Thread,* 48). The novel closes with a reprise of this fantastic image in Maya's mind, as she looks out of the plane in which she and the other families are flying to the United States (at the last minute, Maya adopts a baby whose assigned parents have changed their minds):

---

46. Toby Alice Volkman, "Embodying Chinese Culture: Transnational Adoption in North America," *Social Text* 74 (Spring 2003): 29–55, rpt. in *Cultures of Transnational Adoption,* ed. Toby Alice Volkman (Durham: Duke University Press, 2005), 81–113, quotation at 95. See also Heather Jacobson's skeptical report on the use of the red thread image (*Culture Keeping,* 50, 180–81).
47. Sara K. Dorow, *Transnational Adoption: A Cultural Economy of Race, Gender, and Kinship* (New York: New York University Press, 2006), 192, 296.
48. Ann Hood, *The Red Thread: A Novel* (New York: W. W. Norton, 2010), 123 (hereafter cited in the text).

> Maya almost saw it, that red thread, tangled and curved, connecting each baby to their mother. She blinked. The red thread glimmered and then slowly disappeared. No matter how knotted or tangled it became, at the end of it was the child you were meant to have. (*Red Thread,* 302)

The magically self-disentangling red thread or the trope of "meant to be" transcends all contingencies, even including the last-minute switch of one set of parents for another.

The novel also highlights the trope of adoptive "falling-in-love" by setting up a parallel between an adult courtship plot involving Maya and the plot of the adoptions, eventually including her own. Maya is severely traumatized by the accidental death of her (bio) baby daughter eight years earlier, when the child slipped from her hands after her bath and fell, hitting her head. This loss ended her marriage but also launched her business, when she found that getting unparented babies into the hands of loving parents helped salve her grief. When the novel opens, she reserves her warmest feelings for the hundreds of children she has placed and whose photos adorn her office walls, but a suitor appears, and by the end she has sufficiently forgiven herself to accept both the man and a baby of her own. Prior to the heating up of Maya's romance, another couple's situation calls attention to the proximity between adult and adoptive "falling-in-love." Brooke wants to adopt, but her husband does not; as he puts the problem to himself, "If they didn't adopt a baby, he would lose her. And when the baby arrived and she fell in love with it, he might too" (*Red Thread,* 85).[49] Meanwhile, Maya has a series of nightmares about falling and compulsively recalls her daughter's death, which she calls "the fall" (e.g., 113, 120). The falling aspect of "falling-in-love"—the sudden, surprising, world-altering quality of it—is, in this context, more terrifying than pleasurable. As the romance plot develops, Maya wishes not to "fall in love with him," preferring the safety of her work and solitude; in China, repeating the distinction made by Bartholet, Greene, and Wolff between loving and falling in love with a child, "she did not doubt that she would love her daughter [but] she feared falling in love again." A few pages later, "Maya realized that she could not do it. She could not risk loving another baby. She could not fall from that great height again" (232, 295, 298). But her friends push her forward, she accepts the baby, the predictable occurs—"'Hello daughter,'

49. A subplot involving an ex-wife likewise cites the cliché distinction in adult romance between "love" and "in love" (Hood, *Red Thread,* 197).

she whispered"—and the novel ends with her contented vision of the magical red thread in the sky over the Pacific.

Thus far, *The Red Thread* would seem to be a novelization of Bartholet, Lewis, and the transnational memoirs in *A Love like No Other,* situating middle-class Americans so that their "falling-in-love" with abandoned children from other lands—here, via the magical connection of the red thread—can appear innocent of accusations of imperialist predation or worries about the marketing or instrumentalization of children. The novel, however, has another dimension and another plot line that complicates this reading. In five short italicized sections (amounting to under fifty pages of the three-hundred-page book), set apart from the narrative of Maya and the adopting families and never entering their awareness, the novel tells the stories of the five women in Hunan Province whose babies will end up in the Americans' hands. While following the ups and downs of the adopting couples, the reader holds in her mind the harrowing stories of these women's marriages or love affairs, their pregnancies, their deliveries, their love for their children, their heartbreaking efforts to keep them, and the betrayals of their trust. (A sixth, horrific story is interpolated within the first, told as a warning to the unwilling mother, who, as a result of hearing it, heartbroken, abandons her baby.) Shifting back and forth between these worlds, it is hard not to see the Americans, despite the sympathetic identifications that the narrative also promotes in the reader, as the self-indulgent wealthy, blindly taking advantage of the sufferings and losses of the less privileged, who (in Christina Frank's terms) "produce the world's abandoned babies." Except in the last case, in which the mother is accidentally killed and her grieving widower leaves the baby at an orphanage because he cannot bear to be reminded of her, each of the babies is given up unwillingly because of a combination of poverty, traditional preference for boys, and the one-child policy; the women suffer coercion and betrayal at the hands of husbands, lovers, mothers, and mothers-in-law. One mother, Li Guan, conceals her baby for months although this second child endangers her entire family, finds her baby suddenly stolen from her to be abandoned by her husband, and searches for her lost child every Saturday in the town where she was left. Another mother, Ni Fan, is fifteen years old, unmarried (in love and abandoned by her lover), and terribly poor; she leaves a valuable sweet potato in her baby's wrappings to signify her preciousness. Chen Chen gives birth to twin girls and is forced to abandon the smaller of the two.

When the "referrals" arrive at the agency, and we learn which baby is going to each family, the reader can match the descriptions of the babies with the stories we (but not the families) have been privy to. By the inscrutable yet magical logic of the red thread, the baby of the poorest mother, Ni Fan, goes to the wealthiest and most irritatingly class-conscious mother; the only baby conspicuously at risk for developmental delays, Chen Chen's second twin, goes to the mother who is most fearful of genetic defects. Do these matches prove that the red thread exists and works, because these are the very children these women need, to teach them a lesson, perhaps? Or does the novel ironize the entire concept, whether by so neatly mismatching children and parents or by revealing, through the last-minute substitution of Maya for the couple that drops out, that any randomly selected baby will be the perfect baby for the parent who is ready to be "smitten"? Once having read the stories of the birthmothers, it is hard to look at the novel's fiction of the red thread other than skeptically: so much suffering attends the transformation of these loved babies into available adoptees that only those who are ignorant of their histories—Maya and the other parents—could preserve the illusion of a romantic destiny free of history's bonds. Maya, herself happy, observes the others:

> All of them, happy.
>
> What she could not see were the families they were leaving behind as China disappeared and the ocean stretched before them. (*Red Thread,* 301)

Although the epilogue here gives a nod to each of the birthmothers and to the fifth baby's birth father, briefly glimpsed in the novel's present time grieving and wondering about their lost daughters, it is as if the narrative is protecting Maya and the other parents from this painful knowledge. Evidently, the parents must believe in their daughters' fated links to them, and fall in love with them, in order to parent them.

The narrative presents the red thread as a necessary illusion; otherwise it would be intolerable to hear Maya thinking of "the brave women who had dared to leave their daughters in the hope that there would be a life for them somewhere" and to hear Maya and her friend Emily say "these mothers gave us a gift" and refer to "what they've done for us," all clichéd and egocentric views of the birthmothers' experiences and intentions that are entirely at odds with their stories as Hood tells them (*Red Thread,* 300–301).[50] The narrator also analogizes the "fear" and "bravery" of the adopting families with the fear and bravery of the birthmothers, another callous gesture made possible only by ignorance. The acknowledgments printed at the end of the book reveal that Hood herself, like Maya, suffered the loss of a child and subsequently adopted from China, and she thanks her agency, China Adoption with Love. Serving as an epilogue beyond the epilogue, this information limits the extent to which the red thread concept can be felt to be ironized. And yet the narrative knows more than it allows its highly sympathetic protagonist to know. The knowledge of what is denied by "falling-in-love" and by the romantic myth of the red thread is both there and not there in the novel. The stories of the birthmothers haunt *The Red Thread* in something like the way that Christina Frank's thoughts about her daughter's birthmother as "produce[r]" haunt *A Love like No Other.*

Scott Simon's 2010 *Baby, We Were Meant for Each Other: In Praise of Adoption* interweaves personal memoir about adoption from China with other families' favorable adoption stories. Its sprightly advocacy resembles a lighter version of Bartholet's argument against "barriers" and in favor of transcendent adoptive love. The title invokes one of Bartholet's key tropes ("meant to be"); the book's first sentence—"Adoption is a miracle"—embraces another; and "falling-in-love," with love of the child made explicitly analogous to adult romantic love, dominates the story of Simon's first adoption.[51] He narrates amusingly baby Elise's unstoppable weeping on their first day together and his and his wife's desperate efforts to pacify her. As she finally drops off to sleep, he offers his version of "falling-in-love":

> Caroline and I realized that in the space of an afternoon, our lives had suddenly developed a few new and indisputable truths.
>
> That my wife and I loved each other even more than we had a few hours ago. That we loved no one on earth more than this new, small, squalling, hungry, thirsty, and occasionally ornery human being that was now ours. Our baby had opened new chambers in our hearts. (*Baby,* 9–10)

---

50. Anagnost argues that seeing the child as a "gift" is part of disavowing the economic transactions involved in adoption ("Maternal Labor," 148). Barbara Yngvesson argues that seeing the adoptee as a "gift" reinforces the notion that parenthood means exclusive ownership; see "Placing the 'Gift Child' in Transnational Adoption," *Law and Society Review* 36, no. 2 (2002): 227–56.

51. Scott Simon, *Baby, We Were Meant for Each Other: In Praise of Adoption* (New York: Random House, 2010), 3 (hereafter cited in the text).

As he puts it later, alluding to adoption's appropriation of the red thread myth, the moment he received Elise's photo, "I suddenly felt the tugging of some huge extraordinary cord from the other side of the globe, and I knew that no power on earth would keep us away from that child" (151).

The "miracle" and "meantness" of adoption perform for Simon's book something like the role played by the red thread myth in Hood's novel: they reinforce the belief that transnational adoption operates according to laws beyond human law, rendering unthinkable the mundane transactional realities of adoption. Simon explicates what he means when he says "adoption is a miracle": not just "amazing, terrific," but rather an event "not explicable by natural or scientific laws" and thus "the work of divine agency" (*Baby*, 3). Like Bartholet invoking divine agency in "the miracle that after all the years of wandering I found my way to this particular child" (*Family Bonds*, 22), Simon sustains the metaphor of the "miracle" by alluding first to the book of Genesis (he says he and his wife did not have children "in the traditional, Abraham-and-Sarah-begat manner") and then to Christian ritual: "we cannot imagine anything more remarkable and marvelous than having a stranger put into your arms who becomes, in minutes, your flesh, your blood: your life" (*Baby*, 4). Alluding to marriage vows that turn two individuals into "one flesh," Simon also hints at a bodily transformation like that of the transubstantiation of wine and wafer into blood and flesh. "Meant for," too, confers on the adoptive match extra-human sanction, by implying the intentions of a mind beyond human understanding.

The "miracle" is such a commonplace of adoption narratives that it is a virtual requirement for adoption skeptics to mock it: Eng, for example, writes of the so-called "miraculous transformation" of the Chinese orphan into a US citizen, which in his view "efface[s] the history of this transaction in the global marketplace."[52] In adoption novels to be discussed more fully in chapter 2, Barbara Kingsolver and Gish Jen figure adoption as a miracle early in their works: in *The Bean Trees*, wisteria suddenly blooming out of bare dirt becomes "the Miracle of Dog Doo Park" and supplies an obvious analogy for the thriving of the transplanted child Turtle;[53] in *The Love Wife* Blondie fixates on a clump of "miraculously" large sunflowers that have taken root in her yard despite the seed having merely dropped from the bird feeder.[54] Unlike Simon, however, both novelists also frame these "miracle" images of adoption

52. Eng, "Transnational Adoption," 7, 9. See also H. Jacobson, *Culture Keeping*, 50.

53. Barbara Kingsolver, *The Bean Trees* (New York: Harper Collins, 1988), 152.

54. Gish Jen, *The Love Wife* (New York: Knopf, 2004), 5.

skeptically, Kingsolver by revising the miraculous adoption story to include its history and politics in her later novel *Pigs in Heaven*, Jen by ironizing Blondie's vanity as a mother.

Similarly, memoirist Jeff Gammage takes care to demonstrate his thoughtfulness and realism by disavowing the view that matching is "mystical" or "predetermined . . . by the hand of God": "Me, I don't believe in invisible red threads." Pondering the "perfect match" between his daughter and her new family, he believes instead that "the people at the CCAA [the China Center of Adoption Affairs, where parents' dossiers are paired with those of adoptable children] are really good at their jobs."[55] Even so, he mystifies the agency of the unknown worker who gave Jin Hu to him and his wife: out of the "thousands" of prospective parents, "only we would be granted the joy of her smile and the pleasure of her laugh. . . . I wish I knew who in the government made that decision. If I did, I would kowtow before him, knocking my head on the floor."[56] Similarly, in a scene set at a culture camp that she is attending with her seven-year-old daughter from China, Nancy McCabe describes her irritation with an adult adoptee's view "that families formed by adoption were meant to be, as if . . . God himself had removed children from their birth parents and cultures and given them to us"; her daughter is a pragmatist too, pointing out that "if you didn't have me, you'd have another daughter, and you'd love her, too."[57] And yet twenty pages later, indulging in sentimentality akin to that of Simon, Bartholet, and the contributors to *A Love like No Other*, McCabe celebrates "the miracle by which a lovely, fully formed baby enters your life and becomes your own child."[58] Although like the scholars and novelists, these memoirists seek to distinguish themselves from the pack by debunking the "miracle" and "meant-to-be" views of adoption, they struggle in maintaining this skepticism when they turn to their love for their children.

World-transcending love is the hero of Simon's book, its punchline, its moral. When the two parents worry that their second baby does not match her photograph and fear becoming attached to a child they will be required to exchange for another, the older sister solves the problem by reaching out her arms and saying "softly, 'It doesn't matter'" (*Baby,*

---

55. Jeff Gammage, *China Ghosts: My Daughter's Journey to America, My Passage to Fatherhood* (New York: Harper Collins, 2007), 115–16.

56. Gammage, *China Ghosts,* 113.

57. Nancy McCabe, *Crossing the Blue Willow Bridge: A Journey to My Daughter's Birthplace in China* (Columbia: University of Missouri Press, 2011), 56.

58. McCabe, *Crossing,* 77.

21). Simon follows with a paean to the triumph of adoptive love over blood identity:

> Race, blood, lineage, and nationality don't matter; they're just the way that small minds keep score. All that matters about blood is that it's warm and that it beats through a loving heart. (*Baby,* 21)

Elise's "it doesn't matter" is one of those expressions of love that romantically sweeps away history and circumstances. But what would that kind of love have meant if another set of parents had already fallen in love with her photograph or if this baby were not available for adoption because her birth parents still wanted her? Historically, many children were wrongly adopted from Korean and Vietnamese orphanages when their destitute parents left them for care, intending to return for them. Should the Simons' baby already belong to others, "it doesn't matter," like Bartholet's "I won't let him go," would not be loving but horrifically callous.[59]

And indeed a few pages later Simon narrates a telling anecdote of just such an occurrence. At their first daughter's orphanage an official remarks:

> "Sometimes, one of the workers falls in love with a child. They will take the child and disappear in the middle of the night, and run off hundreds of miles away, because they do not want to give up that child." My wife and I stiffened as he leaned over.
>
> "Don't worry," he cooed with reassurance. "We find them. We deal with them. We bring the children back."
>
> Caroline and I muttered. Small grunts and rumblings to ask only each other, "And throw the poor people who love that child into a dungeon? Why not just let them be?" (*Baby,* 39)

Simon's "mutterings" represent his rooting for "falling-in-love," the romantic view of adoptive love transcending all contingencies; yet what if

---

59. "It doesn't matter" resonates uncomfortably with a scene in Korean adoptee Deann Borshay Liem's documentary film *First Person Plural,* in which her adoptive family recalls that she did not resemble her photo when they met her, age eight, at the airport. "It didn't matter—one of 'em was ours," remarks her older sister. It did matter: she had been switched with another child from the orphanage. See Deann Borshay Liem, dir., *First Person Plural* (San Francisco: National Asian American Telecommunications Association, 2000). See further discussion of this scene in chapter 2.

that child had been the one promised to him? A baby's identity may not "matter" in matters of love, yet such disregard for the law (for Bartholet's despised "barriers") is hard to differentiate from advocacy for kidnap. As at the end of *The Red Thread,* Simon's book seems at once to know and not to know what irreducible contingencies "falling-in-love" may sweep aside.

Among these contingencies, love sweeps aside any worry about child trafficking or economic imperialism. Like Lewis, Simon festively commodifies his children, his first daughter's tears "little jewels," his second daughter a "present" given to his first because "we love her so much" (*Baby,* 7, 22). Lightly brushing past the negative resonances of this claim, Simon sees the presence of so much love negating any possibility that he and Caroline went "shopping for children in the international marketplace," to use Kim Park Nelson's words. Similarly, he boasts of the material comforts that he, as "spoiler-in-chief," can provide his daughters to prove to them that "they are *not* victims" (109–10):

> When I take our daughters out to breakfast, if they so much as look at a bagel, bialy, cinnamon roll, croissant, muffin, or waffle, more food than a family of four would consume in many parts of the world goes onto their plates, and we walk away from the crumbs without a twinge. (*Baby,* 109)

Buying each child "whatever she wanted, *whatever she wanted*" (*Baby,* 12), like Bartholet taking baby Michael shopping as a "symbolic 'claiming' action," is somewhat like placing a sweet potato in an unwillingly abandoned daughter's basket: it demonstrates the high value placed on the child. But what is poignant in the latter case is disturbing in the former, and Simon's tone is both boastful and defensive. The next paragraph opens: "Maybe I should be embarrassed. But . . ." In acknowledging an inverse relationship between his daughters' high value and the poverty and hunger of some other "family of four" (the birth family of one of his daughters, maybe?), Simon both concedes and celebrates his complicity in a global economy that makes one person's loss another's gain. It is as if Simon's book both knows and refuses to know the high price of love.

In the same year that saw the publication of Simon's *Baby, We Were Meant for Each Other* and *The Red Thread,* two scholarly books appeared that offer fresh reflections on the relation between love and money in transnational adoption, reflections that aspire to move the debate beyond the impasse between, on the one hand, the bitter critique of transnational adoption as kidnap or "shopping" put forward by Hubinette,

Nelson, Briggs, and others and, on the other, such defensive apologetics as those of Bartholet, the contributors to *A Love like No Other,* Hood, and Simon. "Falling-in-love" may mask or deny the multiple costs of transnational adoption in the texts we have been considering, yet love is never entirely extricable from economic transactions, as Simon's defensive tone about "spoiling" his kids suggests. Karen Dubinsky and Barbara Yngvesson—responding to Anagnost's challenge, "What would happen if, instead of rituals of decommodification, the specter was confronted head on?"—both endeavor to look undefensively at the economics of transnational adoption. If adoption is inevitably embedded in economic disparities, is it possible nonetheless, without denial or concealment, to find some justification for it?

Writing in *Babies without Borders* about Guatemala, a country whose transnational adoption program is said to have made the nation "synonymous with stealing and selling children," historian Karen Dubinsky traces the sudden shift from a dominant narrative of transnational adoption as "rescue" (which masked imperialist aggression toward vulnerable third world nations) to a dominant narrative of kidnap.[60] She wonders "what knowledge is created" by the long popular history of associating scandal with transnational adoption (*Babies,* 103). Looking closely at the case of Guatemala, after acknowledging the hundreds of children who have gone missing in a war-torn country, she documents since the 1980s the circulation of numerous ungrounded tales of baby trafficking, including for the purpose of organ theft. Unlike Briggs, who focuses on verified instances of kidnap and trafficking, Dubinsky interprets these stories not as the truth about adoption but rather as symptomatic expressions of the experience of oppression by the country's rural poor. Kidnap and trafficking, in other words, are in her view political myths about adoption, as rescue used to be.[61] Although she credits many Guatemalans' beliefs that crimes are being committed, she also observes that critics and reformers have broader political agendas into which "child politics" neatly fits (121). Moreover, she calls these stories "partial" because they do not reflect the as-yet-untold experiences of individual Guatemalan birth-

60. Dubinsky, *Babies without Borders,* 120 (hereafter cited in the text). She dates a shift away from the rescue narrative to the mid-2000s (100).

61. For a related discussion see Bruno Perreau, who argues that the popularity of mass-media stories about child trafficking reveals a fear of adoption itself, especially (in the context of France) its challenge to biogenetic definitions of nationhood; see *Penser l'adoption / Rethinking Adoption: The Pastoral Governance of Gender* (Paris: Presses Universitaires de France, 2012), 1–16.

mothers, whose "hard lives and lack of reproductive choices" may make transnational adoption "an important alternative" for them (125, 124).

Further complicating the picture of Guatemalan "baby-selling," according to an adoption social worker she knows, "some birth mothers she has found receive regular remittances from their children's adopted families," enabling them "to raise their other children" (*Babies,* 126). In these cases, adoption has resulted in material benefits to those who most need them, benefits that cannot be dismissed as corruption. Global economic realities require, Dubinsky argues, setting aside "the myth of the universality of childhood—premised on key concepts such as innocence, dependence, and vulnerability," because it falsely "measures and normalizes the lives of many against the experiences of a tiny few" (130). When critics of transnational adoption complain of the unpaid and unconsenting labor performed by adopted children, they are forgetting that children perform various kinds of work wherever they are, in their birth nations, in their birth families, in orphanages, or in adoptive homes. "In factories, farms, and streets," writes Dubinsky, "child laborers make shrewd calculations that defy their stereotype of mute suffering. . . . We can't move beyond kidnap and rescue until we also move beyond the adult-created lie of universal, innocent childhood" (130). It is not helpful to persist in conjuring childhoods outside of the cash nexus, as we have seen done both by the most severe critics of transnational adoption and by its most ardent defenders.

Like Dubinsky deconstructing this myth of a pre-economic childhood, Barbara Yngvesson sees the celebrated naturalness of the birth relation as a back-formation created only from the standpoint of adoption.[62] Her cautiously positive claims for the market aspect of adoption, in the context of present-day global economic realities, echo and extend Dubinsky's. Looking at transnational adoption to Sweden from India and Ethiopia, Yngvesson finds not just individual financial benefits to individual birthmothers but an entire economy, which she sees as beneficial to the birthmothers as a group, based on the desire of Swedish adopters for foreign children. In the early 2000s, ethically motivated

62. Barbara Yngvesson, *Belonging in an Adopted World: Race, Identity, and Transnational Adoption* (Chicago: University of Chicago Press, 2010), 14–15. The same, Yngvesson argues, is true for nationality: only by being candidates for transnational adoption do abandoned or orphaned children acquire rights that their nation is pledged to protect (by the UN and the Hague Convention). Although their belonging to the birth country may be projected backward onto a time prior to adoption, "*the capacity for belonging . . . is created by the very potential for alienage.* . . . There is no 'Indian' (or 'Columbian' or 'Korean') child prior to its adoption in other nations" (*Belonging,* 58, emphasis in original).

Swedish government efforts to demonetize transnational adoption from India had the effect of cutting off needed support for women and children in the sending country; she speculates that "the construction of an expanding range of children as desirable (for adoption) may contribute (in slow-working ways) to the empowerment of (marginalized) women and children."[63]

With regard to the children themselves, Yngvesson counterintuitively sees their commodification as potentially advantageous too. Citing Marilyn Strathern's observation that "commoditization works . . . as a process of 'making value visible,'" Yngvesson argues that adoption "transformed . . . children who were, in effect, 'priceless' in the sense that they had no apparent value in India—girl children, dark children, other kinds of special-needs children—into resources of the nation to which they belonged."[64] Similarly, the journalist Xinran claims that foreign adoptions brought better care and attention to abandoned baby girls in China, and even so firm a critic of "consuming motherhood" as Barbara Rothman concedes that "given our great respect for property, there are ways in which, in this society at this time, it works in the interests of children to treat them as property."[65] In the adoption process, in Yngvesson's analysis, children acquire not only outer characteristics to distinguish them from others but also the kind of individuality that is seen to reside inside the child:

> The interests and needs of the child (indeed, the concept of a particular entity as "a child" with distinct interests that the nation-state must protect) take shape in the context of transactions between parties (orphanages and agencies, giving and receiving nations, birth and adoptive parents). . . . The "diverse internal qualities" that give any particular child value . . . are elicited or made visible "in dealings with others."[66]

---

63. Yngvesson, *Belonging,* 79, 85. Yngvesson also discusses in detail Jaclyn Aronson's decision to send money back to her birthmother in Korea (161–62).
64. Yngvesson, *Belonging,* 68, citing Marilyn Strathern, "Qualified Value: The Perspective of Gift Exchange," in *Barter, Exchange, and Value: An Anthropological Approach,* ed. Carolyn Humphrey and Stephen Hugh-Jones (Cambridge: Cambridge University Press, 1992), 172.
65. Xinran, *Message from an Unknown Chinese Mother: Stories of Loss and Love,* trans. Nicky Harman (London: Chatto and Windus, 2010), 111–12; Rothman, "Motherhood under Capitalism," 29. Rothman later, in "Caught in the Current," quotes approvingly a remark by her editor Janelle Taylor: "Commodification is not always or only about devaluation of people; it can also sometimes be about creating/asserting/claiming value for people" (287).
66. Yngvesson, *Belonging,* 71, citing Strathern, "Qualified Value," 178–79, 181.

For Yngvesson, the legal market in children in India is, paradoxically, both heinous and indispensable to the visibility and valuation of those children as children. Recall the story of Ni Fan's baby in *The Red Thread:* only as the mother is leaving her baby does she acquire that poignant signifier of value, the sweet potato tucked in the basket. Yngvesson writes, "the market in children does not so much devalue the adoptable child (by commoditizing it), as establish a central condition in constituting its value (its entitlement to political or physical life, or both)."[67]

Looked at through the lenses provided by Dubinsky and Yngvesson, then, the mother's seeing her baby in *I Love You like Crazy Cakes* as a "soft, pink doll," or Simon's calling one daughter a "present" for the other and buying them "whatever [they] wanted" ("they have . . . more toys than FAO Schwartz, and four flavors of premium ice cream in the freezer" [*Baby,* 109]), are instances of the ways in which commodification and financial transactions make visible not only the value but, in Yngvesson's account, the very personhood that these children lacked prior to adoption. Indeed, this is Simon's stated intention despite his defensive tone. By making his daughters feel "privileged" he wants to ensure that they never "feel sorry . . . for themselves," that they are never abject, that they have a "strong" sense of self (110). Yngvesson and Dubinsky cogently address critiques of adoption as "shopping" by defending certain aspects and consequences of the market rather than by denying its existence, as Bartholet does, and it could be said that Simon is making the market work for his children in the spirit of their arguments. But there is an important difference: Yngvesson and Dubinsky assess the effects of the market on entire communities and nations and ask how the market might conceivably benefit such large groups; Simon, by contrast, is concerned exclusively with benefiting two children, his, regardless of whether the gain to his family comes at the expense of others—indeed, he flaunts his daughters' advantage over others. Yngvesson and Dubinsky are also well aware how close their careful analyses come to the old "rescue" narrative, in which foreign adopters confer benefits on children by taking them away. Simon, by contrast, seems willfully unaware of his imperial tone, continuing to the end to insist upon the insignificance of the economy of adoption compared to the overriding power of "love."

Simon also unabashedly celebrates the instrumentalization of his children: what Eng sees as unconsenting labor and Hubinette as slavery. Not by setting them to work in a sweatshop, but by endowing them

67. Yngvesson, *Belonging,* 58.

with every worldly advantage, Simon makes his daughters work for him by performing a service only children can perform, that of allowing Simon and his wife to appear as a family. Or, to borrow Nelson's phrasing, they provide for the Simons a definitive response to the "enormous cultural pressure to complete one's life with family."[68] They also work to display Simon's wealth and status, and they do so in a conventionally neo-Victorian way, by enabling the couple to exhibit its bifurcation into public (male) and private (female) spheres. Culminating the catalog of the children's luxuries (the toys, the wasteful breakfasts) is this: "Most luxurious of all in these times: their mother is at home for them" (*Baby,* 109). While Simon conducts a highly public professional life as broadcaster on National Public Radio, Caroline Simon stays at home. Seen here in explicitly economic terms, the stay-at-home mom is part of the price of the adoption; put on display together, mother and daughters openly signify elevated class status.

But again after acknowledging it, the memoir denies the work being done, just as it both acknowledges and denies the transactions involved in adoption. Toward the end of the book, Simon launches into an argument (recalling Bartholet's) against the marketing and subsidizing (by health insurance) of reproductive technologies that siphon off potential adopters. He disparages the fertility "industry" for catering to those who want to choose their children's hair and eye color; while adoption is viewed as "a good thing to do" despite its high expense, "having children [by birth] has become a business" (*Baby,* 170). He appropriates the high moral ground for adoption, as if adoption were not itself an industry; adoption, he reiterates, is about "falling in love" and "a miracle in our lives" (171, 173). Those who have adopted, he writes on the last page, "must believe in a world in which the tumblers of the universe can click in unfathomable ways" (177). Once again the "miracle," always singular, makes it hard to see the costs, the labor, the work, the transaction; the last words of the book are, "baby, we were meant for each other." Yngvesson, by contrast, with her wider focus on global demographics and economic forces, is dry-eyed about the "miracle" of adoption: "Each adoption points to the contingencies of birth, to the arbitrariness of choice (which family, which nation), and to the fact that any adopted child could have had a different story: there is no 'meant to be' in adoption stories."[69]

I have been arguing that the romantic discourse of "falling-in-love"

68. K. P. Nelson, "Shopping for Children," 89.
69. Yngvesson, *Belonging,* 147.

and a quasi-religious discourse of "miracle" and "meant to be" enable writings by recent adoptive parents to finesse the conceptual and moral obstacles to seeing the market system of adoption, even as they sometimes indirectly acknowledge their participation in it. How can loved children be purchased objects or unpaid workers, if they are with us by magic and are the focus of so much love? There is little common ground between, on the one hand, political critiques of transnational adoption as "shopping for children in the international marketplace" and, on the other, denial—in the name of love—of the existence of a marketplace, although, as we have seen, both positions idealistically imagine a world for children beyond the economic. Yet social science research is beginning to produce careful defenses of transnational adoptees' involvement in economic exchanges, such as Yngvesson's view that "the market in children . . . establish[es] a central condition in constituting [the child's] entitlement to political or physical life, or both."

Some recent adoptive parents' memoirs are looking at the economy of adoption more directly, too: confronting, in Anagnost's words, the "specter" of commodification "head on." Melissa Fay Greene's contribution to *A Love like No Other* isolates and celebrates an ideal "love" between mother and small child, but in her full-length memoir published six years later, after the adoptions of three older boys from Ethiopia, Greene is perfectly frank about the financial contributions she and her husband make to members of one of the birth families. One boy still has not only a distantly related honorary grandmother but also, it later emerges, his birthmother and an older brother; the son had to be sent away, the family explains, because he would have been subject to an honor killing had he stayed home. Money sent to these needy family members could certainly be described as payment for a child, and Greene's narrative casually (even heartlessly, in the manner of Simon's boastful breakfasts out) displays the ease with which her family buys the taken-for-granted American suburban comforts that initially astonish the children from Ethiopia, but these transactions also contribute materially to the securing of the child's transnational identity. "I want her to always be part of his life," remarks Greene as the grandmother explains her poverty and decision to take the child to the American orphanage; "a boy needs his grandmother."[70] Thereafter Greene enables her son to send money back to Ethiopia, locating the child in an economic transaction—we could

70. Greene, *No Biking in the House,* 180; monetary contributions to the mother and brother are described at 271 and 339.

even call it a swaggeringly imperial one—even as it makes his dual identity as Ethiopian American a more readily lived reality.[71] Sending money home is something any good son and grandson might do. At least some contexts reveal the difficulty of separating what Henry James calls "bliss and bale" in the economics of adoption, or possibly the undesirability of doing so.

These recent moves to acknowledge the potential that commodification holds for "claiming value for people" are always at risk of degenerating into mere defenses of the marketplace; to adoption critics, positions such as those taken so cautiously by Dubinsky and Yngvesson and more casually by Greene may look no different from parental self-justifications. Because, as Briggs and others demonstrate, the evils of child kidnapping and trafficking are so great, the violence done to birth parents and birth communities as well as to the children so grave, it is difficult to think clearly about this morally complex issue, yet the adoption community has an obligation to do so. The assumption that children are property—first paternal, more recently familial—stems from the Enlightenment and is a legal principle as well as a cultural tenet arising from capital accumulation. The economic role of children in reproducing class goes back at least to the Industrial Revolution; as we have seen, the imperative to "complete one's life with family" (which compels the childless to "shop") is a Victorian one. Taboos now inhibit the open acknowledgment of these aspects of children's existence, even as children themselves continue both to suffer and to benefit from their economic roles. Therefore adoption narratives, particularly burdened with a responsibility to address these economic realities, tend to disavow and cover them over with the kinds of sentimentality we have observed in Bartholet, Lewis, Hood, and Simon. Could we locate in earlier eras more frank acknowledgment, more open discussion of "shopping for children," even defenses of the market's potential benefits to children that aren't simply parental self-justifications? Classic fiction in English from the eighteenth and nineteenth centuries contains an abundance of orphan protagonists, as well as social markets of various kinds: marriage markets and markets in children, too. The Victorian novel (British and American) dramatizes the tensions between seeing and denying the market in children, and between disparaging and apologizing for it, in ways

71. This situation could be contrasted to Heidi's horror when her Vietnamese birth family asks her for money in Gail Dolgin and Vicente Franco's film *Daughter from Danang* (2002) and compared to an American adoptive family's willingness to contribute financially to a birth family in Changfu Chang's film *The Daughters' Return* (2011).

that can help us think about the moral dimensions of the commodification and instrumentalization of adopted children now.

The second and third sections of this chapter consider some of the long cultural history of exchanging money for children and obliging them to do certain kinds of work, together with the ambivalences that have attended these practices. Tracing this history, I turn to George Eliot's 1861 novel *Silas Marner*, which vigorously denies the connection between money and adoption, only in the end to celebrate the instrumentalization of the adoptee; and to Henry James's 1897 *What Maisie Knew*, which exposes and even embraces that connection as having, in the end, served the child's interests. Reading these novels is intended to provide a fresh perspective on what it might mean to replace "rituals of decommodification" with "confront[ing]" the "specter . . . head on." Although these readings attend to the historical particulars of each novel's social and economic worlds, I also read these novels as if they were commentaries on current adoption debates. *Silas Marner* can be read as a slowed-down, more detailed version of *Baby, We Were Meant for Each Other* that makes it easier to see some of the evasive effects of Simon's sentimentality, while James's novel anticipates in a bolder register some of Yngvesson and Dubinsky's claims for the marketplace's perverse and counterintuitive contributions to constituting children's personhood.

THE VALUE OF A CHILD: SILAS MARNER'S GOLD, THE BABY WITH GOLDEN CURLS, AND EPPIE'S USELESS GARDEN

Just before the momentous scene in *Silas Marner* when a golden-haired toddler appears on Silas's hearth to replace, or so it seems to him, his lost gold coins, the novel provides its only glimpse of this child's birthmother. Soon to be eliminated from the narrative altogether so that her daughter's adoption can proceed unhindered, Molly Farren Cass is vilified as an opium addict and as the holder of unsuitably vindictive feelings toward her husband, Godfrey Cass, on whose neglect she wrongly blames her sufferings. It is New Year's Eve, and she is walking through falling snow toward Godfrey's stately house, where, in the midst of a "great party" for all the local gentry, she intends to reveal "her little child that had its father's hair and eyes," expose the unsavory secret marriage to Godfrey's father, the squire, and shame Godfrey before the entire community.[72] This once-pretty barmaid is so insignificant a character that

72. George Eliot, *Silas Marner* (1861) (London: Penguin, 1996, 2003), 107 (hereafter

the narrator, doling out moral judgments as Eliot's narrators tend to do, sketches her weak villainy with a few brief strokes: "Molly knew that the cause of her dingy rags was not her husband's neglect, but the demon Opium to whom she was enslaved, body and soul." Molly has only one redeeming quality, as the sentence continues: she is "enslaved . . . except in the lingering mother's tenderness that refused to give him her hungry child" (*Silas Marner*, 107). In her last moments, Molly again has the good grace to experience a moment's hesitation before consuming "the black remnant," which leaves her slowly freezing to death in the snow and her child parentless.

What does it mean to say that Molly "refused to give him [the demon Opium] her hungry child"? Given the extended metaphor of enslavement here, in which Opium is personified as a slave owner, "giving" the child would seem to mean giving Opium another "slave" by letting the child become addicted too; in the early nineteenth century, opium was marketed for children's use, under such names as "Street's Infant Quietness."[73] But the metaphor of slavery for drug addiction sets in motion some other possible meanings as well. The slave trade was still legal in Britain during the early years of the nineteenth century when the novel is set; slavery was still practiced in the United States at the time of Eliot's writing (1860–61); and the transatlantic abolition and temperance movements were linked during both periods by the moral evils of their targets, temperance commonly using the metaphor of slavery for alcohol and drug addiction and abolition representing addicts, slaves, and slave owners as sharing an equivalent moral degeneracy.[74] Molly's giving her child to a slave master could therefore suggest a more directly monetary transaction: in order to feed her habit, Molly might perhaps have sold her beautiful child.

Silas Marner is haunted by the possibility of baby selling. I will argue that the novel goes to great lengths to raise and simultaneously quell and then redirect the anxiety that a child could be exchanged for money. Like the narratives by Bartholet, Hood, and Simon discussed in the first section of this chapter, the novel performs "rituals of decommodification" (to use Anagnost's term) and at once acknowledges and disavows—

---

cited in the text). Marianne Novy too emphasizes Molly's vilification and erasure from the novel; see Novy, *Reading Adoption*, 130.

73. Mike Jay, *Emperor of Dreams: Drugs in the Nineteenth Century* (Sawtry, UK: Dedalus, 2000), 73.

74. Susan Zeiger, *Inventing the Addict: Drugs, Race, and Sexuality in Nineteenth-Century British and American Literature* (Amherst: University of Massachusetts Press, 2008), 9, 20–22; see also Richard Davenport-Hines, *The Pursuit of Oblivion: A Global History of Narcotics* (New York: W. W. Norton, 2002).

by covering it over with sentiment—a market in children. But in contrast to these recent narratives, *Silas Marner* more openly acknowledges that, despite or perhaps because of the high valuation placed on "love" in the Victorian period, to love an adopted child well is to instrumentalize it.

In the early years of the nineteenth century, what would likely have become of an actual child such as this nameless toddler, the offspring of a barmaid and a country squire's son (hardly likely to have been legally married, pace Eliot's fairy tale), whether parented by an impoverished drug addict or abandoned to the elements? Nineteenth-century Britons were not likely to be overly concerned with the disposition of a poor and unparented baby. Infant deaths were common, children's lives disposable. George K. Behlmer cites British traditions of family privacy and respect for parental rights in accounting for the casualness of nineteenth-century British attitudes about child abuse and infanticide.[75] In the 1860s, Behlmer reports, judges customarily distinguished between infanticide and murder, giving lesser penalties for the former.[76] Starting in the early eighteenth century, as Ruth Perry shows, land enclosures and industrialization had pushed a growing number of young women from their homes and families even as the kinds of work available to women diminished. Their out-of-wedlock children were more likely to have been considered burdens than saleable commodities; the founding of the Foundling Hospital in London in 1739 was symptomatic, Perry argues, of the increasing surplus of children whose mothers were unable to support them.[77] In the period when Eliot was writing, the 1834 Poor Law had made unmarried mothers solely responsible for their infants, which increased yet again the number of unsupported infants. As Godfrey indicates to Silas, disavowing his paternity over the dead body of his "unhappy hated wife" (*Silas Marner*, 117), in the countryside the normal destination of such a child as well as of her destitute mother would have

75. George K. Behlmer, *Child Abuse and Moral Reform in England, 1870–1908* (Stanford: Stanford University Press, 1982), 12, 15.

76. Behlmer, *Child Abuse*, 20. A Parliamentary Commission on Capital Punishment debated having British law follow France in delimiting a period of time from birth, a "grace period" ranging from three days to three months, during which the murder of a baby would be considered a lesser crime and subject to lesser penalties than would apply in the death of an older child (Behlmer, *Child Abuse*, 20–21). On the frequency of infanticide see also Randolph Trumbach, *Sex and the Gender Revolution: Volume One: Heterosexuality and the Third Gender in Enlightenment London* (Chicago: University of Chicago Press, 1998), 295–301.

77. Ruth Perry, *Novel Relations: The Transformation of Kinship in English Literature and Culture, 1748–1818* (Cambridge: Cambridge University Press, 2004), 55–64, 218–19, 30–31.

been "the parish," care provided by the church and supported by taxes on landowners.[78] Had she been raised by the parish, her likely future would have been in domestic service or, as the century advanced, in factory labor.

When Eliot was writing the novel and Victorian readers were consuming it, however, Victorian moral crusaders such as Thomas Bernardo were representing impoverished girl children as vulnerable to sale by parents for sexual exploitation.[79] By 1885 the "Maiden Tribute" scandal put this fear into wide circulation when two male reformers, posing as traffickers, induced the parents of a young girl to sell her to them. Although Lydia Murdoch shows that Bernardo exaggerated these risks to promote his orphanages, Eliot's hint that Molly might have sold her child resonates with Bernardo's fear mongering. Moreover, in the period in which the novel is set, putting a price on a child would not have been as strange and unsettling an idea as it would have been for readers in 1861. As Deborah Valenze points out (in a chapter titled "The Price of People"), indentured servitude was still common through the eighteenth century, as was also the legal concept of "property in persons," epitomized by but not limited to slavery, legal in Britain until 1807.[80] Children as young as seven were commonly bound as apprentices. Eighteenth-century children could be rented or bought as props for beggars (the more deformed the better), and no law regulated child labor until 1819; children were kidnapped into various trades into the early nineteenth century.[81] Up through 1775 people traded years of their labor in exchange for passage to America; while historians generally view these indentures as freely chosen, they also "have recognized the full extent of unfree labor in a literal 'market' for children in early America."[82] Thus at the moment when the golden-haired toddler steps from her mother's snow-covered arms, she could become anything, from a gently raised daughter of the gentry (were her father to acknowledge her) to an object of ownership or monetary exchange.

---

78. Compare the situation of Oliver Twist, "farmed" as an infant and starved to weakness if not death: Charles Dickens, *Oliver Twist* (1837) (New York: W. W. Norton, 1993), 20. See Laura Peters, *Orphan Texts: Victorian Orphans, Culture and Empire* (Manchester, UK: Manchester University Press, 2000), 6–18, for an account of the conditions of poor orphans' lives in this period.

79. Lydia Murdoch, *Imagined Orphans: Poor Families, Child Welfare, and Contested Citizenship in London* (New Brunswick: Rutgers University Press 2006), 32.

80. Deborah Valenze, *The Social Life of Money in the English Past* (Cambridge: Cambridge University Press, 2003), 241, 224.

81. Valenze, *Social Life,* 235–36, 241.

82. Valenze, *Social Life,* 240, 275, quotation at 255; Zelizer's *Pricing the Priceless Child* covers a later period but records the enduring effects of these norms.

Marianne Novy has persuasively demonstrated that *Silas Marner* advocates for adoption by counterintuitively representing adoption with metaphors drawn from nature and organic growth.[83] Eppie grows like grass and is associated with flowers; her adoption by Silas is made to seem natural in contrast to the legalistic claim her biological father makes at the end of the novel in his unsuccessful bid to recover her as his daughter. In connection with this naturalizing of Eppie's adoption, the novel labors to insist that Silas has not purchased Eppie, even though the novel's most memorable moment is the coincidence that brings the orphaned Eppie with her golden curls to Silas's hearth just days after the theft of his golden guineas. The novel emphasizes the accidental nature of both the loss of money and the gain of a child. Silas did not willingly part with his money, and he is in a passive state of trance when Eppie enters his house. The novel seems to raise, in order to deny it, the possibility that her adoption constitutes the exchange of a child for money.

This raising and denying of the possibility of child sale is embedded in the novel's richly detailed portrait of an era of rapid economic and social change. The novel opens not with the child's abandonment but with Silas Marner's history prior to the events of that snowy New Year's Eve. It begins specifically with Silas's work as a handloom weaver and its integration into the pre-industrial, rural economy of the village of Raveloe, "a village where many of the old echoes still lingered," lying deep in the countryside and "aloof from the currents of industrial energy and Puritan earnestness" of the early nineteenth century (*Silas Marner*, 7, 23). Here is the novel's opening sentence:

> In the days when the spinning wheels hummed busily in the farmhouses—and even great ladies, clothed in silk and thread-lace, had their toy spinning-wheels of polished oak—there might be seen in districts far away among the lanes, or deep in the bosom of the hills, certain pallid, undersized men. (*Silas Marner*, 5)

These "alien"-looking men, handloom weavers, so different from "the brawny country-folk," are only ever to be seen "bent under a heavy bag," carrying either "flaxen thread, or else the long rolls of strong linen spun from that thread." Although the narrative emphasizes the suspicion with which these outsiders are viewed, their work is also said to be "indispens-

83. Novy, *Reading Adoption*, 126; Novy first presented this argument in "Adoption in *Silas Marner* and *Daniel Deronda*," in Novy, *Imagining Adoption*, 35–56.

able" to the domestic labor that made households of this era economically productive, labor that was primarily the responsibility of women.

Soon we meet some of Silas's customers, women from the upper reaches of Raveloe society: Mrs. Osgood, Silas's first Raveloe customer, who hires Silas to weave her table linens from flax spun at home, and her nieces Nancy and Priscilla Lammeter, unquestionably ladies, who nonetheless operate a home dairy as well as doing their own spinning and producing food (meat pies are mentioned) for the household. Even when she is dressed in silk, lace, and jewels for a party, Nancy's hands "bore the traces of butter-making, cheese-crushing, and even still coarser work" (*Silas Marner,* 92). The Lammeter sisters do the baking and manage the household according to their mother's and aunt's old-fashioned standards: they "had been brought up in that way, that they never suffered a pinch of salt to be wasted, and yet everybody in their household had of the best, according to his place" (25). (Mrs. Poyser in *Adam Bede,* set at around the same time as *Silas Marner,* operates a home dairy; she "make[s] one quarter o' the rent, and," through her thriftiness, like that of Nancy Lammeter, "saves[s] th' other quarter."[84]) Such women, whose hard work and careful housekeeping are integral to the Raveloe agricultural economy and to the cultural memory of this time as "Merry England," pay their weaver in gold.

Eliot would have known, and at least some of her readers would have recalled, that in the years between 1800 and 1815 when the novel is set, the amassing of a hoard of golden guineas would have been next to impossible for an individual such as Silas Marner. Although in eighteenth-century Britain paper money was widely understood to represent its exact equivalent in gold, the war with France had necessitated the printing of paper money well beyond the value in gold held in the Bank of England's reserves.[85] Moreover, although in the early nineteenth century "coins . . . (theoretically) embodied the precious metal to which the units of value referred," throughout the eighteenth century the face value of coins was usually lower than the value of the metal of which they were made, and as a result, supplies of gold, silver, and other coin metals had been diminishing, bought up by foreign markets.[86] For these reasons, and as part of the broader transformation of the British

84. George Eliot, *Adam Bede* (1859) (Harmondsworth: Penguin, 1980), 394.

85. Mary Poovey, *Genres of the Credit Economy: Mediating Value in the Eighteenth- and Nineteenth-Century Britain* (Chicago: University of Chicago Press, 2008), 175–76.

86. Mary Poovey, "Introduction," in *The Financial System in Nineteenth-Century Britain,* ed. Mary Poovey (Oxford: Oxford University Press, 2003), 7.

financial system into a credit economy, the Bank Restriction Act had in 1797 suspended the redeemability of paper money and coins for their equivalents in gold or silver.[87] "The Restriction," which extended from 1797 to 1821, while seeming to "violat[e] the promise printed on the face of every note," also "encouraged the proliferation of provincial banks' notes."[88] Thus, Mary Poovey asserts, during these years "a weaver would have been far more likely to be paid in some kind of paper money than in gold," paper probably issued by a local bank.[89] Nonetheless, starting with the table linens for Mrs. Osgood, Silas's rural customers pay him in gold and silver, "five bright guineas" first and combinations of guineas, crowns, and half-crowns thereafter, as if they themselves, traditionalists like Silas, have been hoarding coins since the last century (*Silas Marner,* 17). Paper is never mentioned, nor—so averse is Silas to the very notion of monetary exchange—does Silas ever even "change the silver," in the narrator's peculiar phrasing, using it instead to "suppl[y] his bodily wants" (21), as if the lesser coins produced food and clothing directly without passing through a system of exchanges. The golden guineas he never spends.

Given the unlikelihood of Silas's accumulating so many guineas (272, to be exact, earned over fifteen years), his improbable hoard gains an uncanny dimension for the knowledgeable reader that enhances the magical qualities already attributed to Silas by his superstitious neighbors because of his "strange" habits. The guinea in particular bore a mythic aura as "the only term that represented both an abstract measure of value and a physical coin."[90] First minted from West African gold (from Guinea) in 1663 both to represent and to embody the value of a pound, its value at first floated up and down with the price of gold, exemplifying the equivalence of intrinsic and symbolic monetary value. The guinea had once stood for intrinsic valuation itself: "the late seventeenth century used 'quid' as slang for 'guinea,' derived from 'quiddity,' meaning the 'real nature or essence of a thing.' . . . As a gold coin, the guinea stood for the 'essence' of money."[91] By 1717 its value had been arbitrarily pegged at one pound one shilling and so had ceased to represent intrinsic value; yet Eliot nostalgically revives its older cultural resonances of authenticity, indivisibility, and value itself. Silas hoards the gold coins

87. Poovey, *Financial System,* 8.
88. Poovey, *Genres,* 176.
89. Poovey, *Genres,* 383.
90. Poovey, *Financial System,* 7.
91. Valenze, *Social Life,* 43.

he earns not for their exchange value but for their intrinsic qualities as objects. In his loneliness, he loves "to feel them in his palm, and look at their bright faces, which were all his own" (*Silas Marner,* 17). Of his growing pile of money the narrator remarks, "he began to think it was conscious of him, as his loom was, and he would on no account have exchanged those coins, which had become his familiars" (19). He loves not only their physical presence but also, paradoxically, what they represent by representing nothing. By being, for him, unexchangeable, they represent value itself.

Although the narrator treats his loving animation of the coins as at once pathos-filled and pathological—"the gold had kept his thoughts in an ever-repeated circle, leading to nothing beyond itself" (*Silas Marner,* 125)—the novel prefers Silas's way of treating money to others surveyed in the novel. The novel connects the idea of intrinsic value (of valuing gold for its own sake, not for what it can buy) to the older agricultural economy of Raveloe, and it privileges intrinsic value over exchange value and speculation, which soon make their contrastive appearance through another set of characters, Squire Cass and his family. "It was still that glorious war-time" when high agricultural prices allowed the landed gentry to live well and share their largesse among their neighbors. "For the Raveloe feasts were like the rounds of beef and the barrels of ale—they were on a large scale, and lasted a good while," and within the hierarchical social structure, the "great merry-makings . . . were regarded on all hands as a fine thing for the poor," owing to the spilling over of this abundance (23). Yet the narrator, positioned in a later time, can see the end coming in the "fall of prices" and "currents of industrial energy" that will soon expose this "timeless" rural economy as the last gasp of an outmoded way of life. The ill-natured second son Dunstan is a sign of the changed economy of the future. Through Dunstan, with his "taste for swopping and betting" (24), the narrative indicates distaste for the speculative principles of the new economy. Dunstan is blackmailing his brother Godfrey, extorting cash in exchange for keeping silent about Godfrey's secret marriage. One of the squire's tenant farmers has given his rent to Godfrey, who has given it to Dunstan instead of to the squire; now that the squire is threatening to seize the farmer's property Godfrey must raise a hundred pounds to make good his lie. On the grounds that "I'm a jewel for 'ticing people into bargains" (29), Dunstan persuades Godfrey to let him sell his horse Wildfire. The next day Dunstan, claiming to have "swopped" with Godfrey, arranges to sell Wildfire for 120 pounds; speculating, lying, and "encouraged by confidence in his luck"

(35), Dunstan takes one risk too many and rides Wildfire into a fatal injury. His brutal treatment of the animal epitomizes the immoral new economy, which instrumentalizes all the living beings (human and animal) that were once embedded in a system of non-monetized reciprocal obligations.

In Victorian fiction, speculation is always morally suspect.[92] In this novel, the speculator is also a thief. Walking away from the horse's accident, Dunstan plans to visit Silas and appropriate his hoard of gold. The novel scarcely distinguishes between Dunstan's intention to talk Marner into lending him the gold (on the promise of paying him interest) and his eventual outright theft of the guineas. Dunstan, it is clear, would never have bothered to repay the old man: as he approaches Silas's door,

> he had been imagining ways of cajoling and tempting the weaver to part with the immediate possession of his money for the sake of receiving interest. Dunstan felt as if there must be a little frightening added to the cajolery, for his own arithmetical convictions were not clear enough to afford him any forcible demonstration as to the advantages of interest; and as for security, he regarded it vaguely as a means of cheating a man by making him believe that he would be paid. (*Silas Marner,* 37–38)

When Dunstan finds Silas gone, he simply takes the guineas and leaves.

Silas's door is unlocked for a peculiar reason that Eliot emphasizes by elaborating its details. He has used his heavy metal door key as a counterweight to aid in the hearth cooking of "a small bit of pork." While going out on an errand, he has left this arrangement in place, and his supper cooking, rather than disassemble his arrangement to lock the door. Dunstan thinks the cooking meat signifies Silas's surplus wealth, but, to the contrary, Silas received the pork as a gift from his customer Priscilla Lammeter. Dunstan's theft thus takes advantage of and depends upon Silas's participation in the older, simpler farm economy in which thrift,

92. Tara McGann remarks, "What Victorian novel finds in financial speculation anything other than a sign of social corruption, and which takes a stance other than stinging indictment?" in "Literary Realism in the Wake of Business Cycle Theory: *The Way We Live Now* (1875)," in *Victorian Literature and Finance,* ed. Francis O'Gorman (Oxford: Oxford University Press, 2007), 133–56, quotation at 134. See also Tamara S. Wagner, *Financial Speculation in Victorian Fiction: Plotting Money and the Novel Genre, 1815–1901* (Columbus: Ohio State University Press, 2010). Although Wagner finds more nuance in Victorian representations of speculation, she too highlights the conventional link between speculation and villainy (and notes *Silas Marner*'s allusion to the gold standard [80]).

generosity, gifts, and barter play so large a role. In the value system of the novel, careful housekeeping and generous gift giving are both opposed to speculation and monetary exchange; the practice of thrift links Silas to the Lammeters despite their class differences. That Dunstan's theft is swiftly punished—weighted down by the two heavy bags of gold, he falls into the quarry and drowns—shows that the materiality of the gold (in other words, Silas's view of it) trumps Dunstan's view of it as a medium of exchange and speculation.

This morally suspect view of money is also represented by the dehumanizing mercantile and industrial economies at the novel's urban borders. In the retrospective scenes in Lantern Yard, in the northern industrial city from which Silas was exiled, he was paid weekly rather than, as in Raveloe, by the piece. Coming to him as a weekly wage rather than as the direct equivalent of each product of his labor, money was abstract. Moreover, money was precious for its exchange value: he used to spend part of his wages on the collective expenses of his chapel. (In Lantern Yard, "every penny had its purpose for him," although the hypocrisy and faithlessness of Silas's religious community eventually ironizes that "purpose" [*Silas Marner*, 17].) The urban mercantile economy and its inferior moral values are again glimpsed briefly when the Miss Gunns, "the wine merchant's daughters from Lytherly," appear at Squire Cass's New Year's Eve ball. "Hard-featured" and "dressed in the height of fashion," they wear their clothes too tight and too low-cut, and they displease the narrator by patronizing Nancy Lammeter, who, despite her country accent, her lack of schooling, and her work-coarsened hands, is without doubt "a lady" (90–93). The Miss Gunns, in contrast to the hardworking Miss Lammeters, represent the new economy in which middle-class women display the wealth of their menfolk by their conspicuous consumption and their abstention from productive activity. Dunstan's wastefulness, expensive tastes, and gambling habit link him to the modern city, while Silas's thriftiness and industriousness place him on a continuum with the old-fashioned Lammeters, whose industriousness is interdependent on his. In this context, miserly hoarding is far less pernicious than speculation as a way of treating money; indeed, Silas's love of his coins helps to keep the "sap of affection" flowing in him (20).

Anachronistically substituting gold coins, the stuff of fairy tales, for unromantic but historically more accurate paper bills, and privileging the older farm economy over the newer urban economy, Eliot locates her adoption narrative within an atavistic dream of intrinsic value, the dream or wish that value might inhere in objects themselves and not be determined by market exchange or speculation. This wish is amplified by the novel's representation of a series of other sign systems that form part of the novel's thick description of Raveloe's "timeless" agricultural community, sign systems in which meaning is inherent or literal rather than symbolic or figurative.

At the Rainbow bar, where Silas will shortly appear to announce and seek justice for the theft of his guineas, the conversation among the beer drinkers skips from topic to topic but circles around themes of tradition and the fixed nature of character and class, and it repeatedly reaffirms the self-identity of objects. A disagreement between the farrier and the butcher turns on the question of whether one particular cow ("a red Durham") is the same as itself; the landlord ends it by asserting "the Rainbow's the Rainbow" (*Silas Marner*, 46–47), and at the end of the next chapter he will resolve another argument by asserting that "a fly's a fly" (58). A couple of topics require recourse to nature: one man can't sing because "it's your inside as isn't right made for music" (48), and some people can see ghosts and others cannot in the same way that some can smell strong cheese and others cannot. Family traits are inborn—musicianship runs in Mr. Macey's family—and generations repeat: "the young man—that's the Mr Lammeter as now is . . . soon began to court Miss Osgood, that's the sister o' the Mr Osgood as now is, and a fine handsome lass she was" (50).[93] The conversation stresses the value of traditional lifeways and fixed class positions. A Mr. Cliff, a tailor who bought a large property in the neighborhood, is punished with family deaths and madness for his temerity in daring to step out of his class. Anecdotes that reassuringly confirm the permanency of the social order are ritually repeated. One story has been told so often that "it was listened to as if it had been a favorite tune, and at certain points the puffing of pipes was momentarily suspended, that the listeners might give their whole minds to the expected words" (51–52). This particular story affirms the legality of a marriage ceremony despite the minister's garbling of the spoken words; social order is threatened only to be reaffirmed.

Dismayed by the sudden loss of his guineas, Silas rushes into the bar and accuses the poacher Jem Rodney, who defends himself in these terms: "What could I ha' done with his money? I could as easy steal the parson's surplice, and wear it" (*Silas Marner*, 56). Social positions are so firmly fixed in Raveloe that, as the town ponders the robbery, it occurs to

93. Novy sees a similar moment elsewhere in the novel as a "comic exaggeration" of the townspeople's superstitious belief in heredity that supports the novel's affirmation of adoption (*Reading Adoption*, 127).

no one that Dunstan's disappearance on the same day might be connected. Suspicion falls instead on a peddler recently in the neighborhood, whose social inferiority and foreign looks make him a more natural suspect than the squire's second son. Raveloe assumes that people are what they appear to be and what their natures and inherited positions make them; that like Silas's guineas themselves they are self-identical and that their meanings are self-evident. As the narrator comments a short while later, "time out of mind the Raveloe doctor had been a Kimble: Kimble was inherently a doctor's name" (98).

Self-identity and inherent meaning also characterize the primitive Christianity of the villagers, in whose use of religious signs, similarly, meaning is not referenced or symbolized but rather inherent in the sign itself, in an Adamic or literal language where the words for things are the things themselves. During the dark days after the robbery and just before Christmas, Silas Marner receives a consolatory visit from his neighbor Dolly Winthrop, who hands him a package of "lard-cakes" stamped or pricked with the letters I.H.S. Silas can read these letters, but he does not understand what they mean; Dolly does not know what they mean, either, nor can she even read them, but she knows "they've a good meaning" and indeed that "they're good letters, else they wouldn't be in the church," where she has noticed them also embroidered on the "pulpit-cloth" (*Silas Marner,* 82). Dolly can transmit them accurately without understanding them because she inherited from her husband's mother the stamp with which she, in her day, pricked the letters into her lard cakes. The intrinsic goodness of the letters (it's not just that they have a good meaning, but that they are good) is proven not only by their presence in church and by their association with a line of motherly women, but also by the sensuous palpability of their embodiment. Dolly modestly confesses that although she marks the letters on all her baked goods, "sometimes they won't hold, because o' the rising." The failure of one form of goodness, the legibility of the letters, occurs only because another form of goodness, the yeasty plumpness of the bread, has superseded it. But meaning is not lost: "rising" is what the mysterious letters signify, although Dolly does not know it, for they represent the name of Jesus. When the letters I.H.S. disappear into the crusty curves of a risen loaf, the miraculous and perhaps incomprehensible "rising" to which the letters I.H.S. allude is literalized as (and replaced by) a "rising" that anyone can enjoy. That the letters pricked into the lard cakes "have held better nor common," as Dolly says, suggests that this particular recipe tends to flatness rather than to yeasty roundness and thus that the lard cakes she give Silas resemble unleavened communion wafers, into which the letters I.H.S. are sometimes stamped to this day, though Dolly's cakes are rendered tastier with the addition of fat and spices. The sign is indistinguishable from what it signifies.[94]

Although Silas has no interest in taking communion at church, by sharing her I.H.S.-marked baking with him, Dolly brings Silas into what Q. D. Leavis calls "the true religion of neighborliness," a real and practical communion with fellow human beings.[95] It does not matter what the holy letters signify; what they are intrinsically is good food, a word made bread that physically ties Silas to the community. The transubstantiation that occurs in Catholic communion, if not strictly speaking in the Anglican ritual, takes literal form in this scene. When Silas cannot understand or appreciate the Christmas carol that Dolly's son Aaron sings for him, he can express his gratitude by silently offering Aaron some more lard cake (*Silas Marner*, 85). And just as the novel favors Silas's love of gold as palpable object over other characters' view of money as instrument of exchange or speculation, so the literal goodness of cakes marked I.H.S. is valued over the arbitrary understanding of religious signs in the practice of Lantern Yard's urban fundamentalists. Though Silas's coreligionists aspired to read the Bible literally, claiming its authority for "drawing lots" to determine Silas's guilt or innocence, they convicted him unjustly of theft when they read God's will in random, arbitrarily chosen signs, and they left Silas believing there is "no just God . . . but [only] a God of lies" (13–14).

Despite Dolly's visit, Silas remains desolate and spends a grim Christmas alone in his stone cottage, grieving for his lost gold coins and looking out at "the black frost" and the "half-icy red pool." Now, though the narrative's texture remains realist, the plot turns mythic. Silas's dark week between Christmas and New Year's comes to a fairy tale end when he finds, as if by magic or miracle, his gold coins replaced by the golden curls of a child. And just as in the recent adoption narratives by Bartholet, Hood, and Simon discussed in the first section of this chapter, narratives that likewise depict adoption as a miracle, the novel carefully denies that Silas has made an exchange. The child with the "golden head" (*Silas*

94. Moreover, the letters call attention to themselves as visible shapes because they are both a transliteration of the first three letters of Jesus's name in Greek (copying the look, not the meaning, of the name of Jesus) and the initial letters in Emperor Constantine's heavenly vision of the cross, "In Hoc Signo Vinces."

95. Q. D. Leavis, "Original Penguin Classics Introduction" (1967), in Eliot, *Silas Marner*, 208–39, quotation at 216.

Marner, 109) is the transubstantiation of Silas's lost golden guineas, a word made flesh, like the lard cakes; in Silas's mind she is literally their transformation into another substance.[96] For the narrative insists that the gold has "turned into" Eppie:

> To his blurred vision, it seemed as if there were gold on the floor in front of the hearth. Gold!—his own gold—brought back to him as mysteriously as it had been taken away! . . . The heap of gold seemed to glow and get larger beneath his agitated gaze. He leaned forward at last, and stretched forth his hand; but instead of the hard coin with the familiar resisting outline, his fingers encountered soft warm curls. (*Silas Marner,* 110)

Pondering this mysterious appearance, Silas arrives at a conclusion that is best expressed paratactically. "My money's gone, I don't know where—and this is come from I don't know where" is the formulation Silas settles upon; he says it twice (118, 121). The narrator translates this to mean "that the child was come instead of the gold—that the gold had turned into the child" (122).[97] With these two accounts of this mysterious happening, divided and linked by a dash that might imply either apposition or revision, the narrative emphasizes a relationship of visual similarity that distinctly differs from the kind of relationship in which money might figure. Each of these formulations—"come instead of" and "turned into"—borders on saying that Silas has exchanged his guineas for the child, but the narrator takes care that this is not what they say. His guineas had no exchange value for Silas. The girl is valuable not because she signifies something that remains elsewhere, but because, transubstantiated, she is something: the gold has become her, just as the letters I.H.S. become a literally nourishing communion.

The child's value for Silas is intrinsic and therefore beyond measurement and not subject to exchange. Yet just moments earlier, in her mother's unreliable arms, the child was a shameful secret, of uncertain but nonetheless potentially measurable value. Valued by her mother chiefly as an instrument of revenge or extortion, yet not valued enough (Molly

96. In his reading of biblical hermeneutics in *Silas Marner,* David Carroll uses this term explicitly: "his gold transubstantiated into Eppie's curls before his eyes"; see *George Eliot and the Conflict of Interpretations: A Reading of the Novels* (Cambridge: Cambridge University Press, 1992), 152.

97. Much later, the narrator reports Silas and Eppie's shared story of family formation in this way: Silas "had taken her golden curls for his lost guineas brought back to him" (Eliot, *Silas Marner,* 146), a formulation that almost acknowledges an exchange.

chooses the laudanum over the baby), this child, now suddenly available for adoption, is of radically uncertain value, her value about to be decided in a scene that evokes a marketplace. In her crossing from her mother's cold body to Silas's warm hearth, a potentially terrifying passage that the narrator presents as a cute piece of toddler behavior and covers with the phrase "the ready transition of infancy" (*Silas Marner,* 109), this child moves from one mode of valuation and frame of meaning to another. As George K. Behlmer demonstrates, in 1861 England was in a period of transition with regard to the value of the unparented child.[98] Orphaned or illegitimate children had long been seen as burdens, trash to be disposed of at the birth parent's expense. Five pounds or less was, in this period, the amount typically paid to a "baby farmer" by mothers of illegitimate babies needing to have them taken off their hands; most of these babies soon died from neglect or worse. Indeed, according to Behlmer, "the term 'adoption' increasingly becomes associated with the criminal treatment of illegitimate children."[99] Yet sometimes during the same period available children were also seen as treasures, to be paid for by adoptive parents wanting to add either to their families or to their stable of workers. Discussing advertisements in a late-nineteenth-century newspaper called the *Bazaar, Exchange, and Mart,* Behlmer writes: "Some advertisers were prepared to pay for the right sort of child, while others wished to be compensated for their kindness."[100]

The novel at this point expansively mirrors the unstable value and meaning of unattached children across the nineteenth century, subject to sale and purchase, potentially burdensome as well as potentially valuable. In the scene of the child's public revelation, her perceived value oscillates between trash and treasure as characters from a range of so-

98. George K. Behlmer, *Friends of the Family: The English Home and Its Guardians, 1850–1940* (Stanford: Stanford University Press, 1998). See especially chap. 6, "Artificial Families: The Politics of Adoption," 272–315, which appears revised as "What's Love Got to Do with It? 'Adoption' in Victorian and Edwardian England," in *Adoption in America: Historical Perspectives,* ed. E. Wayne Carp (Ann Arbor: University of Michigan Press, 2002), 82–100.

99. Behlmer, *Friends of the Family,* 274. For the figure of five pounds, see p. 278; this is higher than the parish's subsidy of seven and a half pence a week, or between one and two pounds a year, for the support of Oliver Twist by the baby farmer, but comparable to the offer to pay five pounds to whoever would take Oliver on as apprentice.

100. Behlmer, *Friends of the Family,* 290. Although Behlmer's examples of this two-way street in adoption come mostly from the later nineteenth century, he cites *Silas Marner* as an example of a text displaying radically different views of the parentless child. Viviana Zelizer traces a similar history of the changing value of parentless children in the United States between the late nineteenth and early twentieth centuries (*Pricing the Priceless Child,* 169–200).

cial positions negotiate her disposition. To the squire, both Silas and the child are offenders against social order. Silas, ironically and unintentionally carrying out Molly's plan, has rushed into the midst of the squire's party, where the squire addresses them angrily: "what do you do coming in here in this way?" And Godfrey echoes this devaluation by silently refusing to acknowledge the child as his. Mrs. Kimble (who is the squire's sister and the doctor's wife), bothered by the proximity of "those dingy clothes [to] her own ornamented satin bodice," takes the child for an object to be disposed of: "you'd better leave the child here," she tells Silas; "I'll tell one o' the girls to fetch it" (*Silas Marner,* 115). Yet in dialogue with these characters, Silas reconstructs the valueless child as a precious treasure. To Mrs. Kimble Silas replies, "I can't let it go" because "it's come to me—I've a right to keep it." The narrative of this marketlike scene stresses that Silas had not yet formed an intention about the child: his response is instinctive, and it surprises both himself and Mrs. Kimble. Yet it is foreshadowed by his initial apprehension of the child as transformation of his gold. Desperate to repair the lifelong losses that have culminated in the loss of his gold, Silas is in effect the high bidder for the child, even as the narrative—by making Silas so naïve, so uncalculating—denies there is anything transactional about his part in the scene.

When the scene shifts to Silas's house, where the unknown woman's body has been laid out and the anxious Godfrey has gone to assure himself that it is Molly and that she is dead, the narrator stresses the child's transcendent value. She exhibits

> that wide-gazing calm which makes us older human beings, with our inward turmoil, feel a certain awe in the presence of a little child, such as we feel before some quiet majesty or beauty in the earth or sky. (*Silas Marner,* 118)

Even so, the market value of the child continues to fluctuate. Godfrey, temporarily torn between two opposed poles of valuation, feels both regret and joy that his child does not recognize him, but the words he speaks next determine her real value to him. He asks Silas rhetorically, "You'll take the child to the parish tomorrow?" Silas in response reasserts his "right" to her by way of the child's identification with the gold: "My money's gone, I don't know where—and this is come from I don't know where." Silas is not talking about the child's monetary value to him, but Godfrey turns their conversation into a financial transaction by handing Silas a half guinea "towards finding it clothes." This payment—routine in one sense, given the gentry's traditional patronage of those less well off—echoes the payment that the mother of an unwanted child might give to a baby farmer.

In giving money to Silas, Godfrey silently marks the value he places on being rid of the child. In the next moment Godfrey tries to get public assent to his devaluation of "the tramp's child" by remarking to Mr. Kimble, the doctor, that "the parish isn't likely to quarrel with him for the right to keep the child." But the child's market value is still subject to contestation: Mr. Kimble replies that he "might once have quarreled with him for it myself" although his wife (who in the previous scene found the child's clothes repellently "dingy") is now too old. As the chapter closes, the narrative keeps tracking Godfrey's defensive and self-justifying thoughts, awkwardly repeating the emphatic pun three times in two adjacent sentences:

> He would do everything but own it. Perhaps it would be just as happy in life without being owned by its father, seeing that nobody could tell how things would turn out, and that—is there any other reason wanted?—well, then, that the father would be much happier without owning the child. (*Silas Marner,* 119)

Owning denotes acknowledging, and yet Godfrey's half guinea and his inner promise to provide financial support in return for not "owning" it also construct the child as alienable property, devalued by being equated with fixed sums of money. In Silas's hands, by contrast, the half guinea coin's exchange value dissipates: Silas does not spend Godfrey's money (indeed, we never hear of this coin again) but instead clothes the child in hand-me-downs from Dolly. The child's value for Silas excludes the possibility of being measured in monetary terms. From here on, the novel mobilizes the language of treasure to describe the value of the child—now named Eppie—to Silas, treasure that not only is not associated with monetary exchange but is explicitly identified with the valueless. In the single extended anecdote about Eppie's childhood, when she cuts herself loose from Silas's loom and wanders across the fields to a muddy pond, Silas is "overcome with convulsive joy at finding his treasure again," a treasure whose carefully detailed filthiness recalls the "dingy" appearance that lowered her value for the gentry at the squire's New Year's Eve party (128). What is trash for others is treasure to Silas; her value has been determined in a marketplace that the novel at once invokes and disavows by granting her to the man for whom her value has no measure and for whom the market itself has no existence.

The novel aligns moral value with those who lack concern about money, but that does not mean the novel lacks concern about economic matters. The short second part of the novel, in tracking outcomes for the characters sixteen years later, tracks changes in their economic lives and in their social positions. The novel's fairy tale logic requires that the good man be rewarded for his generous deed, and he is rewarded, and not only in the kind of treasure that has no exchange value. The novel sketches out the economic transformation of the British countryside that took place during the Industrial Revolution, compressing a hundred years or so of change into the thirty years of its narrative. Although the economic formation on which both Silas and the gentry have depended comes to an end, the novel, improbably and ahistorically, places Silas among the beneficiaries of this transformation. It makes his economic and social rise a result of his adoption of Eppie, precisely and ironically because Eppie had no measurable value for him. As in Simon's *Baby, We Were Meant for Each Other,* and as noted in recent critiques such as Nelson's, Eng's, and Anagnost's, the adoptee performs the essential labor of consolidating her parent's class position and his status as a citizen of his community, a task she can perform only because—like Scott Simon's daughters—she seems to do no work at all.

Silas makes no profit from adopting Eppie, despite Godfrey's cash gifts, and the narrative calls attention to Eppie's nil material contribution to household support. Eppie is defined as a nonworker. With its mentions of the parish and the workhouse, the narrative offers reminders that a "tramp's child" might have become a domestic servant or a factory worker. Eppie stays at home with her father, but she conspicuously does not become his apprentice or even his low-skilled helper, as children in eighteenth-century economically productive homes would have done. Surely the well-off Lammeter sisters worked more as children, learning their mother's productive skills, than does this worker's child. Instead, she impedes his work, her care making it harder for him to spend all day at his loom and travel the countryside delivering his products, although the narrative insists that the pleasure and humanization Silas gains more than compensate. In the childhood episode in which she ends up in the mud, she makes herself "like a small mouse" and uses one of Silas's work implements, his scissors, to cut through the "broad strip of linen" with which Silas has secured her to his loom. The narrative thus calls attention to what Eppie subtracts from Silas's means of support, using his very tools to make mischief; moreover, "the weaving must stand still a long while this morning" while Silas cleans her up (*Silas Marner,* 129). In part II of the novel, sixteen years later, Silas ought to be in trouble economically, because "the weaving was going down" and he is the sole support of this lovely, nonworking eighteen-year-old whose chief preoccupation seems to be her "curly auburn hair" (138). Silas and Eppie nonetheless end the novel far better off than they started.

As we have seen, the narrative locates the main events of the novel in a pre-industrial, pre-capitalist rural enclave where reciprocal obligations and mutual dependence link the squire and his tenants and, too, the ladies and the handloom weaver. In part I the narrative tends to present this archaic economy with a mix of nostalgia and impatience, as when, introducing the comfortable life at the squire's, the narrator comments, "the fall of prices had not yet come to carry the race of small squires and yeomen down that road to ruin for which extravagant habits and bad husbandry were plentifully anointing their wheels" (*Silas Marner,* 23). By the time of part II, this set of economic interdependencies is on the decline. The war is over, agricultural prices have fallen, and taxes have risen. Although we hear of no immediate financial troubles for Godfrey and Nancy, who still runs a thrifty household, the Cass family line is coming to an end and with it the traditional riches and dignities of their quasi-feudal way of life. Godfrey is plain Mr. Cass, not having inherited his father's title, and, childless, he has no heir. At the same time, "the weaving was going down too—for there was less and less flax spun" (141), owing to the rise of water- and steam-powered cotton manufacturing; few of the women who once spun their own flax now make their households into centers of economic production.

A still more archaic agricultural economy is represented by the nonfarm labor of Silas's mother, whose way of life has already been swept away before the start of the novel but who is nonetheless remembered at key points. Although Silas was born and raised in a northern industrial city, the narrative remembers his mother as one who once made a living in the countryside by foraging for herbs in the lanes and commons and using them in the practice of medicine. As an unschooled healer, Silas's mother belonged to a tradition stretching back to pre-Christian religious practices and beliefs. Silas, who has inherited his mother's knowledge, is expected by Raveloe to perform like "the Wise Woman at Tarley," who used charms as well as herbs (*Silas Marner,* 18); because he refuses to, the villagers ostracize him, and he abandons his mother's practice. Traveling "the fields and lanes" to deliver his work, Silas "never wandered to the hedge-banks and the lane-side in search of the once familiar herbs" (21–22). His mother's heritage is one of the things he recovers when Eppie's childhood reconnects him to the human and natural world. Not only is Eppie's growth compared to "grass i' May" and her baby clothes to "fresh-sprung herbs" (120–21); soon Silas is taking Eppie for spring walks to pick flowers and listen to the birds, and, "sitting on the banks in this way, Silas began to look for the once familiar herbs again," their leaves bringing him "a sense of crowding remembrances" (126).

Although his mother's vanished way of life returns sentimentalized, as a hobby, not a source of income, other aspects of Silas's economic life recall her archaic reliance on the commons, the long-ago end of which is symbolically repeated within the time span of the novel. (Although the novel does not specify, perhaps the enclosures of the eighteenth century account for his mother's move to the city where Silas was born.) The "Stone-pit" where Silas lives is one of those mythic places in George Eliot novels, like the Red Deeps in *The Mill on the Floss,* that defy realistic depiction. Deep and broad enough for a man to drown in and his body to remain undiscovered for sixteen years, the water-filled declivity formed by this disused quarry is nonetheless level enough that draining it can be expected to produce grazing land for cows. The water is always red, presumably with mud, but perhaps more with the symbolism of sacrifice. The area is also specifically described as "a piece of unenclosed ground" (*Silas Marner,* 34). This means that it is part of that unowned terrain, the commons, where prior to the enclosures of the eighteenth century and the consolidation of land ownership in the hands of fewer and richer individuals, ordinary folk could go to make a living. Ruth Perry argues that women of all classes, but especially poor women, were unequally disadvantaged, compared to men, by the economic, social, legal, and cultural changes that accompanied the rise of industrial capitalism. The enclosures of common land, which forced so many people off the land and into the cities and factories, hit women hardest, she argues, because women more than men had made their livings in the manner of Silas's mother: foraging for food and fuel and grazing animals.[101] That Silas lives on "a piece of unenclosed ground" (he appears to owe no one rent) may account in part for his ability to save so much of his earnings, but the Stone-pit is also represented as primeval and threatening. When Silas

101. Perry, *Novel Relations,* 55–64, 302, 310.

fears that Eppie has fallen in and drowned, the narrative reiterates the description of the Stone-pit as "unenclosed" (127), projecting the obvious unsafety of an unfenced pool onto the commons itself, as if the existence of common land were not a resource for the poor but a danger to them. Thus the novel gently nudges the reader to think favorably about enclosure, the devastating economic practice that threw women like Silas's mother into poverty two generations earlier.

In the present time of part II, despite the passing of these traditional lifeways and economic formations, Silas and Eppie are thriving, their lifestyle distinctly gentrified. When we first see her, Eppie is preoccupied not only by her curly hair but by her desire for a garden: in the quaint Sunday scene that opens part II, Eppie's first words are, "I wish *we* had a little garden, father, with double daisies in" (*Silas Marner,* 138). Silas's encouraging response shows his understanding that making a garden is above all about enclosure. "I could work at taking in a little bit o' the waste, just enough for a root or two o' flowers for you" (139). The conversation is allegorical: as the way of life passes that supported his dying craft, Silas now embraces the new economy that depends on a proprietary boundary between the raw and the cultivated. The act of enclosing a little garden mimics the large-scale enclosures and identifies the interests of this upwardly aspiring family not with the working poor but with their "betters." Eppie does not want to grow flax, food, or anything useful: she wants a flower garden. In addition to flowers, Eppie wants herbs, too—rosemary, bergamot, and thyme—not for their medicinal properties but because they smell sweet; and she wants lavender despite or because she believes it grows "only in the gentlefolks' gardens" (139).

Eppie emphasizes the word "we" in her initial request because she has just been admiring the rectory garden, even though she goes only so far as to say she would like daisies "like Mrs Winthrop's." She wants a garden as a luxury of the kind that her social and economic betters can afford, a garden as charming, decorative, and useless as herself. Eppie is not strong enough to dig the soil or move rocks to make the needed enclosure; Silas is proud that his daughter is "dillicate made" and unable to "carry a stone no bigger than a turnip" (*Silas Marner,* 147). Sturdy Aaron Winthrop, courting her, offers to do the hard physical work. He is the Cass family's paid gardener, and he can bring extra soil as well as "slips of anything; I'm forced to cut no end of 'em when I'm gardening, and throw 'em away mostly" (139). Eppie's physical delicacy, her love of adornment, and her lack of involvement in productive work make her, strangely, more like the Miss Gunns than like any of the women of her own economic class or even the women among the previous generation of "gentlefolk." Eppie is the woman of the future.

While they are planning their garden, discussing the "loose stones" (that is, waste material, apparently unowned) that they can bring from the edge of the water-filled Stone-pit, Silas and Eppie notice that the water is going down. This is happening because Godfrey Cass has traded with Mr. Osgood to obtain this piece of land, which he is draining, we learn later, to help Nancy start a dairy. What had seemed to be a piece of unenclosed commons turns out to have belonged to Mr. Osgood, and now it belongs to an owner who will make use of it for private economic gain. A dairy is economically backward looking, a holdover from the Lammeter sisters' younger days; the old-fashioned Priscilla still loves her dairy and urges Nancy to start her own. But the draining of the Stone-pit also means the consolidation of one landowner's property at the expense of those who may still have relied upon it as a commons.

Before any milk cows can come to graze, however, the completion of the draining brings the momentous discovery of Dunstan's skeleton at the bottom of the pool and with it the revelation that he robbed Silas's guineas sixteen years before. This discovery, which occurs only a few hours after Eppie and Silas's conversation about the garden, restores Silas's guineas to him and confirms the moral bankruptcy of the gentry even as it foreshadows their economic bankruptcy. Although Dunstan was the family's black sheep, Godfrey is ready to absorb his guilt as his own. The narration leading up to the revelation is concerned with the long history of Nancy and Godfrey's childlessness and his disingenuous efforts to persuade her to adopt Eppie, a narration that culminates with Godfrey's guilt: "his conscience, never thoroughly easy about Eppie, now gave his childless home the aspect of a retribution" (*Silas Marner,* 159). When Godfrey brings the news about Dunstan to Nancy, although the "dishonour" of this "kinship with crime" would have been sufficient to account for her husband's distress, Godfrey's guilt spills over into a confession he does not strictly need to make: that he is Eppie's father. In the emotional logic of Godfrey's guilt, his refusal to "own" Eppie—his having decided that "owning" her would be a greater burden than dispensing with her—is equal to Dunstan's theft of the guineas. The remainder of the novel is devoted to working out the meaning of these coinciding events: the enclosure of the commons, the (discovery of the) bankruptcy of the gentry, and the working man's accession to wealth. These are the events that finally establish the value and meaning of Eppie's adoption.

Although every "bright-faced" coin is returned, the value of the gold has changed. Silas and Eppie sit alone with "the recovered gold—the old long-loved gold, ranged in orderly heaps, as Silas used to range it in the days when it was his only joy" (*Silas Marner,* 165). Silas reflects that, although initially he imagined Eppie might be "changed into the gold again," he soon came to feel that it would have been "a curse come again, if it had drove you from me." He is rewarded for his right-mindedness by now having them both. As if by magic, "the money was taken away from me in time; and you see it's been kept—kept till it was wanted for you" (166). His guineas have been saved for him, but the passage of sixteen years has turned them into money with exchange value. "Wanted for you" means that he now values the guineas not for their intrinsic, material properties but as expendable cash. Silas has moved from the old economy to the new.[102]

Meanwhile, Godfrey and Nancy visit Silas, having decided to adopt Eppie. Godfrey speaks patronizingly of owing Silas a "debt" and disparages the stacks of guineas as insufficient "whether it's put out to interest, or you were to live on it as long as it would last," even though Silas points out they represent far more savings than "working-folks" usually amass (*Silas Marner,* 167). Godfrey needs Silas to be poor because he intends to present his adoption of Eppie, and her transformation into "a lady," as a generous transfer of wealth from himself to Silas, through removing the burden of her care and by compensating Silas for having "been at the trouble of bringing her up so well. And it's right you should have every reward for that" (168). Godfrey will even make Eppie his heir: "provide for you as my only child" (171). His condescending attitude signals his desire still to be understood as Silas's class superior; he speaks as though the old rules of patronage binding and dividing rich and poor still applied. But Silas refuses to accept Godfrey's class and economic logic and invokes a different logic of compensation that presupposes their essential equality: "God gave her to me because you turned your back upon

102. As coins, the guineas always held the potential to slip from intrinsic back to figurative or arbitrarily assigned value. When the metal value of a coin is equivalent to its face value, the stamping on the coin should be unnecessary; it is a supplement that opens the possibility of a gap between signifier and signified, a gap denied by the gold standard. The guinea bore the monarch's profile on one side and on the other a shield or shields representing Great Britain and its territories, but it seems unlikely that the "faces" Silas loved were the ugly mugs of the monarch (perhaps George III) stamped on the coins. The "faces" the coins turned toward Silas were "faces" in some other sense, perhaps the same sense in which they were his "unborn children" (*Silas Marner,* 21), so that even when Silas most loved the coins for their intrinsic qualities, his love depended on a gap between the thing and its meaning, the gap on which the new economy depends.

her. . . . When a man turns a blessing from his door, it falls to them as take it in" (169). Godfrey gives up in frustration when Eppie reveals that she is "promised to marry a working-man," minutes after he has invoked this very possibility as a choice that would put her forever out of the reach of his generosity: in that case, "whatever I might do for her, I couldn't make her well-off" (173, 170). In Godfrey's understanding of social strata, Eppie will remain forever one of the working poor.

But Eppie is going to marry Aaron Winthrop, the wheelwright's son, whose upward mobility is signaled both by his increasing workload as the gardener for the gentry (he works for the Casses, the Osgoods, and the rector) and by his tactful way of disparaging the wastefulness of his wealthy customers. The class leveling that Silas angrily frames in moral terms is projected as a practical reality with this marriage. While Aaron will continue to work hard, Eppie's physical delicacy and lack of useful occupation will mark this future family's status as middle class: instead of a productive worker, she is a consumer. She wants a pretty garden filled with "gentlefolks'" plants, a garden that would perform the same function she herself performs by doing no useful work.

Other emblems of the family's projected class rise abound in the final pages of the novel. When Nancy offers to buy her a wedding dress, Eppie has her choice ready: "she had often thought . . . that the perfection of a wedding-dress would be a white cotton, with the tiniest pink sprig at wide intervals" (*Silas Marner,* 181). Daydreaming about her wedding dress, Eppie at least in her fantasy life joins the ranks of the Miss Gunns. It would have been highly unlikely for a working-class woman to marry in white in the period in which the novel is set, and it would still have been unusual in 1860. Wedding clothes, even if made especially for the occasion, would have been of a darker, more practical shade, as no working person could afford to own a dress used only for one occasion; the wedding dress would be in use for years to come. Only in 1840, when Queen Victoria chose a white wedding dress, did the tradition of marrying in white take hold, and then only for those who could afford it. Although her desires settle on cotton rather than silk, Eppie thus proleptically imitates an upper-class custom of the future. Moreover, the newlyweds will live in a cottage that has undergone a class transformation along with its inhabitants. Once a stonecutter's cottage on a commons, then the home workshop of a weaver, now, with new rooms and dignified furniture, it will become a scene of domestic bliss from which a paterfamilias goes out to work. And it has an enclosed flower garden where once it opened onto the rough commons. Even though the reality of these social and cultural formations lies years in the future (in Eliot's present), the house is already Victorian, and the family that lives in it already mimes the Victorian middle class.[103]

Eppie is, then, not just a marker of economic value but economically valuable herself, but this value depends paradoxically on its never being measured or named. Eliot has Silas almost but not quite exchange money for Eppie, and she has Eppie turn down the Casses' lucrative offer, because her economic value needs to be concealed and naturalized. The middle class became hegemonic in Britain's nineteenth century by representing itself as a timeless, natural growth, in contrast to the historically contingent economic practices that actually made its expansion possible. Eppie's adoption and her adult confirmation of that tie, which the novel treats as foundational to this emergent social formation, must seem to be natural occurrences motivated by feeling alone, in order to serve as class-founding myth.[104] By choosing her pure love of Silas and Aaron over Godfrey's money, Eppie performs one of the central functions of the middle-class woman: to demonstrate that middle-class families can afford to care more about morals and feelings than about money. Emotional specialists instead of income producers, middle-class women nonetheless contributed materially to middle-class ascendency. As Mary Poovey writes, the "rhetorical separation of spheres and the image of domesticated, feminized morality were crucial to the consolidation of bourgeois power."[105] This power depended upon the construction of middle-class values and practices as universally human. With Eppie's

103. Among others, Q. D. Leavis and Marianne Novy discuss the novel in terms of the class differences among the characters. Leavis ("Original Penguin Classics Introduction") celebrates the novel for its radical sympathy with the poor villagers. Although she is right that the gentry are portrayed as lacking in moral fiber, the novel in my view does not end with a simple triumph of poor over rich. For Novy, the novel equivocates as to whether or not it is advocating the cross-class ties brought about by adoption: Eppie's looks come from her aristocratic Norman father, but her goodness comes from Silas's care, and she chooses to stay in the class of her mother. See Novy, *Reading Adoption,* 128–31. Neither critic sees the novel, as I do, moving its characters into a third class.

104. For a fuller version of the argument that Eliot's novels universalize the British middle class by naturalizing middle-class Victorian womanhood as timeless womanhood itself, see my "Dinah's Blush, Maggie's Arm: Class, Gender, and Sexuality in George Eliot's Early Novels," *Victorian Studies* 36 (1993): 155–78. After Dinah Morris marries Adam Bede, she stops preaching and becomes a static image of virtue, and the novel ends (much as does *Silas Marner*) with a middle-class family tableau and with the aristocratic family much diminished and possibly heirless.

105. Mary Poovey, *Uneven Developments: The Ideological Work of Gender in Mid-Victorian England* (Chicago: University of Chicago Press, 1988), 10.

class-establishing adoption seeming a natural occurrence, not a deliberate or economically motivated act, the novel is free to disparage the less appealing economic practices (industry and capitalism) that actually made the rise of the middle class possible. Fueled apparently by love alone, Eppie carries her family from its class-defined origins into a universal future, one that is as much enmeshed in economic relations as the past, only without seeming to be so.

Eppie's garden also registers an important change in the novel's signifying systems that parallels and lends support to its economic story. Earlier in the novel, in such instances as the I.H.S.-stamped lard cakes and the literal-minded conversation at the Rainbow Bar, the sameness of sign and referent supported, by echoing it, the claim that both the gold and Eppie bear only intrinsic value and thus cannot be exchanged. In another instance, during Silas's fifteen years alone, when he appears to have become an unfeeling miser who loves nothing beyond his guineas, the narrator tells an anecdote to show that "the sap of affection was not all gone" (*Silas Marner,* 20). Grief stricken by the accidental breakage of the companionable earthenware pot in which he has carried his water for twelve years, Silas "stuck the bits together and propped the ruin in its old place for a memorial" (21). Just as his guineas signify only themselves, Silas makes a memorial that is not different from the object commemorated: a representation in which there is no gap between sign and referent. At the end of the novel, by contrast, Eppie wants to memorialize her long-dead mother using conspicuously figurative forms of representation. Eppie and Silas have long held in high regard the wild furze-bush where Molly's body was found. Planning the enclosure of her garden, Eppie wants to dig up the furze-bush and move it inside. Not only that: "it'll come into the corner, and just against it I'll put snowdrops and crocuses, 'cause Aaron says they won't die out, but 'll always get more and more" (147). Eppie's representational logic moves from metonymy to symbolism here, even as she reaffirms the principle of enclosure. In its arc from the old economy to the new, the novel also moves from intrinsic self-representation to metonymy and then to symbolism, from gold signifying only itself to money exchangeable for home improvements and a white wedding dress.

Although the first part of the novel emphasizes Eppie's intrinsic worth—her almost but not having been exchanged, bought, or sold—her entry into the exchange economy in part II and her eagerness to create symbolism are in keeping with her most conspicuous feature: she herself becomes a symbol. Despite the novel's realist texture (its rustic dances, its muddy lanes and fields) and its refusal of the romance plot that would restore the lost child to her birthright, Q. D. Leavis notes the novel's frequent reception as a "mere moral 'fairy tale'" and "the remarkable stylization of *Marner,* which is really due to its being an extension of the parable form."[106] When the child mysteriously arrives on his hearth, Silas, skilled as he is in biblical exegesis, runs through a series of possible meanings before settling on her identity with his gold. Perhaps the child is his sister returned to him or "a message come to him from that far-off life" in Lantern Yard (*Silas Marner,* 111). Literary critics have followed suit by expanding the number of things Eppie may stand for, the Christ child among them.[107] As a character, Eppie is a cipher. Where a different novel, including any other Eliot novel, would have given the orphan some form of character development, Eppie lacks psychological depth. The novel is very short: one episode alone does the work of showing her childhood, and five out of six chapters in part II represent one day in her eighteenth year. Eliot's lengthy *Felix Holt,* by contrast, creates psychological complexity and slowly elaborated maturation for the heroine torn between loyalty to the world of her adopted father and the attractions of the wealth made available by the discovery of her birth.

As a two-dimensional symbol of immeasurable value, Eppie signifies for Silas love beyond price and, for the changing world of Raveloe, the ascendancy of the social formation that believes in love beyond price. Only by representing pure love that disregards economic concerns can she serve the economic interests of the emergent middle class, in which her father is innocently included and from which he unintentionally benefits. Her task is to facilitate and stand for the transformation of two social formations that are dying out—the rural gentry to which she belongs by birth and the industrious rural poor in which she is raised—into the new social and economic formation that is being born. In her white wedding dress, "she seemed to be attired in pure white, and her hair

106. Leavis, "Original Penguin Classics Introduction," 212, 234. In *Genres of the Credit Ecomony,* Poovey offers a different reading of the novel's balance of realism and romance that depends on accepting that Godfrey is Eppie's "real father" (382) and that Silas is her father only metaphorically.

107. In addition to Christ (from Eppie's arrival near Christmas to save Silas's soul), Harold Fisch proposes the angel who rescues Lot or, at the end of the novel, Ruth. See Fisch, "Biblical Realism in *Silas Marner,*" in *Identity and Ethos: A Festschrift for Sol Liptzin,* ed. Mark H. Gelber (New York: Peter Lang, 1986), 343–60, this dicussion at 345–48. David Carroll links Eppie's name, Hepzibah, to the promise of joy in Isaiah 62; see Carroll, "Reversing the Oracles of Religion" (1967), rpt. in *George Eliot: The Mill on the Floss and Silas Marner: A Casebook,* ed. R. P. Draper (London: Macmillan, 1977), 212.

looked like the dash of gold on a lily" (*Silas Marner,* 181). Eppie looks like a Victorian painting of purity, a costly symbol of such Victorian middle-class values as the belief in domestic women's moral superiority and capacity for pure love, values that can look like luxuries from the point of view of those with insufficient cash. The novel resisted the equation of Eppie with money, only to reveal that resistance to have been a way of calculating value after all. Sacrificing character development to the exigencies of her economic story, Eliot uses the radical social dislocation of adoption—the arbitrary transfer of a child from one social location to another—to imagine the unusual social flexibility necessary to generate a new class out of the remnants of the old. Eppie's value and meaning seemed intrinsic, but their measurement was only being deferred, just as the novel only postpones the exchange value of the golden guineas, which it will now be Eppie's pleasant duty to spend.

Lacking intrinsic character, Eppie adapts at the beginning of her adoption story with eerie, even frightening ease to the move from "Mammy" to Silas. Already abandoned by her mother's neglect, "accustomed to be left to itself for long hours without notice from its mother" (*Silas Marner,* 109), the child calmly accepts her new caretaker. Although the novel formally veers between realist scenes and fairy tale plotting, the crucial moment of her abandonment and adoption, when she adorably totters across the snow-covered space between her mother's freezing body and Silas's warm hearth, is characterized by an aura of magic and freighted symbolism. It is a dark New Year's Eve, the old year about to give way to the new. A series of conspicuous coincidences bring the characters together: Molly just happens to collapse at this precise spot; Silas just happens to be standing in his open doorway looking yearningly out for his guineas when he is rendered unconscious by "the invisible wand of catalepsy." A deep, old magic seems to attend the arrival of this preternaturally happy child. We could call this the magic of the author's guiding hand, or we could call it the "miracle" of adoption that, as we saw in the first section of this chapter, conceals economic transactions and the consolidation of class formations under the guise of "love." Retelling this old story in a modern idiom, Bartholet, Hood, Simon, and others similarly allow adoptive love to cover and defer adoption's economic meanings and functions. The economics may be different now—the economy being concealed is globalized, and the economic story is the consolidation not only of middle-class hegemony but also of the wealth and power of the west and north at the expense of the global south—but adoption's narrative power has not changed.

MAISIE'S PROFIT, OUR PROFIT: THE GOLD COIN, THE TEN-POUND NOTE, THE HIGH GILT VIRGIN, AND THE MEDAL OF SO STRANGE AN ALLOY

While *Silas Marner* denies that Eppie's adoption is a monetary transaction yet subsequently places her at the center of a narrative of economic gain, thus hiding and displacing but not eliminating the economic instrumentalization of the adopted child, Henry James's *What Maisie Knew* acknowledges the exchange of money for a child but eventually transforms the child's instrumentalization for others into a source of transcendent value for herself. A novel about the afterlife of a divorce, *What Maisie Knew* begins with a legal judgment about a child and the economic transactions that flow from it.[108] Although the judge awards sole custody of Maisie to her father—on the grounds that, while the two parents have exhibited characters equally "bespattered," "a lady's complexion . . . might be more regarded as showing the spots"—the judge also requires Beale Farange to return to his ex-wife Ida the money she had earlier provided in child support.[109] Because he fails to do so, the judge alters the custody decree to divide Maisie's time and guardianship equally between her two parents, thus in effect rendering half of Maisie equal to the precise if arbitrary sum of twenty-six hundred pounds. The language of James's ironic narrator could not be more explicit: "His debt was by this arrangement remitted to him and the little girl disposed of in a manner worthy of the judgement-seat of Solomon. She was divided in two and the portions tossed impartially to the disputants" (*What Maisie Knew,* 35).

James's 1907 preface turns this plot device into a metaphor for the novel itself, while also shifting from the language of monetary exchange to that of capital speculation of the kind that Eliot's novel deplores.[110] Describing his plan to write of the sordid relations among the adults from

---

108. Although Marcia Jacobson locates the novel in the popular contemporary genre of the divorce novel, in *Henry James and the Mass Market* (Tuscaloosa: University of Alabama Press, 1983), the novel is more concerned with the search for appropriate parents for Maisie than it is with the causes of the divorce, the more typical (and titillating) subject of the divorce novel.

109. Henry James, *What Maisie Knew* (1897) (London: Penguin, 1985), 35 (hereafter cited in the text). This edition includes James's 1907 "Preface" (23–31).

110. J. Hillis Miller discusses James's preface to *What Maisie Knew* in terms of its linkage of economic, aesthetic, and ethical values in *Versions of Pygmalion* (Cambridge: Harvard University Press, 1990), 29, 52–54, although he does not distinguish as I do here between the language of exchange and that of speculation.

the point of view of the sensitive and observant child, James notes that he would need to "invest her with perceptions easily and almost infinitely quickened" (*What Maisie Knew,* 26). Once this investment has been made, "how could the value of a scheme so finely workable *not* be great" (27)? "Our business," he continues, "is to extract from her current reaction whatever it may be worth" (28). Maisie's perspective yields "profit" for the author because it renders the otherwise banal immoralities of the adults "*appreciable*" (29, 30); their value rises or "appreciates" because James has "invest[ed]" in Maisie. But this "economy of process" (29) does not amount simply to the economic exploitation of Maisie by her author: "our little wonder-working agent" is granted the power to "create, without design, quite fresh elements of this order—contribute, that is, to the formation of a fresh tie, from which it would then . . . proceed to derive great profit" (25). The repeated use here of the term "fresh" echoes Eliot's description of Eppie's naturalizing effect on Silas ("the child created fresh and fresh links . . . reawakening his senses with her fresh life" [*Silas Marner,* 125]). James's jarring linkage of a child's "freshness" to her "profit" measures the distance between the two novels but also suggests something about their affiliation, as James makes explicit what Eliot's novel has an investment in concealing: the unavoidable yet possibly beneficial economics of adoption.

Readers of the novel who note Maisie's objectification and commodification usually see these as forms of abuse.[111] But to note the injustice is not yet to have taken seriously the particularity with which James details Maisie's objectification. The custody judgments reported on the first page establish the kind of object she is initially: paternal property. Late nineteenth-century divorce proceedings, despite legislative changes starting with the Matrimonial Causes Act of 1839, remained under the sway of the eighteenth-century idea of the child as property belonging exclusively to the father, an idea deriving both from pre-modern theories of human conception and from the demands of capital accumulation. Although the Matrimonial Causes Act had established, against a norm

111. For example, and touching briefly on some of the scenes I will discuss here, John Carlos Rowe summarizes: "Maisie's early childhood . . . revolves around her sense of identity as an item of exchange, like the sovereigns the American countess gives her for cab fare or the money Maisie's mother, Ida, starts to give her in Folkestone, only to withdraw the bill;" see *The Other Henry James* (Durham: Duke University Press, 1998), 22. Christine DeVine also proposes Maisie's resemblance to the figure of the child prostitute (which hovers too over *Silas Marner*), a figure especially vivid in the wake of the "Maiden Tribute" scandal of 1885; see "Marginalized Maisie: Social Purity and *What Maisie Knew,*" *Victorian Newsletter* 99 (Spring 2001): 7–15.

of paternal proprietorship of children, the principle of some maternal rights (to visitation rather than custody), as late as 1897 a judge wrote, "nor is the paternal right capable of being bargained away."[112] The 1857 Divorce Reform Act required Chancery to award custody to the "innocent parent," yet paternal rights still prevailed regardless of morals under common law. Moreover, a legal prejudice against adulterous mothers remained even when maternal custody rights would otherwise have been observed, apparently the case with Ida and her more visible "spots," which initially led the judge to award custody to Beale, against what had become by now a norm of awarding custody of young children to their mothers. These heavy penalties for the woman's (and not the man's) adultery, while naturalized by and veiled as Victorian morality, reflect the enduring ideological power of capital accumulation under patrilineage: the heir must be ascertainably the father's. And indeed, Beale is himself the beneficiary of this system, for his money is inherited, although he terminates his line of inheritance by spending everything. Thus the custody decision that launches *What Maisie Knew*—quite apart from the way the parents respond to it—defines Maisie as parental property. As for her equivalence to the twenty-six hundred pounds that has become Beale's "debt" to Ida, because divorce decisions presumed the child to be of value to the custodial parent, value equivalent to property, the noncustodial parent would not have paid support (the reverse of divorce settlement norms today).[113] But it soon becomes quite unclear what Maisie's value really is.

Maisie's identification as a dependent in whom others hold property rights runs through the novel, as when the new Mrs. Beale remarks, in response to Sir Claude's pleased observation that she "really care[s] for" Maisie, "I shall never give up any rights in her that I may consider I've acquired by my own sacrifices. I shall hold very fast to my interest in her" (*What Maisie Knew,* 74). "Really caring" is taken by both Sir Claude and Mrs. Beale to be the same as having an "interest" in her. This language

---

112. Quoted in Lawrence Stone, *The Road to Divorce: England 1530–1987* (Oxford: Oxford University Press, 1990), 174. Historical information on divorce outcomes is from Stone; from Allen Horstman, *Victorian Divorce* (London: Croom Helm, 1985); and from Janice Hubbard Harris, *Edwardian Stories of Divorce* (New Brunswick: Rutgers University Press, 1996). See also Julie Rivkin, *False Positions: The Representational Logics of Henry James's Fiction* (Stanford: Stanford University Press, 1996), 209.

113. Irene Tucker, reading *What Maisie Knew* for its representation of a period of transition with regard to contracts, unpacks the confusing logic of the decision and the appeal on the first page of the novel; see *A Probable State: The Novel, the Contract, and the Jews* (Chicago: University of Chicago Press, 2000).

recurs when Ida mocks Sir Claude's "humbug of 'interest'" in Maisie (125), when, meeting her by accident in Kensington Gardens, Sir Claude claims Maisie is "mine" on the grounds that "I have her from her father" (that is, from Mrs. Beale, her father's "representative"); or when Beale himself recollects, as if from the "dim" past, "what he possessed in her and what, if everything had only—damn it!—been totally different, she might still be able to give him" (149). Mrs. Beale points out at the end that, as the partner and representative of the father, she has "priority" over other claimants (226). At the same time, a more modern language of capital speculation—of investment and return, like that used by James in the preface—runs through the adult characters' language, including even that of the traditionalist governess Mrs. Wix, who, trying to persuade Sir Claude to leave Ida and set up a decent home for her and Maisie, appeals to him on the grounds of sound investment: "What I want to speak of is what you'll *get*—don't you see?—from such an opportunity to take hold. . . . Make her your duty—make her your life: she'll repay you a thousand-fold!" (101). Mrs. Wix has made her own investment: a quarter's salary is owed to her, yet the loss seems money well spent, as "keeping quiet about it put her ladyship, thank heaven, a little in one's power" (102). This power Mrs. Wix draws upon later in the novel, as her investment pays off both financially and morally.

Starting the novel with a precise monetary value attached to her, Maisie could hardly be described, as Eppie is, as a bearer of intrinsic value, and her arbitrary valuation is soon subject to the kind of violent rise and fall that is more often associated with the stock market than with a human life, as indeed Eppie's value, too, actually if less conspicuously fluctuates from trash to treasure. From being fought over, Maisie quickly becomes "disowned." As James summarizes (about the actual child whose fate sparked the story), "whereas each of these persons had at first vindictively desired to keep it from the other, so at present the remarried relative sought now rather to be rid of it . . . which malpractice . . . would of course be repaid and avenged by an equal treachery" (*What Maisie Knew,* 23). Serviceable at first as an innocent bearer of insulting messages, "a ready vessel for bitterness," a "receptacle" into whose memory a vindictive "missive" may be dropped, Maisie soon forms the "determination to be employed no longer" as "messenger of insult" and as a consequence loses her value for her parents (36, 42, 43). Even when she is under their respective roofs, her mother and father leave her with ill-paid and sometimes morally questionable subordinates, while providing little by way of paid-for education or pleasure. Soon, each parent is leaving Maisie too long with the other, Ida feeling "more delight in hurling Maisie at him than in snatching her away" (46). Each parent then delegates her care and custody to his or her "representative," the new step-parents, Mrs. Beale and Sir Claude, who will eventually in turn transfer their obligation (or lose their investment?) to Mrs. Wix, the remaining governess. Having initially been a prize to be contended over, she becomes "unclaimed and untutored," a "burden" to be disposed of like an unwanted baby dispatched to a baby farm.

These rapid shifts in Maisie's valuation, more conspicuous than Eppie's, recall Behlmer's account of contradictory adoption advertisements in late-nineteenth-century periodicals and, too, Zelizer's history of the changing value of parentless children in this period in the United States, except that in Maisie's case the change tends to run in the opposite direction from what the historians might predict. Zelizer sees a gradual shift from a prevalence of baby farmers taking in unwanted children, for a payment of about ten dollars, in the 1870s to a profitable and often open market in babies in the 1920s and 1930s (she quotes a 1939 article in *Collier's:* "'there's gold in selling babies'").[114] And indeed, confusingly, even as they treat her like trash, Ida and Beale are also aware that Maisie is not entirely without value, since they transfer their "interest" in her to others rather than simply abandon her. Soon after her second marriage, Ida tells Maisie that she delegates her care to Sir Claude, or as she puts it, "I've made you over to him," as if Maisie were a check to be endorsed on to the next signatory (*What Maisie Knew,* 89). The novel's prologue ends with an accounting of the three Faranges' finances that details the parents' impecuniousness and establishes Maisie's continuing monetary value: "The child was provided for, thanks to a crafty godmother, a defunct aunt of Beale's, who had left her something in such a manner that the parents could appropriate only the income" (38). Maisie's care ought not to be a financial burden, then, and ought possibly to be profitable; yet Sir Claude remarks that Maisie's finances are even more "involved" than his own, which is apparently saying a lot. The question of her legacy, then, does not settle but only adds another layer of complexity to the question of whether she is a treasure or a burden.

Neither *Silas Marner* nor *What Maisie Knew* romanticizes the "original" family, but in contrast to *Silas Marner*'s naturalization and stabilization of the adoptive family, *What Maisie Knew* replaces Maisie's first fam-

---

114. Behlmer, *Friends of the Family,* 272–315; Zelizer, *Pricing the Priceless Child,* 169–200, quotation at 170.

ily with provisional, shifting assemblages that change rapidly over time. "Undoing the oedipal family," the novel pursues what Julie Rivkin calls a "dynamic of substitution" that renders family roles as positions to be occupied for a time and then abandoned.[115] Maisie's post-biological, serial family is ostentatiously constructed and deconstructed by James in a novel that scarcely notices nature, that privileges compositional symmetry over likelihood, and that James describes as itself a monstrous growth. In the preface, James calls *Maisie* "a tree that spreads beyond any provision its small germ might on a first handling have appeared likely to make for it" (*What Maisie Knew,* 23), one of those "comparative monsters . . . whose narrative mass exceeds their originating germ."[116]

James connects the anti-natural social formations of the story to what he sees as the unnaturalness of its telling. According to Rivkin, James's dismantling of the oedipal family is linked in the novel to his dismantling of the oedipal model of signification: just as there is no proper parent for Maisie, there is no truth to be uncovered by the narrator, only an endless string of ironies. The novel, Rivkin shows, "leaves behind the oedipal model of narration, in which signs owe their meanings to a 'parental' authority of original truth . . . in favor of an ironic model in which there will always be a difference between sign and meaning."[117] In contrast to the mode of signification in which things are what they mean that dominates the first part of *Silas Marner,* or even the orderly symbolism that overtakes the end of that novel, the very idea of representation is called into question by the adulterous stepparents' claiming to be "representative, you know, of Mr Farange and his former wife" (*What Maisie Knew,* 265), a situation in which the representative serves interests far removed from those she or he purportedly represents. But to say that representations or words tend to mean the reverse of what they should mean would be to imply a straightforward system for decoding; instead, words become unreliable and frequently convey at least two incompatible meanings at once.

The terms "real" and "really," for example, are particularly prone to

115. Rivkin, *False Positions,* 122, 127.

116. Sheila Teahan points this out in "*What Maisie Knew* and the Improper Third Person," *Studies in American Fiction* 21 (1993), rpt. in *New Casebooks: The Turn of the Screw and What Maisie Knew,* ed. Neil Cornwell and Maggie Malone (New York: St Martin's Press, 1988), 220–36, quotation at 222.

117. Rivkin, *False Positions,* 142. Rivkin illustrates this principle with a reading of the scene in which Miss Overmore can neither agree nor disagree with the proposition "that [Beale] lies and he knows he lies"; her answer would depend not upon the truth, but upon which of Maisie's parents she is most interested in pleasing.

such inconsistency. Early in his acquaintance with Mrs. Beale, Sir Claude asks Maisie:

> "Do you think she really cares for you?"
>
> "Oh awfully!" Maisie had replied.
>
> "But, I mean, does she love you for yourself, as they call it, don't you know? Is she as fond of you, now, as Mrs Wix?"
>
> The child turned it over. "Oh I'm not every bit Mrs Beale has!" (*What Maisie Knew,* 82–83)

For Maisie, "really" can mean at once "sincerely" ("awfully") and "instrumentally," as she acknowledges to Sir Claude that Mrs. Beale's feelings for her may be inextricable from her use of Maisie (when she was a governess working for Ida) to attract and acquire Beale as a husband, but no less tenacious for that reason. Later, Maisie will resist her father's implication that Mrs. Beale and Sir Claude only love her because she serves as "a jolly good pretext" for their pairing and will "chuck" her once they no longer need her. Maisie understands that instrumental love is not incompatible with what she calls "tremendous" love: when her father points out their "game," she replies, "that's all the more reason . . . for their being kind to me" (154). Words also take up their meanings relationally, adapting, like the adults around Maisie, to the new positions they occupy. Early in the novel, Maisie learns that it is "perfectly proper" for Miss Overmore to live with Beale in her role as Maisie's governess; when the governess accuses Ida of immorality for traveling with a male companion, Maisie "remarked to Miss Overmore that if she should go to her mother perhaps the gentleman might become her tutor." Maisie's idea depends on a principle of relativity: would not her being there "make it right—as right as your being my governess makes it for you to be with papa?" Miss Overmore, insisting on a stable meaning for "real" that would distinguish her from Ida's partner, contends, "You're too sweet! I'm a *real* governess"; to which Maisie replies, insisting on the relative meaning of words, "And couldn't he be a real tutor?" (58–59). As Rivkin observes, Maisie "sees that tutors, like governesses, are not 'real' but can be made or unmade to fit the occasion," a proposition unsettling to Miss Overmore whose claim to propriety is threatened along with her claim to being "real."[118] But Maisie is no more dismayed by the prospect of being tutored by so (un)"real" a tutor than she is by the experience

118. Rivkin, *False Positions,* 145.

of being "really loved" by those for whom she is also instrumentalized as a "pretext."

Just as "real" and "really" can, through the filter of Maisie's trusting consciousness, mean both true and fake at the same time, so the novel's language of economic transactions can bear both literal and figurative meanings, to sometimes startling effect. When Mrs. Beale and others talk about their interest in Maisie, in the examples cited above, it appears their meaning is primarily figurative, pertaining to emotional and moral claims on her time and affections. Yet as we have seen, Maisie's legacy from her great aunt means that whoever has possession of her may also have access to her small means, and when even the relatively trustworthy among her guardians fight over her, it is impossible to rule out pecuniary motivations, as Sir Claude's mention of the legacy to Mrs. Wix on the last page makes clear. These two registers of value, figurative and literal, are constantly becoming entangled with one another, and their confusion goes to the heart of Maisie's condition. Do the adults value her because they love her or because she is a means to some other end, erotic or financial (and, in turn, is the love between the adults ever an end in itself, or is it finally a means toward a financial end, too)? The persistence with which money—as metaphor, as scenic prop, as subject of anxiety—appears in the novel to represent other things suggests that the answer is both: the financial dealings of Maisie's family and friends are inextricable from their emotional dealings, and Maisie is at once loved and instrumentalized.

Maisie's narrator attends closely to who pays or does not pay for what, as Maisie is acutely aware of how little is spent on her, despite what is promised and owed her. The narrative calls consistent attention to her parents' complete failure to pay for her education, as her governess (under whom "she had learned nothing whatever" [*What Maisie Knew,* 75]) morphs into her father's lover and then into the new Mrs. Beale, and as the next governess, Mrs. Wix, defers instruction on "subjects" in favor of studying the adults. ("Her lessons these first days and indeed for long after seemed to be all about Sir Claude" [76].) The possibility of a boarding school is raised and dropped, as are paid-for French lessons and lectures (she attends a few free lectures in the company of Sir Claude). Maisie does not receive pocket money, and she is hyper-aware of her lack and of what things cost. With Mrs. Beale, at the Exhibition, "they had all their time, the couple, for frugal wistful wandering," having eaten a cheap "jam-supper" at home and lacking, now, the sixpences that would admit them to the sideshows; Maisie "press[ed] closer to her friend's pocket, where she hoped for the audible chink of a shilling" (142). Sir Claude's appearances generally mean an abundance of gifts, and once a present of five pounds for Mrs. Wix, although he joins the other adults in skimping on the larger costs. He fails to arrange for music lessons, which he explains are "shockingly dear," yet manages to impress Maisie nonetheless by sending her sheet music valued at precisely five shillings (119).

Expenditure and its absence are always emotionally fraught, and the narrative habitually conflates economic and emotional matters in punning diction that recalls Godfrey's reluctance to "own" Eppie. That their "affairs" are "involved" is a frequent topic among Mrs. Wix, Sir Claude, and Maisie, to the extent that the words become a shorthand through which Maisie, unaware of their erotic connotations, explains various deprivations to herself (*What Maisie Knew,* 95, 102, 120). Maisie tries to understand why she and Sir Claude have made the journey to Boulogne, which the narrator and the adult reader know is the destination of convenience for Britons escaping both financial and erotic entanglements (Sir Claude runs into acquaintances at every turn). She wonders when they will go on to Paris. When Sir Claude replies that it is too expensive, Maisie, drawing on her precocious knowledge of "the dash economic," turns to this familiar phrasing: "'I see, I see.' She smiled up at him. 'Our affairs are involved'" (183). Thinking that this expression, and their journey, bear only economic meanings, Maisie becomes confused when Sir Claude says they may stay only a few days. For Sir Claude, the question of what they can "afford" (198) concerns not only their financial "affairs" but also his affair with Mrs. Beale and his chances of obtaining a divorce from Ida.

Just as financial transactions and the discussions of them bear emotional or moral meanings, so too moral and emotional matters carry financial meanings or are presented through economic metaphors. At the beginning of her affair with Beale, the first of many instances in which the adults make Maisie a "pretext," Miss Overmore explains her surprising appearance at his house (Ida having promised to fire her if she moved there with Maisie) by telling Maisie that she told her father that "she adored his daughter," that "her courage had been rewarded," and that "fortunately your papa appreciates it; he appreciates it *immensely*" (*What Maisie Knew,* 47). Just as "appreciate" here carries both erotic and economic meanings, when Mrs. Wix reaches Boulogne, her intent to "save" Sir Claude has a primarily moral force (save him from Mrs. Beale), yet she embeds this expression in a narrative about "debt," bribery, and payment that mingles actual financial transactions with moral and emotional ones:

> "I say it to [your face], Sir Claude, even though I owe you the very dress on my back and the very shoes on my feet. I owe you everything—that's just the reason; and to pay it back, in profusion, what can that be but what I want?" . . . She manipulated her gown as she talked, she insisted on the items of her debt. "I have nothing of my own, I know . . . nothing but my hold of this little one truth, which is all in the world I can bribe you with: that the pair of you are more to me than all besides, and that if you'll let me help you and save you, . . . I'll work myself to the bone in your service!" (*What Maisie Knew,* 201–2)

Mrs. Wix's debts to Sir Claude are monetary (she calls attention to the dress he has paid for), but the currency in which she can repay him is moral. This speech is her reply to Sir Claude's financial generosity to her and Maisie in France and his promise of still greater "luxury" if she will, in return, "oblige me above all by not making a fuss" about his connection with Mrs. Beale (199). By converting his monetary into her moral currency, Mrs. Wix justifies repaying his costly bribery by denying him the very thing he intended to buy with it; instead, he must purchase his own "sav[ing]," which here connotes financial as well as moral prudence.

Similarly, the narrator translates Maisie's sense of emotional deprivation into the economic terms of a bad financial deal. She tends to pay involuntarily with deprivation "in advance" for future "rewards" that never arrive (*What Maisie Knew,* 120). With the arrival of Mrs. Beale in Boulogne, the narrator again presents Maisie's disappointment in terms of a financial transaction gone bad:

> She put it together with a suspicion that, had she ever in her life had a sovereign changed, would have resembled an impression, baffled by the want of arithmetic, that her change was wrong: she groped about in it that she was perhaps playing the passive part in a case of violent substitution. (*What Maisie Knew,* 225)

All Maisie's deprivations merge here, between the figurative language, into which her actual finances have migrated, and the situation it designates: her lack of sovereigns, her lack of paid-for lessons in arithmetic, and the emotional loss effected by the substitution of Mrs. Beale for Sir Claude.

The relationships surrounding Maisie are discussed and arranged according to an economic logic. Maisie may lack arithmetic, but she has learned to make equations with people. Just as Ida's boyfriend can be a real tutor because Miss Overmore is a real governess, she infuriates Mrs. Wix later by equating her with Mrs. Beale when, to Mrs. Wix's attempt to scandalize Maisie by revealing that Sir Claude pays Mrs. Beale, Maisie retorts, "'doesn't he pay *you* too?'" (*What Maisie Knew,* 210). The changes in Maisie's situation, and the negotiations for the final disposition of her care, are marked by a series of equations involving the procedure called "squaring," or the balancing of one set of needs or demands against another, as if emotions and morals could be counted like money. Soon after Ida "makes" Maisie "over" to Sir Claude, Sir Claude articulates the first of these equations: "I've squared her. . . . Your mother lets me do what I want so long as I let her do what *she* wants" (104–5). A few pages later, Maisie expresses her understanding that the same equation applies to Mr. and Mrs. Beale (114), so that Sir Claude and Mrs. Beale are now free to "make her" their "duty . . . together," although in this new configuration, Mrs. Wix is left out, or not yet "squared" (115, 118). Maisie, energized and empowered by her discovery that she too can participate in "squaring," devises another kind of equation when she tells the captain, whom she has compelled to repeat that he "loves" Ida, "So do *I* then. I do, I do, I do!" (131), her love for her mother—whom in the next sentence she acknowledges "won't have me"—becoming an element in a logical proposition.[119]

These foursquare equations prepare for Mrs. Beale's announcement, in France, of Ida's brutal contract: "She isn't your mamma any longer. . . . Sir Claude has paid her money to cease to be. . . . She lets him off supporting her if he'll let her off supporting you" (*What Maisie Knew,* 228). Maisie sees her final choice, her "settlement" (another term conjoining financial and emotional meanings), as "an impossible sum on a slate" (252), a sum that, like her school subjects of old, she wishes she could defer indefinitely. (A few hours later she sees it as an "exam" [260].) Maisie has prepared for this moment of choice, when alone with Mrs. Wix, by practicing her math: Mrs. Wix asks if she will accept "the two" or "only him alone"; Maisie replies, "him alone or nobody" (231)—"nobody," in this algebra, being the X that equals Mrs. Wix.

---

119. Barbara Eckstein considers Maisie's learning how to "square" as part of her victimization and her efforts to "square" as an adaptation to the moral laxity around her; see "Unsquaring *What Maisie Knew,*" *Henry James Review* 9 (1988): 177–87. I see Maisie's education in "squaring" as empowering, in context.

Given the novel's punning monetary-moral diction and the prevalence of equations and contracts uncertainly located between moral and financial and between literal and figurative—and given, too, that all the characters seem to be in debt—the appearance of actual gold coins comes as a surprise. Their difference from Silas's lovingly treated golden guineas helps to measure the difference in the two novels' representations of adoption and of value. Maisie, acutely aware of her lack of money, is excited by the appearance of coins, and she attends to their physical locations and their intrinsic value much as Silas does. A child, she predictably values the coins she can touch over the checks or contracts representing far greater sums that she cannot see. But in this novel, Silas-like excitement over coins generates pathos rather than stable moral value. At the Exhibition, as we saw, Maisie listens closely and in vain for "the audible chink of a shilling" in Mrs. Beale's pocket. At the end of that long night, after Maisie's final interview with her papa, the countess shoves into Maisie's hand, without counting them, a "cluster of sovereigns" so Maisie can take a cab home (*What Maisie Knew,* 159). These gold coins, which to the countess signify merely her disdain ("stepmothers *don't* pay!"), mean great wealth to Maisie and to the underservant Susan Ash, with whom Maisie considers them on her return home. James devotes two pages to detailing the career of these coins, one taken by Susan in repayment of Maisie's debt to her, then the whole lot later claimed by Mrs. Beale on the pretext of returning it to the countess. Whether the countess is "brown" because she is of African or of some other descent, she is both the wealthiest of the birth parents' paramours and, for Maisie, the least appealing—a barbaric, barely human figure. This oddly excessive racialization means that Maisie never imagines the countess (in contrast to other parental partners) as a potential parent substitute, and thus the allure of her gold, while great, is short-lived.[120] Susan Ash's resentful focus on her lost coin, even while transactions on a

120. For the debate about race in late James, see among others Kenneth W. Warren, *Black and White Strangers: Race and American Literary Realism* (Chicago: University of Chicago Press, 1993), 18–47; and Sarah Blair, *Henry James and the Writing of Race and Nation* (Cambridge: Cambridge University Press, 1996). Walter Benn Michaels insists on the significance of the countess being "brown" (and thus outside US racial categories) in "Jim Crow Henry James?" *Henry James Review* 16, no. 3 (Fall 1995): 289; John Carlos Rowe reviews critical treatment of the countess's race, and offers his own, in *Other Henry James,* 142–53. Those who consider the countess to be black include Toni Morrison; see *Playing in the Dark: Whiteness and the Literary Imagination* (Cambridge: Harvard University Press, 1992). On the possibility that she is Native American, see Kendall Johnson, *Henry James and the Visual* (Cambridge: Cambridge University Press, 2007).

far larger scale are occurring over her and Maisie's heads, helps to identify coins with the young, the dependent, and the servile.

In the next chapter, sitting with Ida on a garden bench in Folkestone, Maisie watches her mother's hand fumbling in a pocket and, recalling the "handful of gold" she so recently gained and lost, watches her pull out a purse. She hears a click; observing microscopically as Ida removes something ("It was not too substantial to be locked with ease in the fold of her ladyship's fingers" [*What Maisie Knew,* 176]), Maisie tries to discern if the object is a sovereign or a shilling. She unwittingly offends her mother (by praising the captain for his adoration of Ida—she cannot keep up with her mother's love life), hears again the click of the purse, and realizes the coin is gone forever. Later, asked by Sir Claude how much Ida was going to give her, Maisie replies:

> "I didn't see. It was very small."
> Sir Claude threw back his head. "Do you mean very little? Sixpence?"

Maisie, "resent"ing this infantilizing suggestion, replies:

> . . . . "It may have been a sovereign."
>
> "Or even," Sir Claude suggested, "a ten-pound note." She flushed at this sudden picture of what she perhaps had lost, and he made it more vivid by adding: "Rolled up in a tight little ball, you know—her way of treating banknotes as if they were curlpapers!" (*What Maisie Knew,* 179)

Although Maisie resents the implication that she cannot distinguish between "little" in size and "small" in value—she does know that a "small" gold coin might still be large in value—she nonetheless had not conceived that the smallest object of all, a crumpled banknote, might carry the largest value. The yearning to stabilize affections and family relations that her superfluous praise of the captain betrays is expressed in her attraction to shiny coins over money abstractly represented on paper or in even more abstract transactions, such as her being "made over" like a check by her mother to Sir Claude. It is as if she were wishing herself back in the universe of part I of *Silas Marner,* where value is intrinsic and unmistakable.

The period in which James wrote the novel was a period of controversy over the gold standard, particularly in the United States. Long gone was the possibility of an economy in which paper money could be redeemed for gold or silver or in which the nation could guarantee that it held bullion reserves equivalent to the face value of the paper it issued, and yet the dream of a gold standard survived in the United States, Walter Benn Michaels argues, equally in "the goldbug demand for a material equivalence between the representation and the objects represented" and in the naturalist fiction of the 1890s.[121] Money, especially paper money, as an essentially symbolic entity "cannot be reduced to the thing it is made of and still remain the thing it is"; by contrast, "the logic of the gold standard" yields "the desire to make yourself equal to your face value, to become gold."[122] In such novels as Frank Norris's *McTeague* (1899), Michaels and Bill Brown both trace the pathological consequences of hoarding gold for its intrinsic value rather than understanding its exchange value. Norris's Trina, in a sour parody of Silas's innocent love of his gold, sells her possessions to obtain gold coins and "counted and recounted it and made little piles of it, and rubbed the gold pieces between the folds of her apron until they shone."[123] Yet characters who think gold is a stay against the flux of market speculation are wrong, as the value of gold itself is subject to the rise and fall of markets. James's amused exposure of Maisie's touching loyalty to and yearning for face value is of a piece with his embrace of a consumer culture that extends to human markets elsewhere in his later fiction.[124] Maisie will soon learn better; speculation (as James points out in his preface to *What Maisie Knew*) will yield "great profit" not only for the author but for the heroine too.

Despite her naïve longing for coins in these scenes, Maisie is also

121. Walter Benn Michaels, *The Gold Standard and the Logic of Naturalism: American Literature at the Turn of the Century* (Berkeley: University of California Press, 1987), 162.
122. Michaels, *Gold Standard,* 21, 22.
123. Bill Brown, *A Sense of Things: The Object Matter of American Literature* (Chicago: University of Chicago Press, 2003), 66, quoting Frank Norris, *McTeague: A Story of San Francisco* (1899) (New York: Penguin, 1982), 209.
124. As Jean-Christophe Agnew demonstrates, *The Golden Bowl* makes characters such as the Prince and Charlotte into consumable objects whose purchase is not an abuse but an exhibit of an authorial power that James celebrates in his heroine; see "The Consuming Vision of Henry James," in *The Culture of Consumption: Critical Essays in American History, 1880–1980,* ed. Richard Wightman Fox and Jackson Lears (New York: Pantheon, 1983), 65–100. See also Brown's revision of Agnew's argument: where Agnew sees the treatment of the Prince as an object of consumption, Brown sees Maggie and Adam Verver collecting and transforming him from a commodity into a possession (*Sense of Things,* 142–75). On the importance of money in James see also Donald Mull, *Henry James's "Sublime Economy": Money as Symbolic Center in the Fiction* (Middleton, CT: Wesleyan University Press, 1973); Jan Dietrichson, *The Image of Money in the American Novel of the Gilded Age* (New York: Humanities Press, 1969); Laurence Holland, *The Expense of Vision: Essays on the Craft of Henry James* (Princeton: Princeton University Press, 1964).

expert in the speculative emotional-financial transactions that rule her life, as the subsequent circulation of the possibly imaginary ten-pound note suggests. On her arrival in Boulogne, Mrs. Wix reports that Ida has given her ten pounds, perhaps the very same crumpled note that Maisie and Sir Claude suppose Ida held between her fingers in Folkestone. "So you see, Maisie, we've not quite lost it," he says (*What Maisie Knew,* 187). Sir Claude initially considers this gift as a benefit to himself or rather to his vision of what is best for Maisie, as if the paper note had finally if circuitously reached its proper destination by functioning like a coin, a physical object as much as a token of exchange. (Is it literally the same note, or a substitution with the same value, or another note altogether? Sir Claude is only guessing what was between Ida's fingers.) Mrs. Wix, by contrast, understands Ida's money to be a payment to her, to help her on her way to France to protect Maisie from the two bad stepparents; perhaps it is even the long-deferred payment (with interest?) of Ida's debt, the coming due of Mrs. Wix's investment in unpaid salary, which the governess shrewdly believed would give her leverage over Ida. Moreover, if possible, Mrs. Wix will turn it toward yet another purpose unintended by Ida (who seeks only to annoy Sir Claude), her plan to "save" Sir Claude. Maisie, too, understands the meaning of the note to have shifted from its supposed original purpose (as a farewell gift to her) to a new one (as an aid to solidifying her relation to Mrs. Wix). Adding to the confusion over this note, Ida's seeming to pay Mrs. Wix to take the burdensome child off her hands appears at odds with her having earlier sold Maisie to Sir Claude. But in the space opened by the indeterminate value of the note, Maisie comes into her own. As we have seen, her conversations with Mrs. Wix, Sir Claude, and Mrs. Beale presuppose her understanding of the "squaring" that computes human relationships in economic terms. In crossing the channel, Maisie has gained a new appreciation of financial abstractions (with their characteristic deferral of value) and their potential to serve her interests. Maisie is about to take part in a final transaction that emancipates her from the painful illusion of organic family and stable (or "face") value.

In the novel's last hours, Maisie and Sir Claude go out to breakfast, leaving Mrs. Beale and Mrs. Wix behind at the hotel (Maisie, ever attentive, watches Sir Claude pay with "a gold piece"), after which they take a long, "dawdl[ing]" walk around the town and on the beach, a walk the purpose of which is to put off the moment of decision (the "choice" that was "there before her like an impossible sum on a slate" [*What Maisie Knew,* 252]), a walk that brings them finally to the train station, on the pretext that Sir Claude wishes to purchase the "Paris papers." He buys so many papers, and buys, too, such an armful of books, "that it would have seemed simpler with such a provision for a nice straight journey through France, just to 'nip,' as she phrased it to herself, into the coupé of the train that, a little further along, stood waiting to start" (253). Each has been harboring the wish that they could simply go off together as a pair, and this train is leaving for Paris. Maisie asks, "Won't you take me?" The porter asks if they want tickets: "*Monsieur veut-il que je les prenne?*" Sir Claude relays the question directly to Maisie, in French ("*Veux-tu bien qu'il en prenne?*"), just as the train is about to leave, whereupon Maisie, who has been taught no French, cries "*Prenny, prenny. Oh prenny!*" (254). Her uncanny grasp of French conjugation is of a piece with her mastery of the economic language of human relations: to ask Sir Claude to pay for train tickets is the same as asking him to live with her alone.[125] As the porter "waited there for the money," Sir Claude chooses to misinterpret Maisie's cry as conceding his wish to live with Mrs. Beale but without Mrs. Wix: "You *have* chosen, then? You'll let her go?" To the contrary, as the train departs, Maisie is finally able to make to Sir Claude her final speculative counteroffer, in the form of yet another equation:

> "I'll let her go if you—if you—
> She faltered; he quickly took her up. "If I, if I—?"
> "If you'll give up Mrs Beale." (*What Maisie Knew,* 254–55)

As Maisie begins to see that she can make her choice, that she is "free," she takes hold of the novel's economic language as agent, not object, of these emotional transactions. In this regard, she anticipates Dubinsky's claim that "child laborers make shrewd calculations that defy their stereotype of mute suffering" and, though her situation differs from that of the children Dubinsky is talking about, the view that we must "move beyond the adult-created lie of universal, innocent childhood" (*Babies,* 130). But before turning to the novel's final "settlement," we must consider one last figure of value that helps to establish Maisie's economic agency.

During the two days when Mrs. Wix and Maisie are alone together in Boulogne, enjoying Sir Claude's bribery in the form of pretty hotel

125. Miller sees her fluency as "the sign of Maisie's sexual maturity" because French is "the language of . . . illicit love" (*Versions of Pygmalion,* 38).

rooms, little glasses of liqueur for Mrs. Wix after their meals, touristic carriage rides, and "sixpences [that] seemed to abound in her life" (*What Maisie Knew*, 202), the two of them develop a fondness for walking up to the old town, with its "quaint and crooked rampart," its "rows of trees, its quiet corners and friendly benches where brown old women in such white-frilled caps and such long gold ear-rings sat and knitted or snoozed" (203), where they sit quietly and talk. From their seat they can see one particular object that, as they talk, so fascinates Maisie, apparently, that the narrator mentions it several times: they look "across at the great dome and the high gilt Virgin of the church" (204). Preoccupying Maisie during these conversations, which turn on their shared love of and plans for Sir Claude, is her worry that, by her silence, because of "her inveterate instinct of keeping the peace," she is tacitly conceding Mrs. Wix's vilification of Mrs. Beale, for whom Maisie still harbors a loyal affection (205). Immediately following a long passage (the paragraph is over a page long) in which the narrator follows the train of Maisie's guilty thoughts (she thinks of herself as "a low sneak," a favored phrase of her birth parents), something slight happens that nonetheless seems to prompt Maisie to speak her thoughts:

> She watched beside Mrs Wix the great gold Madonna, and one of the ear-ringed old women who had been sitting at the end of their bench got up and pottered away.
>
> "Adieu, Mesdames!" said the old woman in a little cracked civil voice—a demonstration by which our friends were so affected that they bobbed up and almost curtseyed to her. They subsided again, and it was shortly after, in a summer hum of French insects and a phase of almost somnolent reverie, that Maisie most had the vision of what it was to shut out from such a perspective so appealing a participant. It had not yet appeared so vast as at that moment, this prospect of statues shining in the blue and of courtesy in romantic forms.
>
> "Why after all should we have to choose between you? Why shouldn't we be four?" she finally demanded. (*What Maisie Knew*, 206)

Possibly, all that the narrator is communicating is that Maisie's appreciation of France has been so heightened by Boulogne's charm that she feels all the worse about leaving Mrs. Beale out of their travel plans. Yet her train of thought about Mrs. Beale seems to be wrapped up in the fixity of her gaze on the golden Madonna, a complex figure that captures the instability of the novel's concluding representations of value.

The vast "gilt Virgin" seems at first to typify France, where gilded surfaces abound, as in "the little white and gold salon [at their hotel] which Maisie thought the loveliest place" (*What Maisie Knew,* 186) and that reminds her of the countess's apartment, another deceptively pretty place. France's combination of deep Catholic piety with pervasive sexual laxity seems well represented by this imposing image of purity with its shining surface covering, presumably, base metal, its "gilt" evoking "guilt." The gold Madonna also seems to represent Mrs. Beale herself, whose commanding presence and whose "grace and charm, her peculiar prettiness," Maisie has just been dwelling on. By associating Mrs. Beale with the statue, with its superficial gilding, Maisie unknowingly acknowledges her mistrust of her stepmother, who, together with Sir Claude himself, has lied to her again and again. The complex figure of the static shining Virgin and the departing old woman captures Maisie's ambivalence toward Mrs. Beale: she yearns for her to stay, yet she fears her shining surfaces; she wishes her to be harmless and, perhaps, to be gone.

The image of the "high gilt Virgin" also echoes earlier images of Maisie's even less trustworthy first parents, whose glamour was long ago exposed as a thin veneer over empty hearts and spent fortunes. They are known for being "awfully good-looking" and for being excessively tall; Ida's presence is so exaggerated that her public appearances amount to "a kind of abuse of visibility." Of Beale Farange the narrator observes that he "had natural decorations, a kind of costume in his vast fair beard, burnished like a gold breastplate, and in the eternal glitter of the teeth . . . that gave him, in every possible situation, the look of the joy of life" (*What Maisie Knew,* 37, 38). Beale's gold and glitter are natural adornments, yet they support the narrator's emphasis on his moral emptiness. Ida is soon revealed to be a bottle blond who changes tints from time to time; seeing her mother after a long separation, Maisie notes that "the principle thing that was different was the tint of her golden hair, which had changed to a coppery red and, with the head it profusely covered, struck the child as now lifted still further aloft" (77). Their parting scene in Folkestone is introduced again by an emphasis on Ida's shining height; Maisie, seated on an outdoor bench, seeing first Ida's gown, must "follow up its stiff sheen—up and up from the ground," in order at last to see and recognize the face (166). Ida represents herself as "good," self-sacrificing, and suffering in silence; she caps her long, self-serving speech to Maisie by claiming to "shine . . . like pure gold" (175). Ida puts forward this simile while surreptitiously opening her purse and extracting the mysterious piece of money that reminds Maisie of her lost "handful of gold" and that she will soon withdraw; it is Maisie's reply to this claim ("That was what the Captain said to me that day, mamma") that prompts Ida's anger and the abrupt end of the interview. Ida's self-proclaimed character of "gold" is ironized by her failure to give Maisie the actual coin or bill that would have (given Maisie's poverty) betokened real kindness. Perhaps as the "high gilt Virgin" draws her gaze again and again in Boulogne, Maisie's mind links it not only to Mrs. Beale but also to her papa and mamma. The golden Madonna stands for all that has fascinated Maisie about her alluring parents and stepparents, even as they have turned to her their deceptive surfaces.

But the golden Madonna is also "*their* gilded Virgin," Maisie's and Mrs. Wix's, a vision they share when alone together (*What Maisie Knew,* 216, emphasis added). Their talks up on the ramparts have covered not only the badness of Mrs. Beale but also the question of whether Maisie possesses a "moral sense." Mrs. Wix is desperate to fortify Maisie against the other pair, and perhaps holding these conversations in the presence of an image of the Virgin—however "French," however morally compromised—is Mrs. Wix's way of underscoring this message. On their third ascent to the bench on the ramparts, on the second day of their solitude, "they wandered again up the hill to the ramparts instead of plunging into distraction with the crowd on the sands or into the sea with the semi-nude bathers. They gazed once more at their gilded Virgin" (216). Here, that the statue of the Virgin is above the town, and that they direct their steps upward rather than down toward the "semi-nude bathers," locates the statue in a moralized geography advocated by Mrs. Wix, where its meaning is not corruption, hypocrisy, or irony but rather moral rectitude.[126] Yet Mrs. Wix cannot control its meanings, its tendency in the context of Boulogne to undermine the ideal it is supposed to represent, just as her high Victorian term "moral sense" inevitably falls victim to self-parody. In this scene Maisie turns her own shining surface toward Mrs. Wix and self-consciously performs the "moral sense" she knows she does not really possess; Mrs. Wix accepts their shared adoration of Sir Claude as its equivalent. Two days later, suffering through the "exam" of trying to meet all three adults' demands, Maisie can only "dimly remember" that she is supposed to have a "moral sense" and makes her choice, finally, on the basis "of something still deeper than a moral sense" (260). Here, "moral sense," which Mrs. Wix may have

---

126. Like Mrs. Wix, Miller thinks the gold Virgin stands for purity (*Versions of Pygmalion,* 59).

thought was unironically represented by the gold Virgin, is exposed as yet another misleading surface.

The "high gilt Virgin" presiding over the city of Boulogne could thus be seen as an emblem not only of "French" deceptiveness in morals but also of the slipperiness of the novel's mode of signification itself, a slipperiness that Maisie finally masters. In contrast to Silas's gold or to Dolly Winthrop's I.H.S.-marked lard cakes, in which the signifier is perfectly identified and merged with the signified, and in contrast to the ideal of the gold standard with its identification of intrinsic and stamped value, the gilded statue of the Virgin represents the ironic disparity between signifier and signified that has characterized the language of *What Maisie Knew*.[127] Everyone lies to Maisie; idealizing rhetoric covers base motives whenever Beale, Ida, or Mrs. Beale utters a word, and even Sir Claude succumbs. But it is not as though Maisie is pure in contrast to the adults' ironic impurity. She loves France and takes to it with uncanny rapidity the minute she arrives; "she had grown older in five minutes and had by the time they reached the hotel recognized in the institutions and manners of France a multitude of affinities and messages" (*What Maisie Knew,* 181). The narrative links her tendency to create an "impression of an excess of the queer something which had seemed to waver so widely between innocence and guilt" with the atmosphere of Boulogne, where for Maisie there was "no wavering: she recognized, she understood, she adored and took possession" (182). Maisie has been living in a virtual France all her life, but now she can have its pleasures as well as its confusions. For Maisie early learned the advantage in recognizing the difference between inside and outside. At the beginning of the novel, the narrator links her decision not to carry her parents' messages to her discovery of "an inner self, or, in other words, of concealment" (43). Maisie experiences a "moral revolution" when she discovers that she can hear things but not repeat them, receive commands but not obey them, know things but not reveal them.[128] "The high gilt Virgin" with its evident disjuncture between inner and outer may then be a figure not only for

127. Similarly, Bill Brown notes the difference between Trina's gold, whose "quiddity . . . Trina fights to preserve," and the giant gilded tooth, which ceases to be a tooth and becomes a table when it no longer hangs outside as the sign for the dentist office (*Sense of Things,* 68, 78).

128. On Maisie's "inner self" see Rivkin, *False Positions,* 140–43. In contrast to this view of Maisie's learning to master the indeterminacy of language, J. Hillis Miller sees Maisie as herself a figure for undecidability; see "Is There an Ethics of Reading?" in *Reading Narrative: Form, Ethics, Ideology,* ed. James Phelan (Columbus: Ohio State University Press, 1989), 79–101.

the lying adults around her but also for Maisie's mature yet uncorrupt understanding of linguistically mediated social relations and her newfound ability to use language's self-division toward her own ends.

Maisie's "inner self" becomes so complex yet so "conceal[ed]" that she defies the comprehension not only of the adults but of her narrator, who toward the end of the novel more than once confesses his inadequacy to report her thoughts ("I so despair of courting her noiseless mental footsteps. . . . I am not sure that Maisie had not even a dim discernment" [*What Maisie Knew,* 212]). Maisie's self-possession is also reflected, as readers of the novel have often observed, in the novel's last pages' consisting almost exclusively of dialogue and the barest stage directions. The narrator gives up his authority over Maisie's thoughts and can only, with Mrs. Wix, wonder at Maisie's spoken claim, "Oh I know!," echoing this claim but not providing a referent for it in the novel's final words, "what Maisie knew."[129]

Fittingly, then, the fourth and final time the gilded Virgin is mentioned, it appears not in the narrator's setting of a scene but in Maisie's quoted speech. Her way of speaking of it confirms its linkage in her thoughts with her "impossible sum," the conundrum of how and with whom to live. When Maisie and Sir Claude return to the hotel after failing to elope to Paris, they observe signs that Mrs. Wix is leaving (her "battered old box" with "a big painted W" in the hotel hallway), and Maisie offers her companion a way to effect her proposed bargain. If Sir Claude undertakes to break with Mrs. Beale, Maisie offers to "go straight out with you again and not come back till" Mrs. Wix has gone, or, as she elaborates,

> "I'll stay out till the boat has gone. I'll go up to the old rampart."
>
> "The old rampart?"
>
> "I'll sit on that old bench where you see the gold Virgin."
>
> "The gold Virgin?" he vaguely echoed. But it brought his eyes back to her as if after an instant he could see the place and the thing she named—could see her sitting there alone. "While I break with Mrs Beale?" (*What Maisie Knew,* 256)

129. On Maisie's "speak[ing] for herself," see Rivkin, *False Positions,* 159–62. Miller, noting the same withdrawal of the narrator, sees her "unknowability" as indicating Maisie's "escape," her "freedom," and by extension her death (*Versions of Pygmalion,* 55–56, 69–74).

Maisie then amends her proposal: Sir Claude should "do as I do" and simply "go out and wait . . . till they both have gone" (256–57). But Sir Claude ends the conversation by simultaneously remarking that "Mrs Beale will never go" and opening the door to the hotel room, where Mrs. Beale will soon end any possibility of this plan taking effect. Sir Claude's slowness in this conversation, and the narrator's hedging about whether he pictures Maisie sitting alone with the gilt Virgin or only pretends to do so ("as if . . . he could see"), measures Maisie's distance from Sir Claude and the independent development of her private and inward vision. Maisie uses the remembered view of the gold Virgin as a shorthand or placeholder for the complexity of her thoughts about her choice, thoughts into which neither Sir Claude nor the narrator can enter. (If I were to hazard a guess, her thoughts might run something like this: I will ally myself with the gold Virgin in doing something that means differently on the inside and on the outside.)

In the heated four-way conversation that follows in the hotel room, which sometimes devolves into slapstick shovings and snatchings that recall Maisie's ambiguous value as both "burden" and "prize," Maisie initially adheres to the bargain she proposed to Sir Claude. Tearfully she insists that she did not simply make a stand for propriety (Sir Claude wants to celebrate as "beautiful" what he thinks is Maisie's "refusal" to give up Mrs. Wix), but rather that "I said I would [give up Mrs. Wix] if *he'd* give up—!" (*What Maisie Knew,* 262), an equation in which each term depends on the other. The stepparents attempt to impose on her a different equation that presumes not relative but absolute values. Mrs. Beale, on the grounds that "we're representative, you know, of Mr Farange and his former wife," and invoking the goldbug assumption that the representative is the same as the thing represented, claims, "I'm your mother now. . . . And he's your father" (265). But the stepparents represent the parents and can assume their relational names only as long as they remain married to them, and as long as they remain married, their living with each other is outside the law and therefore hardly parental, as Mrs. Wix is quick to point out. A representational system involving perfect identity between the signifier or "representative" and the signified has never functioned in the world of *Maisie;* like the gilt Virgin, Mrs. Beale can only pretend to intrinsic meaning and value. With her superior understanding of the relativistic economy of these relationships, and with her stronger grasp of signification's disparity between signifier and signified, Maisie follows the sequential displacements of one "representative" after another logically to her own emancipation.[130] Maisie completes the equation she had formulated prior to Sir Claude's return, "him alone or nobody": on the last page Maisie leaves with that nobody, Mrs. Wix.

The ways in which Maisie uses the allegorical figure of the gilt Virgin help to indicate that she has escaped the fate of becoming allegorical herself.[131] In contrast to Eppie's representation as a cipher and her transformation at the end of *Silas Marner* into a stable emblem of Victorian purity ("she seemed to be attired in pure white, and her hair looked like the dash of gold on a lily"), James's heroine is endowed with interiority that can only be represented by how little of it shows on the outside. As a static figure of virtue, the gilt Virgin is Eppie inside out: instead of gold transformed into a human girl, it is a human figure turned into gold. But the gilt Virgin's meanings, like Eppie's in the marketlike scene in part I and unlike Eppie's at the end, are multiple and mobile, and Maisie, deploying signification's elusiveness, escapes fixity of meaning as she leaves Boulogne. Her cryptic final "Oh I know!" resists decoding even as it names a space of private meanings. As Rivkin argues, "what Maisie gains . . . is what Sir Claude has acknowledged: she is unique. In renouncing the family, she finally ceases to be the agent of other characters' projects of representation."[132] Although both novels pursue what Rivkin calls a "dynamic of substitution," Eppie, gold's substitute, finally freezes into place in an allegorical tableau about the rise of the middle class; Maisie, by contrast, openly exchanged and passed from hand to hand (her value rising or falling with every exchange), ends by escaping allegorization as she becomes an agent rather than a pawn in the last of the series of economic transactions that might have confined her within others' instrumentalizing intentions but did not. "We *can't* work her in," exclaims Sir Claude, admitting defeat as he celebrates her resistant subjectivity, the "great profit" James's preface allocates to his heroine (*What Maisie Knew,* 264, 25). Whether or not Maisie and Mrs. Wix will have the benefit as well of Maisie's "means" (the great aunt's legacy that the unre-

130. Thus, my reading of the novel's conclusion, like Rivkin's, is closer to that of Juliet Mitchell, who celebrates Maisie's independence and freedom, than to that of, e.g., Eckstein, who sees Maisie "trapped" and impoverished: "Maisie has learned discretion, and in doing so she has become a discrete, an autonomous person"; see "*What Maisie Knew:* Portrait of the Artist as Young Girl," in *The Air of Reality: New Essays on Henry James,* ed. John Goode (London: Methuen, 1972), 168–89, quotation at 169.

131. Miller, however, sees Maisie as a statue (like Galatea) made by both James and Sir Claude, although he also grants Maisie the powers of an artist and the freedom to escape (*Versions of Pygmalion,* 46–51, 65).

132. Rivkin, *False Positions,* 159.

liable Sir Claude now undertakes to "get . . . back"), Maisie moves from being a passive item of paternal property in the old economy to becoming a modern speculator in her own right.

Rereading the novel a decade after writing it, James, as we have seen, emphasizes this vision of Maisie as a speculator who, along with the narrator, derives "profit" from investing her goodness in the banal badness of the others. As we have seen, Maisie's nostalgia for some semblance of normative family relations is captured fleetingly in her yearning for gold coins (and the stable form of signification they emblematize), but the yearning gives way to her more complex appreciation of economic speculation and the alternative analogy it provides for her ever-shifting situation. One of James's most conspicuous figures in the preface is an image that, in the context of the persistent economic metaphors, seems coinlike, and yet it is neither gold nor a coin. James describes in this way the close relationship of "bliss and bale" that is to be found in Maisie's "terribly mixed" experience: "so dangling before us for ever that bright hard medal, of so strange an alloy, one face of which is somebody's right and ease and the other somebody's pain and wrong" (*What Maisie Knew,* 25). As Miller points out, the figure is "absurd," for its "obverse face contradicts its reverse" and, if it is a coin, it "could never be currency, since it has a positive value on one side and a negative value on the other."[133] Although Miller reads "alloy" to mean that each face is a made from a different metal—"let us say gold on one side and lead on the other"—and thus that the ending grants Maisie "bliss" and leaves Sir Claude and Mrs. Beale with the "bale" (since she is in the right, the pleasures of renunciation are great, and her departure will likely divide the guilty pair), the medal could instead be composed of one substance, uniformly "bright" and "hard," and yet that substance "so strange an alloy" that it permits opposite appearances on the medal's two sides.

As much as it both suggests and refuses to function as a coin, this "medal" also evokes betting and speculation, for example, in George Eliot's *Daniel Deronda,* where early scenes juxtapose gambling and bank failure and where the heroine, the "fair gambler," is led by a sudden plunge into poverty (owing to her bank's bad investments) to wrong another woman by marrying the villain. Gwendolen's moral development is shown through the metaphor of gambling and speculation as she learns to wish not to "gain [from] another's loss"; moreover, she finds that her

133. Miller, *Versions of Pygmalion,* 58.

gain has become indistinguishable from her own loss.[134] In *Maisie,* the image of the medal depicts not so much Maisie's gain at the expense of others' losses, as Maisie's "mixed" experience, the readiness with which right and wrong, pain and ease can be mixed together and felt simultaneously. If the golden guinea with a face value equal to its metal value represents the dream of the gold standard, whereby signs are what they signify, the "medal of so strange an alloy" is the gold standard's nightmare (or parody), in which its printed faces bear no single meaning and its value as metal cannot be measured. How could it ever be said that Maisie gets either the bliss or the bale alone or that Sir Claude does so? The unaccountable "mixture" or "alloy" of loss and gain is her speculator's reward.

If Eliot uses adoption, with its enormous potential for social relocation, to imagine and naturalize the beginnings of a new economic and social class, James uses adoption to imagine a "fresh" form of human subjectivity detached from biogenetic family and from "truth." Although both novels imagine social worlds in which genealogy ceases to count, they use adoption stories to different ends: Eliot to celebrate the middle-class nuclear family, James to ironize its demise; and Eliot's relative coyness about Eppie's economic value contrasts with James's striking openness about Maisie's. Nonetheless, these novels' representations of the constructive uses to which the economic transactions involved in adoption may be put exhibit the Victorians' ability, greater than ours, to speak of the monetary as well as the social value of an adoptable child's life, to avoid "rituals of decommodification" and instead to "confront" commodification "head on." *Silas Marner* articulates the powerful wish that human value and meaning might be intrinsic and beyond price, and like a slowed-down and franker version of *Baby, We Were Meant for Each Other,* it dramatizes the process of concealing the market in children under the name of "love" even as its ending makes clear what economic interests "love" serves. It makes visible the economic subtext of its own claim that love is all: its utility for consolidating Victorian middle-class hegemony; therefore it helps make visible the somewhat different economic subtext of contemporary adoption "love" stories. *Silas Marner* also exposes the human cost of that artfully obscured claim: as an allegory of love and integrity, Eppie has no character, no psychological complexity. *What Maisie Knew,* by contrast, imagines a rich interiority emerging plausibly from the crudities of the marketplace, and thus it resonates with and lends

134. George Eliot, *Daniel Deronda* (1876) (London: Penguin, 1995), 322, 337.

conceptual support to Yngvesson's and Dubinsky's cautious twenty-first-century defenses of "the market in children" as, paradoxically, helping to bring a child's valued personhood and agency into existence. These Victorian novels can aid twenty-first-century readers to contemplate the almost unimaginable thought of children benefiting from their participation in such a market.

2 / SEARCHES AND ORIGINS

Life stories of adopted people often have complex narrative lines, since to the already insurmountable difficulty of any human effort to know and fix one's origin is often added the extra difficulty of lack of information about birth parents, date, and place: all the small and large particulars we have in mind when we expect the answer to "where are you from?" to help answer the question "who are you?" Starting in the 1970s, with the emergence of the adoptee rights and open adoption movements, with the contested practice of placing minority children out of their birth communities, with newer practices of transnational adoption modeled on these existing practices, and with the broad international acceptance of the 1989 United Nations Convention on the Rights of the Child and of the 1993 Hague Convention on Intercountry Adoption based on it, which promise parentless children the right to the formation of an identity linked to their culture of origin,[1] popular adoption culture in the United States has placed a high value on knowledge of personal (familial, genetic) origins. In most cases access to such knowledge is thwarted, however, whether by law or by circumstance, so adoptive families generate doubles and substitutes. Adoption day is celebrated as well as the sometimes conjectural birthday; narratives of the adoption trip or first encounter are told in place of birth stories. In the case of transnational, transracial, or transethnic adoption, parents construct a simulacrum of the "birth culture" (or, in Alice Diver's recent phrase, "inherent biogenetic culture") by providing role models of the child's race or ethnicity and incorporating, into family life, cultural fragments (holidays, food, clothing) that are meant to be authentic but that are, inevitably, trans-

1. Barbara Yngvesson points out that the UN Convention emphasizes such rights more than does the Hague Convention, which stresses the termination of the birth family relation and the adoptee's full integration into the adoptive family. Both documents are self-contradictory in this regard. See Yngvesson, *Belonging in an Adopted World: Race, Identity, and Transnational Adoption* (Chicago: University of Chicago Press, 2010), 19.

lated and hybridized.[2] Transnational adoptive families embark on "roots trips" to the scenes where an origin might be reconstructed. In the case of US domestic adoptions, adult adoptees search for birth parents.

Searches and roots trips make origins seem knowable, memorable, and documentable, yet again and again in the narratives of such journeys, origins are fictionally constructed in the face of admissions that they cannot otherwise be known. Search narratives, like the epic quest plots on which as Barbara Melosh points out they are modeled, never arrive where the searcher wants:[3] the past is another country, and you cannot go there. Because western cultures tend to equate biological origins with identity, roots trips and searches are expected to provide what nothing can provide: certain knowledge of who you are.[4] Anyone might recognize that identity and the origins that supposedly ground it are artifacts, but the adopted and those who think about them may be particularly well positioned to do so.

Like Donna Haraway's cyborg, the figure of the adoptee reveals that no one, adopted or not, can sustain an organic connection to an origin. And yet the adoptee, unlike the cyborg, is pressured to pursue a quest for identity by seeking access to his or her origins, which are usually represented as materialized in a place or embodied in a person. As discussed in the introduction, Eleana Kim, for example, finds that "adoptees who may not want to find their roots or who are not involved in a search of origins are often viewed as being repressed or in denial."[5] Kimberly Leighton argues that adoptees are told they suffer from "genealogical

---

2. For the commonly used yet oxymoronic phrase "birth culture," see, e.g., Susan Tompkins, "The Changing Outlook on Transracial Adoption," in *A Passage to the Heart: Writings from Families with Children from China,* ed. Amy Klatzkin (St. Paul: Yeong and Yeong, 1999), 275–77, quotation at 276. For "inherent biogenetic culture," see Alice Diver, "Conceptualizing the 'Right' to Avoid Origin Deprivation: International Law and Domestic Implementation," *Adoption & Culture* 3 (2012): 141–80.
3. Barbara Melosh, "Adoption Stories: Autobiographical Narrative and the Politics of Identity," in *Adoption in America: Historical Perspectives,* ed. E. Wayne Carp (Ann Arbor: University of Michigan Press, 2002), 218–45, this topic at 228–29; on search narratives as quest plots, and the searcher as hero, see also Emily Hipchen and Jill Deans, "Introduction: Adoption Life Writing: Origins and Other Ghosts," *a/b: Auto/Biography Studies* 18 (2003): 163–70; and Marianne Novy, *Reading Adoption: Family and Difference in Fiction and Drama* (Ann Arbor: University of Michigan Press, 2005), 45.
4. On the assumption in western culture that birth determines identity, see, e.g., Northrop Frye, *The Secular Scripture: A Study of the Structure of Romance* (Cambridge: Harvard University Press, 1976).
5. Eleana J. Kim, *Adopted Territory: Transnational Korean Adoptees and the Politics of Belonging* (Durham: Duke University Press, 2010), 91.

bewilderment" and must want to know "who their 'real parents' are," even though their distress arises not from lack of knowledge of heredity but from bias against "the social acceptance of adoption as a mode of family-making as good as biological reproduction."[6] Adoptees are peculiarly burdened, in popular adoption culture, with this obligation to find, know, and grasp material origins. Addressing in this chapter a range of recent works of fiction and autobiography about origins—some from the point of view of adoptees, others by parents on behalf of their adopted children—and looking at them through the lenses of narrative theory and trauma theory, I argue that the quest for literal origins ultimately gives way to an understanding of the figurative—indeed, fantasmatic—nature of origins. In these works the search for an unavailable origin compels imaginative work that itself constitutes identity.

To say that adoption is a fiction-generating machine is not to contrast it categorically to non-adoptive family formation, but rather to claim that it presents in a particularly acute form the problem of the unknowability of origins and the common tendency to address that problem with fiction making. As Judith Butler writes of human subjects generally, "the irrecoverability of an original referent does not destroy narrative; it produces it 'in a fictional direction.'" And because "I cannot be present to a temporality that precedes my own capacity for self-reflection, . . . I am always recuperating, reconstructing, and I am left to fictionalize and fabulate origins I cannot know."[7] In this chapter, I discuss some narrative consequences that flow from adoption's orientation toward a knowledge about the past that is intensely but apprehensively sought and that is not finally available. I argue that adoptive origins and origin stories are not discovered in the past so much as they are created in, and for, the present.

CREATING ORIGINS IN NARRATIVE THEORY, TRAUMA THEORY, AND ADOPTION NARRATIVES

Narrative theory at least since Roland Barthes has identified the story of Oedipus—his search for the truth about his parentage, his trust in

6. Kimberly Leighton, "Addressing the Harms of Not Knowing One's Heredity: Lessons from Genealogical Bewilderment," *Adoption & Culture* 3 (2012): 63–107, quotations at 68, 87.

7. Judith Butler, *Giving an Account of Oneself* (New York: Fordham University Press, 2005), 37, 39.

language to tell that truth—as the paradigm of storytelling itself.[8] That this key western narrative is a story about adoption is a secret hidden in plain view. As Marianne Novy points out, adoption memoirs often reference Oedipus the adoptee, but literary theorists, starting as they do with Freud's view of the story as everyman's fantasy, have for the most part overlooked the adoption theme.[9] For most readers, Oedipus's abandonment and "sealed records" adoption merely comprise the mechanism by which he is induced to commit his celebrated crimes. But the uncovering of adoption at and as the fountainhead of narrative theory is suggestive for thinking both about adoption and about storytelling itself. As we have seen in chapter 1, Julie Rivkin shows in her reading of *What Maisie Knew* how the dismantling of oedipal family structure can also undo the cause-and-effect sequences of oedipal narrative, and (see the introduction) Judith Butler proposes Antigone as the founding figure of a new psychoanalytic theory that would defy the heteronormativity founded on Oedipus's narrative. Both these critics take the Oedipus story to represent linear causality and truth in narrative, and they highlight alternatives to it.[10]

Taking this line of criticism in another direction, though without taking any special notice of the adoption theme, J. Hillis Miller influentially reads *Oedipus the King* against the grain as offering in itself a demonstration of the unattainability of truth and origins. Building on the classical scholarship of Sandor Goodheart, who showed that *Oedipus the King* does not finally prove Oedipus's guilt, Miller emphasizes the implausibility of the coincidences on which the denouement—the recognition of the alleged truth—of *Oedipus the King* depends.[11] For Miller, the play dramatizes the failure of ends to proceed logically or deterministically

---

8. See, e.g., J. Hillis Miller, *Reading Narrative* (Norman: University of Oklahoma Press, 1998), 3–45; and Julie Rivkin, *False Positions: The Representational Logics of Henry James's Fiction* (Stanford: Stanford University Press, 1996), 122–24.

9. Novy, *Reading Adoption,* 7, 37–39. Exploring alternatives to Oedipus as a model for thinking about adoption, Novy proposes Euripides's pro-adoption play *Ion* (*Reading Adoption,* 50–52).

10. As do other feminist scholars who have been seeking in women's writing alternatives to the Oedipus story's androcentrism as well as its linearity: see, e.g., Susan Stanford Friedman, "Lyric Subversion of Narrative in Women's Writing: Virginia Woolf and the Tyranny of Plot," in *Reading Narrative: Form, Ethics, Ideology,* ed. James Phelan (Columbus: Ohio State University Press, 1989), 162–85; and Susan Winnett, "Coming Unstrung: Women, Men, Narrative, and Principles of Pleasure," *PMLA* 105 (1990): 505–18.

11. Sandor Goodheart, "Oedipus and Laius's Many Murderers," *Diacritics* 8, no. 1 (Mar. 1978): 55–71.

from origins. Like the adoption narratives discussed in this chapter, Oedipus goes backward in time, trying out various theories about his birth and then stringing together an unlikely series of events to make up the origins narrative on which he irrationally settles, the narrative that has come to stand, improbably, for truth itself. It is Oedipus's adoption, his departure from the oedipal family and its causal logic, that allows his story to stand for the undoing of that logic. Perhaps the scandal of his story is not incest and parricide but adoption, which requires him to spin such racy yarns about his origins and their presumed but not proven consequences and which can stand as a paradigm for all such retrospective and doubtful figurings of origins. But as it has been taken up by the adopted to stand for loss of and yearning for origins, Oedipus's adoption story can also be used to quarrel with such deconstructive appropriations and to assert, to the contrary, the urgency of the quest for truth.

Building on his reading of Oedipus, Miller generalizes about the elusiveness and constitutive fictionality of origins. With reference to writers as diverse as Trollope, Valery, Hegel, Derrida, and Said, Miller writes:

> The paradox of beginning is that one must have something solidly present and preexistant, some generative source of authority, on which the development of a new story may be based. That antecedent foundation needs in its turn some prior foundation, in an infinite regress. . . . Any beginning in narrative cunningly covers a gap, an absence at the origin.[12]

Miller uses deconstructive reading here to show the impossibility of origins. Although he is also interested in the stories that rest on such thinly if "cunningly" covered gaps, his language about origins is categorical: the "regress" is "infinite," there is "an absence at the origin." To read his argument, presented as it is in so calm and genial a tone, is to be swayed by the pleasure of feeling scales drop from one's eyes and intellectual skies open up. But the adopted, including Oedipus, are haunted by the conviction that there is an origin. They do not necessarily find the "absence at the origin" intellectually or personally liberatory. Instead, adoption narratives are generally about the work of making an origin, which is often the work of refusing to accept a view such as Miller's. While Miller's magisterial view offers an astringent corrective to what are often false and sentimental (if arduously sought) truth claims about origins in

12. Miller, *Reading Narrative,* 57–58.

adoption, it also does not sufficiently account for the imaginative work and emotional labor such claims can perform. Two recent narratological studies of stories thematically related to adoption suggest how Miller's observation about origins might apply, but with an adjustment of emphasis and tone, to the case of adoptive origins.

Catherine Romagnolo, reading Amy Tan's *The Joy Luck Club,* a novel of severe personal and cultural dislocations, reveals how ideologically freighted as well as elusive various kinds of narrative beginnings, especially "causal beginnings," can be.[13] Drawing on the skepticism of postcolonial and feminist theorists such as Homi Bhabha and Trinh Minh-Ha, who debunk the possibility as well as the political desirability of cultural authenticity because of the invidious hierarchies it can foster, Romagnolo argues that contemporary novels may, through the ideological mobilization of formal devices, likewise expose as a dangerous fantasy the dream of recovering authentic origins. Tan, she argues, countering "a fixation" among advocates of Asian American culture "on reclaiming authentic origins [that] can occlude the experiences of marginalized members of a community," destabilizes narrative beginnings by structuring her novel around multiple plots and points of view, in order to "critique the very concept of origins [and] illuminate the discursive constructedness of authenticity, origins, and identity."[14] According to Romagnolo, origins in Tan's novel are multiple and undecidable, but they nonetheless matter to the characters. Several older women search for something from the past (much as the adopted do), and although Romagnolo shows how the novel destabilizes or even "repudiates the existence of [each quest's] goal," she also stresses "the importance of the histories of these characters to their ongoing sense of agency." Origins may be "irretrievable," and for politically salutary reasons, but that makes the action of their incomplete reconstruction all the more vital.[15]

Taking a related approach to the "discursive constructedness of . . . origins," Mark E. Workman moves narrative theory even closer to some specific characteristics of adoption narratives. Workman observes that certain personal narratives with "obscured beginnings" are "'flawed' because of the narrator's awareness of and preoccupation with an originary event that the narrator strives to envelop within her story but that lies

13. Catherine Romagnolo, "Narrative Beginnings in Amy Tan's *The Joy Luck Club:* A Feminist Study," *Studies in the Novel* 35 (2003): 89–108, quotation at 92.

14. Romagnolo, "Narrative Beginnings," 91, 90.

15. Romagnolo, "Narrative Beginnings," 96, 97.

beyond her narratival grasp."[16] Workman's exemplary "flawed" narratives (recorded anecdotes rather than literary texts) are those of sexual jealousy, which compels imaginative reconstruction of an unexperienced event, and trauma, which compels imaginative reconstruction of an unremembered or uncomprehended event. The sequence of birth and abandonment prior to adoption has been linked to both of Workman's paradigmatic narratives, and so when it comes to adapting Miller's categorical remarks about "absence at the origin" to the specific case of adoption, Workman's thesis offers a particularly apt guide. Even more than in Romagnolo's reading of Tan, the emphasis in Workman's texts and in adoption narratives falls less on "absence at the origin" and more on creative, if compulsive, acts of reconstructing origins; origins are felt to be "obscured," not absent. As we have seen, adoptive parents often describe their feelings about meeting their children as falling in love; like Workman's jealous lovers, such parents may feel compelled to imagine primal scenes they missed. For example, in Kathleen Tolan's play *Memory House,* the adoptive mother, narrating the adoption story, says, "then I fell in love"; when the cynical teenage daughter picks a fight about the mother's supposed disregard for the birth family and place of origin, the mother counters—confirming Workman's thesis—by insisting that she thought constantly about the birthmother.[17]

The linkage of adoption to trauma is more complex, since infant relinquishment is not only like trauma (an unremembered yet life-altering event): it has itself been called a form of trauma by such popular theorists of adoption as Nancy Verrier and Betty Jean Lifton. While Romagnolo explains why stable, knowable origins are unlikely (if sometimes desperately sought) in narratives involving personal or cultural dislocations, Workman's specific concern with the reconstruction of traumatic origins can highlight the generative aspects of adoption narratives. Like (or as) trauma narratives, adoption narratives are often obsessively oriented toward an irretrievable past, and like (or as) trauma, adoption compels the creation of plausible if not verifiable narratives. Narratives of trauma and adoption (therapeutic and otherwise) are best understood not as about the unearthing of the veridical past, nor yet again about revealing the past to be what Miller calls the "absence at the origin," but about the creation of something new. I turn now to trauma theory to suggest how its handling of origins might contribute to our understanding of adoption narratives.

---

16. Mark Workman, "Obscured Beginnings in Personal Narratives of Sexual Jealousy and Trauma," *Narrative* 12 (2004): 249–62, quotation at 249.
17. Produced at the Playwrights' Horizons theater in New York, May 2005.

Adoption writers such as Verrier and Lifton subscribe to a theory of adoption as trauma that roughly corresponds to the theory of trauma as "unclaimed experience" articulated by Cathy Caruth, Shoshana Felman, Dori Laub, Bessel Van der Kolk, and others in the early 1990s. (This is the definition of trauma on which Workman relies.) For Lifton, the adopted are "wounded psychically."[18] In Verrier's view, any separation from the biological mother from the moment of birth onward, whether for relinquishment or merely for medical treatment, produces a "primal wound" that manifests itself in numbed affect, anxiety, depression, lifelong difficulty in trusting others, and the same intrusions and constrictions suffered by survivors of wars, the Holocaust, or childhood sexual abuse. As post-traumatic stress disorder (PTSD) sufferers, in Verrier's view, the adopted act out rather than consciously recall their abandonment. Not only do the adopted experience "possession by the past," to borrow Caruth's formulation: its "insistent reenactments . . . bear witness to a past that was never fully experienced as it occurred [and] that is not yet fully owned."[19] Verrier tells an anecdote, for example, of an adoptee who helplessly mimed her own abandonment by her birthmother.[20] Lifton describes adoption as a disease not unlike the condition of survivors of Hiroshima: "we walk around seemingly normal like everyone else, but we've got taboos, guilts, and repressions lodging like radiation inside us" (*Twice Born,* 156).[21] For Caruth and her fellow authors and the primary research on which they draw, such as that of analyst Pierre Janet, trauma has physical effects, as it does for Verrier's and Lifton's adoptees, and it creates a "traumatic memory" system filled with literal but unrepresentable memories separate from the "narrative memory" that is available to conscious recall.[22] The difficult task of the survivor and the therapist or witness is to move the traumatic event from the former to the latter,

---

18. Betty Jean Lifton, *Twice Born: Memoirs of an Adopted Daughter* (New York: McGraw Hill, 1975), 165 (hereafter cited in the text).
19. Cathy Caruth, "Recapturing the Past: Introduction," in *Trauma: Explorations in Memory,* ed. Cathy Caruth (Baltimore: Johns Hopkins University Press, 1995), 151–57, quotation at 151. This account of trauma theory draws also on Caruth, *Unclaimed Experience: Trauma, Narrative, and History* (Baltimore: Johns Hopkins University Press, 1996), and on Shoshana Felman and Dori Laub, *Testimony: Crises of Witnessing in Literature, Psychoanalysis, and History* (New York: Routledge, 1992).
20. Nancy Verrier, *The Primal Wound: Understanding the Adopted Child* (Baltimore: Gateway Press, 1993), 151 (hereafter cited in the text).
21. Lifton also sees the adopted and their birth parents as just as much in need of reunion as families separated by the Holocaust (*Twice Born,* 220–21, 227).
22. Bessel A. Van der Kolk and Onno van der Hart, "The Intrusive Past: The Flexibility of Memory and the Engraving of Trauma," in Caruth, *Trauma,* 158–82, quotation at 160.

where it can be integrated into the sufferer's overall life narrative. Similarly, Verrier claims that the adoptee, even a days-old infant, remembers her abandonment, with memories that are deeply buried "in the psyche and cells" (*Primal Wound,* 16). The task for therapy, in Verrier as in Caruth, is to articulate and narrate what at first seems non-narratable.

Used as a model for narrative, Verrier's account of trauma would imply that the story of the past should and can be accurately told. Just as Caruth finds that "the images of traumatic reenactment remain absolutely accurate and precise," Verrier emphasizes the literality of the trauma's residues. Unlike Caruth, however, with her deconstructive skepticism about the difficulties involved in narrating and integrating traumatic memories lodged in images that are "largely inaccessible to conscious recall," Verrier has little doubt that therapy can retrieve the past.[23] But in Verrier's writing, this therapeutic work involves a surprisingly high degree of fiction making. When an infant arrives in its adoptive home, for example, Verrier encourages the parents to interpret any "unexplained sadness or crying" as "expressions of the child's loss of the biological mother. . . . It would be important to empathize with the loss and to talk about it—put it into words for him" (*Primal Wound,* 119). Perhaps so, but the parents could also be making this up, obliging the child to mourn a loss she does not feel.

Moreover, Verrier's strategies for mourning also entail some unacknowledged temporal dislocations. Verrier urges the adopted to search for their birthmothers, and she calls this "searching for that biological past," as though a living and inevitably much changed human being could somehow make present or embody the past (*Primal Wound,* 153–54). This temporal confusion is common to many search narratives. As Barbara Yngvesson writes: "The search for roots assumes a past is there, if we can just find the right file, the right papers, or the right person."[24] But as Lifton says of her own search, "the past was not there waiting to receive me" (*Twice Born,* 118). Verrier elides such questions as why searching for the biological past would be a good idea or what it should accomplish. She emphasizes instead that if everyone speaks honestly about "what they are truly feeling" in the present, all will go well: "These feelings do not have to be denied or apologized for. But if they are not owned, they will be projected upon another member of the triad" (*Primal Wound,* 166–67).

23. Caruth, "Recapturing the Past," 151.

24. Barbara Yngvesson, "Going 'Home': Adoption, Loss of Bearings, and the Mythology of Roots," *Social Text* 74 (Spring 2003): 7–27, rpt. in *Cultures of Transnational Adoption,* ed. Toby Alice Volkman (Durham: Duke University Press, 2005), 25–48, quotation at 32 (hereafter cited in the text).

In other words, for the "unclaimed experience" of the past of Caruth's, Felman's, and Laub's model, Verrier substitutes feelings in the present that must and can far more easily be "owned." "How is it possible . . . to gain access to a traumatic history?" asks Caruth.[25] Verrier's inadvertent answer is that there is no history; there is only the present. Her literalism about the past (her insistence that it can be retrieved) has the paradoxical effect (because it cannot be retrieved) of making history disappear.

A turn from Caruth's to Ruth Leys's account of trauma suggests a different (indeed explicitly opposed) paradigm for what it would mean to say that adoption is like trauma or is trauma, a paradigm that can better account for the fiction making and focus on the present in Verrier. In the realm of trauma theory, Leys is arguing for something like what Miller argues for in narrative, that origins are inventions, neither recoverable nor verifiable. Leys rereads a series of early trauma analysts including Pierre Janet to reveal a longstanding shift in focus from the truth of what really happened in the past to creative constructions in the present, and from efforts to retrieve memory to the beneficial effects of forgetting. In Janet's writings, Leys argues,

> patients acquired the ability to produce an account of themselves that conformed to certain requirements of temporal ordering but that did not necessarily entail a process of self-recognition. . . . If narration cures, it does so not because it infallibly gives the patient access to a primordially personal truth but because it makes possible a form of self-understanding even in the absence of empirical verification.[26]

Curative "narrative memory," in other words, could very well be fictional, prompted by the doctor's suggestions or even by narrative conventions: "certain requirements of temporal ordering." Ferenczi, even more strikingly, believing the traumatic origin to be irrecoverable, Leys says, "subscribed to a notion of lying, or simulation . . . encouraging the patient to *feign* or *simulate* the traumatic scene or origin" (*Trauma,* 13). Leys traces this line of thinking on to the British World War II psychiatrist William Sargant, who discovered that being induced by drugs to relive "invented situations," indeed "false memories" suggested by the doctor, worked just as well to cure shell-shocked patients as the reliving of an actual incident (202–3).

---

25. Caruth, "Recapturing the Past," 151.
26. Ruth Leys, *Trauma: A Genealogy* (Chicago: University of Chicago Press, 2000), 117 (hereafter cited in the text).

With Leys's emphasis on the figurative, possibly fictive, and present-time nature of traumatic "recall," a different model for adoption narrative emerges, one in which claims to reveal the truth of the past are replaced by the narration of an emotionally satisfying but probably fictional story about the present. Rather than expecting to retrieve the veridical origin (either the traumatic moment of relinquishment or maternal and cultural origins prior to that moment), the adopted and their families could understand themselves as inventing helpful fictions about those irretrievable historical moments. Judith Butler argues that "the narrative reconstruction of a life *cannot* be the goal of psychoanalysis," because the self doing the reconstructing will always be at a remove from the self that is the object of knowledge; "the origin is made available only retroactively, and through the screen of fantasy."[27] Workman says ruefully at the end of his essay that personal narratives that seem self-revelatory may really only be a "comforting but . . . dissembling ruse."[28] But why not accept such ruses?

In adoption memoirs, the stakes involved in searching for an authentic origin can be very high: the author recounts her search not only for a narrative about her past but also for her identity, and the high value placed on truth-telling serves as an implicit guarantee that she will choose truth over fiction at every opportunity. Yet even the most stringently honest memoirs cannot fail to resort not only to fictional techniques in telling their stories but also to fiction in constructing the very origin whose truth is so painstakingly sought. Lifton's *Twice Born* is a classic adoption memoir, one of the earliest in the recent wave of such memoirs that accompanied and helped to launch the open adoption and search movements. Lifton, with a distinctly negative tone, calls the lives of the adopted "fictitious" (*Twice Born,* 4). Adopted at two but not told of the adoption until she was seven (and even then lied to about her birth parents), she "impersonat[es]" the child her parents were unable to bear (29), endures a childhood filled with empty rituals and pretense, and lives in an "illusion" (218) created by her adoptive mother. In opposition to this "fictitious" life Lifton posits a primal "need for origins" (248), a compulsion to search for the truth about one's birth, and she compares the discovery of that truth to the gradual exposure of "a mummy bound in layers of shroud, wrapped in years of secrets, mysteries, lies, deceptions, confabulations, mythology" (191). She begins her memoir

27. Butler, *Giving an Account,* 52–53.

28. Workman, "Obscured Beginnings," 261.

with her adoptive mother's fabrication of a story, based on a novel, about her married birth parents' tragic deaths (from shell-shock and grief), a story that bore no relation to what Lifton eventually discovered, that her unmarried parents were both alive when she began her search. Lifton compares her mother's fabrication explicitly to that of literary fiction: "What easier way to get rid of excess characters than to kill them off from the beginning. (Novelists have been known to be just as ruthless if it will help them get on with their action)" (12). The memoir is plotted as a quest to uncover the secret truth hidden behind the fiction.

The line separating (desired) truth from (harmful) fiction soon blurs, however. With chapter titles such as "Into the Maze," borrowed from the myth of the Minotaur, the book associates fiction not just with lies but with the author's positive efforts to uncover and replace those lies. Because of her mother's tales and her own imaginings, "an adoptee's natural parents never completely lose the aura of fantasy, both positive and negative, which once surrounded them, even after they are found" (*Twice Born,* 17). Not only is fantasy her adoptive mother's way of life, but it has also been her own, not just in childhood but even after she learns the identities of her birth parents, in phrasings suggesting that as an adoptee she may not have been searching for the truth after all: "all adoptees have an unconscious fantasy when they are searching that they are following a path that leads to *home*"; if "there is no gingerbread house with Mommy and Daddy waiting inside with presents under the family tree," and she cautions adoptees against investing in such fantasies, that does not mean she has not imagined there would be such a house (233). She represents herself through Greek and Japanese myths, identifies with Oedipus, analogizes her secret to the Minotaur hiding in the labyrinth, and sees herself in the Japanese shape-changing "kappa" (60). The comparison of her story to that of Oedipus presumes that both are about the concealment and eventual recovery of the truth, yet it also exhibits her practice of deferring the meaning of her story to that of preexisting fictional narratives.

When Lifton, discovering her mother's falsehood, decides to find out what really happened, her formulation of her project suggests not so much the replacement of fiction with truth as the substitution of one story for another: "I no longer wanted to live in [my mother's] fantasy world. I wanted myth and reality to merge" (*Twice Born,* 85). Although she concludes this passage expressing her wish "to be real," why call for myth and reality to merge, rather than for myth to give way to reality? The facts revealed by the adoption agency become the basis for new speculations ("Such is the fiction the adopted invent" [91]; "Now it was my turn to revise the script" [92]) that are not unlike both the adoptive mother's yarn and the "gingerbread house" fantasy Lifton later confesses to. Momentarily ambivalent about continuing her search, she fears losing not only "the poetic fantasy [of the birthmother] you've created in your mind" (93) but also the "reality of my adoptive family unit—the only family I had ever known" (94), a reality heretofore defined as "fictitious." Fictional and real trade places; competing fictions become competing realities.

Told she needs therapy to cure her of her need to know, Lifton turns to Helene Deutsch, who tells her—in a phrasing strikingly echoed by Leys's reading of Janet, Ferenczi, and Sargant—that "the myth becomes integrated into one's life and psychology and is as good as the real history" (*Twice Born,* 98). Lifton rejects Deutsch's conclusion that her need to search is neurotic, yet their analyses of the situation are not far apart. Valuing the fictional positively, she recognizes that her birthmother "had been more nurturing as the ghostly mother of my fantasy than as a reality in life," where she became "disappointed" by the "defeated" woman she met (139). Confirming that her adopted (yet "fictitious") self feels real to her, she consigns her birth self to the realm of fiction:

> Many adoptees take their original names when they learn them, discarding the other like a snake sheds its skin. I have no desire to take mine. Blanche is a fictional character in a fairy tale. (*Twice Born,* 181)

"Fictional" comes to cover a surprisingly large portion of what Lifton initially terms "reality."

If the truth Lifton believes she will reach about herself and her birthmother proves not only elusive but positively fictive, her biological father, who in her adoptive mother's fabrication "had had a concrete, shell-shocked reality," becomes "nonexistent" once she opens the files (*Twice Born,* 92). A shadowy figure her birthmother does not want her to find, dead by the time Lifton begins to search for him in 1973, he is, momentarily, the "absence" Miller locates "at the origin." But Lifton's desire quickly resumes its creative work. He is already, she finds, a legend: a former bootlegger, an "Adonis [who] always had a beautiful woman on his arm" (197), a figure she comprehends by comparing him to Fitzgerald's Gatsby. She contacts his best friend, who agrees to meet her at, of all places, Plymouth Rock. Lifton recognizes the mythic dimensions of this choice:

> A novelist could have done no better than Sammy in choosing Plymouth Rock for our rendezvous. Here where the traveler comes to seek the pilgrim father, I came to find my bootlegging father, hoping to trap that perfidious ghost. (*Twice Born*, 200)

In Sammy's tales "Boots emerged as a cross between Jesse James and Don Juan," a striving immigrant "akin in spirit to those intrepid founding fathers who had forged their way through an unknown land" (201). Plymouth serves to amplify the grandeur of Lifton's search, as though her personal origin were synonymous with the nation's.[29] Yet Plymouth Rock (with its present-day "honky-tonk tone" and phony landmarks [200]) amounts to a legend of origination, a fiction generated by a national need for "the pilgrim father" much as Sammy elaborates his tales to meet Lifton's desire.

Once Lifton has related her father's story, the narrative returns to her troubled relationships with her two mothers, both of whom insist on maintaining the secrecy of the adoption and both of whom Lifton eventually defies by writing and publishing *Twice Born*. Again, although she appears to contrast her allegiance to the truth to her mothers' need for softening fictions, Lifton stands for fabrication, too. She is proud that she and her birthmother "are writing a new page of the adoption story even while we talk" (*Twice Born*, 228). They debate the meaning of the term "natural" (229), each claiming it to justify her own impulses (toward openness or secrecy), thus opening to interpretation a term that might seem synonymous with authenticity. Lifton concedes that her position is not the only one grounded in nature: nature, she allows, "is not determinative" (233); "the biological tie is divested of some of nature's components" (234). Finally, she concludes with the benefits of adoptive self-fabrication. What she has gained in the end, she concedes, is not a true or real self (her habitual terms) but a made self. Her husband remarks, "I would say that if one is twice born, one has to carve out a new self distinct from the one society assigned you." Lifton replies: "It [adoption] had allowed me to create myself" (252).

Unraveling the line between fictitious and factual, Lifton defines the adoptee as "twice born." Where there are two origins, as in Romagnolo's reading of multiple origins in Tan's novel, neither can be claimed as authentic, and the very idea of authenticity becomes untenable. In Lifton

29. Similarly, Jean Strauss's film *Adopted: For the Life of Me* accompanies the announcement of the opening of sealed birth records in Massachusetts with a brief shot of the public road sign for Plymouth Rock.

as in Tan this situation has positive and negative resonances: an individual may value highly her sense of history even if the text that contains it concedes the groundlessness of any attempt at truth. If *Oedipus the King* can model both the quest for an adoptee's past and the inescapable fictitiousness of the resulting narrative, then the adoptee who frames her quest as Oedipus's embraces truth and fiction together.

INVENTED AUTHENTICITY AND ORIGINS IN RECENT AMERICAN ADOPTION FICTION

In Lifton, and even more in the adoption narratives to be discussed next, the compulsion to search for origins becomes a compulsion to create them, even as a contradictory desire for or belief in authenticity may remain strong. I turn now to some recent works of adoption fiction—four novels and a play—that exhibit complexly the tug between veridical and fictional theories of narrating lost origins: Toni Morrison's *Tar Baby;* Barbara Kingsolver's *The Bean Trees* and *Pigs in Heaven;* Sherman Alexie's *Indian Killer;* Gish Jen's *The Love Wife;* and Rolin Jones's play about Chinese adoption, *The Intelligent Design of Jenny Chow.* These works of fiction represent a range of topics and subject positions in transracial and transnational US adoption and span the period of greatest controversy on the subject, but they share—and I believe they are representative in sharing—similar approaches to the problem of adoptive origins. In these works, origins are fictions produced by and temporally sequential to the present.

A fast way to sketch this narrative pattern is to review Cynthia Chase's deconstructive reading of George Eliot's *Daniel Deronda,* in which, according to Chase, the adopted hero's biological and cultural origins are produced by the exigencies of his adult present, in which he can live a satisfactory life only if he turns out to have been born a Jew.[30] (Hans Meyrick refers elsewhere in the novel to "the present causes of past effects."[31]) Nearing its conclusion, the novel grants him that desired past, complete with birthmother and birth culture, calling attention to its nonce creation of that past by overlooking the fact that, in Chase's view, if Deronda really was supposed to be Jewish from the start, he had most likely only to observe, marked on his male body, the sign of his race. *What Maisie*

30. Cynthia Chase, "The Decomposition of the Elephants: Double-Reading *Daniel Deronda,*" *PMLA* 93 (1978): 215–27.

31. George Eliot, *Daniel Deronda* (1876) (London: Penguin, 1995), 641.

Knew presents a similar paradigm of temporal inversions brought about by adoption: in Rivkin's view, Maisie becomes the origin of new family formations (such as the tie between her father and her governess, who becomes her stepmother) rather than finding her origin in an existing family, so that causal and narrative sequences often run in reverse.[32] Or we could recall Oedipus, in Miller's reading, inventing a past to solve a possibly unrelated present mystery, the plague's cause. In works of fiction written in the contemporary context of debates over the potential injustice of transracial and transnational adoption, the explicit invention of adoptive origins exists in tension with claims that authentic origins can be found and stabilized. Nonetheless, these novels exhibit, and accept, what Eliot calls "the make-believe of a beginning" for their adopted protagonists and their families.

Toni Morrison's 1981 *Tar Baby* uses an adoption story to represent and explore questions of racial identity, deracination, and origins. In doing so it ambivalently reflects the 1970s–1980s discourse opposing transracial adoption and favoring "roots."[33] Even though the novel's "yalla" heroine Jadine was orphaned at the age of twelve by her mother's death, so that her birth itself is not the mystery, her adoption mobilizes throughout the

32. "The undoing of the oedipal family enacted in the novel not only deprives social roles and class origins of their power to determine identity, but also alters the narrative sequences by which those social orders are maintained" (Rivkin, *False Positions,* 145).

33. Works participating in and analyzing the debate over transracial adoption include: Rita J. Simon and Howard Altstein, *Transracial Adoption* (New York: John Wiley and Sons, 1977), which includes the National Association of Black Social Workers position paper of Apr. 1972 opposing transracial placements, which sparked the controversy (50–52); Ricki Solinger, *Wake Up Little Susie: Single Pregnancy and Race before* Roe v. Wade (New York: Routledge, 1992), and *Beggars and Choosers* (New York: Hill and Wang, 2001); Elizabeth Bartholet, *Family Bonds: Adoption and the Politics of Parenting* (Boston: Houghton Mifflin, 1993), and *Nobody's Children: Abuse and Neglect, Foster Drift, and the Adoption Alternative* (Boston: Beacon Press, 1999), which mount strong arguments in favor of racial mixing in US and transnational adoption; Sandra Patton, *BirthMarks: Transracial Adoption in Contemporary America* (New York: New York University Press, 2000), which argues that the NABSW was defending the black community against the 1965 Moynihan Report (153–55, 173–74); Dorothy Roberts, *Shattered Bonds: The Color of Child Welfare* (New York: Basic Books, 2001); Hawley Fogg-Davis, *The Ethics of Transracial Adoption* (Ithaca: Cornell University Press, 2002); Randall Kennedy, *Interracial Intimacies: Sex, Marriage, Identity, and Adoption* (New York: Pantheon, 2003); Barbara Katz Rothman, *Weaving a Family: Untangling Race and Adoption* (Boston: Beacon Press, 2005); Pamela Anne Quiroz, *Adoption in a Color-Blind Society* (Lanham, MD: Rowman and Littlefield, 2007); and Laura Briggs, *Somebody's Children: The Politics of Transracial and Transnational Adoption* (Durham: Duke University Press, 2012), which expands upon Patton's defense of the NABSW by arguing that it defended black mothers against their scapegoating by opponents of the Civil Rights Movement.

novel a series of meditations on origins, their loss and ambiguous reconstruction.[34] Jadine has been ineffectively adopted by two sets of people: her black aunt and uncle and their white employer, who sent her to college and now dines with her in his splendidly remote Caribbean island home while her aunt and uncle cook and serve.[35] With two families yet, in effect, none, Jadine is rootless and a believer in self-making. She cultivates only the surface appearance of blackness that makes her a successful model and object of white male desire in Paris and New York; she appears to care less about her aunt and uncle than about her new coat made from the skins of black baby seals.

Despite or because of this commitment to inauthenticity, Jadine is haunted by visions of the traditional black womanhood that her adoptive raising has both saved her from and denied her. The "vision" of a woman with "skin like tar against the canary yellow dress" (*Tar Baby,* 45), a woman of "unphotographable beauty" (46) holding up three eggs accusingly and then spitting at her, sends Jadine on her journey from Paris back to wherever home might be. The down-and-out hero Son represents and introduces her to black folk culture, rooted in the all-black Florida town of Eloe that he loves but that she finds "Paleolithic" (257) in its poverty and backwardness, a place where night is "the blackest nothing she had ever seen" (251). He dreams, and tries to make Jadine too dream, of "the fat black ladies in white dresses minding the pie table in the basement of the church" (119). Constructing "a new childhood" (229) for her that he hopes will repair her rootlessness, attempting to insert black traditions into her unconscious, he temporarily makes her feel "unorphaned" (229). In her eyes, however, his favored signifiers of blackness are murderous traps. The Isle des Chevaliers' "swamp women" (184) nearly pull her down to her death, and Son's dream of ladies around the pie table transmutes in Jadine's mind into a nightmare of black mothers and sexual women, the "night women" (262)—including the woman in

34. Toni Morrison, *Tar Baby* (New York: Knopf, 1981), 155 (hereafter cited in the text).

35. See Marilyn Sanders Mobley for a reading that begins with Jadine's double adoption but reaches opposite conclusions from mine about Morrison's representations of authentic origins: "Narrative Dilemma: Jadine as Cultural Orphan in *Tar Baby,*" in *Toni Morrison: Critical Perspectives Past and Present,* ed. Henry Louis Gates and K. A. Appiah (New York: Amistad, 1993), 284–92. Cynthia Callahan's reading of the novel focuses on the "complex sense of self" that Jadine develops because of her double adoption: "Given her two adoptive families, Jade's tendency to identify with both white and black worlds is, perhaps, the most 'authentic' option available to her": *Kin of Another Kind: Transracial Adoption in American Literature* (Ann Arbor: University of Michigan Press, 2011), 99.

yellow, her aunt Ondine, and her own dead mother—who hold out their breasts and eggs accusingly.

The novel thus seems to draw on popular trauma theory (approximately that of Verrier and of Caruth, et al.) in representing the consequences of Jadine's orphanhood and adoption. When the narrative has Jadine thinking, "Mama how could you be with [the night women]. You left me you died you didn't care enough about me to stay alive" (*Tar Baby,* 261), her lost and incompletely mourned mother seems to break through the barrier of repression and intrusively haunt the present. Authenticity is linked through blackness to night and dreams, and Morrison dedicates her book to a list of women who "knew their true and ancient properties."

But Morrison represents Jadine's rejection of traditional black womanhood with evenhandedness, granting some merit to Jadine's argument for education and professional work, an interminable argument with Son that ends in their separation. Moreover, the swamp women themselves are, incongruously, promoters not only of female "sacred properties" but also of adoption. Surprised that Jadine is "fighting to get away from them," they are "mindful . . . of their value . . . knowing . . . that they alone could hold together the stones of pyramids and the rushes of Moses's crib" (*Tar Baby,* 183). Moses's mother made him "an ark of bulrushes and daubed it with slime and with pitch" (Exodus 2:3, King James version) when she sent him down the river to be adopted by Pharoah's daughter. The mud that adheres to Jadine's legs appears to be "pitch," a term connected to the woman in yellow with her "skin like tar" and her authentic, premodern look, but it is also linked both to Moses's adoption story and to the novel's title. At first "tar baby" seems to reference Jadine's alluring but superficial blackness, but here it alludes to the swamp women, the woman in yellow, and the novel's other female figures of black authenticity. The tar baby is not, or not only, the deliberately self-fashioned Jadine but also those who claim an ideal yet unlivable authenticity. The hallucinatory "night women" may thus be both an intrusion by the traumatically lost mother and a conspicuously phony-sounding simulacrum of authentic origins. Two more race women, Thérèse and Alma Estée, likewise represent black authenticity ambiguously: although Thérèse's breasts still magically give milk and, though blind, she can steer a boat in the dark, she is not the wise crone she at first appears, and Alma Estée's only desire is a "russet wig" (288). The novel produces a series of figures of authenticity that are both admired and ironized.

Son, in contrast to Jadine, seems to have, know, and enjoy a stable origin. After eight years hiding from the law, he is joyfully reunited with friends and family in Eloe. And yet for Son, too, a figure of authentic origins turns at least potentially nightmarish. At the very end, in fog and darkness, Thérèse takes him to the Isle des Chevaliers, where he hopes to find Jadine. Dropping him off not on the inhabited part of the island, where Jadine would likely be found, but on the wild, dockless "far side," Thérèse compels Son to feel and smell his way along a "bridge" of ocean rocks to reach the shore. She insists that these rocks form a line: "Climb to it and the next one is right behind, then another and another like a road. Then the land" (*Tar Baby,* 305). Recalling the rocky causeway extending to the Isle of Slingers in Hardy's *The Well-Beloved,* a line of rocks signifying direct genealogical descent in a novel about a man who falls in love with three identical generations of mothers and daughters, this line of rocks seems to demarcate the direct route back to a native, unadulterated past.[36] For Thérèse, the back of the island is the domain of the legendary race of black, blind, naked, primeval "chevaliers" who "mate" with the "swamp women" and perpetually "race those horses . . . all over the hills" (306). For her level-headed nephew Gideon, however, the legend of the blind chevaliers is just a cover story for the mundane reality of syphilis. The chevaliers thus occupy an ambiguous space between sordid fiction and mythic if crazed authenticity. Leaving Son on the first rock, Thérèse forces him to "choose" the pure, originary chevaliers over the deracinated Jadine. At first he is terrified and reluctant, but the last sentences are ambiguous. Son appears to reach the shore, stand up, and begin to walk; "Then he ran. Lickety-split. . . . Lickety-lickety-lickety-split" (306). Has he become one with the blind, racing chevaliers? Was he all along one of them, a fantasy of ancestral black purity, another "tar baby" luring Jadine into the swamp? Does his transformation into a legend mean a descent into madness or death or a sublime elevation? Either way, authenticity is conspicuously figured as fictional.

Morrison's adoption novel reveals both the appeal and the risk of romantic fictions of racial origins. Through the subject matter of adoption—Jadine's position between two sets of nonoriginal parents—the novel denaturalizes such origins, to expose their fictive creation in response to different characters' needs and the ways in which they might

36. Hardy's celebration of direct genetic descent is likewise in tension with what is known of his forging and fictionalizing his own genealogy; see Tess O'Toole, *Genealogy and Fiction in Hardy: Family Lineage and Narrative Lines* (New York: St. Martin's Press, 1997).

both serve and fail to serve the present. Morrison gestures admiringly toward racial authenticity in the abstract, yet she does not suggest that authentic origins could be retrieved or restored; in this novel, fictive origins are the only origins there are. Reflecting obliquely on the contemporaneous debate over the merits of transracial adoption, the novel does not so much take sides as question the terms in which the debate is conducted.

Written a decade after *Tar Baby,* Barbara Kingsolver's two novels about the adoption of a Cherokee child by a white woman from Kentucky are among the most frequently studied fictional representations of transracial adoption. Explicitly engaged in the debate about the politics of whites adopting Native children, *The Bean Trees* and *Pigs in Heaven* have been examined time and again for the accuracy and the politics of their depiction of such adoptions.[37] These novels construct origins retroactively, however, as if in fulfillment of Homer Noline's wish in *Animal Dreams* (the novel Kingsolver wrote in between the two adoption novels) to change his own racial origin: "If you change the present enough, history will bend to accommodate it."[38] In *The Bean Trees* an unnamed Cherokee woman places in the front seat of the protagonist Taylor Greer's car a child who exhibits the physical and emotional signs not only of neglect but of violent sexual abuse. Seeking legally to adopt this child, whom she names Turtle, Taylor must produce exactly the kind of factual evidence of the past that is so hard to come by in trauma narratives as well as in adoption: in this case, firm evidence of voluntary relinquishment or orphanhood. All Taylor knows about Turtle's birth is that it occurred "in a Plymouth," a story that seems generated after the fact as an echo of the subsequent moment when Turtle appears in Taylor's car.[39] As an echo, this Plymouth origin story serves to undo the difference between adoption and birth, making the adoption the original of which the birth is the copy. Moreover, as in Lifton's *Twice Born,* "Plymouth" signifies a grand myth of US national origins: Plymouth is everyone's generic origin and so no one individual's. The term's irony is amplified in this context through the meaning of Plymouth for Native Americans: not a celebrat-

37. Mary Lyndon Shanley discusses the history of Native transracial, transnational adoption in the United States in *Making Babies, Making Families: What Matters Most in an Age of Reproductive Technologies, Surrogacy, Adoption, and Same-Sex and Unwed Parents* (Boston: Beacon Press, 2001), 25–38. See also Kennedy, *Interracial Intimacies,* 480–518; and Briggs, *Somebody's Children,* 59–93.
38. Barbara Kingsolver, *Animal Dreams* (New York: Harper Collins, 1990), 288.
39. Barbara Kingsolver, *The Bean Trees* (New York: Harper Collins, 1988), 24 (hereafter cited in the text).

ed national origin but a mourned endpoint of autonomous sovereignty. Whether birth in a Plymouth gives Turtle the upward mobility of immigrants such as the pilgrims or Lifton's father or a beginning that contains its own demise, its mythic dimensions give Turtle a fantasmatic origin.

The conditions of Turtle's being placed in the car further the conflation of adoption and birth by mimicking birth. The child emerges from a pink blanket that, wrapping her and her aunt together, simulates a maternal body. Rewrapped alone in the pink blanket in Taylor's car, the silent child is, like a newborn, not yet a human subject: Taylor cannot tell if she is a baby or a child, boy or girl, alive or dead. Taylor points out, oddly, that the pink blanket is "exactly like" one she and her Mama have at home, as if to suggest that if, in this post-adoption birth, a blanket is a body, that body could well have been Taylor's own. Much of the novel thereafter is devoted to showing the process by which the unmaternal Taylor gradually becomes Turtle's loving and protective mother.

Unable to determine Turtle's biological roots, Taylor acquires adoption papers through a fictional subterfuge, when she poses a Guatemalan refugee couple as the relinquishing birth parents. This simulation functions as an effective emotional truth not only for Turtle and Taylor but also for the grieving refugees themselves, whose own daughter has been kidnapped and lost to adoption. Marianne Novy points out that *The Bean Trees* advocates for adoption by advocating for accepting substitutes at every level. Just as in Ruth Leys's reading of trauma theorists Janet, Ferenczi, and Sargant, simulation does as well as or better than knowledge of the hidden truth to heal whatever trauma these characters have suffered.

Kingsolver was chastised by readers, however, for so lightheartedly assigning the Native Turtle to a non-Native mother and for her apparent ignorance of the 1978 Indian Child Welfare Act that, responding to a long history of widespread state-sponsored kidnappings, creates and protects the rights of Native tribes to control the placement of abandoned Native children.[40] Five years later she published *Pigs in Heaven*, which ostensibly

40. For discussion of Kingsolver's novels in the context of the ICWA, see Kristina Fagan, "Adoption as National Fantasy in Barbara Kingsolver's *Pigs in Heaven* and Margaret Lawrence's *The Diviners*," in *Imagining Adoption: Essays on Literature and Culture*, ed. Marianne Novy (Ann Arbor: University of Michigan Press, 2001), 251–66; Pauline Turner Strong, "To Forget Their Tongue, Their Name, and Their Whole Relation: Captivity, Extra-Tribal Adoption, and the Indian Child Welfare Act," in *Relative Values: Reconfiguring Kinship Studies*, ed. Sarah Franklin and Susan McKinnon (Durham: Duke University Press, 2001), 468–93; Callahan, *Kin of Another Kind*, 110–21; and Novy, *Reading Adoption*, 188–213.

repudiates the earlier novel's fraudulent adoption and its embrace of explicitly fictional origin stories (the Plymouth story, the acted scene of relinquishment). Seeming to peel back that veil of once-satisfactory fictions, the second novel reveals what counts as Turtle's real history and ancestry: her wistfully deracinated Cherokee grandfather Cash Stillwater and the tribal extended family members who, in the view of the tribal lawyer Annawake, herself a grieving witness to the kidnapping of her twin brother, are the proper guardians of the orphaned child.

Pigs in Heaven does not simply reject Leys's theory of traumatic origins (or Miller's parallel theory of narrative origins) in favor of Caruth's or Verrier's, as it were, figures and fictions in favor of literalism and truth. As in Romagnolo's and Workman's readings, narratives of origins searches highlight their inventiveness even while acknowledging how attractive a belief in literal retrievability can be. Through the use of omniscient narration to represent almost all possible points of view, and through a narrative contrivance that rivals Taylor's earlier staging of the fake relinquishment, a contrivance calling attention to the novel as a work of fiction, Kingsolver, as many readers have noted, resolves the conflicting claims of the birth family and of Taylor's maternal love by arranging for literal and simulated origins to converge in the courtship and projected marriage of Taylor's mother and Turtle's biological grandfather.

This convergence, which recalls Lifton's "I wanted myth and reality to merge," is made possible not just by Kingsolver's elaborate plot contrivance but also by her rewriting of her characters' histories to support the new story. In *Pigs in Heaven* the birth family history Kingsolver devises for Turtle does not match the history hinted at in *The Bean Trees* but, instead, fulfills the narrative and ethical requirements of the new story. The first novel, under the sign of realism, had emphasized Turtle's abandonment and sexual abuse by an unidentified family member: Turtle herself is one great trauma symptom, with her silence and repetitive acting-out behavior. The second novel replaces this ominous and undiplomatic vision of Turtle's past with positive and timeless evocations of Cherokee culture and extended family, through such present-time scenes as the traditional stomp dance and the bucolic lake where Annawake's wise uncle Ledger lives. Nowhere does this novel account for the abuse that marked Turtle's mind and body in *The Bean Trees;* although Taylor recalls it in defending her right to adopt, the narrative never goes there, instead leaving stand the inference that the central trauma was her loss of her birthmother and birth culture. Taylor's ignorance of Turtle's inherited lactose intolerance, for example, looms disproportionately large as a sign of Taylor's new-minted inadequacy as a mother. A series of brief, repeated notations convey the bare information that Cash's daughter Alma drove her car into the river, leaving her baby to the care of her alcoholic sister and her abusive boyfriend. That the novel keeps repeating this information without developing it into a narrative suggests how deliberately the novel is trying to forget the past implied in *The Bean Trees. Pigs in Heaven* also gives Turtle just one extant immediate family member, the clean-living Cash Stillwater. The complex, ambivalent figure of the aunt from *The Bean Trees* has vanished, replaced by idealized examples of nurturant extended family. The later novel invents for Turtle a past worth reclaiming, yet the inventedness of that past is always evident.

As in *Twice Born,* the adopted child's original name (revealed long after we know her by her new name) seems less true to the character and more fictional than her adopted name. Just as Lifton says her original name "Blanche" is "a fictional character in a fairy tale," *Pigs in Heaven* has Turtle originally named "Lacey" after a character on television.[41] "Turtle" is coded as the more authentic name, both because it describes the child's leading characteristic (her attachment to her mother), rather than referencing someone else's (generic, white) fantasy, and also because it sounds authentically Native. Taylor's ability to give Turtle her true name helps to establish adopted identity as authentic and retroactively to associate her origins with fiction. The name Turtle, however, may also allude to the old joke about Native cosmology ("If the world rests on the back of a turtle, what does the turtle stand on?" "It's turtles all the way down") and so may also reference the naïvete of belief in groundedness. Miller's "infinite regress," the categorical impossibility of origins, remains visible in the novel's uneasy forging of authenticity.

Generated by the present time of Kingsolver's political anxieties, the conspicuously fabricated character of Turtle's community of origin in *Pigs in Heaven* is part of a pattern of retroactively produced pasts in both novels. In *The Bean Trees,* the adoption story emerges in response to the requirements of Taylor's first-person narrative, requirements deriving from her need for a new past. She has left her roots in Kentucky, driving west until she can reinvent herself with a new name and a new home. When she more or less stumbles upon the Cherokee reservation, Taylor reveals that she and her mother Alice are part Cherokee with "head rights" to enroll in the Cherokee Nation (*Bean Trees,* 18). Just be-

---

41. Barbara Kingsolver, *Pigs in Heaven* (New York: Harper Collins, 1993), 322 (hereafter cited in the text).

fore the child is placed in her car, Taylor buys a postcard of two Native women whom she resembles enough that she plans to write "here's us" on it and send it to her mother (20). In one of the novel's many reverse chronologies, Taylor and her mother become retroactively the originals for a representation that they are, instead, soon to imitate. The Native child so suddenly appearing on Taylor's front seat thus literalizes at once Taylor's own intended rebirth (both she and her new daughter gain new names, and these names echo each other) and her latent Native ancestry. When Taylor finally mails the postcard she writes, "I found my head rights, Mama. They're coming with me" (32). That is, Turtle is Taylor's ancestry come alive. Almost like one of Nancy Verrier's adoptees "searching for that biological past," or Lifton wistfully recalling her wish to find "the past . . . there waiting to receive me," Taylor finds in Turtle her own desirable alternative origin story, a story in which she comes not from alienated Appalachian poverty but from an open-armed Native community. In *Pigs in Heaven* Alice becomes Cherokee—acquires that past, that ancestry—because of present circumstances, her falling in love with Cash and her effort to support her daughter's claim to Turtle. Theoretically one-quarter Cherokee from birth, Alice is not actually, functionally Cherokee until her child needs her to be. Kingsolver has racial origins not so much trump as echo or copy the later-formed, but discursively and emotionally prior, ties of adoptive love. Blood ties from the past are produced by the exigencies of the present.

Because Turtle thus originates not in her own but in Taylor's story, despite the political imperative for *Pigs in Heaven* to retrieve Turtle's roots, the emphasis of the story is not on Turtle's origins but on Turtle as Taylor's belated origin. Despite Kingsolver and her audience agreeing that the novels should accurately reflect Native life, from the start of *The Bean Trees* the entire plot of abandonment, adoption, search, and reunion is propelled not by allegiance to historical truth but by the narrative requirements of the white female protagonist. Readers, such as Kristina Fagan, who are critical of the politics of *The Bean Trees* and *Pigs in Heaven* have identified this aspect of the narrative—that Taylor comes first and that the Native community serves her needs, rather than her benefiting it—as its most politically egregious feature. Although at the end Taylor suffers in having to share custody of Turtle with Cash—giving up "the absolute power of motherhood . . . makes her feel infinitely small and alone"—her nightmarish experience of life on the run, isolated and poor, leads her affirmatively to choose the community that now surrounds her. She fleetingly considers driving off again with Turtle, but "from now until the end of time she is connected to this family that's parading down Main St., Heaven. . . . If she gets separated from the others now, she'll never know how her life is going to come out" (*Pigs in Heaven,* 341–42). Turtle's return to the reservation serves to connect Taylor with the ancestral community she now needs to have come from.

Despite the good intentions with which Kingsolver set out in *Pigs in Heaven* to restore Turtle to her community of origin and to show respect for the autonomy of Native communities, the novel undermines those intentions through its unavoidable failure to treat as truthful Turtle's originally depicted past and its construction, instead, of a happy fable of all-embracing extended family that meets the needs of the present. Just as Jadine's having two adoptive families leaves her with no roots and with a skeptical view of myths of black rootedness that the narrative itself partially endorses, Turtle's two contradictory origin stories call attention to the inventedness of both, the first one an unsympathetic white fantasy of reservation alcoholism and abuse, the second a utopian fantasy of Native harmoniousness. The novel ends with Cash shooting his TV: ostensibly a demonstration of his love for the TV-phobic Alice, this gesture also signals a repudiation of fiction (the fantasy world of characters with names like "Lacey") and thus the novel's belated allegiance to a theory of veridical origins that it has every step of the way violated.

Sherman Alexie's 1996 novel *Indian Killer* responds to Kingsolver's utopian (and, in Alexie's view, "colonial"[42]) compromise over Native adoption with a far grimmer picture of adoption as one of a menu of ways in which Native children can become deracinated and grievously harmed. Like *Tar Baby,* the novel uses adoption to tell a larger story about, indeed to allegorize, racial alienation. Genetic essentialism makes the adopted character as much a Native as those who grow up in Native families: just as Turtle has the digestive tract of the authentic Cherokee she unequivocally appears to be, John looks the part of the generic big Indian brave, and in both cases identity is equated with the body. Nonetheless, the novel uses adoption to highlight the elusiveness and constructedness of origins. It refrains from suggesting that retrieving authentic origins would cure the ills of the adopted or of any of the other deracinated characters. With its conspicuously fictive myths of origins and authenticity, the novel anticipates Leighton's thesis that whatever the adopted may suffer is not caused by "genealogical bewilderment,"

42. Sherman Alexie, interview with Joelle Fraser; copyright 2001 by the *Iowa Review.* www.english.illinois.edu/maps/poets/a_f/alexie/fraser.htm.

and the cure is therefore not to be found in the recovery of authentic heredity.

John Smith, raised since infancy by a white couple in Seattle, becomes schizophrenic and eventually kills himself after mutilating a white man he has identified as the source of his troubles. He knows nothing about his origins except that his birthmother was fourteen; his generic, founding-father name, like "Plymouth" in Lifton and Kingsolver, ironically signifies his lack of stable origin or identity. His story seems to represent an "absence at the origin" that is felt not as liberatory but as dehumanizing. His parents' worthy efforts to connect him with his birth culture only increase his sense of belonging nowhere, in part because no one knows what tribe he was born into. The novel opens with his fantasy about his birth and adoption: in a scene that begins in gritty realism but that devolves into paranoid fantasy, a helicopter, firing military guns as it leaves the ground, takes him directly from his yearning mother's body to his adoptive parents. Thereafter, the novel periodically introduces idyllic scenes of "How He Imagines His Life on the Reservation,"[43] but it undercuts these idylls of authenticity by juxtaposing them to scenes from the life of a minor character, King, a wanderer among the homeless urban Indians of Seattle. King's early history—happy childhood on the reservation, promising departure for college—exactly resembles John's fantasy life but leads to the same dead end where John's real life takes him: abandonment of college, loss of bearings, and psychosis. John's efforts to track down his origins are futile: he hitchhikes randomly to reservations hoping to run into his birthmother; at the Hupa reservation he hires a guide to show him the legendary female sasquatch, a figure who, like Morrison's swamp women and chevaliers, stands for an appealing but elusively fictive racial authenticity. John's search for his origin also echoes the suicidal wandering of his friend Father Duncan, a Native Jesuit priest and sometime same-race role model so torn by conflicting allegiances that he finally walks off into the desert and disappears.

Thematically, the novel centers on a series of incidents that raise the question of who speaks for Native people. The novel's central action concerns an unidentified and possibly magical figure who performs ritual murders of white men, scalping them and leaving owl feathers. "The killer" (pronouns are never used) also kidnaps a white child, in a reversal of the state-sponsored kidnappings John suspects he fell victim to.

43. Two chapters bear this title; see Sherman Alexie, *Indian Killer* (New York: Warner Books, 1998), 43, 287 (hereafter cited in the text).

These symbolic acts appear to express the angers of the novel's Native characters at the same time that, thanks to a right-wing radio host, they prompt a race war between white and Native gangs. After his suicide, John is falsely identified as the Indian Killer by the man he disfigures, the white, Indian-wannabe novelist Jack Wilson, who has been writing a novel titled *Indian Killer* and who writes John into his novel as the perpetrator. (This misidentification was compounded when early reviews of Alexie's novel missed the point and mistook John for the killer.) Wilson is doubled in the novel by Professor Clarence Mather, who arouses the ire of the Native students in his classes for appropriating Native voices and claiming that whites can understand and represent Native experiences. Wilson likewise exploits his contacts with Natives and has achieved literary success—his white readers praise him for "see[ing] so clearly into the Indian mind"—by inventing a clichéd detective hero, Aristotle Little Hawk (*Indian Killer,* 266). The first time he sees John, Wilson exhibits his penchant for appropriation by observing that John resembles his fictional hero, an imperial view that John protests: later, when John slashes Wilson's face, John tells him, "Let me, let us, have our own pain" (411). In identifying Wilson as the source of pain, the novel shows that John understands the power of cultural appropriation and misrepresentation. He wants to tell his own story, although he can only write it inarticulately in the mark he places indelibly on Wilson's face. By dying, he leaves white men to misconstrue his story yet again. The novel does not (cannot) say what a true representation would be, for if the Indian Killer speaks for Native angers, he, she, or it also exposes John to a grievous misrepresentation.

Indian Killer treats the idea of authentic origins less lightly than do Kingsolver's novels. Of the novels considered in this chapter, it has by far the most politically and ethically at stake in advocating for the reclamation of authentic origins and in rejecting views such as Miller's, Leys's, or Leighton's. Whereas Alice Greer and even Taylor (should she choose to) can become Cherokee retroactively, because they possess token quantities of Cherokee "blood" but more because they might simply want to, Wilson is mocked throughout the novel for believing that one Native ancestor gives him the right to pose as a Shilshomish Indian and speak for Native people. John's inchoate anger at Wilson's misrepresentations is sparked by that of the novel's most articulate urban Indian, Marie Polatkin, who talks back to Mather and stages a protest, witnessed by John, at a Wilson reading. Arguing with Mather about his enthusiasm for what he calls Wilson's "authentic and traditional view of the Indian world," she expresses a radically essentialist view of literary representation: "How can Wilson present an authentic and traditional view of the Indian world if he isn't authentic and traditional himself?" (*Indian Killer,* 66; see also 312). With a dig at Kingsolver's white characters, she rhetorically asks why "all of these so-called Indian writers claim membership in tribes with poor records of membership? Cherokee, Shilshomish?" (67). The novel's conscience and the most resilient among the urban Indians, she makes a good case for essentializing views of race and culture.

Yet Marie's essentialism about Native origins and identity is undermined when she herself questions the assumption that the Indian Killer is Native and male and not a woman or, say, a white trying to start a race war (*Indian Killer,* 247, 332–33).[44] Despite the essentialism that makes John inarguably Indian and the seriousness with which the novel weighs the felt loss of Native origins, the novel also questions authenticity as a trope of Native self-representation. Only the deracinated characters yearn for and fantasmatically construct authentic origins. Like King, Marie had the reservation childhood John missed, but she couldn't leave fast enough; only now that she is away does she defend Native lifeways, objecting to Wilson and Mather and staging a prohibited powwow. Despite this apparent change of heart, she devotes her energies to feeding Seattle's ethnically diverse homeless rather than returning home. She mocks familiar images of Native authenticity that have become hopelessly entangled in white appropriations: "I'm not some demure little Indian woman healer talking spider this, spider that, am I? . . . I'm talking like a twentieth-century Indian woman" (247). "Spider this, spider that" represents the kind of manufactured authenticity that makes "Turtle" sound like a more "authentic" Native name than "Lacey." Like John, Marie wants to reclaim the right to represent her and other Natives' anger at their dispossession, yet she has little interest in the origin that dispossession refers back to, knowing that that origin has been irretrievably overtaken by white fantasy. In this regard, Marie anticipates the "contingent essentialism" of the Korean adoptees interviewed by Eleana Kim, who identify as Korean adoptees without taking much interest in Korean national identity.

Similarly, in one of John's imagined scenes, life on the reservation leads to yearning to move off it. This imaginary self "had known he wanted to go to college when he was three years old" because of his appreciation of books, which he equates with knowledge of "life outside the

44. Callahan's reading of the novel likewise (though on different grounds) emphasizes the "undercut[ting]" of Marie's professed essentialism, which she sees as Marie's "strategic" compensation for her insecure identity; see Callahan's discussion of Alexie in *Kin of Another Kind,* 121–28, quotations at 125.

reservation" (*Indian Killer,* 291). The grounded self he imagines having, had he grown up on the reservation, is free to experiment with contingencies of identity that link identity to words, for John thinks of himself and his birthmother in textual terms as "paragraphs that belonged next to each other:"

> The paragraph was a fence that held words. All the words inside a paragraph had a reason for being together. They shared a common history. John began to see the entire world in paragraphs. He knew the United States was a paragraph within the world. He knew his reservation was a paragraph within the United States. His house was a paragraph distinct from the houses to the west and north. Inside the house, his mother was a paragraph, completely separate from the paragraph of John. But he also knew that he shared genetics and common experiences with his mother, that they were paragraphs that belonged next to each other. John saw his tribe as a series of paragraphs that all had the same theme. (*Indian Killer,* 291)

Placing "genetics," "common experiences," and "words" and "paragraphs" together in this way, equating people with words (words in a paragraph have a "common history" just as he and his mother have "common experiences"), and alluding to the kind of writing one might study in an off-reservation college (Joyce's *Portrait of the Artist as a Young Man,* say), this lyrical passage exhibits tension between, on the one hand, loyalty to genetic family and, on the other, the fluidity of literary textuality. If persons and nations are words and paragraphs, they may be rewritten, and the relations of words to meanings may be indefinitely rearranged.

This textual fluidity appears to the imaginary reservation-raised John (and perhaps to Alexie himself: the passage reappears almost verbatim in an autobiographical essay[45]) as a dream of freedom, but from the perspective of John the character, it is the nightmare actuality from which he is unable to awake, a nightmare in which there are only representations, all of them wrong. Like Lifton's *Twice Born,* which claims that the lives of the adopted are "fictitious" yet which also renders the recovered origin in fictional terms, Alexie's novel laments the loss of authentic origins yet imagines no more favorable way to express them than to portray them, highly figuratively, as figures of speech. Traumatized without a doubt by the circumstances of his adoption, John nonetheless could not be cured

45. Sherman Alexie, "Superman and Me," *Los Angeles Times,* Apr. 19, 1998.

by recovering his authentic place, for in the novel that place exists only in and as words.

Like *Tar Baby* ending with Son's apparent transformation into a mythical black chevalier, *Indian Killer* ends by evoking magic realism to represent racial authenticity. Moreover, the Indian Killer's apparent authenticity is shown to be not the origin but the effect of collective modern Native anger. The last scene witnesses the killer at night in an Indian cemetery, masked, singing a song that summons flocks of owls, dancing a dance "over five hundred years old," and teaching the dance and song to "hundreds" of Indians (*Indian Killer,* 420). Earlier, although the killer has been portrayed as human, the kidnapped child testifies that his kidnapper was neither man nor woman, but rather "it was a bird" (324). The final paragraph calls attention to the killer's disguise: "The killer believes in all masks, in this wooden mask. . . . With this mask, with this mystery, the killer can dance forever" (420). Subject to multiple and conflicting interpretations and misconstructions throughout the novel, the killer (like the trope of Native authenticity itself) appears finally as the exclusive function of fantasies and desires, both white and Native. Authenticity takes its revenge, but only through misrepresentations, the only kind of representation that authenticity, in this novel, can achieve.

Gish Jen's novel *The Love Wife* makes the case for roots searching as an imaginative activity not likely to achieve veridical results not so much by showing characters literally making up origin stories as by questioning such categories as authentic and inauthentic, natural and unnatural, and by representing fantasized origins as capable of their own subversively, even exuberantly, fictive plotting. In the world of this novel, transnational and transracial adoption is a normal part of contemporary well-to-do family formation. The family in the novel comprises an Anglo American wife (Blondie, once Jane), her Chinese American husband Carnegie, and their three children: Lizzy, of Asian but not necessarily Chinese background, adopted in the United States; Wendy, adopted in China; and Bailey, the natural-born son, a "mutt," according to Carnegie's recently deceased Chinese mother, whose powerful presence continues to hover over the interracial family whose construction she vigorously opposed.[46] The title character, Lan, said to be distantly related to

46. Gish Jen, *The Love Wife* (New York: Knopf, 2004), 161 (hereafter cited in the text). For historical and sociological analysis of adoption from China since the early 1990s, see Kay Ann Johnson, *Wanting a Daughter, Needing a Son: Abandonment, Adoption, and Orphanage Care in China* (St. Paul: Yeong and Yeong, 2004); and Sara Dorow, *Transnational Adoption: A Cultural Economy of Race, Gender, and Kinship* (New York: New York University Press, 2006).

Carnegie, enters the family as the Chinese nanny, the upper-middle-class suburban solution to adopted children's apparent need for links to their roots. The novel gently mocks the parents' earlier clichéd attempts, such as "concentrating the chinoiserie in the adopted children's bedrooms," insisting on Chinese culture camp, joining the FCC (Families with Children from China, with its creative promotion of Panda Festivals, calligraphy workshops, Chinese dance classes, and a host of other opportunities to identify positively as a person from China), and doing the Chinese holidays; "how mightily we had strived to build her self-esteem" with Asian dolls and "multiracial crayons" (*Love Wife,* 206).[47] Carnegie and Blondie have clumsily required Lizzy to identify as Chinese, because it is convenient to have two girls that "match" (107), but her identity as Chinese is entirely fictitious. Each daughter has a hybrid Chinese identity imposed on her, and growing up requires each to invent her own idea of China and to decide what part China will play in her self-composition.

As a representation and agent of Chinese roots, Lan is a greater success than the parents' other offerings: the girls like her Chinese food and exotic tales, she fosters Wendy's interest in her Chinese identity and her spoken Mandarin, and she provides the alternate mother figure that any set of rebellious teenagers might enjoy. But her effect on the family is also disastrous. One boyfriend, a thuggish type "like a grade-B movie," abuses her (*Love Wife,* 298); the other, whom she marries, dies in an arson fire, leaving her three months pregnant; and the novel strongly hints that she sleeps with her employer as she nearly precipitates a division of the family along its ethnic faultline. Because Lan looks the part of the children's mother even though she is not genetically related to them, the girls speculate that she could be their "real" mother, whereupon Lizzy calls her blond mother a "fake." Coming home one day, Blondie sees the rest of her family seated around the dining table all quietly working on separate computers, all sipping tea from lidded cups, Lan "in my

47. For discussion of adoptive parents' efforts to preserve and promote Chinese "birth culture," see Toby Alice Volkman, "Embodying Chinese Culture: Transnational Adoption in North America," *Social Text* 74 (Spring 2003): 29–55, rpt. in Volkman, *Cultures of Transnational Adoption,* 81–113; Heather Jacobson, *Culture Keeping: White Mothers, International Adoption, and the Negotiation of Family Difference* (Nashville: Vanderbilt University Press, 2008); and Lori Delale-O'Connor, "Learning to Be Me: The Role of Adoptee Culture Camps in Teaching Adopted Children Their Birth Culture," *Adoption & Culture* 2 (2009): 204–25. On the role of roots trips in these efforts, see Debra Jacobs, Iris Chin Ponte, and Leslie Kim Wang, eds., *From Home to Homeland: What Adoptive Families Need to Know before Making a Return Trip to China* (St. Paul: Yeong and Yeong, 2010).

seat," the whole scene "how much more natural . . . than the one that included me" (257). Later Blondie and Bailey move out, and the family bifurcates into "two natural-looking households," although in Carnegie's view they are all "missing quite keenly our true motley splendor" (368). In a parodic echo of US adoption culture's conflation of biological birth, genetic heritage, and "birth culture," Lan's role in the novel, as a kind of avatar of the birthmother, is to represent ethnic and racial roots as natural and as indistinguishable from genetic heritage and to cast adoption as unnatural fakery. The sections of narrative written from Lan's point of view appear in italics, just as Hood italicizes her Chinese birthmothers' stories, to remind the reader that Lan thinks in a different language from other narrators and to underscore Lan's function, to represent intrinsic difference as she stands in for the absent, nearly unimaginable birthmother. In his reading of the novel, Mark Jerng cites the scene around the table as evidence for the view that "the fantasy of the genetic . . . haunt[s] [the] desire to de-essentialize family."[48]

Lan has joined the family for another reason as well. Carnegie, remorseful over having rejected everything Chinese while his mother was alive—he failed to learn Mandarin, he married Blondie—now desperately wants to own her seventeen-generation family genealogy, which she has left to Wendy on condition that Lan move in with them and restore to the family its missing Chineseness. In Blondie's sardonic view, Lan is "the wife you should have married," sent by Mama Wong from beyond the grave (*Love Wife*, 195). Moreover, with her authentic Chinese look and style and her heartrending tales of suffering during the Cultural Revolution, Lan seems to represent ethnic and national authenticity itself. When the long-awaited genealogy finally arrives at the end of the novel (the plot is structured around the wait for the book), it reveals that Lan is Mama Wong's biological daughter, abandoned in China, and that Carnegie was adopted. This news oddly vindicates Lan as the "real" parent of the Asian daughters while Blondie and Carnegie become classified together as "fake," both adopted and adopting. This illusion holds sway despite the fact that the girls' own birth genealogies are not at all illuminated by these melodramatic revelations, so powerful is Mama Wong's haunting presence and capacity to control the meaning of authenticity.

But the novel does not simply value biological authenticity and the

48. Mark C. Jerng, *Claiming Others: Transracial Adoption and National Belonging* (Minneapolis: University of Minnesota Press, 2010), 234; Jerng discusses how similarity of appearance gets refigured as biological connection by the various characters (239–42).

recovery of roots over the "motley splendor" of the mixed-race family formed by adoption. Lan's coming to occupy the position of the "authentic" or "natural" is ostentatiously a narrative trick, because the narrative conceals her filiation for so long and because it links her to the gothic figure of Mama Wong's ghost. And she becomes the girls' authentic if not biological aunt only if Carnegie's adoption is accepted as a fully authentic family form, too: her authenticity depends on his and cannot exceed it. Although Carnegie ironically turns up the evidence of his adoption while searching for confirmation of his biological roots, the genealogy book shows that adoption runs in the family (and is an accepted part of Chinese lineage) by revealing how many sons have been adopted over the centuries in order to maintain the family name. Possibly even in Mama Wong's own lineage the line is not genetic but adoptive ("Look! In this generation, only one family had sons, all the rest had to adopt a son from somewhere else" [*Love Wife,* 371–72]). The apparently factual-beyond-doubt genealogy blossoms into a cornucopia of fictions, as Chinese definitions of family clash with western (biogenetic) ones. Julia Watson argues that genealogy generally contrasts with autobiography in its conservative resistance to revision,[49] yet Jen here enlists genealogy to do the work of grounding its own ungrounding. Carnegie's adoption, in this context, grants him more ancient Chinese family authenticity, not less, even as it radically redefines authenticity to include the made-up, what appears in the modern US context as the inauthentic.

Redefining origins as a text, the novel also casts strong doubt on the value of roots essentialism by refuting normative claims about the value of roots travel and of sentimental views of the home country. At age four, Lizzy experienced the trip to adopt Wendy in China as the roots trip from hell (Lizzy is injured when the family car is flipped by a mob). And when Lizzy, under the sway of Lan's enthusiastic lectures, sentimentalizes China, Blondie replies, "And what about Tiananmen Square?", a question that resonates with Lan's own revelations about the horrors of the Cultural Revolution (*Love Wife,* 215). Rejecting the romanticization of Chinese origins, the novel rejects the ethnically separatist solution that it shows the family toying with when Blondie and Bailey move out. What looks "natural" is only an appearance and may not reflect the characters' needs and desires: Blondie's Asian family cannot do without her, and besides, she is the family's most expert China hand and its most fluent

49. Julia Watson, "Ordering the Family: Genealogy as Autobiographical Pedigree," in *Getting a Life: Everyday Uses of Autobiography,* ed. Sidonie Smith and Julia Watson (Minneapolis: University of Minnesota Press, 1996), 297–323.

Mandarin speaker. The novel values Lan's Chinese identity while confirming that the artificial or "fake" can also be real. Mama Wong stands for and advocates fixed, knowable, and genetically inherited ethnic and national identity, yet for that very reason she views her son's biological child Bailey as unnatural and sees her adopted grandchild Wendy as the authentic heir. The novel scrambles the categories of authentic and inauthentic, removing the boundary between them and dizzyingly redistributing their assignments in counterintuitive, postmodern ways.

It also endorses a kind of radical and fictional self-creation, not so much in the trajectories of the adopted children as in that of Lan. While the novel only sketchily indicates the adopted daughters' eventual strategies for navigating their ethnic and racial identities, Lan's lurid adventures in romance and capitalism occupy much of the final quarter of the novel, where the plot becomes as improbable and melodramatic as one of the gothic tales with which she once fascinated the children. From the start, Lan embodies, ambiguously, the genuine otherness of China and the family's collective fantasy about Chinese origins. A figure at once of authenticity and of fictionality, Lan eventually leads a life in the United States that starts to follow the narrative paradigm of her own stories, mostly involving violence and victimization, as she takes control of a narrative she first entered on others' terms. That she acquires a center of subjectivity of her own apart from her role in the suburban family may account for the criticism that Jen received for this apparently awkward narrative swerve.[50] Possibly it makes readers uncomfortable that a figure representing roots and therefore the exotic past should develop a future of her own. And her scarcely believable adventures, spun out in a gothic style, pose a threat to the literary genre of suburban realism into which most of the novel fits. As Lan herself becomes Americanized and leaves behind both the needs of the family that hired her and the Chinese roots she was hired to represent, the novel suggests that the hybrid Chinese cultural identity that US adoptive families invent can assume an unpredictable life of its own, one that affirms fiction and self-invention over truth and allegiance to the past.

Rolin Jones's 2003 play *The Intelligent Design of Jenny Chow* makes graphically explicit some features of the works considered so far. It shares *The Love Wife*'s mix of irreverence and seriousness in representing roots searches in adoption, and it shares the novel's anti-essentialism too. In

50. See, e.g., Jennifer Schuessler, "Family Values," review of *The Love Wife,* by Gish Jen, *New York Review of Books,* Jan. 13, 2005, 16–17.

contrast to the suburban realism of *The Love Wife,* however, *The Intelligent Design of Jenny Chow* uses an antic strain of futuristic science fiction first to finesse the impossibility of finding origins in China and then to explore the limitations of such a roots search, even should it attain its literal goal. Ultimately the play suggests that an adoptee's efforts are better expended on a different sort of search and on invention rather than discovery.

Jennifer Marcus, a brilliant but agoraphobic twenty-two-year-old adoptee from China, hates her workaholic, demanding mother Adele, whose tough love only intensifies Jennifer's disability. Jennifer initially imagines, in the familiar and essentialist fantasy that motivates many roots searches, that all would be well if only she could find "my real mother" and connect with "the lives we were supposed to be living" back in China.[51] She induces a Mormon missionary to locate her birthmother and then—in a darkly hilarious subterfuge involving the Department of Defense, Raytheon, and her former science teacher—engineers a missile-powered, multilingual, lifelike robot, Jenny Chow, to make contact on her behalf with her birthmother. Jennifer has no interest in birth culture, the orphanage where she spent her first six months, learning Mandarin, or any of the rest of what constitutes normative roots searching in the early twenty-first century; Jenny carries out Jennifer's desire to make straight for the birthmother by flying directly to her doorstep. Jennifer (in her room at home) experiences this contact through the mechanisms of virtual reality, but like the results of many more ordinary searches, the experience is crushingly disappointing. After secretively acknowledging what she takes to be her biological child, the birthmother closes the door in Jenny's face, an action that is all the more dismaying to Jennifer because it repeats Adele's pushing her out of the door at home. Compulsively copying this action, Jennifer rejects Jenny on her return, and Jenny flies away, destination unknown. Jennifer guiltily tries to get her back; the play ends in uncertainty as to whether Jennifer will find Jenny and what she will do with her if she succeeds.

Jennifer's compulsive agoraphobia economically sums up both the affective disorder that afflicts some adoptees (more typically those adopted after infancy) who cannot handle physical or emotional intimacy and, as well, her ambivalence, despite her apparently single-minded drive, about making contact with her birthmother. She desperately wants to meet her birthmother, but she cannot tolerate the idea of doing so in

51. Rolin Jones, *The Intelligent Design of Jenny Chow: An Instant Message with Excitable Music,* first performed 2003 (New York: Dramatists' Play Service, 2006), 18 (hereafter cited in the text).

person. Although she immensely enjoys the long-distance internet work, instant messaging, and high-level engineering that finding the address and then building the robot entail, she is suddenly afraid at the moment of sending Jenny off to China. She barely knows what she wants Jenny to do and say when she reaches the birthmother's home or what she hopes will happen next. She both wants and does not want to touch her birthmother, finally touching her in one rapturous but virtual hug. Linking and maintaining the separation between Jennifer and her birthmother, Jenny quite literally embodies Jennifer's defensiveness. Jennifer reengineers spy satellites and other defensive weapons for the Department of Defense in exchange for periodic shipments of the robot body parts and other electronic gear that she needs to build Jenny and that her supplier assumes she is using to build military robots for South (or possibly North—chillingly, he doesn't care) Korea. The questionable military defenses that enable her robot seem an apt metaphor for her own psychic defenses.

In making Jenny, Jennifer realizes two conventional understandings about adoptive life: the common fantasy of living two lives (the one she has led in California since the age of six months and the life she was "supposed to be living" in China); and the sense that the lives of the adopted are artifacts, "fictitious," to use Lifton's term, not from nature. As in *The Love Wife,* the fact of adoption makes authentic and inauthentic, artificial and "real," exchange places. As Jennifer's stand-in and envoy to what she considers to be her "real life," Jenny is Jennifer's real self. But since Jennifer thinks of herself as artificial, that real self is also necessarily an artificial self. In this regard, Jennifer is just a few steps beyond the Korean adoptees in Eleana Kim's study, who use technology (the internet) to create community—the "collective personhood" of the adopted—and to assert transnational identity, when they use their Korean names as online tags.[52] Jennifer imitates robots in her own tic-ridden bodily style; her personality seeming to copy that of a robot, Jennifer is a copy of a copy with no original, and Jenny is both a copy of that copy and the original copy that Jennifer copies. But Jenny is more "real" than Jennifer in another sense, too. Compared with the anxious, robotic, agoraphobic Jennifer, Jenny is her polar opposite: ever smiling, adventurous, invulnerable, fearless, and better able to express emotion. The robot does not understand what a mother is, yet she grasps immediately the emotional force of her exchange with the birthmother.

52. Kim, *Adopted Territory,* 86, 89.

"Something has happened," she remarks spontaneously, uncannily, and (as acted in the 2003 New Haven production) very movingly after Jennifer's birthmother has closed the door in her face (*Jenny Chow,* 60). Just as her coming to life in Jennifer's room—first with jerky robotic movements, then with increasingly human moves—is a thrilling moment in the theater, so is this mysterious attainment of clumsy yet unmistakably human feeling. She develops complexity and empathy, and when she returns to Jennifer's room she tries to help Jennifer through the rage in which Jennifer eventually expels her.

Although the play might have been plotted and thematically organized around Jennifer's roots search, the plot instead revolves around the search for Jenny that starts at the play's end. Framed as Jennifer's IM exchange with the bounty hunter she has hired to locate Jenny, the play begins with Jenny's disappearance and goes back in time to explain how she came into being. Thus the play displaces one birth and its attendant search in favor of another "birth" and search. Roles and players circulate here: Jennifer acts the part of all-powerful, rejecting mother to the creature she has made, as if to take revenge on the two mothers who have left her so unhappy; Jennifer expels Jenny just as her two mothers have traumatically expelled her. Kicking her alter ego out of the house, Jennifer symbolically preempts her mothers' ability to hurt her; by this emotional logic, in seeking to get Jenny back, she is trying to fix the damage her mothers have done to her. And Jennifer's search for her alternate self, perhaps her more authentic self (that is, her more authentically artificial self), perhaps also her better self, substitutes for and becomes more important than the roots search on which she initially embarked. The play debunks the illusion that finding the birthmother would produce the desired feeling of wholeness or realness. It suggests instead that self-invention is both more challenging and more rewarding. Jenny is going to be harder to find than the birthmother, as well as more worth finding; her body is a weapon, and she loves to fly, yet she is the part of herself that Jennifer most needs.

Like Gish Jen's characters uncertain where to locate the line between the authentic and the inauthentic but discovering narrative self-invention, Jennifer discovers that searching for the self she has invented, not for the birthmother who constitutes only an illusion of wholeness, is the most urgent of her tasks. Jenny is linked both to the power of invention and to Asian (not US) power, since Jennifer maintains the fiction that Jenny's body parts are going into weaponry for Korea, just as Lan's Chinese identity is associated both with extravagant fictionality and with the aggressive capitalism of Mama Wong, whose arrival in the United States amounts to a kind of reverse imperialism. Most important, however, all these texts show that the adoptive self is a made thing, itself a provisional point of origin for a new family configuration.

Like Haraway's cyborg, Jenny is a positive figure for non-blood kinship. Capable of human emotions, caring and responsive, Jenny the robot with her superb capacity for flight also represents liberation from the divisive anguish of blood, roots, and genes. As the freely imagined alter ego of a transnational adoptee harmed by the illusion that she could be cured of all ills by finding her birthmother, Jenny represents the capacity for self-invention that may be the adoptee's secret blessing. Similarly, Lan, who enters Jen's novel as a stick figure of essentialist, literalist American assumptions about roots, ends the novel demonstrating the powerful and constructive fictiveness of origins. Along with the critique and ungrounding of veridical origins that we have observed in the novels by Morrison, Kingsolver, and Alexie, these figures help to highlight the positive value of the fictions of the adopted self and of adoptive origins that are implicitly and ambivalently generated not only in novels about adoption but also in adoption memoirs, to which the last section of this chapter turns.

Recognizing the fictitiousness of much of what passes for knowledge about adoptive origins is more than just a healthy acceptance of limits. As Elizabeth Alice Honig argues, return journeys provide not certainties but rather occasions for revising fictional life narratives. The texts discussed so far provide troubling yet inspiring new paradigms for what Betty Jean Lifton said years ago when she claimed that her adoption—despite the loss, the "identity hunger," the feeling of unbelonging—also "allowed me to create myself" (*Twice Born,* 252). Like Jeanette Winterson having to be a writer to "trace . . . the imprint of another life," to be adopted and to have one's own story to create and tell may be to find oneself in a position of great power. As their children mature, Honig writes, adoptive parents discover "the inadequacy of their own narratives of their child's alternative life" and learn to "accept that their child will invent entirely different and utterly personal fictions of their own, fictions essential to identity."[53] If fictions are essentially what the adopted have to call their own, then stories about the positive value of fiction making in adoption may be among the most useful. The works discussed

53. Elizabeth Alice Honig, "Phantom Lives, Narratives of Possibility," in Volkman, *Cultures of Transnational Adoption,* 213–22, quotation p. 220.

here affirm the power of storytelling in adoption, the power and indeed the necessity of self-invention.

RETURN MEMOIRS AND FICTIVE ORIGINS

Lifton's discovery of the undecidability of her origins and the tensions we have observed in works of fiction about origins and authenticity strongly parallel, both in content and in ambivalent affect, recent arguments in social and cultural theory against the possibility of recovering authentic personal or cultural origins, whether for the adopted or for diasporic and postcolonial subjects. For example, Norma Alarcón writes, of a Gloria Anzaldúa poem about "this fear that she won't find the way back": "The quest for a true self and identity . . . has given way to the realization that there is no fixed identity. 'I,' or 'She' as observed by Anzaldúa, is composed of multiple layers without necessarily yielding an uncontested 'origin.'"[54] Yet what seems liberatory for Alarcón is not simply so in the Anzaldúa poem on which she comments. In the same ambivalent spirit, Barbara Yngvesson and Maureen Mahoney, arguing for the complexity of adoptees' stories about their origins, cite Stuart Hall's disillusioned account of stable, ascertainable origins: "there is no homeland 'waiting back there for the new ethnics to rediscover it.' Rather, this past, this homeland . . . 'is something that has to be told. It is narrated. It is grasped through desire. It is grasped through reconstruction.'"[55] Aimed at debunking harmful illusions, such a statement also acknowledges the creative power of the "desire" for origins. For adoptees as for diasporic subjects, the origin may be not so much an actual geographic starting point as a back-formation created by desire in the present. And yet the prospect of visiting an actual geographic homeland can exert a powerful allure. Adoption places the dearly held aims of a population with strong motives for believing in the recoverability of origins in productive tension with the liberatory agendas of those who would, just as reason-

54. Norma Alarcón, "Chicana Feminism: In the Tracks of 'The' Native Woman," in *Between Woman and Nation: Nationalisms, Transnational Feminisms, and the State,* ed. Caren Kaplan, Norma Alarcón, and Minoo Moallem (Durham: Duke University Press, 2000), 65.

55. Barbara Yngvesson and Maureen A. Mahoney, "'As One Should, Ought and Wants to Be': Belonging and Authenticity in Identity Narratives," *Theory, Culture and Society* 17, no. 6 (2000): 77–110, quotation at 102; they quote Stuart Hall, "The Local and the Global: Globalization and Ethnicity," in *Culture, Globalization, and the World-System,* ed. A. D. King (Minneapolis: University of Minnesota Press, 1997), 38.

ably, deauthorize authenticity and origins in the name of rejecting intellectually spurious and politically oppressive hierarchies. For example, Kimberly Leighton's critique of "genealogical bewilderment" (as a way of misnaming the distress caused by social biases against nonconforming families) implies that origins searches and returns cannot solve anything, and yet the same issue of *Adoption & Culture* in which Leighton's essay appears also contains Alice Diver's argument for an internationally recognized right "to avoid origin deprivation."

In the midst of these contradictions, adoptees have been making return journeys. Recent US social norms around ethnic identity, meshing with the popular understanding that transnational adoptees need to form an identity linked to their culture of origin, not only make return journeys imaginable but raise high expectations for them. Although many transnational adoptees in the United States express a powerful need to reconnect with some aspect of their origin, whether by identifying culturally with their birth nation, by returning to their birthplace, or by searching for their birth parents, some social theorists have questioned the apparently seamless logic connecting this felt need to its apparently obvious sequelae: return, search, and reunion. Barbara Yngvesson argues that the lived reality of transnational adoptees is an experience of being "pulled" between two locations and two identities. She explains how little can be taken for granted about the meaning of a place of origin: of the painful story of an adoptee who returned to Korea and found her birthmother she writes:

> This narrative illuminates the powerful pull of a discourse of identity and the "returns" (to an origin) that identity requires, while at the same time pointing toward a more complex story of movement between (temporary) locations, of desire that is shaped by hegemonies of race, blood, and nation, and of the impossibility of ever fully belonging in the places where we find ourselves.[56]

Studying roots trips undertaken by Swedish children adopted from Chile, trips modeled on the quest plot to restore the adoptee's missing part or fill an internal void, Yngvesson found that these returns "unsettle the idea that such journeys of self-realization are likely to produce completion for the adoptee," an idea put forward by, among others, Lifton, for

56. Yngvesson, *Belonging*, 163.

whom they constitute "a journey toward wholeness."[57] Rather, she found a "loss of bearings" and "the precariousness of 'I am'" ("Going 'Home,'" 27, 28), for return trips are returns to scenes of abandonment more than they can be recoveries of a lost part.

But even more, "laying claim to the past in this way may shake up identity in the very moment of grounding it by revealing the interruptions, contradictions, and breaks through which the process we know as 'identity' takes shape," Yngvesson writes ("Going 'Home,'" 32). In other words, identity can be constituted by, and not just despite, the loss that, in an older framework, might seem to inhibit its development. Under the impression that they have a "hole in their lives that must be filled if they are to be whole people" (36), believing that once they meet their birthmothers they will finally know themselves, the traveling adoptees do ironically come to know themselves, although not as rooted wholes but rather as split subjects. The roots trips, Yngvesson writes, "create gaps" rather than healing them as travelers hope, because they "materialize a moment of abandonment by a return to the physical spaces (orphanages, foster homes, and courtrooms) in which this break was made concrete" (36). Discovering that they will never be "fully integrated" anywhere, roots travelers "confront" not only the impossibility of "a coherent 'I'" but also "the illusion of autonomous families, nations, and selves on which this 'I' is contingent" (37). In this formulation, Yngvesson implies that every "I"—and not just adopted ones—needs to recognize the impossibility, or at least the illusory foundations, of its own coherence; the adopted are positioned to make visible the impossibility that all humans share.

Yngvesson reports in detail her participant-observation of a roots trip when an eighteen-year-old she calls Clara travels with her Swedish mother to the part of Chile where she was born, to meet her birthmother. Clara says, soon after this meeting:

> It was as though, because I have always had a hole inside, or however one might say it, and then when I saw her, immediately I cried and then it [the hole] was filled again. I still don't understand that feeling, that it went so fast. I was almost a little scared. ("Going 'Home,'" 40, brackets in original)

57. Yngvesson, "Going 'Home,'" 27, quoting Betty Jean Lifton, *The Journey of the Adopted Self: A Quest for Wholeness* (New York: Basic Books, 1994).

Although Clara's words about filling a hole seem to conform to the conventional image of adoption as a lack that must be made whole, Clara speaks of the hole "always" inside her, suggesting that she knows that "hole" to be identity-conferring rather than identity-depriving. Moreover, she says, oddly, that when she saw her birthmother, "the hole was filled *again*" (emphasis added), as if it had been filled, suddenly emptied, and refilled; that she didn't and doesn't understand the feeling; and that it frightened her. Possibly the birthmother's inevitable failure to match Clara's imaginary picture of her increases the emptiness of the hole, which is then "filled again" as Clara recovers her composure. Clara's remarks thus suggest not that her life was a vacancy waiting to be filled with the presence of the birthmother, but rather that the unfathomable, even scary, moment of seeing the birthmother has made, or remade, the hole. This reading is confirmed by what Yngvesson reports Clara says next:

> It felt good, partly because I could speak Swedish with my mother from Sweden, and then I had you, who could translate. I felt supported to have Mamma along, someone from Sweden. It was something one could return to, that one wasn't alone in Chile. ("Going 'Home,'" 40)

To be with her birthmother was, affectively, to be alone. (The complex and important matter of what the birthmother may have been experiencing lies outside the scope of Yngvesson's research.) Clara is happier with the birthmother's gift of a rosary, which she likes and calls "something . . . that one can make something of [later], on one's own" (41, brackets in original). Contrary to the hope held out by "missing organ" adoption discourse, Clara does not find in the birthmother's presence the replenishment of loss; instead, she prefers to "make something" in solitude and to "return" to a psychological location that is now identified with the adoptive family. The "something" she will make, the adoptee's self-making, is the gift of her experience of rupture.

Yngvesson's study resonates with many other experiences and representations of transnational roots trips and searches. Although much of the writing on searches presupposes both the desirability and the possibility of literally recovering lost origins and of making organic connections to the past that would give the searcher feelings of wholeness and belonging, gaining visibility has been a counterview that such searches are valuable efforts that cannot, however, achieve the literal restoration that they were once expected to provide. Instead, searchers find a "shake up" of identity that reveals identity to be a work in progress, a work that demands a high degree of creativity. Researchers appreciate the importance of narrative in the construction of adoptive identities, as when Sara Dorow names as her subject "the discursive work found in the narratives people tell to and about children adopted from China, because . . . identity narratives . . . are meant to bring coherence and unity to identity, telling us who we are."[58] The "fictitious," the term Betty Jean Lifton used pejoratively long ago to characterize the lives of the adopted, is itself beginning to be seen as a source of positive value in the adoption community. Some key studies of transnational adoption are taking seriously the idea put forward by literary and cultural theorists that origins are best understood as fabrications.

Writing about transnational adoption, Honig stresses the fictional nature of the stories the adopted and their parents entertain about origins:

> Each life stage generates new narratives that are always only fictions. . . . Return journeys . . . are so important and yet so difficult because they are moments when a somewhat settled narrative of possibility is strikingly tested against a great deal of new information, and almost certainly has to be revised. That revision cannot, however, be confused with resolution. . . . The alternative past remains always only a fiction.[59]

These "strong fictions," or psychologically necessary fantasies, include the notion, omnipresent particularly in the discourse of US-China adoption, that cultural origins can be recovered, even when birth parents cannot be found. Ann Anagnost argues that the Chinese culture that parents construct for their children tends to be "purely celebratory and devoid of history," a fantasy version of origins.[60] As Gish Jen's Carnegie ruefully points out, families can take pleasure in pretending to create cultural roots by joining the FCC and decorating with "chinoiserie." For Volkman, adoptive parents' vivid interest in Chinese culture represents their effort to compensate for the lack of information about birth parents;[61] possibly, to the contrary, a focus on culture helps to distance the threatening idea that actual birth parents might still exist. Either way, as Dorow

58. Dorow, *Transnational Adoption,* 27.

59. Honig, "Phantom Lives," 216.

60. Ann Anagnost, "Scenes of Misrecognition: Maternal Citizenship in the Age of Transnational Adoption," *Positions* 8 (2000): 389–421, esp. 390–91; see also Honig, "Phantom Lives," 217.

61. Volkman, "Embodying Chinese Culture," 96–97.

and others point out, the imperative to construct a "birth culture" for adopted children—a cultural formation with little relation to whatever the child would have experienced had she stayed in China—dovetails all too neatly with the fantasmatic pleasures of US consumer culture.[62] Heather Jacobson, too, points out that "this framing of culture as attractive, necessary, and innate to the child is the professionally prescribed position of the adoption industry" and a "marketing strategy" that appeals to a well-off clientele whose "cultural practices," however, in the words of one parent, are "'not really Chinese culture' but rather 'FCC culture.'"[63]

Return journeys or roots trips, along with reconstructions of the "birth culture," are a part of the fiction-generating machine that transnational adoption has become. In the narratives of such journeys, origins are (to cite Stuart Hall's words again) "grasped through desire [and] reconstruction," fictionally constructed since they cannot otherwise be known. To return to Romagnolo, Workman, and Leys and the models they offer of the discursive construction of obscured or traumatic origins: whether or not lack of connection to birth parents and to cultural origins is itself traumatic, the desire for origins generates a tremendous creative power, even if fictions, and not some stable, singular truth about the past, are what that desire produces.

I now turn to some search and return memoirs, all of them about east Asia, which has produced the largest body of such literature so far. First I survey works by parents conducting searches or roots trips in China on behalf of their young children: short reflections from *A Passage to the Heart* and other anthologies and some full-length memoirs: Emily Prager's *Wuhu Diary,* Jeff Gammage's *China Ghosts,* and Nancy McCabe's *Crossing the Blue Willow Bridge.* Next I consider works by adult adoptees returning to Korea and to Taiwan: three book-length memoirs—Jane Jeong Trenka's *The Language of Blood,* Katy Robinson's *A Single Square Picture,* and Mei-Ling Hopgood's *Lucky Girl;* a film—Deann Borshay Liem's *First Person Plural;* and some short memoirs collected in the volumes *Voices from Another Place* and *Seeds from a Silent Tree.* In the first set of memoirs, the parent-narrators set out with the assumption that their children from China need access to their origins so as to achieve an or-

62. Dorow, *Transnational Adoption,* 42–44; see also Eleana Kim's critique of "the new generation of adoptive parents with children from Asia [who] focus on the progressive choices they have made to . . . educate their children in their cultural heritage," mostly in the form of "multiculuralist consumer practices," choices dismissed by some adult Korean adoptees as worse than useless (*Adopted Territory,* 117, also 92).

63. Jacobson, *Culture Keeping,* 54, 123.

ganic link to the veridical past, but over the course of their travels they are obliged to shed this assumption and accept instead the undecidable, fictional nature of the origin for which they search. The children, as characters in these memoirs, tend to accept and enjoy the fictitiousness of origins more readily than do the parents, much as works of fiction present fiction making as the best tool for conceiving of and connecting with a much-desired but unavailable past. The return memoirs by adult adoptees begin with expectations raised high by imaginary versions of the home country, fictions and idealizations that are debunked by experience and are later replaced, in qualified ways, by the acts of writing or filmmaking.

A Passage to the Heart is an anthology of short commentaries and memoirs from newsletters published by the FCC during the 1990s. Most though not all of the selections reveal normatively essentialist attitudes toward origins and identity. One representative contributor states that these children "will always be Chinese," referring presumably not to citizenship but to the visual markers of race.[64] For this reason they must be taught their cultural, national, and racial origins for proper "identity development,"[65] as if the meaning of "Chinese" were singular, stable, knowable, and teachable. But when it comes to conducting roots searches or thinking about birth parents, the hoped-for certainties about race and culture give way to more or less openly acknowledged invention. In one piece titled "The Importance of Loving Your Child's Birth Mother," a parent recalls speculating about "how beautiful and smart she must be, how sad her life must be," and this parent urges "you and your child [to] fantasize about her."[66] Social worker and parent Jane Brown, who earlier in the book emphasizes the importance of teaching "racial identity," encourages parents "to make guesses" because of "our children's need to identify positively with their birth parents and to feel as strongly as possible that they were cared for all along their route to us," even though there is no way of knowing.[67] Parents must invent birth parents in order

64. John Bowen, "Chinese Language Instruction for Children," in Klatzkin, *Passage to the Heart,* 248–51, quotation at 249.

65. Patricia Gorman, "The Korean Adoption Experience: A Look into Our Future?" in Klatzkin, *Passage to the Heart,* 271–74, quotation at 273.

66. Susan Tompkins, "The Importance of Loving Your Child's Birth Mother," in Klatzkin, *Passage to the Heart,* 313–15, quotation at 314–15.

67. Jane Brown, "The Importance of Cultural Education," in Klatzkin, *Passage to the Heart,* 239–42, quotation at 239; Brown, "Did Our Children's Birth Parents Love Them?" in Klatzkin, *Passage to the Heart,* 316–19, quotation at 317–18. See also Volkman's discussion of Jane Brown and of the imperative to make up birth parents: "Introduction: New Geographies of Kinship," in Volkman, *Cultures of Transnational Adoption,* 1–22, this point at 16, and "Embodying Chinese Culture," 105.

for their children to grieve properly. *A Passage to the Heart* thus undermines its opening claims for the possibility and the value of retrieving veridical origins by acknowledging that fiction making plays a key role in the search for and constitution of origins.

In a more recent collection, *The Lucky Ones: Our Stories of Adopting Children from China,* one adoptive father recalls how he noticed the lack of "mystery stories for Asian kids" and gave his first daughter's name to the detective heroine of the young adult novel series he then started to write; in the excerpt from *Bullets on the Bund* that appears in this anthology, he invents for his adopted young heroine a fictional birthmother anguished by being forced to give up her daughter and promising, at parting with her infant, "your mama will always love you." Thus a parent vividly imagines and popularizes the birthmother all adoptees are expected to wish for.[68] Other adoptive parents who are positioned to give advice encourage fictionalizing origins, echoing Jane Brown in *Passage to the Heart.* The anthology with the no-nonsense title *Adoption Parenting: Creating a Toolbox, Building Connections* contains an essay by Jean MacLeod called "Parenting with Narratives" that opens with these words: "Once upon a time is a magical phrase that conjures up a faraway world from long, long ago. For our internationally adopted children, it is also a phrase that bridges the huge chasm between their early lives and who they are now."[69] MacLeod encourages making up stories as well as reading works of fantasy with young children; in the same subsection of the anthology, Sheena Macrae encourages families to "talk what-ifs": to enable growing children to speculate on "possibilities that might have been" and to create their own stories that might differ from their parents'.[70] This encouragement to invent shares space in the anthology with pieces on DNA testing and on homeland tours and other essays that presuppose knowable, locatable origins.

Emily Prager's *Wuhu Diary: On Taking My Adopted Daughter Back to Her Hometown in China* both expresses a yearning for access to origins that it presumes to be knowable and implicitly and ambivalently acknowledges the fictive, indeterminate nature of those origins. So firm is the confi-

---

68. Steve Whan, "*Bullets on the Bund:* An Excerpt," in *The Lucky Ones: Our Stories of Adopting Children from China,* ed. Ann Rauhala (Toronto: ECW Press, 2008), 119–24, quotation at 124.
69. Jean MacLeod, "Parenting with Narratives: the A, B, C's of Adoption Stories," in *Adoption Parenting: Creating a Toolbox, Building Connections,* ed. Jean MacLeod and Sheena Macrae (Warren, NJ: EMP Press, 2006–7), 228–37, quotation at 228.
70. Sheena Macrae, "What If's . . . ," in MacLeod and Macrae, *Adoption Parenting,* 232. For more examples of imagining origins coupled with practical advice on returns, see Jacobs, Ponte, and Wang, *From Home to Homeland.*

dence of Prager's narrator in the determining power of biological origins that she imagines her four-year-old daughter has no need to learn Chinese history because "maybe all that history is encoded in her DNA."[71] (This confusion of history with biology is given a comic turn by Shanti Fry, who notes that during her "endless pregnancy" of waiting to adopt, she read Chinese history when, as she realized ruefully when the baby arrived, she should have been reading *What to Expect the First Year.*[72]) Prager attributes not only Lulu's pretty looks but her social characteristics to her genetic heritage. As mother and daughter get acquainted with the city of Wuhu, where Lulu was abandoned as a days-old infant and where she spent her first seven months in an orphanage, Prager realizes that her daughter "really is *Wuhuren*" (*Wuhu Diary,* 97), a person whose character can be explained by noting that she is from Wuhu. Prager has very high expectations both for her ability as a researcher to pin down Lulu's origins and for Lulu's genetic "instincts" to reconnect her with her birthplace.

The narrative of *Wuhu Diary* is structured as a quest plot, although the closer they get to Lulu's origins, the further those origins recede and the more readily the narrator—Prager is a novelist—makes things up. Prager wants Lulu to get to know her place of origin by living and attending preschool there for a few months; she herself sets out to locate and document any traces she can find of Lulu's existence before the adoption. Prager hopes, in a telling metaphor, to reconstruct something akin to Lulu's genetic heritage: "If paleontologists can build a race from just a jawbone, surely we can glimpse a mother and father from an entire town" (*Wuhu Diary,* 40). By analogy to "building a race from a jawbone," the "entire town" is the racial indicator leading to genetic identification of Lulu's birth parents. But just as paleontologists must "build," speculatively, from the traces they find, so too Prager is building Lulu's past. Prager does not so much discover as "build" a determining heritage for Lulu. For example, in an early scene a piano in the train station calls up Prager's theory about Lulu's "long, slender fingers" and her musicality: "I imagine this musical family she must have come from. I see them on a summer night, outside near the rice fields, under the clear, bright stars. . . . They are always laughing" (50). So sure is Prager of this fantasy that she wonders only if it was the mother or the father who passed on this trait. On the train, passing rice farms, she convinces herself that

71. Emily Prager, *Wuhu Diary: On Taking My Adopted Daughter Back to Her Hometown in China* (New York: Random House, 2001), 32 (hereafter cited in the text).

72. Shanti Fry, "Surviving Waiting Parenthood," in Klatzkin, *Passage to the Heart,* 2–4, quotation at 4.

Lulu must have been born in such a place: "I imagine my farm-loving, animal-loving, plant-loving, water-loving daughter opening her infant eyes to this perfect view" (52).

Confidently deducing Lulu's past in this way, Prager nonetheless quixotically seeks external corroboration, but external facts prove to be less reliable and appealing than her daydreams, and Prager winds up settling for a complex tissue of fictions. She and Lulu possess a note allegedly from Lulu's birthmother; warned that such notes are sometimes the fabrications of orphanage directors hoping to please adoptive parents, Prager decides to believe in it anyway. From a description of the bridge where Lulu was abandoned and found, Prager locates and photographs what later turns out to be the wrong one, but through much of the narrative she makes rich symbolic use of this bridge anyway, because it connects an ancient outdoor market to an area of newly developed department stores. Discovering this (wrong) bridge, Prager describes her process of regretfully replacing a prior mental picture of what she hoped it would look like (in a pastoral vein) with its actual modern appearance, but the reader knows that its modernity is a convenient symbol. When the replacement image turns out to be false, too, and Prager is shown the right one, she points even this solid fact in the direction of a fiction possibly derived from the ending of *Pigs in Heaven.* Contemplating the possibility that Lulu's birth family might locate her if these accurate details are published in a news story, Prager writes, "From terror, I segue into fantasy, and now Lu is spending summers in Wuhu with my in-laws (her birth parents) and I'm learning from them to cook and garden" (*Wuhu Diary,* 221–22).

Similarly, Lulu's orphanage has been torn down and replaced; Prager takes Lulu to visit not the replacement (from which they are officially barred) but a different one, pretending that it is the original orphanage, a charming place that contrasts strikingly with the drab and forbidding orphanage built to replace Lulu's. They have a lovely time; Prager fabricates for Lulu an experience of origins about which Lulu can say, "I'll remember where I was adopted" (201). The place they visit is a substitute for a substitute; Lulu's pleasure comes not from finding her origin but from her mother's choice of one fiction over another and her power to dramatize this fiction and make it real.

At the same time, Prager is learning that even the few facts she thought she could count on are probably fictions as well. There are no files with hidden truths about Lulu, nor was there a special-duty nurse who might have specific memories of Lulu, despite the alleged evidence of a photograph. Prager accepts instead the speculations (about the birth parents) of a possibly fraudulent journalist on the basis of documents he may or may not have seen. Replacing the pastoral fantasy she developed in the train on the way to Wuhu, Prager builds a new certainty, that the birth parents were probably factory workers, probably aged around thirty, from an industrial development outside of the city. But despite, or because of, her pleasurable dream of spending summers with the family, Prager declines to pursue this new lead, making excuses for why she and Lulu must leave right away for the United States. Although Prager indicates that she and Lulu intend one day to restart their search, she has by now provided her daughter with such satisfactory emotional experiences that the uncovering of factual origins has become irrelevant. On the train taking them away from Wuhu, they gaze "as one" at factories, speculating about Lulu's origins there just as Prager, on the way in, had gazed at the rice farms and invented an origin narrative befitting them (233). The plot drives, then, not toward a climactic reunion with the birth family but, in effect, toward the consolidation of Prager's fictions of origination and toward the development of the mother's and daughter's skills as fiction makers, ever on the move from one origin fiction to the next.

Although Prager does not explicitly acknowledge the fictional nature of her own findings, throughout the narrative she depicts and celebrates Lulu's exuberantly creative representations of scenes from her early life. These instances of Lulu's creative "psychic work" are among the most moving features of the memoir, and they underscore the necessity of fiction making for the process of searching for origins. In contrast to her mother and to the adults who write in the brief memoirs discussed above, Lulu rushes straight for simulacra, knowing how well they serve her purposes. Charming and fluent in Mandarin, Lulu creates a wholly fictive Wuhuren "family" out of the kindly local hotel staff (*Wuhu Diary,* 128–29, 142, 156–57), complete with Baba (father) and Mama. She also devises a rescue fantasy game about her adoption in which her mother is obliged to play the part of Captain Hook, tying Lulu up again and again and making her walk the plank, so that she can "escape again and again" (139). Lulu's transformation of her own passive role into an active one and the fluid circulation of roles is characteristic of a series of games Prager reports Lulu devised as a younger child, in which she and her mother would take turns giving birth to Lulu or to a baby doll, sometimes throwing the baby away or seeing it get stolen. The most enduring of these games, Prager recalls, was the "Panda game," in which three Pandas took turns being the birthmother, the baby, and the adoptive mother: "For months we played with the pandas. Sometimes I was the birth mother, sometimes she was. Mostly she was the baby. We both gave her away and readopted her many times over" (29). Like the stuffed pandas, the trip to Wuhu provides the occasion for valuable imaginative work, but it is not China or Wuhu itself that Lulu needs. What she and her mother both need is permission to invent satisfying stories about Lulu's origins.

Threaded through this many-stranded story about storytelling is a disturbing subplot about the North Atlantic Treaty Organization (NATO) bombing of the Chinese embassy in Belgrade, which killed three Chinese journalists in May 1999, during Prager's stay in Wuhu. The news, which is presented in Chinese media as an act of American aggression, arouses anti-American sentiment on the streets of Wuhu and leads Prager to keep Lulu inside the hotel more than she says she would have liked. As if defending against the argument that transnational adoption is itself a form of imperial exploitation and aggression, Prager, despite her sympathy with the victims' families, defends NATO and the United States and expresses the wish that the United States had had "a democratic influence" on China after World War II (*Wuhu Diary,* 116). Siding with the United States, Prager refuses to believe that the bombing was deliberate, and she turns the bombing to her and Lulu's advantage as fiction makers. The bombing keeps Prager and her daughter inside the hotel and focuses and encourages Lulu's imaginative work in creating her "family" there, and the bombing also becomes Prager's reason for not seeking the birth parents in the industrial area that seems promising at the end of the book, so that Prager and Lulu can hold onto their latest imaginary vision of Lulu's origins. Prager's narrative thus aligns US imperialism with an implied preference for her and Lulu's fictions of Chinese origins over the prospect of actually meeting Lulu's birth parents. This situation recalls Clara's preference, in Yngvesson's essay, for "mak[ing] something" at a distance from the Chilean birthmother whose emotionally charged presence makes Clara feel "alone." In Clara's story and in Lulu and Prager's, as in the imaginary making of Jenny Chow, an undercurrent of sadness, even violence, accompanies the recognition that origins are being created by the adoptee at home, not found in the country of origin.

Prager's narrator persists in her claim to want to find Lulu's actual origins, yet her text's repeated celebration of the healing work of imagination acknowledges the great value of adoptive fictions, along with their cost. *Wuhu Diary* exhibits the creative lengths to which it is possible and sometimes desirable to go—including the reversal of temporal and causal sequences—in the endeavor to make or reconstruct an origin that meets present needs. Similarly, in his *China Ghosts: My Daughter's Journey to America, My Passage to Fatherhood,* Jeff Gammage tries and fails to find his first daughter's birth parents or any information about them. Like Prager, but at far greater length and more explicitly, he extrapolates her parents from Jin Yu's qualities (her mother must be beautiful, witty, and smart) and, on the basis of fragmentary information—the name of the alley where she was found, the weather that August day, a description of the clothes she wore—devises "a dozen or more" speculative narratives to replace the knowledge he cannot acquire.[73] In chapter 9 he launches into a narrative so vivid and detailed that, although he has announced he is only "pretend[ing]" to "know everything" (*China Ghosts,* 137), a reader could not be blamed for believing this work of fiction. Writing, like Ann Hood in *The Red Thread* and like Steve Whan in *Bullets on the Bund,* from the birthmother's point of view and dramatizing her poignant feelings as well as her actions, Gammage creates a plausible scenario (a young couple needing a son, the mother regretfully taking the bus and waiting till she sees her daughter found) that he spins out for four pages, only to replace it with older or younger mothers and a variety of situations and motives. The information, gleaned from internet research, that there were thunderstorms that day in Xiangtan "allows me to more fully imagine that day, that moment when her mother set her down and walked away" (146). Attributing to her the feelings he would have ("devastated"), worrying that she is still grieving, "again and again I take that journey with her" (149); "a woman I've never met moves through my life like a ghost" (151) as he imagines her imagining him and "wonder[ing] about the fate of her child" (152).

Nonetheless, he explains why he gives up trying to find her, not even taking out an ad in a local newspaper (he does not want to endanger the birth parents, and besides, it is Jin Yu's search, not his): like Prager stopping short in her search, like Christina Frank in *A Love like No Other* downplaying her own concern about the birthmother, he settles instead for imaginative identification and his own creative acts of "wonder[ing]." Later in the book, when after persisting in contacting the China Center of Adoption Affairs (CCAA) he has acquired a copy of the "birth note," a spare twenty-three-character notation of the day and time of birth, he

73. Jeff Gammage, *China Ghosts: My Daughter's Journey to America, My Passage to Fatherhood* (New York: Harper Collins, 2007), 142 (hereafter cited in the text).

imagines disproportionately elaborate and emotional scenes of writing even as he reaffirms his decision not to search and projects safely into the future a melodramatic claim: "Someday . . . I will track her down" (*China Ghosts*, 212). The writer as hero displaces the object of his imagined quest.

Nancy McCabe, author of two parent memoirs, creates a persona for herself that is more skeptical and less sentimental than Prager's or Gammage's. She admits to doubt about exaggerated claims for the transformative effects of culture camp and homeland trips, describing her daughter Sophie "rolling her eyes" at "testimonials like the ones in the book *From Home to Homeland*" ("miraculous conversion narratives," in Sophie's mocking view).[74] Nonetheless she and Sophie participate in both, and McCabe also finds more remnants of Sophie's early life than do Prager and Gammage. Rather than fantasizing about the birth parents, she uses a photograph to identify and locate someone else who makes a concrete link to Sophie's past: a kindly man who served as an informal foster parent while Sophie was at the orphanage, who traveled with her from the orphanage on her adoption day, and who still remembers her with fondness. Orphanage personnel also help the travelers visit the village where Sophie was found.

In this section of the narrative, however, McCabe departs from her usual level-headed tone. Like Prager she arrives with a misconception about Sophie's "finding place": it was not a police station, as she had first been told, but the marshy edge of a pond where two men came to fish early one morning and found a baby in the reeds. The conjectural police station steps "have loomed so large in my imagination, even now it takes me a few seconds to let the image go and replace it with new ones" once she becomes convinced of the new story (*Crossing*, 177). Noting "how biblical, how mythical" this new location is (178), McCabe proceeds to embroider her mental picture of her baby among the reeds. Because a new apartment building now stands where their guide tells them the pond once was, McCabe, like Prager and Gammage, must invent the place for herself, despite her worry that "all of this is too romanticized, too sentimental" (179). She builds her imagined scene from various sources: Moses floating in a basket; a Paul Simon song; and a silk picture she purchased earlier on the trip in Beijing, of a full moon floating above "the shimmery, silvery blue and gray scene of the edge of the pond"

74. Nancy McCabe, *Crossing the Blue Willow Bridge: A Journey to My Daughter's Birthplace in China* (Columbia: University of Missouri Press, 2011), 19, 186; see also 54–56 (hereafter cited in the text).

(179), an ekphrasis that blurs the distinction between the work of art and the formerly actual, now imagined, scene that resembles it. Claiming that the picture and the song "echo my daughter's beginnings" (180), she implies there is something uncanny in her having been attracted to them before she knew the story of the pond and the fishermen. But it could equally be said that only by means of already extant works of art can she retrospectively construct her daughter's origins.

These memoirs reflect searches and returns that are framed and staged, generally on behalf of children, by parents or social workers. I now turn to memoirs by adult adoptees who, prior to traveling "home," may have fictionally constructed ideal versions of their birth parents and of their place of origin and who find their expectations challenged by the experience of return. As we have seen, the relation of a transnational adoptee to her nation of origin may be a vexed one. Although the children in the memoirs just discussed (Lulu Prager, Jin Yu Gammage, Sophie McCabe, and others unnamed) express a generalized enthusiasm and curiosity about China that is not particularly connected to political realities, Blondie's point in *The Love Wife* that China means Tiananmen Square as well as tasty food, Jennifer Marcus's disregard for the difference between South and North Korea and her sending in effect a missile to China, as well as Prager's conflict over the Chinese response to the embassy bombing in 1999, are all reminders that returns require adults to replace a nostalgic fantasy of the country of origin with a more complex recognition of, among other things, international political tensions and mutually exclusive national loyalties.[75]

What does it mean for an adult adoptee to return to the country from which she departed as a baby, of whose language and customs she has no memory? To the unknown mother who has for decades been "an act of imagination"?[76] For those adopted as older children, taught in an assimilationist era to deny their memories, will a "roots trip" be a welcome return to the comfort of a once-loved home, or, especially if there is a language barrier, will it only activate a painful sense of loss? What do adoptees seek when they go "home," and what is gained and what is lost

75. Jacqueline Stevens advocates for a new model of citizenship that might accommodate transnational adoptees' movements and identifications across national boundaries; see "Citizenship to Go," *New York Times,* May 17, 2012; see also her *States without Nations: Citizenship for Mortals* (New York: Columbia University Press, 2010).

76. Laurel Kendall, "Birth Mothers and Imaginary Lives," in Volkman, *Cultures of Transnational Adoption,* 162–81, quotation at 164.

in replacing a dream of reunion and belonging with the experience of return? In some cases, the returning adoptee seeks refuge from a lifelong sense of dislocation, or worse, arising from the contradictory imperatives in the United States to assimilate and to retain and embody racial and national difference. Korean adoptees Jane Jeong Trenka, Katy Robinson, and Deann Borshay Liem all describe experiences of sexist racism suffered in the 1970s and 1980s in homogeneous white communities where their efforts to blend in could never succeed. In their works and other return memoirs, Korea is imagined as a place of nondifference and acceptance where such injustices could not occur. Fostering such hopes, the South Korean government, recognizing in the children sent abroad a potential economic resource, encouraged return visits starting in the 1990s. In 1997 the Overseas Koreans Foundation (OKF) was created, as part of the Ministry of Foreign Affairs and Trade, to promote "blood ties that cannot be severed."[77] Government-sponsored homeland tours flourished; popular TV shows staged reunions;[78] individual families as well as the state sought forgiveness and financial help from their restored children. Yet the place of origin seldom matches adoptees' hopes or provides the returning adoptee with a simple sense of belonging; indeed, it can nightmarishly mirror the situation the adoptee seeks to escape.

The OKF has contributed to producing, in the view of Eleana Kim, not more loyal Koreans, but instead, through the disidentification wrought by the government's inappropriate demands, a virtual "nation" made up of individuals from all over the world who, gathering periodically starting in 1999, identify with one another not as Koreans but as Korean adoptees.[79] Kim stresses the adoptees' agency in creating and defining norms for this community, and "KAD nation" is a positive element in many lives.[80] Nonetheless, it also names a form of permanent homelessness for those alienated from their adoptive countries yet not finding a sense of true belonging in Korea. Like the Chilean adoptees Yngvesson studied, for whom seeing their homelands and meeting their

77. Eleana J. Kim, "Wedding Citizenship and Culture: Korean Adoptees and the Global Family of Korea," in Volkman, *Cultures of Transnational Adoption,* 49–80, quotation at 62.

78. See Elise Prebin, "Looking for 'Lost' Children in South Korea," *Adoption & Culture* 2 (2009): 227–63; and Kim, *Adopted Territory,* 177.

79. Kim, "Wedding Citizenship and Culture," 59–60, 71; see also Kim, *Adopted Territory,* throughout.

80. Sunny Jo coined the term; see "The Making of KAD Nation," in *Outsiders Within: Writing on Transracial Adoption,* ed. Jane Jeong Trenka, Julia Chinyere Oparah, and Sun Yung Shin (Cambridge: South End Press, 2006), 285–90.

birthmothers produced not wholeness, as they hoped, but confusion, a "shake up [of] identity" rather than a securing of it ("Going 'Home,'" 32), adoptees who return to Korea often find the experience confusing. Seoul is home to a sizable community of returned adoptees, among whom Trenka writes of having lived for three years. In her haunting second memoir *Fugitive Visions,* they live fragile, marginal lives, cut off from their adoptive families yet unable or unwilling to assimilate into Korean life.[81] Prone to alcoholism, they meet in the English- and French-speaking bars; suicides, according to Trenka, are not uncommon.[82] Although at least for English speakers jobs are relatively easy to find, the sense of belonging many had hoped for proves more elusive. According to Kim,

> many adoptees . . . fantasized about Korea as a site of plenitude and true familial or ethnic belonging, [yet] any fantasies that adoptees may have harbored about their ability to be Korean or to be fully accepted in their homeland were easily disrupted by their encounters with the dominant ethnic nationalism that equates Koreanness with cultural, linguistic, and ethnic homogeneity.[83]

The scopic sexist racism that angered and harmed Korean adoptees in the United States is not necessarily remedied by their being in a place where, at last, they seem to look like everyone else. Many find themselves subjected to a nationalistic form of racism when disparaged for forgetting Korean language and customs and for looking American.[84] They also encounter Korean forms of androcentrism and sexism that they experience as even more toxic than those they suffered in the United States.

Korean culture, like American, defines kinship primarily through "blood" or genetic ties. But whereas in US adoption discourse blood kinship paradoxically becomes the dominant metaphor for severing a child's biological ties and reassigning her new kin, "*as-if-begotten,*" in Judith Modell's phrase, among the Korean families in the memoirs blood

81. Jane Jeong Trenka, *Fugitive Visions: An Adoptee's Return to Korea* (St. Paul: Graywolf Press, 2009) (hereafter cited in the text).
82. See also Kim, *Adopted Territory,* 198–202.
83. Kim, *Adopted Territory,* 186.
84. See, e.g., Leah Kim Sieck, "A True Daughter," in *Voices from Another Place: A Collection of Works from a Generation Born in Korea and Adopted to Other Countries,* ed. Susan Soon-Keum Cox (St. Paul: Yeong and Yeong, 1999), 84–91, this point at 85. See also Kim, "Wedding Citizenship and Culture," 65–66; Kim, *Adopted Territory,* 187–98.

ties are understood to be so strong as to be inviolable. Children who have lived for twenty or thirty years as members of US families are greeted upon their return as if no break had occurred. Parents under economic and other kinds of stress placed children in orphanages and even agreed to their adoption abroad because they thought that only thus could their children be safe, fed, and educated; they could not imagine or anticipate that their children would, by law and US custom, cease to be theirs, often disappearing untraceably. "My mother," writes Trenka, "had no idea we would be separated for twenty-three years, that international adoption is not some kind of extended study-abroad program" (*Fugitive Visions,* 98). On returning to Korea, these adoptees encounter the powerful discourse of blood both as the expectation that they will now rejoin the family and resume being Korean—as if Korean language, cultural knowledge, and body style were in their blood—and as the expression of a patriarchal belief system that confounds their US liberal feminist assumptions about personal autonomy. They flee US sexist racism only to find even more explicit sexisms in Korea, where among their parents' generations traditional (in this case, Confucian) gender norms and hierarchies are far more openly enforced than in the United States. They find subservient, often abused, wives and mothers and the expectation that they too will give up their independent American ways to become Korean-female. "It is good to be a man in Korea," a male Korean adoptee tells Katy Robinson. "I need to find myself a good traditional Korean wife to take home with me."[85]

Many children were relinquished or abandoned for reasons of sexism. Boys were preferred, and girls might be mistreated or abandoned in situations where a boy might have been treasured and kept. Trenka and an older sister were sent to America because their mother, herself bearing disfiguring scars from her husband's violence, feared for her daughters' lives: "My own Umma told me that if she had kept me, I would have been either dead or a beggar. She told me the stories of how my father beat me about the head and my head turned black and blue, how he threw me from a window, how she was homeless and slept on the streets."[86] Trenka notes the irony of her having, on account of a psychopath who stalks her, "experienced the fear that my mother had given me away to escape," a fear of misogynist violence that may have locally specific causes but

85. Katy Robinson, *A Single Square Picture: A Korean Adoptee's Search for Her Roots* (New York: Berkley Books, 2002), 175 (hereafter cited in the text).

86. Jane Jeong Trenka, *The Language of Blood: A Memoir* (St. Paul: Borealis Books, 2003), 200 (hereafter cited in the text).

whose effects cross national borders (*Language of Blood,* 69). Time and again, adoptees learn that their birthmothers, left partnerless by death or by sexual betrayal, had to give them up because a single mother had no social standing and no way to earn a livelihood. Eleana Kim writes that, despite a 1991 change in the law giving some rights to mothers, "birth mothers . . . represent the most subordinated groups in an entrenched patriarchy and misogynistic state welfare system."[87] After the accidental death of her father, writes one adoptee, her mother "tried to support us by selling insurance, books and other things. She tried for almost three years . . . but like tens of thousands of single mothers in Korea's patrilineal society and poverty of the 1970s, she found it impossible and turned to U.S. adoption."[88] Still sadder, another adoptee's mother "left my dad because he was an alcoholic and beat her. She left to save her life. She couldn't take me with her because I was the property of my father."[89]

Although these assertions of male privilege and patriarchal authority stem from Korean law and tradition, the intensity and cruelty of their recent expression appear sometimes to be motivated by a defensive nationalism that responds to decades of imperial subjugation followed by divisive war and then the International Monetary Fund (IMF) crisis of the 1980s. Trenka, analyzing her father's violence in the context of a nation of failed, alcoholic men (all the beggars in Seoul, she says, are men), reports that with their light skin, she and her sister were "assumed to be half-American in a public setting such as this, packed with . . . American soldiers carrying rifles who ate meat every day" (*Fugitive Visions,* 134–35). Her father raged against what he took to be his wife's unfaithfulness to him and to the nation, and he raged against the children who seemed to make it visible. In Deann Borshay Liem's autobiographical documentary film *First Person Plural,* too, the Korean older brother identifies the family honor with that of the nation when he delivers a face-saving speech that echoes the official South Korean line about foreign adoption: Deann was not "abandoned" but rather "sent away" to enjoy "better opportunities" and to get an education. The tearful mother at

87. Kim, "Wedding Citizenship and Culture," 72; for a somewhat more optimistic view of Korean birthmothers' situations, see Kendall, "Birth Mothers and Imaginary Lives." Social supports for single mothers, however, remain notoriously lacking.

88. Crystal Lee Hyun Joo Chappell, "Now I'm Found," in *Seeds from a Silent Tree: An Anthology by Korean Adoptees,* ed. Tonya Bishoff and Jo Rankin (Glendale, CA: Pandal Press, 1997), 124–35, quotation at 131.

89. Mea Han Nelson-Wang, "Purpose," in Cox, *Voices from Another Place,* 64–66, quotation at 64; for a similar story see Tonya Keith, "A Journey Back," in *Voices from Another Place,* 32–40.

first parrots his words, dutifully supporting the young patriarch; yet at other times, departing from the script, she weeps and tells Deann that she has felt "endless heartache" and acknowledges that her daughter's "pain was indescribable."[90] Daughters returning to Korea often struggle to hear their mothers' broken, discredited voices behind the loudspeaker of public and private male authority.

Nonetheless, temporarily, or in adoptees' dreams, refound birthmothers and the cultural values linked to them may soothe away the scopic sexist racism of the United States and the patriarchal sexism of Korea. Rediscovering the taste and smell of Korean food can provide the greatest pleasure of a return trip, and returning adoptees tend to locate in outdoor food markets their fantasies of suddenly recognizing and reuniting with their lost birthmothers.[91] When families reunite, the mothers press homemade food on their children. Touch, too, is often imagined as the sign of maternal presence. Katy Robinson wistfully recalls "the way she combed my hair and cut my bangs, pasting down wisps of hair with a lick of her finger" (*Single Square Picture,* 294). One short return memoir ends with two dreamscapes in which the writer is climbing a mountain in the dark and sees herself as a baby, glowing blue in the moonlight; then, closing her eyes and praying to the mother she never found, she holds her hand out in the dark, and, "after a while, I feel her grasp my hand."[92]

Trenka, who does find refuge with her mother and sisters in *The Language of Blood,* describes a nearly womblike contact that mutes the visual and accentuates intimate bodily contact and care. On arriving at the Seoul airport, released from the visual violence of "cameras flashing in shocking explosions," she writes, "I was pushed onto a bus with my mother," who could not stop weeping and who "clutched my hand tightly and didn't let go." The bus ride is like a journey down the birth canal for both of them: "in my memory, we are suspended together in the blackness, all by ourselves, with nothing to say, no words to say it" (*Language of Blood,* 98–99). Umma's stories about her perilous babyhood penetrate her daughter physically, and she reinforces them with touch: "She showed me her breasts to tell me that she loved me and had nursed me. I touched her old woman's depleted breasts, as she asked. *Touch me here, where I gave myself to you. I made you with my own body,* she seemed to

90. Deann Borshay Liem, dir., *First Person Plural* (San Francisco: National Asian American Telecommunications Association, 2000).

91. See, e.g., Kimberly Kyung Hee Stock, "My *Han,*" in Cox, *Voices from Another Place,* 96–104, this point at 96.

92. Sieck, "True Daughter," 91.

say" (102). When Umma gives her daughter a bath, "the water is warm as birthwater"; Umma squats, in laboring position, and "washes me hard and quickly, with so much ardor it hurts, and I become a child again" (107). The bath, like the bus ride, enacts her rebirth as her mother's baby, and these deep physical pleasures seem to repair the injury of abandonment.

Are long dreamed-of maternal feeding and touch sufficient remedies for the suffering inflicted on adoptees by androcentric regimes? For the highly articulate, communicative daughters who author these memoirs, they can be both comforting and frustrating. The mothers refuse to honor adult boundaries. On her first visit to Seoul, Trenka expects to spend an "orderly week" with her tour group before turning her attention to her birth family, but Umma keeps appearing at the hotel room of "her baby," "bearing plastic bags crammed full of tomatoes and watermelon—far more than I could ever eat" (*Language of Blood*, 100, 99). Especially when there is no or little shared language, mother and daughter resort to tears and caresses, forms of communication that wear thin after the first overwhelming moments. As David Eng points out, Liem manages her confusion about having both a Korean and an American mother by distributing, one to each, the roles of preoedipal and of symbolic mother, but neither is satisfactory.[93] Liem's American family inhabits a scopic symbolic domain: the film opens with a survey of her father's art photographs, and that she herself is making a film aligns her with her father's viewpoint, despite the harm she sustained from the US culture of the gaze. When she visits her birth family, by contrast, "my body remembers something, but my mind is resistant"; her communications with her mother are limited to touches, hugs, and tears; and she finds herself unable to relearn Korean. The rediscovery of the long-sought preoedipal mother turns from a source of comfort into a source of frustration.

Although Trenka (unlike Liem) celebrates the restoration of her preoedipal mother, it cannot last. By the time of her third visit to Korea, her mother is dying of metastatic brain cancer, which appears in the narrative as the result of long years of abuse and poverty. She requires the constant care of her daughters, and Trenka moves into the hospital with her sisters to reciprocate Umma's wordless maternal care. "I rubbed your back, where you had carried me," she writes; "I came to know your body" and to learn that "I am a daughter after your body and after your

93. David Eng, "Transnational Adoption and Queer Diasporas," *Social Text* 76 (2003): 1–37.

heart. Even if I fail to create you again with words, I will carry you with me, in the language of blood" (*Language of Blood,* 139–40). This semiotic "language of blood" links the returned daughter to the preoedipal mother. The father was the violent intruder who inscribed his dominion in the form of scars on the mother's and sisters' bodies. The language of blood, by contrast, is the wordless bond between mother and daughter that transcends their geographic and linguistic distance.[94] But this relationship can be perfected only after Umma's death, when linguistic and cultural barriers fall away. Toward the end of the memoir Trenka writes:

> Now that you are dead, you are more near to me. You've always been so far away, halfway across the earth in your basement apartment in Seoul, me here in Minnesota trying so hard to learn your language and failing. . . . But now, I talk to you all the time. I talk to you in English, and I think I hear you talking to me in English, or in emotions, or maybe it is something else, but I can understand it. I have dreams now. They are in Korean, and they must be from you. (*Language of Blood,* 192)

The memoir ends with a lyrical fantasy vision of Umma taking her daughter's hand—"Umma's hand is hot and plump, the way it used to be, and she holds on too tight, the way she always did"—and flying, together with Trenka's imaginary baby daughter, like butterflies into a gorgeously evoked stratosphere (220). The language of blood here is translated from wordless maternal bodily contact into the writer's distinctive literary style, in which she does "create [her mother] again with words." An alternative to silencing paternal force, this maternal language authorizes Trenka's emergent voice. But the maternal language itself is impermanent, going unmentioned in Trenka's second memoir, a book whose literary form is even more stylish and stylized than that of the first. The daughter has established her own language, no longer tied to the mother's body.

How different Trenka's "language of blood" is from the language of "blood" in Katy Robinson's *A Single Square Picture,* where blood refers to the patriarchal preoccupation with bloodlines, blood descent, scopic identity (son and grandson are carbon copies of the father), legitimate birth, and the violent control of women's lives upon which these preoccupations depend. Robinson reads the Korean bloodline in an explic-

94. In a contrasting view, Jerng sees Trenka's *The Language of Blood* responding to the imperative to find identity "within one's body" by showing that "blood" is a metaphorical language, not an ontological reality (*Claiming Others,* 150).

itly feminist framework. Although she had been eager to get to Korea, where she imagined she would fit in and feel at home, "I am grateful I didn't have to grow up a dutiful girl in Korea," she writes home to her American mother. "I am reading a collection of folktales and the moral of every story is for the wife to sacrifice herself for her husband and in-laws" (*Single Square Picture,* 184). She discovers that Korean gender hierarchy accounts both for her relinquishment (at age seven) by her unmarried mother and for her difficulty now in locating her birthmother. Welcomed effusively to Korea by her birth father and his son, her (legitimate) older half-brother, she feels estranged by their sentimental presumptions of intimacy ("Your brother loves you very much," a translator tells Robinson; "since you and your brother share the same blood, he feels very close to you"), combined with their "heartless[ness]," her term for their active efforts to keep her from finding her birthmother (*Single Square Picture,* 140, 197).

For father and son, the birthmother represents a threat to what is, after all, a fragile patriarchal authority. Robinson's memoir is populated by women who were forced to accept their husbands' and lovers' infidelities and their socially and economically devastating desertions. To the men—like the South Korean government itself, which in 1998 apologized for allowing foreign adoptions and then went on permitting the practice—these outcomes exhibit both their masculine prerogative (of which they are proud) and masculine shame (the father keeps confessing his failures as a father). Robinson experiences the resulting culturally sanctioned disparagement of women firsthand: as she prepares to meet her father, her local hosts require her to "comply with the standards of a proper *Korean* daughter," demanding that she dress up, curl her hair, apply makeup, and purchase a deferential gift (*Single Square Picture,* 43). Often in her father's company she feels infantilized: "I felt my independence and American identity dissolve with each passing second I spent with him" (119). Father and son control Robinson's actions while she is in Korea by appropriating her search for her mother: they promise to make inquiries but fail to do so. By having "erased" her mother, Robinson thinks, they believe they can erase paternal shame (197).

Finally Robinson understands that her mother may not want to be found, for the same reason she gave her child up: the exposure of the illegitimate birth could compromise whatever new life she has been able to arrange. When Robinson recalls and speculates about her birthmother, and when she meets other abused wives and mothers, she counters their "erasure" by recalling and imagining touch, taste, smell, and sound. In her intensely tactile memory of the airport where she is to board the plane for America, when her mother is told to let her daughter go,

> her hand releases my fingers, shoots up my arm, and grips my shoulder. As she does this, I feel a shot of panic travel up my chest. . . . But another eternity passes before my mother releases her clawlike grip on my shoulder bone and moves her hand to cover her eyes. (*Single Square Picture,* 3)

Sharing bodily sensations, mother and daughter cannot part, but they do. Trying to soothe herself, she "clung to the scent of roasted seaweed and peppery *kimchee,* the feel of my grandmother's body next to mine, and the last look on my mother's face" (1) Later, in the United States, staring at the Polaroid taken of the three of them in the airport, she cannot recognize herself, as if her connectedness to her mother and grandmother depended on other senses besides sight. In her fantasy of reunion, her mother holds her and "answers all of my questions as if reading my mind, [with] no need for a translator" (*Single Square Picture,* 132–33). Very like Trenka's "language of blood," this dream of unalienated, unmediated contact with her mother's mind and body always ends "with a sense of completion and wholeness." But it is a dream that cannot be realized.

Although Robinson never meets her mother, she acquires a "surrogate Korean mother" (her father's first wife), who, like Trenka's Umma, pinches, squeezes, and pats her and stuffs her with food (*Single Square Picture,* 206). Robinson, in turn, trying to tell her she is beautiful, mispronounces the Korean word and calls her "delicious" (211). But the squeezing, delicious mother represents not so much the long-sought mother of Katy's hopes as the patriarchal system that both creates and destroys her. This woman and her daughter-in-law never sit down to eat with her son, Robinson's half-brother, who barks orders into the kitchen and never offers to help. Robinson is horrified by the two women's traditional Korean female servitude and by the first wife's continued shame and grief over having been deserted thirty years before. She disintegrates in tears because the presence of the mistress's daughter reminds her of their family's "demoted status" and "reopen[s] old wounds" (215, 220). As in *First Person Plural,* the nurturing, preoedipal mother reveals her lack of social power, her pathetic and understandable yet deeply unappealing loyalty to the father's law.

Robinson soon develops a symptom. Her vision blurs; she has a detached retina. This turn of events is linked both literally and figuratively to her search for her mother, which she now must abandon (just as Prager and Lulu abandon their search in Wuhu). The Korean doctor says her condition is hereditary; with excellent eyesight on her father's side, her weak eyes must come from her mother. Only by falling ill, evidently, can she gain accurate information about her mother. This "sick joke" (*Single Square Picture,* 250) anticipates the irony that Trenka's greatest intimacy with her Umma is occasioned by Umma's fatal illness. Delirious, lying together on the floor and stroking her daughter's hair, Umma calls her "*Ipun eggi*" or "pretty baby," her mind going back to her daughter's birth twenty-five years earlier (*Language of Blood,* 150). Although Trenka takes great pleasure in this revelation of her mother's love, for Robinson Korean motherhood, including the maternal touches, tastes, and smells that were once so laden with positive value, begins to lose its aura of safety and comfort. A farewell visit to the half brother revives the image of the grandmother as domestic slave, doing too much hand laundry, making too much kimchee. Finally, Robinson reviews her fragmentary memories of her mother: she "can almost feel the warmth of her love," yet their closeness is also frightening. Late one night, she recalls, she awoke to hear her mother and grandmother arguing about her and then saw her mother run to the bathroom to vomit on the floor:

> Seeing my mother slumped over like that, still sobbing as she choked and spat, suddenly flipped my own stomach upside down. I sensed her desperation and knew that it somehow involved me. I ran to the bathroom and found myself squatting next to my mother, getting sick just as she had a moment earlier. (*Single Square Picture,* 295)

This remembered bodily connection epitomizes the mother's equivocal legacy: like the inheritance of weak eyes, it is about damage as much as about love.

In Mei-Ling Hopgood's memoir *Lucky Girl,* too, the Taiwanese birth family's life revolves around what the author terms her father's "obsession" with patrilineage arising from his Confucian belief that "only a son could be counted on to support the parents when they were old. . . . Only a son could perpetuate the name and bloodline, and worship and care for a father's spirit properly."[95] Mei-Ling was given up for adoption because she was the family's sixth-born daughter. Her father, too poor to support a large family and holding out for the birth of a son, tried to

95. Mei-Ling Hopgood, *Lucky Girl: A Memoir* (Chapel Hill: Algonquin Books of Chapel Hill, 2009), 29 (hereafter cited in the text).

give away each of his daughters after the first three (giving the fourth a name meaning "no more girls") and succeeded with two of them: Mei-Ling, who went to a US family, and the youngest sister, adopted in Switzerland. A son was born after the first two daughters, but his cleft palate rendered him monstrous in the eyes of his father, and a few days after his birth he was left alone to die. The family adopted a boy shortly before Mei-Ling's birth; offered drugs to dry up her milk, Ma declined so that she could nurse the newly arrived one-year-old. When this son turned out to be "slow," and despite the brilliance and resourcefulness of the six daughters who remained in the family, Ba tried again for a male heir: by the time of the author's latest visit to Taiwan, Ba's eight-year-old son by another woman is living with the family, minimally cared for by Ma but ignored and called "The Boy" by his older half sisters, who resent their father's bad behavior and coercive ways. Ba obliges Mei-Ling to acknowledge this son by commanding him to call her *jiejie;* this performative represents his power over the family in a specifically symbolic register. Indeed, the father's control of the mother's life is almost absolute: abused for her failure to produce an adequate son, Ma accepted Ba's horrific choice to kill the first boy, and although she disagreed with him, she also could not stop his efforts to give up the girls. That she even now does nothing to protest Ba's imposition of his illegitimate son on the household irritates Mei-Ling, who wavers between pitying her mother for being "traditional Chinese" and disparaging her for her lack of self-esteem.

Whereas paternal violence and sexual misconduct in *A Single Square Picture* and in *The Language of Blood* lead to empathy for and tactile connection with the mother's body and the good foods with which it is associated, Mei-Ling—with her American impatience with failures in self-determination—cannot muster much more than pity for her birthmother. Although early in the memoir (as in all the others) the smell and taste of local food is a source of great pleasure, and her love of food helps her "fit right in" in Taiwan and enjoy her first visit as a "feeding frenzy" (*Lucky Girl,* 96), as Mei-Ling gets more deeply acquainted with the family's troubles, the associations among the mother, food, and the body become increasingly negative. In contrast to the overload of mostly unsavory knowledge she gains from and about her domineering father, Mei-Ling finds her mother "remained a mystery . . . . a kind of shadow figure, almost unknowable. She and I could be standing together, even touching, but I always felt as if a piece of soundproof glass divided us" (190). So Mei-Ling takes her mother on a trip to mainland China, with a younger sister along as translator and guide, with the express goal of getting her mother's attention. Yet as she spends more time with her, her mother's body and the foods with which she is associated are represented as sources of disgust. Ma, along with other bus passengers, bargains for fresh fruit to eat on the ride but leaves the leftovers on the bus to rot and "stink" (204). Like other tour members, Ma belches and farts at the table; a survivor of cervical cancer, Ma must use the bathroom frequently, her two daughters taking turns shepherding her to the variously disgusting latrines the memoir describes in detail. Ma's answers to her daughter's probing questions reveal a memory that is "fading and jumbled" (206). Their companionship leads not to intimacy but near to alienation.

Instead of the mother's body providing hoped-for intimacy and relief from patriarchal power, patriarchal power seems to have reduced Ma to a body whose degradation her daughter cannot transcend and that cannot be compensated for by nourishment, intimate touch, or care. In the only early photograph of mother and daughter together, taken on the day Mei-Ling left Taiwan for the United States, an orphanage caregiver is holding the baby, and Ma stands nearby, only tentatively touching the baby from whom the father's mandate divides her. On first meeting at Chiang Kai-shek Airport, Ma and Mei-Ling share hugs, sobs, and hand squeezes "for an awkward instant," but soon "Ma turned away, trying to compose herself" (*Lucky Girl,* 91). On the trip to China, only a few scattered moments provide Mei-Ling with anything like the sense of closeness that she hoped for. The common unpleasantness of mosquito bites provides one such rare opportunity: "'You have my skin,' Ma said, observing me. 'That's why they like you'" (209). A particularly bad bite allows Ma to provide the bodily care she might have provided to a child: "She rubbed the salve gently on my bite and looked up at me. . . . / 'Better?' / 'Sure,' I said, and it was. And for a second I felt that we recognized each other: a mother, a daughter, and a mosquito bite" (210).

The mother's death in *The Language of Blood,* her remoteness in *Lucky Girl* and in *First Person Plural* (Liem says she now "admit[s] she's not my mother"), her erasure and Robinson's resignation about it in *A Single Square Picture:* found or not, the long-sought birthmother in each case cannot resolve the daughter's battles either with American scopic sexist racisms or with Korean nationalist patriarchy. Through these frustrating returns, the daughters come to understand the violence that damaged their mothers' lives, that necessitated their own relinquishment and adoption, and that lives on in the persistence of the sexual double standard and of cultural biases toward sons.

The birthmothers and grandmothers want married daughters with grandchildren, to continue the family line, to bear the burden of gender that has formed and deformed them, and to vindicate their own lives. And the memoirists generously comply, even as they frame their compliance in terms that gently underscore the unbridgeable distance between them. Liem's film ends in figurative compliance with the mother's wish, with a still shot of Liem with her husband and baby, as if the filmmaker had stepped momentarily from behind the camera to sign her work not only as artist but also as wife and mother. Robinson and Trenka likewise incorporate figurative babies into their conclusions in ways that nonetheless emphatically underscore their self-definitions as writers. In her memoir's last lines, Robinson mentally resolves her ambivalence about the longed-for yet dangerous maternal body by identifying not with her birthmother's body but with her stories. She imagines her birthmother with the younger children Robinson hopes she bore, patient with them because she "understands the ache of first love and the fickle hearts of handsome men much more than her children will ever know. Her children will doubt her, just as she doubted her own mother and my child will someday doubt me"; being able to pass on her mother's and grandmother's stories makes a "cycle that will connect generations of women, Korean and American" (*Single Square Picture,* 296–97). Like Trenka, she can manage the heartbreaking absence of her birthmother by positioning her as the authorizing ground of her writing. The publication of Trenka's second memoir treats Umma as a distant memory and has nothing to say of the desired grandchild who was imagined so vividly in flight at the end of *The Language of Blood,* but its high style confirms Trenka's vocation as a writer. While Robinson shapes her maternal genealogy into an engine of narrative continuity, Trenka turns the maternal "language of blood" into lyrical prose.

Like Robinson concluding with her legacy of maternal narratives, and, too, like Trenka coming to terms with her birthmother's death by enjoying a fantasy relationship that rises beyond the limitations of their lived realities, Hopgood resolves her story by celebrating her own powers as a writer. Now the mother of a seven-month-old girl with plans to adopt another child, she writes: "I offer my voice to the chorus of ancestors. I am not the son who can perpetuate the family name, but I can tell our story. I am not the heir that Ba wanted, but I, too, can be a keeper of our history. I choose to continue the narrative in my own way" (*Lucky Girl,* 244). Origins may not be graspable, but they can be written.

3 / MARKED BODIES AND IDENTITY

As we have seen, the place of origin is unlikely to provide a returning adoptee with a simple sense of belonging. Expectations raised by the idealizing of origins cannot be met, but they are raised high by the belief that birth confers identity. Although adoptees' desire for connection to their nation and culture of origin is widespread globally, its acute expression in the United States can be traced to peculiarly American contradictions around race, racialized appearance, and blood, contradictions that are often denied and disavowed. The belief that birth confers identity means that identity is understood to arise not from racial interpellation or from other forms of lived experience, but instead from an internal endowment that remains intact within the body through life, regardless of experience. Yet that internal, embodied endowment is only knowable through racially signifying appearance, appearance that can only take its meaning from social interactions. Adoptions—transnational, transracial, but also same-race domestic adoptions—raise questions about the alignment of identity and bodily appearance that this chapter explores.

Growing up in all-white communities in the 1960s, 1970s, and 1980s, the adult Korean adoptees who began producing memoirs in the 1990s, some of which are discussed in chapter 2, were bound by two opposing unspoken laws: the imperative to assimilate in a society that claimed and wished to be colorblind and the iron law of racism that singles out skin color and facial configuration as the most salient factors in personal identity. Many memoirists including those discussed at the end of chapter 2 describe the violent racisms they encountered, despite their best efforts to conform and their parents' denials of racial difference or of racism. This account is typical:

> Raised by white parents in a predominantly white town, I considered myself to be white. Other saw me differently, though. People stared at me as if I were an alien and children asked if I could see through my

> "Chinese, slant eyes." The worst episodes were when teenage boys surrounded me on the school bus and yelled obscenities and racial slurs at me. My race shouldn't have mattered, I thought, because it didn't matter to my friends and family.[1]

How you look is what you are, these transplanted children quickly discovered—a social truth recognized in the representations of Kingsolver's Turtle, for example, or Alexie's John Smith—and yet their new families were devoted to denying difference. Pamela Anne Quiroz explains the racism arising from the contradiction between ideological colorblindness and the practice of racial hierarchization in adoption: "by claiming to ignore racial hierarchy even as it assists in sustaining it, . . . adoption in the United States illustrates the emergence of a new form of color-blind racism in our society that allows whites to argue that race no longer matters even as their adoption practices clearly demonstrate that it does."[2]

In *First Person Plural,* adoptive family members unapologetically recall acting out, in the name of love, what for Deann Borshay Liem was the cruelty of colorblind adoption in a racist society. They were able only to see that the child at the airport was Asian, and they failed to notice that she was not the child in the photos they had received over a period of years, an exchange of identities of great significance to the child herself. In her sister Denise's laughing recollection, "I think mother went up to the wrong person. . . . It didn't matter. I mean, one of 'em was ours [mother laughs]."[3] In another scene in the film her brother Duncan congratulates himself on his blindness: "You don't have the family eyes, but I don't care; you got the family smile. Color and look doesn't make any difference. It's who y'are; you're my sister." In these comments, race is both highlighted and denied. Liem recalls her father making a joke of this contradiction: "people used to stare and . . . ask us, is she your daughter? . . . Then I would say, of course she is, we look just alike, don't we? [laughs]."[4] On leaving home for college, Liem fell into a "deep de-

1. Crystal Lee Hyun Joo Chappell, "Now I'm Found," in *Seeds from a Silent Tree: An Anthology by Korean Adoptees,* ed. Tonya Bishoff and Jo Rankin (Glendale, CA: Pandal Press, 1997), 124–35, quotation at 126.
2. Pamela Anne Quiroz, *Adoption in a Color-Blind Society* (Lanham, MD: Rowman and Littlefield, 2007), 80.
3. Deann Borshay Liem, dir., *First Person Plural* (San Francisco: National Asian American Telecommunications Association, 2000).
4. Deann Borshay [Liem], "Remembering the Way Home: A Documentary Video Proposal," in Bishoff and Rankin, *Seeds from a Silent Tree,* 116–20, quotation here at 117, quotation in next sentence at 118.

pression" on account of this coupling of racism and denial and the uncompleted mourning for her birth family that accompanied it.

The racism from which these adoptees suffered often came in a specifically gendered form. In the passage by Crystal Lee Hyun Joo Chappell quoted above, the teenage boys yell not just "racial slurs" but "obscenities" too. The visuality of American race and racism was exacerbated by the intensive policing of appearance for US girls and women. Efforts to normalize their appearance (permed hair, makeup, eyelid surgery) are reported by women adoptees though rarely by men; many recall as children hating to be photographed or to see themselves in a mirror.[5] *First Person Plural* documents, with vivid archival images, Liem's teenage efforts, as head cheerleader and prom queen, to create and maintain a "happy American façade" by rendering her face, hair, and body style white-American; but not even plastic surgery made her feel secure.[6]

In *The Language of Blood,* Jane Jeong Trenka reports an extreme form of sexualized racism when, in college, she is pursued for months by a white male stalker who calls her "nothing but a Korean in a white man's society,"[7] videotapes her through her dorm window, follows her to her parents' home, wrecks the house, and attempts to shoot her father. He is eventually jailed, his car having been found stocked with paraphernalia for a horrendous crime. This episode leaves an enduring psychic scar, for Jane blames herself. The threat of sexual violence is hardly unique to Korean adoptees or to Asian women; specific to Trenka as a transracial adoptee is her psychic vulnerability, unable as she is to claim securely the Korean identity that can thus be turned against her as a weapon.

Trenka's is an extreme case, yet it helps make visible the scopic sexist racism that troubled the young lives of so many who came from Korea in those early waves of adoption. Interpellated as Asian-female yet misled by denial and unprepared for the virulent biases that would surround them outside their homes, many adoptees grew alienated from their parents and communities. Looking different in a looks-based culture motivated many returns, as suggested by Katy Robinson's childhood letter to her adoptive mother, from *A Single Square Picture:* "Do you know what it feels

5. On transnational adoptees' "shock" at seeing themselves in the mirror, because in their white surroundings they have had to "forget" their racially distinct looks, see Barbara Yngvesson and Susan Bibler Coutin, "Backed by Papers: Undoing Persons, Histories, and Return," *American Ethnologist* 33, no. 2 (2006): 177–90, quotations at 180–81.

6. Liem, *First Person Plural;* Liem, "Remembering the Way Home," 118.

7. Jane Jeong Trenka, *The Language of Blood: A Memoir* (St. Paul: Borealis Books, 2003), 73.

Figure 1. Deann as prom queen. From Deann Borshay Liem, *First Person Plural.*

like to have an Asian shell while longing to be white just like you? Well, I am not one of you. . . . I am Korean and I want to find out what that means."[8] Trenka, too, traces her initial desire to return to Korea in part to her harrowing experience with the stalker, and in her second memoir she attributes her later choice to move there to her divorce from the husband who, like the stalker, turned out to care more for an eroticized "Asian woman" fantasy than for Jane herself.

Given the changes in racial norms surrounding transracial and transnational adoptions, such as the celebration of multiculturalism, difference, and identity by the parents of children coming from China and elsewhere since the early 1990s, it might be expected that such dysphoric misalignments between appearance and identity as Trenka, Chappell, and Liem recall would occur less often. Like the fictional parents in *The Love Wife,* many parents try to inoculate against external and internal-

8. Katy Robinson, *A Single Square Picture: A Korean Adoptee's Search for Her Roots* (New York: Berkley Books, 2002), 36.

ized racism by fostering positive non-white identity, often using "culture" or "heritage" as a "proxy" for race and as a source of upbeat images and practices around which to foster racial identity. Many assert the positive value of affirming difference and of firmly linking racialized appearance to a notionally inherited "birth culture," as when an adult adoptee from Vietnam writes, as if addressing a young transnationally adopted child: "'You come from a different country, rich with heritage and the spirits of your ancestors. You carry that within your soul, and in your appearance.'"[9] Sometimes "heritage" is simply a euphemism for racialized appearance, as when a mother writes that her four-year-old "loved having a chance to spend time with others who shared her heritage."[10] Nancy McCabe, having "paid attention to a generation of adult Korean adoptees who caution white parents not to ignore difference," knows that "colorblindness and assimilation are no longer regarded as healthy." For her, racialized appearance and culture are the same: when she claims, "I embraced her differences," she is talking about race but also explaining why she saved up money for a trip to China.[11]

Nonetheless the problem reported by Trenka and others persists, if in subtler forms: such "culture keeping," as Heather Jacobson points out, can produce the opposite of the desired effect, by accentuating differences that make a child vulnerable to racism.[12] As Kimberly Leighton puts the problem in her critique of adoptees' so-called "genealogical bewilderment" and the affirmations of racial identity and "birth culture" that it motivates, this essentializing idea

> simultaneously recognizes those whose membership in a particular race might be unclear, while it reaffirms the reality of racial membership, a double act the aim of which appears to be the promotion of the health of bewildered adoptees and the effect of which is the pathologization of adoption itself.[13]

---

9. Indigo Williams, "What I Wanted to Hear: Being Different in an All White Family," in *Adoption Parenting: Creating a Toolbox, Building Connections,* ed. Jean MacLeod and Sheena Macrae (Warren, NJ: EMK Press, 2006–7), 311.
10. Cindy Champnella, "Lessons I Learned from a 4 Year-Old," in MacLeod and Macrae, *Adoption Parenting,* 344–43, quotation at 341.
11. Nancy McCabe, *Crossing the Blue Willow Bridge: A Journey to My Daughter's Birthplace in China* (Columbia: University of Missouri Press, 2011), 19.
12. Heather Jacobson, *Culture Keeping: White Mothers, International Adoption, and the Negotiation of Family Difference* (Nashville: Vanderbilt University Press, 2008), 174. Jacobson discusses the idea that culture serves as a "proxy" for race (109).
13. Kimberly Leighton, "Addressing the Harms of Not Knowing One's Heredity: Lessons from Genealogical Bewilderment," *Adoption & Culture* 3 (2012): 63–107, quotation at 92.

For Leighton, the norms expressed by the idea of "genealogical bewilderment" serve to police racial boundaries and deny the reality of non-biogenetic families; it presupposes "that race is something that both is and should be reproduced."[14] Adoptees since 1991 from China are expected to form dual identities, white and Chinese, with their Chinese identities distinguishing them from the white families and communities with which they are also asked to identify. As David Eng points out, multiculturalism can denigrate rather than affirm difference by affirming only those differences that are palatable to mainstream US culture[15] or, as Jacobson points out, that fit into busy middle-class family schedules without fundamentally altering a traditionally Anglo American way of life.[16] In *The Love Wife,* Blondie cannot understand why Wendy is not thrilled that her class is doing a unit on China, but Wendy wants no part of anything that singles her out as different. She knows that racialized difference invites, not solves, racism. Jeff Gammage's *China Ghosts* affirms his daughters' roots in China yet also celebrates Jin Yu's six-year-old fondness for impersonating Disney princesses (her favorite is Belle) in a "sparkling dress-up gown" and "plastic high heels"; the image eerily echoes Liem's archival photo of herself as prom queen in tiara and glossy curls.[17] Despite the wish that a child might benefit from having two identities, and despite the identity affirmations promised by "culture keeping," the image suggests to the contrary how whiteness can remain hyperidealized for transracial adoptees.

Affirmations of "birth culture" are supposed not only to help ward off racism but also to compensate for an adoptee's feeling of loss, but as Cynthia Callahan points out, such affirmations disable rather than aid Sherman Alexie's John Smith in *Indian Killer,* who is raised with enough awareness of Native culture, and of the ways in which his appearance

---

14. Leighton, "Addressing the Harms," 77.

15. David L. Eng, *The Feeling of Kinship: Queer Liberalism and the Racialization of Intimacy* (Durham: Duke University Press, 2010), 2–12. Analogously, see Barbara Yngvesson's criticisms of Sweden's multiculturalist policies toward immigrants, including adopted children, which alienate and "other" the immigrant in the name of respecting cultural and linguistic differences: *Belonging in an Adopted World: Race, Identity, and Transnational Adoption* (Chicago: University of Chicago Press, 2010), 102–3. These critiques are anticipated by Toby Alice Volkman, "Embodying Chinese Culture: Transnational Adoption in North America," *Social Text* 74 (Spring 2003): 29–55, rpt. in *Cultures of Transnational Adoption,* ed. Toby Alice Volkman (Durham: Duke University Press, 2005), 81–113; and by Sara K. Dorow, *Transnational Adoption: A Cultural Economy of Race, Gender, and Kinship* (New York: New York University Press, 2006).

16. Jacobson, *Culture Keeping,* 107–24.

17. Jeff Gammage, *China Ghosts: My Daughter's Journey to American, My Passage to Fatherhood* (New York: Harper, 2007), 214–16, 219.

marks him as racially other, to understand that he is missing something. For Callahan, the novel "critiques the practice of cultural preservation advocated by adoption professionals as a way of offsetting adoption's losses by creating a sense of cultural identity."[18] There is no knowing, much less replacing, what feels to the adoptee to have been lost, especially if, as Leighton maintains, the feeling of loss is itself an artifact of racism's policing of racial boundaries and definitions of the family. By seeming to replace something lost and so denying that suffering has occurred, well-intended affirmations of identity based on "birth culture" may make life harder. Although the requirement to assimilate and be happy about it prevented Deann Borshay Liem from grieving the family, culture, and nation she felt she had lost and thus led to depression, the multicultural practices put in place by the adoptive parents of the 1990s and 2000s may, paradoxically, have the same results for some adoptees.

Looking "different" in a looks-based culture means that, for teenagers, much of the anxiety over racial identity still concerns appearance: the disparity between, on the one hand, their ethnic or racial looks, which raise what Jacobson calls "ethnic expectations," and, on the other, their acculturation in white families and communities. As one of Jacobson's parent interviewees remarks, "life is a lot easier if you look like who you are."[19] In published writing by adopted teenagers in the *Journal of Families with Children from China* and in *Pieces of Me: Who Do I Want To Be? Voices for and by Adopted Teens,* many poems and brief memoirs include some mention of the struggle to locate or create identity in the visual field. A poem that appeared in both publications opens:

> My inner identity has been discovered
> As my shadow has travelled to a new place.[20]

In this poem, written by fifteen-year-old Chloe Berger about "her first trip back to her birth country, Guatemala," identity is achieved when the "missing piece" of adoption is restored, and that "piece" is knowledge about the meaning of her appearance. The poem continues:

18. Cynthia Callahan, *Kin of Another Kind: Transracial Adoption in American Literature* (Ann Arbor: University of Michigan Press, 2011), 124.
19. Jacobson, *Culture Keeping,* 72.
20. Chloe Lauren America Berger, "Inner Soul," *Journal of Families with Children from China* 1, no. 1 (Spring 2009): 29, where it appeared as part of a preview of *Pieces of Me;* also published in *Pieces of Me: Who Do I Want To Be? Voices for and by Adopted Teens,* ed. Robert L. Ballard (Warren, NJ: EMK Press, 2009), 105.

My hair is still dark. I am still short.
Yet something has changed, it's different.
A new piece of the thousand-piece puzzle—found!
I know who I am by looking above
I am Latina, I am Jewish, I am Mayan

After reviewing and celebrating the speaker's multiple identifications, the poem concludes, "in reality I am only one thing / I am unique, I am me." Like this one, many poems and short memoirs by young adoptees end with assertions of achieved wholeness and identity that seem produced more by the demands of literary form (the piece needs to end somehow) than by persuasively represented feeling. In Chloe Berger's poem, "I know who I am" by "looking above," which a couple of lines later is glossed by stars, sun, and moon; but since the words "looking above" are followed immediately by the listing of three ethnic identities, and since in *Pieces of Me* the top of the page bears a photograph of the author, "looking" and even "looking above" seem to point first to the author's appearance. I know who I am, the poem seems to say, for this reason: since I have seen people who look like me in my birth country, I now know how to read my own looks.

Yet this kind of assertion is often undermined by experience, as the effortful optimism of Berger's conclusion predicts. Fourteen-year-old Mei Lan Fogarty, writing in the 2009 "Kids' Issue" of the *Journal of Families with Children from China,* describes feeling "wrong" when, even growing up in multiethnic New York City, she feels she does not "fit in" and must constantly fend off strangers' "ignorant" interpellations of her as "Japanese or Korean":[21] "I stick out like a sore thumb . . . when I go places with my 'typical American family.' . . . So many times I wonder what life would be like with my biological mother in China, or as a biological daughter to my parents." Hoping to "fit in" better where "almost everyone 'looks' like me," she visits China but discovers she still stands out, in this case for her American aura: "Even in China where I could not look more Chinese, I still felt as though I . . . did not belong." (Hong Kong suits her better; she meets people like herself who look Chinese and speak English; and she ends on a tentatively affirmative note: "I know who I am and where I most belong, or at least I am getting there.") The

21. Mei Lan Fogarty, "Homeward Bound," *Journal of Families with Children from China* 1, no. 2 (Fall 2009): 22. See also Abigail Jie-Mei Ren Scott, "Racial Identity," *Journal of Families with Children from China* 1, no. 2 (Fall 2009): 25, for a similar expression of discomfort in various locations and a similar closing claim that all is well.

problem stems from her having had the illusion, presented so hopefully in Berger's poem, that identity is the same as appearance; she is misled by this notion into thinking that she will feel at home and feel "at home with [her]self" when she can mingle with those she resembles. Similarly, many adoptees express the wish either to look like their adoptive parents (Katy Robinson recalls watching her mother apply makeup in the mirror and saying to her, "I would give anything to look like you"[22]) or to fit in in their home countries ("I was ashamed because I was Korean blood, and I didn't know anything about Korea"[23]). Social norms require appearance to match identity.

Is what you look like who you are? As often as they describe searching for their families or places of origin, adoptees describe searching for physical signs on and in their bodies—or searching for the right interpretation of such visible signs—that would establish their identities beyond doubt and beyond the vicissitudes of adoption. In the belief, or wish, that they are who they are by and from birth, they (and sometimes their parents and others who care for them and represent them) seek out signs inhering in their bodies or, in the absence of inborn signs, early acquired marks that might perform the same function: signs that, rightly decoded, would tell them who they are. In Europe and Britain, foundling stories often concern the child whose outward appearance or markings lead to identification of his origin and identity: Joseph Andrews has his birthmark, Oliver Twist his face, Harry Potter his scar. In the United States, habits of racialization mean that skin color and other epidermal signs are presumed both to determine and to reveal identity.[24] For adoptees, however, epidermal signs are sometimes misleading and confusing. Judith Butler critiques the normative expectation that "we manifest and maintain self-identity at all times and require that others do the same";[25] adoptees are among those who may most vividly embody

---

22. Robinson, *Single Square Picture,* 87.

23. Ami Nafzger, in *Once They Hear My Name: Korean Adoptees and Their Journeys Toward Identity,* ed. Ellen Lee, Marilyn Lammert, and Mary Ann Hess (Silver Spring, MD: Tamarisk Books, 2008), 30.

24. In support of this view, anthropologist Signe Howell argues that seeking to reconnect with origins is a product of specifically American preoccupations with autonomous individuality and with race, by claiming that transnational adoptees in Norway seldom express such a wish as intensely, although Scandinavians have been active in creating Korean adoptee identity: "Return Journeys and the Search for Roots: Contradictory Values Concerning Identity," in *International Adoption: Global Inequalities and the Circulation of Children,* ed. Diana Marre and Laura Briggs (New York: New York University Press, 2009), 256–70, this discussion at 258–61.

25. Judith Butler, *Giving an Account of Oneself* (New York: Fordham University Press, 2005), 42.

this critique, even as any teenager might, to the contrary, reasonably feel the need to "know who I am" and to be able to perform that identity clearly in public.

In this chapter I argue that there is a link among loss, visual appearance, and identity, but not always the direct one that is imagined by the young writers I have been quoting and the adults who advise them. Identity is not necessarily to be found or created by the assumption or resumption of the social identity encoded in appearance. Instead, just as origins may be invented in the aftermath of trauma, identity can stem from loss itself, as those adoptees who claim their identity as adopted (rather than as derived from an origin) have recognized. If adoption involves injury, that injury is not only what takes away identity: it may also be the foundation of it. Injury and loss produce their own visual markers, markers that may function in the same identity-conferring way as the kinds of visual signs that are inborn. Traveling across demographic groups not usually considered together (domestic and transnational adoptees, transracial and race-matched adoptees), as well as across genres of representation (memoirs short and long, fiction, advice literature, sociology, history), this chapter explores adoptees' wishful searches for legible signs of identity, the crises that ensue when inborn signs fail to bear intrinsic meanings, and some complex pathways by which loss may lead to identity by way of the visual signs of injury.

IS WHAT YOU LOOK LIKE WHO YOU ARE? VISIBLE RACE, MARKED BLOOD, FAMILY RESEMBLANCE, AND THE UNCERTAINTY OF ADOPTED IDENTITY

Transracial adoptees are interpellated in racialist and often racist ways into the social category matching their racial appearance, and yet they may not possess the secure sense of belonging on which racial identity depends. Just as Chloe Berger, Mei Lan Fogarty, and other young transnational adoptees of color must continuously question the relation between their looks and their identity, black transracial adoptees in the United States are expected to be black, maybe even more than South American and Asian adoptees are expected to be who they appear to be. And yet to look black is not the same as to be black or to feel secure in a black identity. The discourse of racialization creates the expectation that skin tone can be read as a sign of inborn and immutable identity, but the recent historical experience of transracial adoption reveals that "ethnic expectations" can be hard for adoptees to meet. As Jacobson points out, parents, children, and adoption professionals may believe that racial and ethnic identity is innate, yet "the construction of social identities, even those that are popularly seen as ascribed at birth . . . require effort and labor."[26] As a consequence, the social practice of transracial adoption has long been troubled by debates over whether black or biracial children must be raised in black households in order to learn the black identity that can only be acquired environmentally or whether, by contrast, racial appearance and personal identity as formed in the family can be disarticulated without harm to the child.[27]

In Phil Bertelsen's documentary film *Outside Looking In: Transracial Adoption in America,* the filmmaker, himself transracially adopted, attempts to foster in his transracially adopted nephew (also named Phil, his white sister's child) a positive sense of African American identity. He wants to counter his sister's claim that race does not matter and to compensate for the boy's consequent lack of African American identity. Taking young Phil on a visit to Harlem, Bertelsen knows his impulse comes from projecting his needs onto this younger version of himself: he ironizes his attempts "to put something in him that was missing in me" and laughs at his failed attempt to show him the Apollo theater (he was "next door playing with the new Play Station"). Yet back home in Tucson, Phil asks of his nephew, "Please describe to me who you are, what you look like."[28] While Bertelsen's question insists on an absolute synonymity between appearance and identity, the boy refuses his uncle's terms, answering literal-mindedly, "I'm brownish black, I'm eleven years old . . ." Although Bertelsen has seemed to mock his own normative definitions of racial identity (he knows that to be black in the United States in the year 2000 does not require veneration of the Harlem of the 1950s), he also refuses to acknowledge that there could be a livable gap between appearance and identity. Bertelsen wants the mark of race to determine identity, because he himself feels lacking ("something . . . that was missing in me"). He wishes that looking black had given him a black inside. His nephew, however, does not feel this need—or does not feel it yet.

In such contemporary documentary sources—films, interviews, memoirs—adoptees express a range of views and feelings about the real

26. Jacobson, *Culture Keeping,* 72, 58.

27. See chap, 2, note 33, for a review of some of the works participating in and commenting on this controversy, sparked by the National Association of Black Social Workers in 1972 calling for an end to transracial adoptions.

28. Phil Bertelsen, *Outside Looking In: Transracial Adoption in America,* written and dir. Phil Bertelson, prod. Katy Chevigny, exec. prod. Quincy Jones Media Group, film, 57 minutes (Arts Engine/Big Mouth/Independent Television Service, 2001).

Figure 2. "Describe to me who you are, what you look like." From Phil Bertelsen, *Outside Looking In: Transracial Adoption in America.*

or potential disjunction between what they look like to others and what they feel themselves to be. On the one hand, the disarticulation of identity from racial signs may feel like freedom and self-determination; on the other, it may feel disorienting and may strike others as a form of false consciousness. In *BirthMarks,* her study of transracial adoption based on interviews with adoptees, parents, and social workers and on her own experiences as an adoptee, Sandra Patton is by no means essentialist in her assumptions about adoptive racial identity. She understands transracial adoptees' racial identities to be necessarily fluid, subject to a variety of influences, and evolving over time rather than fixed. Because their "identities are forged without genealogical patterns," and because of their "discursive roots and routes" and their experience of racial hybridity and boundary-crossing, transracial adoptees' stories in Patton's view tend to reflect the constructedness of racial categories with particular acuteness.[29] She means "discursive roots" literally: adoptees sometimes possess "origin narratives beginning in a public agency rather than a hu-

29. Sandra Patton, *BirthMarks: Transracial Adoption in Contemporary America* (New York: New York University Press, 2000), 6, 21 (hereafter cited in the text).

man body," narratives that "begin with an anonymous infant written into being by a social worker in a secret file" (*BirthMarks*, 21, 33). In a chapter titled "Navigating Racial Routes,"[30] Patton quotes at length and discusses a series of interviews about racial identity with adoptees who share Patton's personal sense that, because of growing up without biological kin, "our identities were not 'natural,' but rather, contingent and constructed. We knew that we could easily have grown up in other families, and thus have been entirely different from the selves we now knew" (80).

Among the contingencies and constructions that constitute adoptive identity is race. "Skin color," Patton continues, served "to highlight the gaps between actual skin tone and the constructed categories of Black and White." Black and white are constructs, and Patton has been suggesting that assignment of children of whatever "skin tone" to one or the other of these categories is one of the contingencies that family placement by state or private agencies may arbitrarily determine. She also points out that skin color and "culture" are not the same: interviewing Cat Benton, who identifies with all three categories ("biracial, Black and White" [*BirthMarks*, 82]) and resists the societal imperative to choose one, Patton comments that "there was an interesting slippage between her biological definition as biracial—having one Black and one White birth parent—and the cultural familiarity with both groups that she acquired as a member of a White family living in a racially diverse neighborhood" (83). She is also careful to describe genetics as a "cultural discourse" rather than as innately meaningful scientific fact (113). In other words, Patton does not take it for granted that "biological definition" or skin color determines culture or identity.

Nonetheless, Patton also reflexively treats adoptees with varying degrees of African descent as if their African Americanness had an essential reality that underlies and undermines whatever "contingent and constructed" racial identities they have negotiated for themselves in their complex and unique social situations. Some interviewees have very light skin; one shows Patton that "unless she was tanned, it was very difficult to tell she was African American" (*BirthMarks*, 80). In making this comment, Patton implies that, despite the potentially vital gaps between color and identity, and despite her frequently reiterated assertion that racial categories are constructed, an individual either is or is not African

30. Hawley Fogg-Davis's book, published two years after Patton's, also uses the metaphor of navigation for transracial adoptees' active process of racialization in contrast to the traditional notion of race as an inborn heritage; see *The Ethics of Transracial Adoption* (Ithaca: Cornell University Press, 2002).

American, and by blood inheritance essentially: it can be difficult to discern (it requires subtle reading of the skin), but it cannot be doubted.

In this context, Patton introduces Kristin Rhineholt, a transracial adoptee raised "by White parents in a nearly all-White Pennsylvania community" and, in Patton's terms, "strongly White-identified" (*BirthMarks* 86, 71–72). In proof of this Patton says that "Kristin unquestioningly accepted stereotypes associating African Americans with poverty" and that her parents "did not teach her to recognize racist stereotypes" (72, 73). Patton's chief example of Rhineholt's ignorance about stereotypes emerges from a conversation about *Little Black Sambo,* which Patton acknowledges she has not read but which she knows to be a compendium of racist stereotypes. Kristin defends her mother's having read it to her as a child; "I like it," she comments. Although she knows "people are appalled" by this book, "*I don't see what other people see*" (72–73, emphasis in original). For Patton, Rhineholt's failure to "see what other people see" betrays her ignorance about racist stereotypes and her parents' failure to equip her with racial "survival skills." Could it mean something else, though? A child's reading with her mother is a complex social experience, and in the same conversation Rhineholt reports that her mother also "used to do voices to Brer Rabbit" (72). Even in southern white author Joel Chandler Harris's retellings (Rhineholt's mother's most likely source), Brer Rabbit is a witty trickster figure from African tradition; Bannerman's Sambo, too, despite the inexcusable racial labeling, is a successful (South Asian, not African or African American) trickster who looks on as the foolish tigers quarrel themselves into nonentity, enabling him to recover his fine clothes and bring the butter home to his mother. (Patton, not having read the book, mischaracterizes it: "The thrust of the plot is that Sambo is stupid enough to allow tigers to repeatedly trick him out of the new clothes his mother has just given him" [72].) These Reconstruction and Jim Crow–era books may have been unfortunate choices, since there were plenty of race-positive alternatives during Rhineholt's childhood in the 1970s, yet her mother may not have simply been imparting racist stereotypes to her child. What if "not see[ing] what other people see" means a difference of view, not a deficiency?

Patton contrasts Rhineholt unfavorably to transracial adoptees raised in households that taught "critical race skills" and "survival skills." Andrea Bailey, for example, adopted from Africa by two white Africa scholars who were "committed to movements for social justice . . . [,] had been given a solid foundation that included an understanding of racism and oppression, as well as an appreciation of African and African American cultures" (*BirthMarks,* 73). And yet Bailey discusses with Patton her ongoing "identity problems" and her "anger": "though her parents did 'all the right things' with regard to race, she still struggled over her racial identity and the sense that she did not belong anywhere socially" (81). Patton's interviewees express a range of feelings about the contingency and constructedness of their identities; some, like Bailey, struggle to claim one stable identity, while others—typically the lighter-skinned, biracial adoptees in the group—celebrate their multiple identifications. Samantha Bennett, for example, who can be "taken for" Jewish, East Indian, or Mexican, depending on where she is, finds her unreadable racial identity "something I could play with" (76). Rhineholt actually seems happier and more stable with her improbable white identification than interviewees such as Bailey whom Patton sees more favorably.[31]

Despite Patton's eloquent theorizing about the contingency of racial identity and the non-identity between skin tone and culture, she cannot see past Rhineholt's skin to accept Rhineholt's sense of herself. In the following exchange, Rhineholt has been describing her parents' insistence on standard English at home and her black friends' surprise that she does not share their idiom.

SANDI: So do people tell you you "sound White"?
KRISTIN: Oh yeah. Like I don't think anybody would ever mistake me for being Black if they never saw me. Never. Never in a million years.
SANDI: Huh. That's interesting though, the way you put that—"mistake" you for being Black. Like you're not really—
KRISTIN: That's true.
SANDI: That's interesting. A little slippage there.
KRISTIN: Yeah. Okay, rewind.
SANDI: Well, so, play with that a little bit. I mean *what are you*? . . . How do you self-identify?
KRISTIN: Well. [pause]
SANDI: Or who are you?

31. In some ways Rhineholt's situation is like that of someone who is racially passing, and I do not disagree with Patton that her life could be difficult. For an interesting parallel, see Yvette Christiansë's complex defense of a woman of color who passed in apartheid South Africa, building a livable identity from disavowal: "Passing Away: The Unspeakable (Losses) of Postapartheid South Africa," in *Loss: The Politics of Mourning,* ed. David L. Eng and David Kazanjian (Berkeley: University of California Press, 2003), 372–95.

KRISTIN: [pause] I would probably say I am White with very, very dark skin. (*BirthMarks,* 86–87, emphasis in original)

Patton insists here that Rhineholt is "really" black and requires her to acknowledge her error in failing to recall this fact: Rhineholt is not allowed to speak of others "mistaking" her for black. While in the interview with Cat Benton, Patton criticizes the "slippage" from skin color to culture as an intellectually sloppy category error, here Patton criticizes Rhineholt's "slippage" in failing to equate skin tone with identity. Patton's imposition of this norm (Rhineholt is "really" black) makes it very difficult for Rhineholt to speak honestly thereafter or even to speak: the transcript shows her pausing again and again. When Patton reformulates Rhineholt's discreditable position in abstract terms, it sounds just like Patton's own view from a few pages earlier, when she was talking with Cat Benton: "That's a really powerful statement. So in a sense, you're saying you're making a real distinction between skin color and the way you see the world" (87). According to Patton's theory, it ought to be possible for Rhineholt to assent to this and embrace the way she lives out this distinction. But Rhineholt has already conceded that "obviously everyone knows, 'cause they look at me," and she stumbles and pauses in trying to reply. Patton follows up by confirming that she indeed denies the "distinction between skin color and the way you see the world," asking, "what does it mean to be *really* Black in that perspective?" In this way she indicates that she and Rhineholt both know she is "really Black" and Rhineholt is only pretending to herself about being white.[32]

Kristin Rhineholt's contestation of the reality written on her skin may strike readers as delusional, and yet her resistance to Patton's line of questioning makes visible and puts into crisis Patton's wish that particular skin tones would consistently bear the intrinsic meaning of particular racial identities. If only identity followed genetically, automatically, and organically from skin tone, then adoption would not create the unstable, shifting identities Patton's interviewees report. Patton often celebrates her interviewees' skill in navigating these instabilities, and she patiently analyzes the complexity with which identities can be found to be constructed, and yet passages such as this one suggest an underlying wish for a simple, essential correspondence between genetically inherited looks and social and cultural identity.

32. Patton does the same thing in the interview with Samantha Bennett, the "truth" of whose half-black identity is revealed only after decades of concealment by social workers and adoptive parents.

The encounter between Patton and Kristin Rhineholt in *BirthMarks* mirrors an encounter in another scholarly work by a transracial adoptee published in the same year, *In Their Own Voices: Transracial Adoptees Tell Their Stories,* comprising interviews that Rhonda Roorda conducted with other transracial adoptees and including her own interview with her coeditor. Here, as in *BirthMarks,* an adoptee's resistance to assuming the racial role into which he has been interpellated both challenges and activates the interviewer's insistence on the fixed meaning of racial signs. One of the book's interview subjects, Keith Bigelow, who was adopted at age five by a white family and who identifies as black, nonetheless refuses to identify as African American on these grounds:

> I'd be saying that I believe I have current roots in Africa, that that's where my tradition comes from, that's where I was born. . . . Some would argue that our lineage is from Africa. But I don't believe that I have to identify myself as an African American because of it.[33]

His identity and the counterintuitive narrative of origins that underpins it (to paraphrase, I am black, but my forebears did not come from Africa), which disarticulate blackness from black culture, make little sense relative to US norms of racialization. Contrary to Bigelow's strong sense of self, Roorda insists that "you've basically been stripped of your culture and your heritage because of the family with whom you lived" (*In Their Own Voices,* 226). Her questions keep after him to confess an investment in African American culture that he does not share:

> RR: As a father, is it important that your daughter be raised in the African American community?
> KB: It's important that she be exposed to many communities, not just the African American community. We'll do our part to ensure that aspects of the African American culture are there for her to explore herself.
> RR: Why is exposing your daughter to the African American culture important? (*In Their Own Voices,* 221)

Or again later:

33. Rita J. Simon and Rhonda M. Roorda, eds., *In Their Own Voices: Transracial Adoptees Tell Their Stories* (New York: Columbia University Press, 2000), 225 (hereafter cited in the text).

RR: The National Association of Black Social Workers has taken a strong position against transracial adoption. In most cases they say that transracial adoption does not expose the child to his or her ethnicity. What do you think?

KB: . . . Eating the traditional black food of the South isn't the "end" all and "be" all of being black.

RR: But isn't partaking of these traditional foods a part of what makes up the black community?

KB: It's a part of the black tradition, but it doesn't determine one's success or failure. (*In Their Own Voices,* 223)

Refusing genetic or epidermal definitions of identity, he also refuses to accept Roorda's view that because of adoption he has been "stripped of [his] culture and [his] heritage."

Bigelow answers Roorda's charge by asserting, counterintuitively, that he is "more black then they'll ever be" because he had to think so deliberately about himself (*In Their Own Voices,* 226). As "different," he had to "make a way out of no way. This is an education you can't get as a black individual raised in a black family" (227). He credits his mother for helping him think through his responses to racism at school. "We'd work it through . . . intellectually," he says. Instead of yearning for his birth mother or the same-race role model Roorda wishes he had had, Bigelow values the instruction his white mother taught herself to offer him more highly than the visual racial mirroring she could not provide. Nonetheless, Roorda's closing questions continue to insist that he conform to her picture of black identity: "Who is Keith . . . Keith, but are you black?" (230–31). Bigelow counters this insistence by emphasizing his sense of personal empowerment from being able to choose among an array of social roles. "Yes, I am black . . . I can go to the store and get my greens and boil 'em . . . I can use my euphonics when I need to or my vernacular black English Ebonics when I want to. But I can also assume a businessman's mentality and speak like someone who has an education and wants to be successful" (231). Bigelow's remarks may sound—as they clearly do to Roorda, and as Kristin Rhineholt's do to Patton—like self-hating racism: both Bigelow and Rhineholt accept racist stereotypes of blacks as poor, undereducated, and failed. Nonetheless Bigelow's definition of blackness as a role he can assume at will and, more broadly, as the capacity to play various social roles, rather than as a genetically given identity, works for him and productively troubles his interviewer's normative views of black identity.

Although both Roorda and Patton take transracial adoption as their subject, one of the most striking interviews in Patton's book is with a white woman adopted by white parents, and this is ironically the interview that gives *BirthMarks* its title. As for most of Patton's interview subjects, skin tone was the most salient feature in determining her placement, yet Thorley Richardson was troubled by her official status as *un*marked. Although to have skin of any color, including white, would seem self-evidently to be racially marked, within the discourse of transracial adoption only certain aspects of physical appearance constitute marks. Rather than appreciating the privilege attached to the status of "unmarked," Richardson reveals its negative value for her. After describing having been "matched" as a baby in 1965, she goes on:

> So this idea of it just being so easy to pick me out of one place and put me down in another, and just having me fit in without any seams seems strange to me. . . . The most oft-adopted children in that time were babies without any marks or physical problems. So I think that made me feel that kind of the absence of a *birthmark*—made it kind of easy for me to just be transplanted into another family. . . . The idea that I didn't have any distinguishing marks, that there wasn't anything distinguishable about *me* physically always bothered me. (*BirthMarks,* 19)

In the analysis prompted by this passage, Patton reviews the history of matching in adoption, using Richardson's remarks to underscore the historical differentiation between black, mixed-race, and disabled children on the one hand as the "marked" and, on the other, white children as the "unmarked." The passage and her discussion of it take their place in her presentation of "the *literal* social construction" (21) of races and identities in transracial adoption. But Patton does not mention the most striking feature of the passage, which is Richardson's yearning to have been physically, visibly marked: to have some distinguishing feature that would have sustained a single, unmistakable identity from birth through her life as an adopted person. Whiteness does not count.

By silently including Richardson's expression of this wish while not commenting on it, Patton seems at once to acknowledge and to disavow what appears to be her own wish. She ends this section abruptly by turning from the politics of "marked" and "unmarked" to the birthmark as metaphor for the adoptee's psychic losses: for children matched to same-race families, "the birthmarks of difference stemming from adoption were only internal, yet deeply felt" (*BirthMarks,* 20). This change of subject, with the elevation of "birthmark" from literal to figurative, is in keeping with Patton's emphasis on the discursive rather than the biological constitution of identities, and yet Richardson's wish is for an external, visible sign, a wish Patton seems to ignore. It is here that Patton first mentions her own adoption, which appeared to match an "unmarked" child with a white family, although she much later learned that she was born "half Jewish." Perhaps, like Richardson, Patton wished for a racial "birthmark" that would declare her identity to all who saw her, and yet she does not say so directly. Later in the book, faced with Kristin Rhineholt's refusal to see the unmistakable visual signs of her own race, Patton exhibits her frustration, as we have seen. Is it a kind of envy? Perplexed about her own unmarked ethnicity, she quotes herself casually asking someone, "What does it mean then that I'm supposedly half-Jewish, but didn't grow up with that cultural knowledge?" (91); to this her interlocutor replies, "It means you would have been killed in Nazi Germany." This arresting remark (the reader surely expects a polite reply about the flexible relation nowadays between birth and identity) allows Patton to conclude her discussion of Rhineholt by commenting, "racial hatred operates on absolutes. . . . Transracial adoptees do not have the choice of defining themselves out of the category Black" (92). Although she has elsewhere celebrated the deftness of biracial adoptees' racial navigation, she slams Rhineholt's denial of the essential meaning of her skin color up against the wall of genocidal racism, to which there can be no reply apart from the hope that genocidal racism not be permitted to be the overriding determinant of all human identity.

If a work of social analysis can be said to have an unconscious, perhaps, like Richardson, Patton's text is expressing a wish, on behalf of its author, for a racial "birthmark" that would declare her identity to herself as well as to others, even when such marks make their bearers painfully vulnerable. Wishing to have been able to know herself as Jewish from birth onward, she is troubled by Rhineholt's contrary racial self-definition that denies the legibility of epidermal racial signs. Similarly, an adoption advice book airs the pitfalls of "invisible adoption" (what used to be called "matching"): a child who can pass for her parents' biological offspring may feel that "reminders that she looks like [her adoptive parents] belittle her genetic heritage and discount the value of her birth family."[34] The very notion of an "invisible adoption" seems to

34. Karen Holt, "Invisible Adoption: My Child Is Just Like Me," in MacLeod and Macrae, *Adoption Parenting*, 330–31.

call out for a mark of difference that would clearly indicate the identity of the person who bears it on her body.

Although both Roorda and Patton interview individuals who value the room to navigate their racial identities enabled by their ambiguous racial appearance and their mixed or non-normative socialization, the tendency of both books is to confirm norms of racialized identity. These writers, I am arguing, like filmmaker Phil Bertelsen, express a wish for adoptees to share a more deeply felt alignment between racialized appearance and personal identity. To recall the succinct formulation Jacobson records, "life is a lot easier if you look like who you are."

Sometimes, however, instead of external marks, signs presumed to lie within the body—DNA, blood, cells, bones—embody the wish for a marked, intrinsically meaningful body, a body that is coextensive with psychological and social identity. Since the arrival of DNA testing, which has led to reunions between separated parents and children and (with less certainty) between birth siblings, hopes for determinative signs of identity often accumulate around evidence of objectively measurable chemical signs. But such signs are only the most recent form of hopes traditionally invested in the figure of "blood," an imaginary construct of the foundational, the biologically irrefutable and real, that is often based on the marks of appearance that it is thought to originate.

For example, Trace A. DeMeyer, a "Lost Bird" raised in a white home with no knowledge of her ancestry, describes her conviction throughout her childhood that she must be Native: "No one ever said I was Indian. I just knew."[35] Her yearning to discover physical signs of this identity is fulfilled when a DNA test confirms the identity of her birth father, whose mother was Shawnee-Cherokee. "Indian Country is ancient," she writes; in her romantic view, "our cells are identical to those of our ancestors of 30,000 years ago" (*One Small Sacrifice*, 9). This counterfactual claim about her cells and her insistence that she "knew" from some internal source draw on the literary genre of magic realism; referring to Alexie among others, Seo-Young Chu describes as "science fiction" (specifically, "telepathy") the belief in the physical transmissibility and heritability of memory.[36] Perhaps surprisingly, DeMeyer never claims that she

35. Trace A. DeMeyer, *One Small Sacrifice: Lost Children of the Indian Adoption Projects* (Greenfield, MA: [self-published], 2010), 44, also 158 (hereafter cited in the text).

36. Chu's examples include the "postmemory han" that Jane Jeong Trenka claims she receives in utero from her mother, and she links Trenka's and other Korean Americans' representations of "postmemory han" with the embodied inheritance of ancestral suffering in Alexie and in Octavia Butler. See Seo-Young Chu, "Science Fiction and

looks Native; rather, whatever marks her identity is internal. DeMeyer's belief in the innateness of her Native identity arises from her present needs: knowing she had been abandoned was an "injury which felt like an open wound" (*One Small Sacrifice*, 14), and she constructs around that injury the genetic legacy and the distinctive "cells" that alone can repair this wound, she feels, by providing the foundation for a Native identity she experiences as innate. While enrollment in the Cherokee nation requires documentary evidence, she asks: "Does a piece of paper, a name on a roll, or our blood make us Cherokee? All I have of my Cherokee culture are questions, and the voices I feel in my bones" (160). The imagined marking and expressivity of "blood" and "bones" are produced by the wish to restore, stabilize, and ground a desperately desired identity.

Belief in the value of blood connection and in the derivation of identity from blood is the centerpiece of adoptee rights advocacy. Betty Jean Lifton writes: "Most people take their blood relatedness as much for granted as the air they breathe. . . . I have come to believe in the course of my research that it is unnatural for members of the human species to grow up separated from and without knowledge of their natural clan."[37] And indeed it is a commonplace in personal writings by adoptees to express yearning for or celebration of blood connection and to link core identity to blood. Having just met her "blood mother and father," Angie Johnston (a domestic, same-race adoptee) recognizes in her bond with her own newborn baby "the importance of blood coursing through my flesh" and knows that "she would always carry me, through her blood, for the rest of her life."[38] Similarly birthmother Meredith Hall meditates on "cellular" connections between mother and child:

> Women carry fetal cells from all the babies they have carried. . . . My three children are carried in my bloodstream still . . . Their cells crossing permeable boundaries and joining mine, [they] float every day through my body, part of me. . . . The mother's cells are also carried in the child. . . . Every day I spent longing for my lost child. . . . I moved in his bloodstream, part of him.[39]

Postmemory Han in Contemporary Korean American Literature," *MELUS* 33, no. 4 (Winter 2008): 97–121; the term "postmemory" comes from Marianne Hirsch, *Family Frames: Photography, Narrative, and Postmemory* (Cambridge: Harvard University Press, 1997).

37. Betty Jean Lifton, *Journey of the Adopted Self: A Quest for Wholeness* (New York: Basic Books, 1994), 67, 8.

38. Angie Johnston, "Blood Matters," in Ballard, *Pieces of Me*, 36–37, quotation at 37.

39. Meredith Hall, *Without a Map: A Memoir* (Boston: Beacon Press, 2007), 176–77.

The young adoptees writing about their experiences in *Pieces of Me* and the *Journal of Families with Children from China* reflect this normative assumption about the importance of blood connection and the presumed link between appearance and blood. One teenager writes of missing her "birth mom" because she looks "at my friends and their parents and I'm amazed by how alike some of them look" and wants "to look like my parents and my family"; in her extended family of blonds with "grayish blue eyes . . . I sometimes think that I don't belong there because I'm not blood related to them."[40]

Against such a view, Mark Jerng argues that claims about "blood" reveal an effort to represent as internal or intrinsic an identity that can only be constituted by relations with others. For example, the attribution of "black blood" to Faulkner's ambiguously raced adoptee Joe Christmas, Jerng argues, follows rather than precedes (much less causes) the relationships and interactions that produce it as a necessity.[41] Discussing the 1989 United Nations Convention on the Rights of the Child, which declares "the right of the child to preserve his or her identity," Jerng points out that "biological, normative kinship" is assumed to be, although it is not inherently, "the condition for personhood," and birth and genetic identity are tacitly allowed to "stand in for a placed-ness in nation, family, and race that exceeds the biological."[42] The identity that the child has a right to preserve is mistakenly understood as "immanent in the assumed . . . integrity of the person."[43] But, Jerng continues,

> Precisely because identity is *not* something inherent in the person but is guaranteed by something elsewhere . . . the right to know one's identity is a right *to* others, a right to a larger community that will ensure the personhood in question. The right to know one's identity . . . is not just a mission of inward self-discovery but a process of making claims on others for protection and preservation.[44]

Lamenting (for human subjects generally) the idealization of the auton-

40. Eliza Louise Danjian Scofield, "A Challenging Problem and How I Solved It," *Journal of Families with Children from China* 2, no. 2 (Fall 2010): 50.

41. Mark Jerng, *Claiming Others: Transracial Adoption and National Belonging* (Minneapolis: University of Minnesota Press, 2010), 105–12.

42. Jerng, *Claiming Others,* 143–45.

43. Jerng, *Claiming Others,* 146; see also Yngvesson's critique of the idea of the rights-bearing child as requiring that the child be thought of as "an entity *separable* from the family"; this "individualist discourse . . . entails risks for children" (*Belonging,* 49–50).

44. Jerng, *Claiming Others,* 146.

omous, self-contained "I," Judith Butler insists that, in the formation of the subject, "*I am my relation to you* . . . given over to a 'you' without whom I cannot be and upon whom I depend to survive."[45] For Jerng, observing how adopted identity involves especially conspicuous acts of "claiming others," "blood" is a projection of the social onto the body that misdefines identity as the product of preexisting genetic inheritance.

Although the figure of "blood" represents inherited identity as internal to the body, while marked appearance figures inherited identity as external, these signs of innate identity are often interchangeable, as their meanings, uses, and valuations are interdependent. To share blood is to share looks; to find those who look like you is to find your blood kin and, as well, to find who you are. But internal and external marks are signs of one another in an often confusing inversion of cause and effect. Physical resemblance, not only shared skin tone but also similarity of facial features and body type, is thought to serve as a marker of innate identity, the outward sign of internal, blood, or genetic connection (as Indigo Williams puts it, "You carry [your heritage] within your soul, and in your appearance"). And yet until recently, blood or genes have been knowable only by, and are therefore effectively produced by, appearance, just as, in DeMeyer's narrative, knowledge about "ancient" Native cells can only be inferred from other evidence. Among families who have adopted from China, DNA testing of suspected biological siblings is only initiated after photographs have provided evidence of physical similarity (and then the DNA evidence is often inconclusive).[46] In this circular way, blood and genetic connections are constructed on the basis of visible similarities that, however, we value only because we think they signify or are produced by genes and blood.

The wish for appearance to confer identity and meaning has a long history of intersection with beliefs about blood and genetic connection; looking at earlier representations of such wishes and beliefs can shed light on the wishful element of such beliefs as they persist in the present. As Marianne Novy and others have noted, nineteenth-century British fiction about orphans and adoptees—inheritors of the romance tradition of the miraculous foundling story—is filled with exact, compelling,

45. Judith Butler, *Giving an Account of Oneself,* 81, emphasis in original.

46. See e.g. Susan Rittenhouse, "Finding an Unexpected Sibling," in MacLeod and Macrae, *Adoption Parenting,* 215. See also *China Connection: A Newsletter for New England Families Who Have Adopted Children from China* 11, no. 2 (Dec. 2005) (special issue devoted to siblings).

and identity-conferring family resemblances.[47] Oliver Twist is instantly recognizable. Not only does Mr. Brownlow, on first seeing Oliver, notice his resemblance to an old friend, but also he sees Oliver as the "living copy" of what will later be revealed to be a portrait of Oliver's long-dead mother: "The eyes, the head, the mouth; every feature was the same. The expression was, for the instant, so precisely alike, that the minutest line seemed copied with a startling accuracy."[48] As Goldie Morgentaler points out, this resemblance not only provides the clue to Oliver's true (birth) identity but also accounts for the virtuous character that has remained intact despite his harsh upbringing, his "essential self [and] internal identity, which has been fixed at birth," because "Oliver is what he has inherited."[49] The resemblance is striking enough, and in the world of Dickens's novel such evidence counts as reliable enough, that the plot takes a decisive turn here: henceforward Mr. Brownlow will seek the restoration of Oliver's birthright. George Eliot's Daniel Deronda, similarly, is instantly recognizable to his grandfather's old friend Joseph Kalonymos when Deronda, not yet aware that he is a Jew, visits the synagogue in Frankfurt and the two are seated, by coincidence, side by side. Although Deronda, questioned, shakes off Kalonymos's touch and his hint that Deronda is Jewish, Kalonymos knows who Deronda is, despite having been told, decades before, that his friend's grandson was dead. Again, this uncanny identification by appearance is so certain that on the strength of it Kalonymos takes steps to prompt Deronda's momentous meeting with his mother and to ensure his inheritance of his grandfather's papers and, with them, his ambitions for the Jews. And although Eliot emphasizes the permanent difference that Deronda's upbringing as an English gentleman has made, Deronda's instinctive affinity for Mirah and Mordecai makes it clear that his Jewishness is innate in his character.

Discredited nineteenth-century theories of reproduction account for the frequency of such uncanny resemblances, in which "internal identity" is duplicated from one generation to the next and is rendered visually recognizable by a duplication of facial features. According to Mor-

47. See, e.g., Marianne Novy's discussion of Dickens in *Reading Adoption: Family and Difference in Fiction and Drama* (Ann Arbor: University of Michigan Press, 2005), 94–119.

48. Charles Dickens, *Oliver Twist* (1837–38) (New York: W. W. Norton, 1993), 86.

49. Goldie Morgentaler, *Dickens and Heredity: When Like Begets Like* (New York: St. Martin's, 2000), 44, 39. For a contrasting emphasis, on Dickens's orphans' oedipal hostility toward their birth fathers rather than on their biogenetic ties, see Anny Sadrin, *Parentage and Inheritance in the Novels of Charles Dickens* (Cambridge: Cambridge University Press, 1994).

gentaler, Oliver's heredity reflects the early nineteenth-century belief in "preformation," the theory that the essence of every human being was formed at the Creation, even though Dickens also believed that children represented the blending of two parents' heritages, a belief that, along with the existence of mixed-race persons, Morgentaler points out, would seem to undermine the premises of preformation.[50] The coinciding of inner character and outer appearance is a given of nineteenth-century fiction as in, for example, the routine use of phrenology to depict character. Nineteenth-century literature abounds with examples both of the heritability of "internal identity" and of striking corporeal similarities between successive generations of the same biogenetic family. Like Oliver and his mother, Esther Summerson and Lady Deadlock in Dickens's *Bleak House* appear to be each other's exact physical duplicate, recognize one another as mother and daughter when they meet by coincidence, and are recognized as such by others. Dickens is full of such "intuitive recognitions" resulting from an epidermalized blood tie. Morgentaler argues that the idea that identity might be a product of biogenetic inheritance that is marked by visual signs on the body survived twentieth-century scientific discoveries about the biology of heredity: "The idea that parents and children are bound by invisible, near-mystical bonds was common in the nineteenth century, and persists into our own time."[51]

Racial links are often emphasized: as Marianne Novy points out, the fair hair that Eppie in *Silas Marner* has inherited from her birth father (even though her face is not like his) sets her apart from the rest of the village, both of them Normans whose blood has not much mingled with the darker blood of the local Saxon peasantry.[52] The classic British foundling plot, driven by the reunion of the child with the original family and the restoration of birthright, affirms race and class boundaries by confirming that the birth line is the proper place for the child in an era when "races" were distinguished along a multitude of now-invisible ethnic and class lines.[53] Laura Peters, arguing that Victorian orphans often served as scapegoats, expelled to define and police the imperial boundary between native and foreign, sees Oliver Twist's exact mirroring of his

50. Morgentaler, *Dickens and Heredity*, 13.
51. Morgentaler, *Dickens and Heredity*, 92.
52. Similarly, in Mary Shelley's *Frankenstein* the blond hair of the orphaned Elizabeth marks her as aristocratic by birth and distinguishes her from the peasants who have raised her.
53. Hereditary aristocracies were classes defined by bloodline; see Morgentaler, *Dickens and Heredity*, 143.

parents' appearance as essentially racial, defining his membership in the imperial race and distinguishing him from such dark-featured evildoers as Fagin and Monks.[54]

Adoptees frequently express a wish, in searching, to find those who look like them, not just because appearance is believed to index blood but because of the widely held belief that we need human mirrors in order to become human. Korean adoptee Todd Knowlton writes, "When I imagined meeting my father I thought I was going to be looking in the mirror. Everyone who yearns to find his or her birth family talks about that. They think, 'I really want to find someone that looks like me.'"[55] This expectation is normative in adoption discourse, both in terms of family resemblances and in terms of racialized looks. Adoptee Kelli Ann Smith writes in *Pieces of Me,* "the fact that I don't look like anyone I love really bothers me." Meeting her birthmother at the age of thirteen "was like looking into a mirror. I was the spitting image of my birthmom . . . We have the same nose, same eyes, and the same chin. . . . I LOOKED LIKE SOMEONE!"[56] Commenting on the needs of transracial adoptees, A. R. Sakaeda writes, "Our children must see themselves mirrored in the faces of their peers, their neighbors, their teachers and their school environment. It is tremendously isolating for children of color to be in environments in which they do not see reflections of themselves."[57] Cheri Register glosses the "fundamental human longing . . . for a family with whom we feel total affinity" as the adoptee's longing for "people who resemble him."[58] Unknown birth parents are assumed to resemble the adoptee, not only racially but with regard to specific facial features: "The next time your young child asks you what his birthparents look like . . . say that . . . he can look in the mirror."[59] In Changfu Chang's documentary film *Sofia's Journey,* fourteen-year-old Sofia Robinson, "glad" when told that she exactly resembles the birthmother she yearns for but cannot find, draws self-portraits in an effort to picture her: "When I look

54. Laura Peters, *Orphan Texts: Victorian Orphans, Culture and Empire* (Manchester, UK: Manchester University Press, 2000), 41.

55. Todd Knowlton, in Lee, Lammert, and Hess, *Once They Hear My Name,* 51–74, quotation at 63.

56. Kelli Ann Smith, "Which One of These Is Not Like the Other?" in Ballard, *Pieces of Me,* 91.

57. A. R. Sakaeda, "The Color Connection: Transracial Adoptive Families," in MacLeod and Macrae, *Adoption Parenting,* 310–18, quotation at 314.

58. Cheri Register, *Beyond Good Intentions: A Mother Reflects on Raising Internationally Adopted Children* (St. Paul: Yeong and Yeong, 2005), 16.

59. Cheryl Leppert, "In Front of the Mirror," in MacLeod and Macrae, *Adoption Parenting,* 181.

Figure 3. Sofia's drawing of her birthmother based on her own appearance. From Changfu Chang, *Sofia's Journey*.

in the mirror I try and look at myself older so I can kind of see her."[60] J. David Velleman asserts that when adoptees feel compelled to search for biological parents, "they are searching for the closest thing to a mirror in which to catch an external and candid view of what they are like in more than mere appearance. Not knowing any biological relatives must be like wandering in a world without reflective surfaces, permanently self-blind."[61] For Velleman, to see and know those whom you physically resemble is to know yourself.

The notion that only blood-related humans can serve as mirrors for one another is hard to sustain when examined closely. Since no one but an identical twin ever looks exactly like another human being, what does "the closest thing to a mirror" mean? All humans share similarities; wouldn't it be enough to be raised by another human being? Or do humans see themselves in same-race, but not in other-race, faces? Wouldn't it be enough, then, to be raised by someone of the same race? Does that mean that mixed-race children suffer if raised by either of their own parents (one black, say, and one white)? If it means a more particularized

60. *Sofia's Journey: Searching for Birth Parents* (series 1), written, dir., and prod. by Dr. Changfu Chang, film, 45 minutes (2011), www.lovewithoutboundaries.com.

61. James David Velleman, "Family History," *Philosophical Papers* 34, no. 3 (2005): 368, quoted in Jerng, *Claiming Others*, 212.

resemblance as to shape and placement of facial features, what constitutes a sufficient degree of resemblance? What adult face looks enough like any child's? The practice of "matching" in adoption was supposed to allow children to pass for their parents' biological offspring, and in terms of Sakaeda's and Register's demands for same-race mirror-families for transracially adopted children, "matching" ought to have provided adequate mirrors for same-race adoptees. Yet Patton's same-race interviewee Thorley Richardson is nonetheless left wishing for an identifying mark, and neither Lifton nor Velleman considers adoptive "matching" to provide a sufficiently exact "mirror." But by this same logic, children biologically related to their parents are harmed every day if they do not happen to share the same features. Appearance, then, seems to be only a proxy for a deeper, not otherwise visible, blood connection; yet such a connection, as we have seen, is knowable only by appearance.

Moreover, Velleman's claim (and others' similar claims) that a human mirror that physically resembles the subject is a necessity for human development appears to depend upon a misreading of the psychological concept of "the mirror stage." According to Lacan, for a young child to see him- or herself in a mirror is to misidentify with an illusory wholeness, not to become authentically whole, which is impossible in his view. Wholeness—whether discovered in an actual mirror or in the metaphoric mirror of a human face—is only ever an imaginary construction, however necessary that construction may be. Human creatures find and make adequate (or inadequate) mirrors from the materials at hand; a literally mirroring birth family may be irrelevant. An adult adoptee may still yearn for a more precisely similar human mirror, but if the rediscovery of biological relatives confers a sense of wholeness, it is not because they inherently have the power to do so, but because the adoptee, by desiring it, makes it so.

A spirited response from advocates of adoption has met Velleman's claims, a response that answers advice literature such as Sakaeda's and Register's as well. Jerng calls Velleman's a "magical way of thinking."[62] Charlotte Witt argues that family resemblances depend on family stories as much as on "observable appearances" and that their meanings depend on social relations: "Family resemblances are part of a family's mythology, and they serve various purposes: bonding family members, explaining behavior, assigning blame. . . . Family resemblances are re-

62. Jerng, *Claiming Others,* 216.

lational properties."[63] While Witt refutes Velleman's claim for the superiority of biologically related over adoptive families, Kimberly Leighton argues against Velleman on the grounds that identity derives not from appearance but from experience—in her case, the experience of having been adopted. Identity is not a substance or essence that "can then be transmitted to others, assuring that, like property itself, the property that is the identity will continue on."[64] Because her family wished to remain silent about her adoption, and because apparently she could and did pass as biologically related, "the markings of my bodily identity could, without being talked about, be 'read' *as if* they had the same meanings, the same imagined history as those bodies of my relatives."[65] But, she continues, "I do not mean to suggest that bodily markings are in some sense real, that they reflect some natural meaning (or identity) which exists pre-culturally and is then expressed through language." Her appearance derived meaning from her adoptive family's words and silences about it. Her struggle was not to find the "real" meaning of her appearance by finding those whom she "really" resembled, but rather (as we have seen in the introduction), by speaking about having been adopted, to make space for her identity by "claiming a position of difference."[66]

Similarly, adoption scholar and memoirist Emily Hipchen demystifies family resemblance, both taking pleasure in discovering those whom she resembles and observing time and again that resemblance is a consequence, not a cause, of family connection and therefore not a source of identity. As for Leighton, identity originates in a different phase of the adoption narrative and resides in what each writer refers to as her "difference."

Adopted at six months, meeting her biological parents and then the rest of her birth clan in her thirties, Hipchen sorts through the complex questions raised by her adoptive beginnings. "I" refers both to Mary Beth Delany, the infant daughter of Joe Bari and Anna Delany, and to

63. Charlotte Witt, "Family Resemblances: Adoption, Personal Identity, and Genetic Essentialism," in *Adoption Matters: Philosophical and Feminist Essays,* ed. Sally Haslanger and Charlotte Witt (Ithaca: Cornell University Press, 2005), 135–45, quotation at 141.

64. Kimberly Leighton, "Being Adopted and Being a Philosopher: Exploring Identity and the 'Desire to Know' Differently," in Haslanger and Witt, *Adoption Matters,* 146–70, quotation at 154. See also her more recent critique of Erich Wellisch's claim that "lack of genealogy prohibits [adoptees] from developing a complete body-image," which seems logically to require only the presence of other human beings, not of biogenetically related ones: "Addressing the Harms," 74–75.

65. Leighton, "Being Adopted," 152.

66. Leighton, "Being Adopted," 156.

the person who was "reborn in a courtroom . . . Emily Ann Hipchen. Me."[67] When she meets her birth family (her birth parents eventually married and raised a large family together), it is clear to all from her appearance that she is a Bari. Comparing her body to her sister's, "our eyes . . . are Bari-brown; our hair, she says, is Bari-colored." Eyes, hands, eyebrows, and hair are identical. Initially, the "connection" seems "easy":

> Because I was born of the same parents, I am her family, and she is mine—it is as easy as all that. . . . We are all blood-kin, related. Even the courts make this distinction, awarding patrimony after DNA tests which I would pass, inevitably. (*Coming Apart,* 30)

"Every drop of our blood came from the same source," she later reflects (90). "And yet," she continues,

> had I stepped off that plane I took into Seattle, and she not known I was coming, she would never have recognized me. Never. Those Bari-eyes would have met mine perhaps, then slid away again without admitting me, without that jolt that knowing they are Bari-eyes gives us both when we see them. (*Coming Apart,* 30)

"So," she concludes, "because I am a Bari, I look like one." That is, physical resemblance without the social cues and the family narrative would not be enough to make her part of this family. At the same time, because she looks like a Bari, she is one; but would she therefore not have been a Bari "had I not looked like them?" (31). Her looks suddenly seem at once essential (an expression of Bari "blood" and DNA) and meaningless. She tries to imagine the person she would have become had she remained Mary Beth Delany, but that self is "a potentiality I can't fathom." Even her appearance would be different. "She has my face, vaguely . . . but . . . since faces are made not only of flesh but of expression, I can't see her" (41). Curiously, given how Bari-like she apparently actually looks, this remark suggests that, had she been raised a Bari (that unimaginable "potentiality"), she might have looked less Bari-like than she does now. Appearance is no simple expression of blood or genes.

When she returns pages later to the scene of her arrival at the airport (the memoir's structure is highly recursive), she reflects both on the ties

67. Emily Hipchen, *Coming Apart Together: Fragments from an Adoption: A Memoir* (Teaneck, NJ: Literate Chigger Press, 2005), 20–21 (hereafter cited in the text).

of shared blood and looks and on the lack of shared family history, her distance from "that unspoken understanding all those years together allows them" (*Coming Apart,* 90). She both enjoys the sudden intimacy with this large family and mistrusts what seems to be the presumption behind it: "It feels so uncanny to me, the way these Baris all have of believing they know what they can't know, of believing they understand me and have insights into me" (108). This experience is sufficiently disturbing that she comes to doubt her own skepticism and the scholarly rationality that are fundamental to her lived identity. This passage continues:

> . . . and they can't, surely, not with so little experience of me, can they? Is there something they can see because we share the same genes, the same bodies—something years of experience are only a substitute for? (*Coming Apart,* 108)

Hipchen is thrown into this state of mind (compelled to give credence to a sort of telepathy) by her attendance at a major Bari family event: the wedding of one of her birth brothers. As family photos appear projected on multiple screens at the wedding reception, Hipchen suddenly sees her own face, hugely magnified, multiplied, and surrounded by the faces of her birth family, in a blowup of a photo taken when they first met at the Seattle airport. Not only is the image repeated on screen after screen; she also sees her face "repeating the faces of my brothers and sisters, my mother and father, my aunt my niece my nephew, in the picture and in the flesh where they stand and sit all around me" (106). Rather than feeling warmly embraced by this experience of familial mirroring, she says, "something snapped," and she had to leave the room.

> It was as if I no longer recognized myself, as if in being so much a Bari, I ceased to be Emily. As if my face and body no longer belonged to me but were so widely shared that I couldn't separate me from them. I wanted my face back, I wanted to be different again. (*Coming Apart,* 106)

The family resemblance and the telepathic connections presumed to derive from it make her feel less rather than more like herself. As she says later to her aunt Beth, Anna's sister, "It is difficult, you know, seeing my face walking around everywhere" (128).

And yet in the very conversation in which she confides this feeling of loss of self, she also discovers a deep affinity with Aunt Beth, who, like Emily, left her family at age eighteen to escape an abusive father.

Perhaps, with their shared experience, they share a family tie in some more-than-skin-deep way. But the episode ends equivocally, with Beth apparently expressing reservations about Emily's inclusion in the family. Just as for Leighton, "difference," and the possibility of alienation as well as alliance that it implies, is a more viable source of identity than the "mirroring" of shared looks prioritized by Velleman and desired by adoptees such as Todd Knowlton and Kelli Ann Smith.

Hipchen's discovery of the clan whose looks mirror hers leads not to a discovery or affirmation of identity but to its temporary suspension. Another daughter's memoir, Kate St. Vincent Vogl's *Lost and Found: A Memoir of Mothers,* like Hipchen's calls attention to the constructedness of family resemblance and, like Hipchen's, finds the renewed connection to birth parents a source not of identity, but of "identity theft."[68] Vogl's recognition of her resemblance to her birth family is slight and follows long years of reacquaintance. Grieving for her beloved and recently deceased adoptive mother, the memoirist initially sees no resemblance between herself and her birthmother, her (deceased) birth father, or anyone in their families. On meeting her birth father's family she writes, "Is there no one out there who looks like me? . . . So much for recognizing long lost relatives while walking down the street" (*Lost and Found,* 105). Found by her birthmother, Val, she never felt the need to search, she says, perhaps because she has "[her] mother's easy smile, [her] dad's Italian eyes" (8): she had in her adopted family the mirror she needed already. Vogl emphasizes her resemblance to her mourned mother (she reprints photos in the memoir to support this claim), and she researches and writes a genealogy not of her own biological line, but of her mother's.

Because Val found her through an obituary for her mother, Vogl repeatedly claims that her mother sent Val to her from beyond the grave. Melancholic grief for her mother (and not the more typical adoptee's grief over lost origins) prevents her from seeing Val as a relation, much less as a mirroring mother. Only ten years after their reunion does Vogl notice for the first time that they have matching facial moles. At their first meeting, Vogl notices a similarity in how they move their hands (*Lost and Found,* 38), yet she undermines the identity-conferring power of this connection by vaguely imagining inheritances everywhere. Perhaps she inherits her love of writing from her birth father, who was an

68. Kate St. Vincent Vogl, *Lost and Found: A Memoir of Mothers* (St. Cloud, MN: North Star Press of St. Cloud, 2009), xi (hereafter cited in the text).

artist; next she wonders if "self-doubt, like hand gestures, can be passed down as well" (50), and she doggedly records the kinds of coincidences that might link any randomly selected pair of people (it is "uncanny" how much she is like her mother because both like peanut butter [113]). Nearing the end of her story, she does see some facial resemblances. Val's daughter (Vogl's half sister by birth) "had her mother's chin. And mine" (157); she can see in another person what she cannot directly see in Val. At an extended family wedding, Vogl meets a distant relation and again sees something: "She could be my long lost relative. Finally, I thought. After all these years." But "Val didn't see the resemblance" (205). Shared looks, if they can be discerned at all here, neither shape nor confirm identity.

Catherine McKinley's *The Book of Sarahs* follows the more conventional structure of an adoptee memoir established by Lifton, in that the author, discontented with her upbringing, searches in young adulthood for her birth family. She might thus be expected to search for mirroring faces in the way that Knowlton, Smith, and others search, and indeed, at the start she does. A transracial adoptee with one black and one white (later found to be Jewish) birth parent, raised in a white family embedded in a white community, McKinley searches not only for the alternative family she has idealized in her imagination but also for a sense of rootedness in black culture; in this regard she is not unlike some of the interview subjects in *BirthMarks* and *In Their Own Voices.* Growing up in the 1970s in a small New England town, she gained some knowledge of and access to contemporary black culture from books, attendance at a local A.M.E. church, and trips to Boston with a black friend. From an early age, McKinley says she looked for black women whom she thought looked like her and who might be her birthmother. For years she carried with her a photograph of a woman she once saw selling indigo cloth in a park in Providence, a woman whose association with African culture and with Ntozake Shange's fictional character Indigo matched McKinley's fantasy and whose "oval face . . . was not unlike my own."[69] This photograph, displayed in her room at boarding school and college, allowed her to masquerade as the daughter of a black mother:

I called her Mattie, a name I'd read in those narratives of Southern child-

69. Catherine E. McKinley, *The Book of Sarahs: A Family in Parts* (New York: Counterpoint, 2002), 29 (hereafter cited in the text). She refers to Ntozake Shange's novel *Sassafras, Cypress and Indigo* (New York: St. Martin's Press, 1982).

> hoods where the archetypal Black mother was recast again and again. I'm sure that the anger toward my family made Mattie even more attractive. . . . Mattie stood up to the ever-elaborate stories of who she was and why we were apart. An adoptee's boon is that she can imagine and reimagine herself into any life. (*Book of Sarahs,* 30)

Told "again and again how much I looked like my 'mother'" (30–31), even after she reveals that she has been lying, McKinley discards the photo of Mattie only when she meets another African American woman, Rhae, at a party in Accra, Ghana, a woman whose attractiveness and sympathy reawaken McKinley's capacity to endow a stranger with "an almost reflexive fantasy: *Maybe Rhae is my birth mother. Maybe that is why she was so interested in my story and wants to keep in touch with me*" (25–26). Mirroring appearance is a feature of McKinley's fantasized birthmothers.

As her family dissociates ever further from her attempts to establish her black identity, McKinley decides in her early twenties to initiate a "search for my birth family [that] would be everything by way of a remedy to my sense of loss" (*Book of Sarahs,* 85). Now, as her search begins to turn up information about her birth parents—including the fact that her birthmother is white and Jewish—the correlation between appearance and identity begins to fragment. A friend who wants to help her "integrate" "this new dimension . . . into my imaginings and my fragile sense of a new self" (92) shows her pictures of famous African Americans with a Jewish parent and remarks, "See how classically Black and Jewish you are. . . . If you never get anywhere with [the search], you still have some kind of identity papers. You know your mother really has to be Jewish" (93). But looking at the pictures, McKinley notes, "if someone lined up some photos of Arabs or South Asians or Latins, the case might also be made for my similarity to them" (93). Her black/Jewish identity appears on her face only as a consequence of her knowledge of it. Later, during a period in which she mistakenly believes her birth father to be from Cape Verde, she meets some Cape Verdeans who, on hearing this story, tell her she looks Cape Verdean (158–62).

After years of imagining an idealized "Jewish approximation of a Black mother" (*Book of Sarahs,* 125) and then after months of phone calls, McKinley and her birthmother finally meet. A photograph in the mail had revealed "the arch of my jaw, the same oval face, the flat tip of my nose," and a cousin has noted these similarities too (150, 137). Now, comparing their bodies in Logan airport, McKinley sees similarities along with differences: "I had her exact hips and feet; my breasts were thankfully smaller. I was glad to inherit those legs, but I'd have to watch my belly" (152). (Estie is also able to see the birth father in her face.) Yet McKinley knows she could not have recognized Estie as her mother without prior knowledge. In 1989 they were both living in Jamaica and used to visit the same bookstore: "I thought about the occasional American women I had encountered. Would I have been able to recognize myself in her then? I'm sure I would not have. I was focused too intently on my fantasies of Mattie" (156). Imaginative need and stories, not physical appearance, create the mirroring relationship of child and mother.

Several months of deepening acquaintance with Estie, Estie's partner Mac, and their nine-year-old daughter Sarah follow, including two visits to their semi-dysfunctional home in Jamaica and a difficult visit by Sarah to McKinley in New York. It becomes clear that Estie is emotionally fragile and offers Sarah's companionship in place of her own because she cannot tolerate the intensity of the reunion. Sarah, everyone notices, closely resembles her older half sister: looking like "mis-sized twins," Catherine seems to Sarah "a big me" (*Book of Sarahs,* 193, 168). Thus Sarah is doubling for her mother, McKinley too is doubling for Sarah's mother (who neglects her and leaves her too long on McKinley's hands), while McKinley (named Sarah at birth) imagines herself in Sarah's place as Estie's true daughter.

Her place in the family seems not only assured but overdetermined, yet it is never enough. McKinley finds herself "making myself more a part of Estie and Sarah" by reshaping her "WASPy," athletic body to match theirs, suddenly gaining weight partly to conform to "a Black woman's ideal" with a "coffee table backside," but more so as to mimic "fat" Estie and "chunky" Sarah (*Book of Sarahs,* 198): "As my body began to fill out, I felt a powerful kind of intimacy with Estie and Sarah that I felt desperate for." But because these relationships are so difficult, because of her disappointment in Estie,

> all the comfort of that flesh now began to feel sarcophagus-like. I would look at myself in the mirror and see Estie, and I'd feel angry at my image.
>
> After I saw Estie in the flesh, I never saw myself the same way again. During the months that followed, my face became like the broken matter in a kaleidoscope's lens. The lines of my face were shattered, and the lens was shifting again and again. (*Book of Sarahs,* 198)

In reflecting on this experience McKinley offers two contrasting interpretations that read like the debate between Velleman and Lifton, on the one hand, and Jerng, Witt, and Leighton, on the other. On the one hand, she claims this "shattering" "was not a violent interruption; it was pleasurable" (199) to see her features anew, composed of parts of Estie and Sarah's faces:

> I enjoyed those parts of myself in a way I hadn't before. It made me think of how subtly *privileged* people are to come into the world so definitely attached to a people—if not a tribe, then at least persons whose image they reflect. (*Book of Sarahs,* 199, emphasis in original)

On the other hand, in the next paragraph,

> I was also getting a glimpse of how *free* I had been before—in my imagination, in my ability to see myself outside of everyone I was attached to.
>
> Now I would be standing in the shower and I would feel an urge to hurt myself—I wanted to dash my head against the edge of the tub and kill that part of me that was her—the now-pudgy, depressed Jewish woman who had become so immobilized by the past. (*Book of Sarahs,* 199, emphasis in original)

Feeling trapped by her resemblance to Estie, McKinley feels contrastingly grateful for her independence from her adoptive mother and "the troubles her genes had handed her," and she concludes that "it must be torture to grow up never feeling free of other people's legacy—however proud or horrifying." In the end she needs to detach herself from the mirror image her birthmother has become for her.

The mirroring and merging with Estie and Sarah come to an abrupt end when McKinley discovers that there was yet another Sarah, a child born to Estie four years before her and also given up for adoption. This redoubling of her identity amounts to a kind of "identity theft" (to use Vogl's term), because the stories she assumed were about her own birth turn out to have been about the prior Sarah. This crisis arises soon after she locates her birth father, Al, and it precipitates a search for the first Sarah and a shift of attention to Al and his family, as well as detachment from Estie and Sarah. In a concluding chapter entitled "Aftershock," McKinley acknowledges that searching for her birth parents, which began in loss and mourning, did not end her grief. Instead, it dismantled her identity and left, for a time, nothing in its place. "I had disrupted who I was" in order to recover her lost family:

> I had stopped everything else to have them. I had been on my way to being a woman—working hard and having love and ambitions and friends and trying to make the kind of life I wanted for myself—and somehow, believing I was enlarging that, I had cut off from myself. (*Book of Sarahs,* 264)

Relapsing into melancholy, she dreams of cutting herself (as she had years before) and fears "that I was destined to be some part of Estie's emotional self" (266).

Her way back out of this melancholy ingeniously reverses the figure of the mirror:

> I took a Polaroid picture of myself every night and put the series near my bed. When I woke up, I would look at them and have a conversation with myself. "This is who you are. This is what you've accomplished. You are good in these ways. You struggle in these ways. . . ." And what kept me going were those images and my feeling that I wanted to love the person in them. (*Book of Sarahs,* 266)

The cure achieved by seeing herself as herself and not as part of someone else is confirmed by an epilogue in which she expresses measured appreciation of all those—"WASP and Jew and Choctaw and Africa"—who "mark me with ferocity" (288). Although she still feels their connections to her as a form of aggression if not violence ("ferocity"), she keeps close by her a photo of each of her families, in each of which she appears at the center (289). Identity is forged by placing herself at the center of her line of vision and resisting the temptation to confuse herself with others, despite the family resemblances.

MARKS OF LOSS: SCARS, SCARWORDS, LOVE MARKS, AND MELANCHOLIC IDENTITY

McKinley's evocation of the pain that can accompany identifying marks raises in a fresh way the question of why reconnection with birth families and communities can arouse such ambivalent feelings. An adoptee may feel herself to be marked by what she has lost. Skin tone or facial features, or projected markings of blood or bone, may provide visual links to the families and communities into which she was born but to which she is no longer connected. Thus Hipchen's and McKinley's memoirs echo Victorian adoption plots of family resemblance, and a child who wants to know what her birth parents look like is told to look in the mirror. An adoptee may wish to find herself so marked, to find her appearance legible and identity conferring, as in the case of Thorley Richardson or Phil Bertelsen, or to find others so marked, as do Patton and Roorda. (Bigelow and Rhineholt, by contrast, do not.) In these cases, the adoptee's goal is to recover the original context and meaning of those visual marks—to find the mother whose facial features are the originals of her own, say, or the ethnic community that shares her racialized looks—and hence to establish an identity that matches the familial and social meanings of those marks.

Doing so is expected to bring closure to grief, although it does not always work this way, as the memoirs by Hipchen, Vogl, and McKinley suggest, and as the effortfully cheerful endings of the shorter memoirs by younger writers suggest as well. An adoptee may also feel herself marked and identified by loss itself, by what was or now feels like the violent rupture of essential ties. Whether the feeling of loss or even the memory of trauma are actual records of separation from birth family and community prior to adoption, or whether they are the after-effects of racism or prejudice against non-biogenetic family that accompany adoption, pain leaves marks, as well as prompting such fictions about origins as are discussed in chapter 2. Because the visual traces of injury are difficult to distinguish from marks that promise a connection to what was lost, adoptees may find themselves establishing identity on the basis not of a recovered connection to what they lost, but on the basis of loss or the feeling of loss itself. Just as McKinley connects her sometime practice (or dream) of cutting to her adoption, adoptees may be drawn to what would also cause or preserve pain. Because these two different kinds of marks are sometimes one and the same, reconnection does not always lead to cure. The sign of connection may be the sign of loss; to track down connections may lead to repeating traumatic experiences, too.

In *The Book of Sarahs,* remedy is hard to distinguish from injury when various kin "mark" McKinley "with ferocity," on the one hand offering identity-conferring family ties, on the other hand endangering her sense of who she is. Hipchen and Vogl, too, feel as much threatened as rewarded by their birth families' mirroring likenesses. The wish to be indelibly marked as part of a blood clan may arise to redress loss and pain, but it may also produce or perpetuate pain, so closely bound together are the lost and the loss. Recovered birth family may, far from providing a cure, seem like the source of pain. But if recovering a source of identity can feel like a loss, loss can also become a foundation of identity. As we have seen in chapter 2, the "primal wound," the most widely circulating metaphor for the lifelong experience of a child abandoned or given up for adoption, names the adoptee's sensation of missing a piece, a limb, or an internal organ, a loss equivalent to the destruction of identity and identification. While adoption scholars such as Yngvesson, Volkman, Howell, and Leighton have expressed skepticism about claims such as Verrier's and Lifton's as to the inevitability and profundity of the primal wound, there can be no doubt as to the frequency and sincerity with which adoptees evoke its aptness to their experiences. The narrative flowing from this diagnosis generally leads to searching for the missing part so as to reestablish birth identity. But these wounds can themselves become constitutive of identity. If Trace DeMeyer's having been abandoned as a baby was an "injury which felt like an open wound" (*One Small Sacrifice*, 14), the marks she imagines her blood and bones bear are scars formed over that primal wound. They preserve the wound rather than erase it and, paradoxically, provide her with the foundation for an identity: not the identity she would have had had she been raised in her biological father's Native community, but the one she bears at present as the author of *One Small Sacrifice*. Such scars may preserve and make visible a loss that no grieving can cure, or can want to cure. A mark, especially if it is literally or symbolically a scar, can compensate for—because it forms in the place of—the wound of loss.

Scholars working within the tradition of Freudian psychoanalytic theory have, since the 1990s, been exploring the key role played by melancholy in forming subjectivity and identity, for adoptees and others. "All identities are built on loss," state David Eng and Shinhee Han; Anne Anlin Cheng asks "for politics to accommodate a concept of identity based on constitutive loss."[70] In *The Psychic Life of Power*, Judith Butler influentially revised Freud's well-known contrast between successfully completed mourning and pathological, interminable melancholy by reading

70. David L. Eng and Shinhee Han, "A Dialogue on Racial Melancholia," *Psychoanalytic Dialogues: A Journal of Relational Perspectives* 10, no. 4 (2000): 667–700; rpt. in Eng and Kazanjian, *Loss*, 343–71, quotation at 363; Anne Anlin Cheng, *The Melancholy of Race: Psychoanalysis, Assimilation, and Hidden Grief* (New York: Oxford University Press, 2001), 25 (hereafter cited in the text). In my account of Eng and Cheng's theories of racial melancholy I also draw on David L. Eng, "Transnational Adoption and Queer Diasporas," *Social Text* 76 (Fall 2003): 1–37, and on the book into which this work was later incorporated, *The Feeling of Kinship: Queer Liberalism and the Racialization of Intimacy* (Durham: Duke University Press, 2010).

it against his later view, in *The Ego and the Id,* that melancholy is a necessary precondition of ego formation. An infant's psyche, she explains, does not form into a subject with an interior until it suffers a painful loss, at which point it places within itself a version or image of what was lost, thus "setting up . . . an inner world."[71] Melancholy can follow upon the loss of a loved person or of an idea; when the image of what was lost is placed inside the psyche, the subject can then forget or deny that loss has occurred. What makes melancholy a form of illness is that the anger that the bereft subject feels toward the lost person or idea must be redirected toward the self, where what remains of the lost object now resides.

Building on Butler's view of melancholy as psychically productive, David Eng (writing sometimes with psychotherapist Shinhee Han) and Anne Anlin Cheng have developed theories of a specifically racial melancholy, in which what is lost or repressed and then both incorporated and denied is racial otherness. In Freud, the lost object is reviled chiefly because it went away in defiance of the subject's love for it; in the theory of racial melancholy, it becomes despicable for sociopolitical reasons as well. Both writers read as melancholic the attitude of whites in the United States, who, having repressed the centrality of black and other non-white subjects to creating the nation, have then denied this racist repression through the ideology of colorblindness.[72] But Eng and Cheng devote most of their attention to articulating racial melancholy from the point of view of the minority subject. For Eng, first- or second-generation assimilation is intrinsically melancholic because it entails two kinds of loss: loss of the unattainable ideal of conformity to white Americanness on the one hand, and, on the other, loss, via mandatory repudiation, of Asianness. In Eng's view, "the model minority stereotype" through which assimilation is attempted "works, then, as a melancholic mechanism facilitating the erasure and loss of repressed Asian American histories and identities. These histories and identities can return only as a type

---

71. Judith Butler, *The Psychic Life of Power: Theories in Subjection* (Stanford: Stanford University Press, 1997), 179. Butler builds on this reading of melancholy a theory of queer subjectivity.

72. In this view of white melancholy, as both acknowledge, they are anticipated by Toni Morrison's reading of canonical American literature as haunted by the repression of black subjects; see *Playing in the Dark: Whiteness and the Literary Imagination* (Cambridge: Harvard University Press, 1992). (None of these writers mentions a repression still more deeply buried, that of Native Americans.) Paul Gilroy's *Postcolonial Melancholia* (New York: Columbia University Press, 2005) treats similarly the melancholia arising from white Britain's violent denial of its racial others.

of ghostly presence."[73] The Asian American subject splits and denigrates the images of Asianness that he or she nonetheless still holds secretly within, "forgotten but not gone."

Cheng, too, traces Freud's shifting account of melancholy, arriving at the succinct formulation, "the history of the ego is thus the history of its losses" (*Melancholy of Race,* 8). And like Eng, Cheng highlights the pathological ambivalence of melancholy, the mix of love and resentment toward what has been lost. "The melancholic is not melancholic because he or she has lost something," she writes, "but because he or she has introjected that which he or she now reviles"; the minoritized subject suffers from "having to incorporate and encrypt both an impossible ideal and a denigrated self" (*Melancholy of Race,* 9, 72).[74] Like Eng, she criticizes the ideology of colorblindness for its willful denial of racism and hence its racist effects.[75] But whereas Eng sees assimilation as a melancholy process, Cheng characterizes as melancholy racial identity itself. She worries, for example, that forming a racial identity around anti-racism, as African Americans did with "the Black is Beautiful credo" of the 1970s, can grant too much to the power of injury:

> While this urge to reclaim racial beauty has always seemed to say more about the keenness of the hurt than a cure, it is even more disturbing to find certain leftist, anti-assimilation advocates today speaking from a position that eerily echoes racist enunciations: the rhetoric of solidarity speaking in the rhetoric of isolation. (*Melancholy of Race,* 5)

Hawley Fogg-Davis, too, objects to "racial solidity" in her discussion of transracial adoptees' "racial navigation."[76] While Eng likewise notes that racialization is both "a collective injury" and an "individual harm" (*Feeling of Kinship,* 5), Cheng zeroes in on the uncertain merit of

---

73. Eng and Han, "Dialogue," 347–48. The quotation in the next sentence is from Joseph Roach, *Cities of the Dead: Circum-Atlantic Performance* (New York: Columbia University Press, 1996), 2, qtd. in Eng, *The Feeling of Kinship,* 18.

74. I use the term *incorporation* here as a synonym for *introjection*; although Freud and Freudians observe a distinction, Cheng points out that it is as hard to maintain as is Freud's distinction between mourning and melancholia: *Melancholy of Race,* 95–98.

75. Yngvesson, using Cheng's account of racial melancholia, finds the same complex grief in Swedish adoptees from Ethiopia in response to the nation's contradictory messages for immigrants of color; see *Belonging,* 141.

76. Fogg-Davis, *Ethics of Transracial Adoption.* See also Walter Benn Michaels, *Our America: Nativism, Modernism, and Pluralism* (Durham: Duke University Press, 1995), for a critique of racial identity as reproducing the racism of "the nativist project of racializing America" (13).

racial identities and racial pride that are often proposed as antidotes to racism. She attributes the "seducti[ve]" (7) solidification and naturalization of racial identities—white as well as black and Asian—to melancholic ambivalence. Racial melancholia, she argues, experienced "as a kind of ambulatory despair or manic euphoria[,] conditions life for the disenfranchised and, indeed, constitutes their identity and shapes their subjectivity" (23–24). She later elaborates on the "pathological euphoria of hyphenated subjects . . . whereby the euphoria of double identity often conceals the pain of dividedness" (71). To claim, even "euphorically," a strong racial identity, then, may be a sign of incorporated racism and thus of loss.

The melancholy that Eng and Cheng track through readings of such immigrant texts as Maxine Hong Kingston's *The Woman Warrior* appears in particularly vivid ways in the stories of adoptees, those whose identities are racialized and those whose are not, as if all adoptees were "hyphenated subjects." Eng reads *First Person Plural* and Eng and Han analyze case histories of troubled transnational adoptees to uncover the damage inflicted on transnational adoptees by internalized racism or, in psychoanalytic terms, by the melancholic incorporation of the Asian as object of loathing. If non-adopted Asian Americans and African Americans suffer melancholic losses owing to their devaluation as racial others, how much more vulnerable are transracial and transnational adoptees, whose racial identifications may be far more uncertain or negative. For example, the ambivalence about the self and the racially marked body that Eng, Eng and Han, and Cheng analyze seems aptly to describe McKinley's near-pathological ambivalence toward her own physique (marked as both Jewish and black) when she reshapes her body to resemble that of the mother who disavowed her. Diagnosing herself explicitly as melancholic, she loves and hates her own body because that is where her loved and hated mother—not only an incorporated psychic image of her, but her genetic material expressing itself through her body—resides. She experiences a melancholy attachment to the visual mark of what she lost. She reviles the mother she incorporates both because she left and because her body—overweight, ill, and ethnically minoritized—represents social devaluation.

Other adoptees' stories characterize even more explicitly than McKinley's the pain and injury arising from loss and installed in the identity formed from it. Adoption is represented in and on the body sometimes not just by ambivalent incorporations of what was lost, but by signs of injury marking the moment of loss or violent rupture. A scar or mark that at once preserves, covers, and calls attention to a moment of violent rupture can form the basis of melancholic identity by corporealizing the loss itself, locating it in or on the body. (Thus Harry Potter gets his identity from his scar long before he encounters the illusory wholeness of his look-alike family in the alluring Mirror of Erised.) In the readings that follow, I extend Butler's, Eng's, and Cheng's accounts of "identities . . . built on loss" to describe narratives of adoptees whose melancholic identities are not all explicitly racialized, but who share an inheritance of injurious loss made visible on their bodies.

In a short memoir titled "My Birthmark: Finding My Real Family," Gerard Wozek recalls his childhood belief that his birthmark (a dark spot below his navel) doubly links him to his birth mother, by expressing both her genetic legacy and, contradictorily, her grief about not being able to keep him. Subscribing to the folk belief that birthmarks are the imprint of the mother's thwarted desire during gestation (in this case, her desire to keep her son), and mistakenly believing that a birthmark is also heritable in the same way that facial features are, he recalls that he

> would imagine walking in a crowd of strangers, and suddenly out of the corner of my eye, I would see a striking birthmark on a woman's forearm or neck or ankle that would match mine completely. Then I would look into her eyes and instantly recognize her as being the mother who was unable to keep me.[77]

Identity here is constructed not just through inherited appearance but through inherited pain. Although at the end of the memoir Wozek claims he now interprets his birthmark not as the sign of his birthmother's frustration but as the mark of her loving kiss, this adolescent daydream suggests how closely intertwined a wish for an indelible mark of physical identification may be with a wish for the incorporation and preservation, not the termination, of loss and pain. His identity as the marked son of his mother forms because of, not despite, their shared pain.

A long literary tradition represents orphaned and adopted children being identified by marks of damage on their bodies that link them to their birth parents. According to the story that Oedipus comes to believe about his origins,[78] Oedipus's birth father, King Laius, "pierced his

---

77. Gerard Wozek, "My Birthmark: Finding My Real Family," in Ballard, *Pieces of Me,* 6–8, quotation at 7.

78. See chap. 2 for the argument that this origin story is Oedipus's fiction, assembled from incomplete evidence. The validity of Oedipus's interpretation of his wound, like that of adoptees' experience of loss and pain, does not depend on objective verification of "what really happened"; its validity lies in its subjective, emotional truth.

ankles" as an infant before he and Jocasta, fearing the prophecy that the child would grow up to kill his father, abandoned him to die on a mountainside. His wounded feet became his name, Oedipus, which means "swollen foot," although the name remains a dead metaphor (Tiresias: "A deadly footed, double striking curse . . . shall drive you forth") until Oedipus's history becomes joined to the mystery of Laius's murder. The messenger from Corinth describes how he received the baby from Laius's herdsman:

> OEDIPUS: What ailed me when you took me in your arms?
> MESSENGER: In that your ankles should be witnesses.
> OEDIPUS: Why do you speak of that old pain?
> MESSENGER: I loosed you;
> the tendons of your feet were pierced and fettered,— . . .
> So that from this you're called your present name.[79]

What appears as a visual sign to the messenger and others corresponds to an internal sensation (pain) and thence to personal identity (even to an "inner world," as in Freud and Butler), despite or even because of Oedipus's disavowal ("that old pain"). In self-defense or anticipatory revenge, according to this story, Laius at once marks Oedipus, gives him his identity, and determines the future course of his life. Although the twentieth-century adoptees' search movement relied on the figure of Oedipus to dramatize the claim that adoptees need to know who their birth parents are in order to know themselves, it is not recovering his lost connection to his birth parents that enables him to know himself so much as his interpreting his wound: the feeling of injurious loss itself, rather than lost objects, makes Oedipus who he is.[80] When Oedipus finally accepts the meaning of his scar, he confirms that identity by repeating the action memorialized by the scar. Punishing himself by piercing his own eyes, he mimics (what be believes to have been) Laius's piercing action from long ago.[81] Although Laius, in this story, had no intention of conferring

---

79. Sophocles, *Oedipus the King,* trans. David Grene, in *Sophocles I* (Chicago: University of Chicago Press, 1954), 28, 55.

80. On the problems with the search movement's reading of Oedipus, and on this theory's limitations for making sense of some adoptees' experience of locating their birth parents, see Novy, *Reading Adoption,* 48.

81. The original Greek uses the same words for both piercings, and the same word (*arthra,* or articulation) characterizes the ankles and the eyeballs. Odysseus, too, is recognizable by a scar from a boar hunt in his youth; like Oedipus, Odysseus's name and identity compress this painful marking.

an identity on his child—quite the opposite, he wanted to sever their ties and de-identify Oedipus as his son—the injury, ironically, both creates and signposts Oedipus's identity.

From a psychological point of view, there may be little difference for the adoptee between marks of pain sorrowfully, unwillingly, or even unknowingly passed on, such as in Wozek's story, and marks of injury felt to be actively inflicted, such as in Oedipus's. The violence that Oedipus both suffers and inflicts could be read as an adoptee's melancholic symptoms: loss of birth parents may feel like an injury aggressively inflicted, and the melancholy subject's response is to perpetuate the grievance, lashing out not only at others but also at the self, where the loved and reviled object now resides. Like McKinley, some of the young contributors to *Pieces of Me* blame on adoption their self-harming practice of cutting, attributing it to a compulsion to continue rescoring the wound of loss. A teen adopted at age five from India writes that he would cut himself with razor blades and then "cut again and re-open the scars when they started to heal"; once he "carved some swear words into my arm."[82] An adult Korean adoptee who contributes several poems scattered through the volume describes adoption as "The grief / The rage / The unbelievable, undying, unending loss" and claims that "We, who were / left in trash cans / . . . hurt ourselves / To feel alive" and to "test" others' love. Of the loss of a lover she writes, "The cut heals faster / numbs quicker / but the scar remains."[83] These writers' compulsive self-harming suggests that, as for Oedipus, repeating the moment of violent rupture is a self-defining as well as a self-destroying practice. As in "My Birthmark" or *Oedipus the King,* these adoptees melancholically both lament the primal wound and prevent its cure, preserving it visibly marked on the skin, where it constitutes identity.

Louise Erdrich's short story "The Years of My Birth" offers a strikingly literal account of an adoptee's choice to damage herself that succinctly confirms the pattern I am tracing here. The first-person speaker, Tuffy, born deformed and abandoned as a consequence, raised by a loving family yet lonely as an adult, elects to donate a kidney to her biological twin, who was kept and raised by their mother, even though he wants to die and rudely rejects her offer. The request comes from the birthmother, whose unconcealed partiality for her son revives the pain Tuffy pretends not to feel. Despite her claim to be content—she thanks her brother for

82. Sadan Rollings, "Why I Cut Myself," in Ballard, *Pieces of Me,* 59–60.
83. Kim Eun Mi Young, "Two Worlds," "The Test," and "How Do I Move Into the Light," in Ballard, *Pieces of Me,* 73, 60, 148.

crushing her in the womb, as she has had the happier life of the two—Tuffy apparently still feels the loss and needs to enact it in a literally visceral way.[84]

The volume *Pieces of Me* vividly plays out not only thematically but graphically this vision of adoption as the melancholic preservation of the primal wound, in which the wound is both the problem to be lamented and the solution to be preserved. Wozek's memoir appears first in the volume, as if the figure of the birthmark were first among those "pieces" from which adoptees assemble a sense of identity: a "piece" that permanently preserves its production by injury. Extending the "missing piece" theory of adoption, the book's section titles include "Stolen Pieces," "Gathering the Pieces," "Where Do These Pieces Go?" And the book has been designed to resemble a collage, an assemblage of brief "pieces," sometimes two on a page, with wildly varying typefaces, a scattering of inconsistent graphic decorations, and some selections printed as if on Post-Its or notepaper torn and taped to the page. One entry describes and demonstrates the therapeutic use of collage-making for a teenager in trouble,[85] and the cover (like those of the anthology *Outsiders Within* and Callahan's *Kin of Another Kind*) features images of jigsaw puzzle pieces as part of its collage design. This imagery of puzzles, missing pieces, and collage reflects widespread use of this set of related tropes. Birthmother Mary Ann Cohen explains how making a collage can serve as art therapy for adoptees in an essay that opens, "Of all modes of art, adoption most resembles the collage: a collection of mixed materials, already pre-existing, brought together to make something new."[86] The "missing piece" is a common title.[87]

While the "puzzle" metaphor and editorial comments introducing each section imply optimistically that wholeness and completion will be possible for all, the title *Pieces of Me* was chosen in a contest, the winning entry based on Angel Coldiron's highly ambivalent prose meditation about psychic puzzle pieces:

---

84. Louise Erdrich, "The Years of My Birth," *New Yorker,* Jan. 10, 2011, 64–68.

85. Lauren Hamilton, "The Collage," in Ballard, *Pieces of Me,* 110.

86. Mary Ann Cohen, "An Adoption Collage: Putting the Pieces Together," in MacLeod and Macrae, *Adoption Parenting,* 251–52.

87. For a few among many examples, an advice book by Paul Drake and Beth Sherrill features puzzle pieces on the cover and bears the title *Missing Pieces: How to Find Birth Parents and Adopted Children—A Search and Reunion Guide* (Berwyn Heights, MD: Heritage Books, 2004), and a web resource called "Finding the Missing Pieces: Helping Adopted Children Cope with Grief and Loss" is available through www.adoptionlearningpartner.org, as cited in MacLeod and Macrae, *Adoption Parenting,* 489.

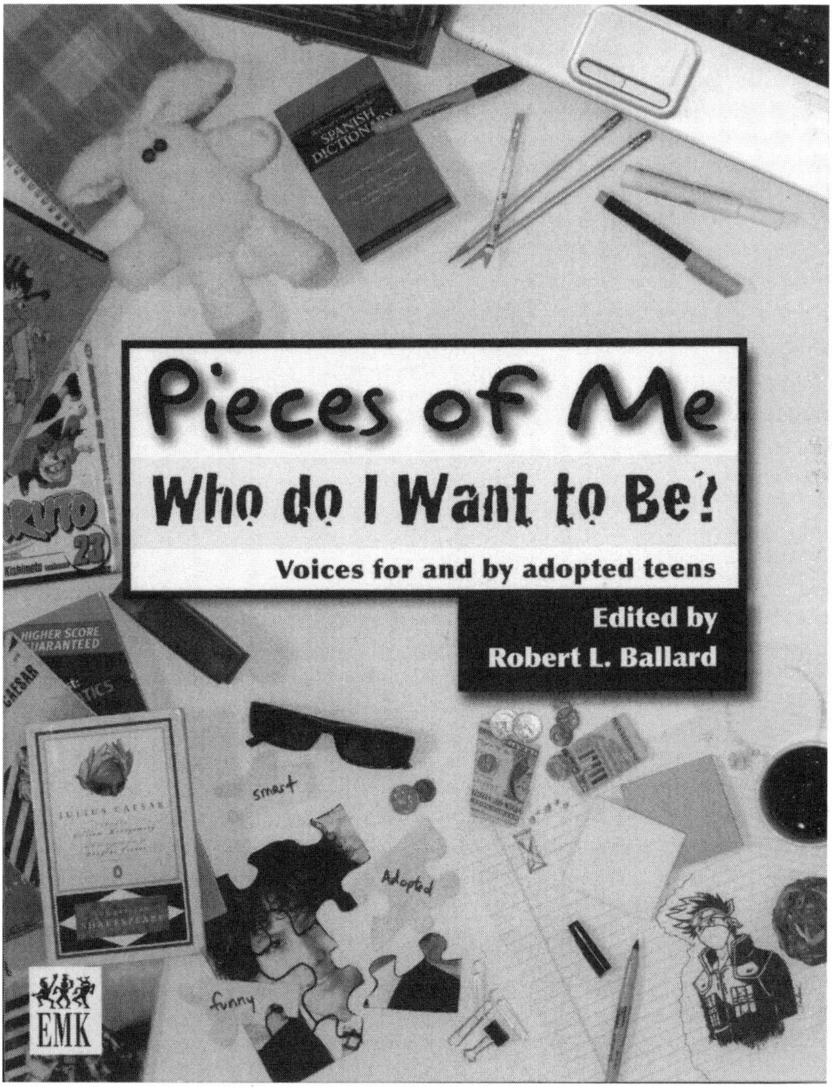

Figure 4. Cover art representing adoption as a collage with puzzle pieces. From *Pieces of Me: Who Do I Want To Be? Voices for and by Adopted Teens,* edited by Robert L. Ballard.

> I have some pieces that have rained down from heaven. I have picked some shattered pieces up off of the floor. I have some pieces that have come from explosions of anger and some from implosions of depression.[88]

Although this text ends optimistically ("I am putting the puzzle together"), Coldiron's other contribution to the book is a terrifying account of her inability to separate from an abusive lover (she fears for her life) because "I cannot deal with the pain of the wounds that were inflicted when I was an infant. The wounds are too deep. The pain is too much."[89] This narrative of unhealed wounds and endless, self-destructive grief is a vivid instance of adoptive melancholy and suggests—with the volume's narratives about cutting and other self-destructive behaviors—the dark underside of the optimistic "pieces of the puzzle" metaphor: wounds that not only never heal but that also, melancholically, characterize who the writer is. Two of Ballard's young contributors died before the book went to press; the book seems barely to contain the injuries that it reports and to which it melancholically clings.

The editor himself, Robert L. Ballard, was adopted as an infant during the US exit from Vietnam in 1975. In her history of "Operation Babylift," journalist Dana Sachs uncovers numerous cases in which children's identities were confused or falsified either through mismanagement or by design and the children wrongly made available for adoption; she argues that the United States failed to live up to the 1949 Geneva convention on children orphaned or displaced by war, which calls for repatriation and the reuniting of children with their families, and she reports on children's traumatic losses and birth parents' agonizing choices and frustrated searches.[90] She also tells a series of what she terms "scar stories" in which physical marks are expected to help in recovering birth identities and families. Where documents are vulnerable to error or malpractice, bodily marks can persist through time and accident.[91] Sachs opens the

88. Angel Coldiron, "The Lifelong Journey," in Ballard, *Pieces of Me,* 78.

89. Angel Coldiron, "Cost of Connection: My Life," in Ballard, *Pieces of Me,* 67.

90. Dana Sachs, *The Life We Were Given: Operation Babylift, International Adoption, and the Children of War in Vietnam* (Boston: Beacon Press, 2010). See also Aimee Phan's fictional reconstruction of the lives of Babylift orphans and adoptees, agency workers, and one birthmother, drawing on some of the same sources Sachs used: *We Should Never Meet: Stories* (New York: St. Martin's Press, 2004).

91. Websites, including one for Vietnam, allow searching children and parents to describe identifying scars and birthmarks as aids to identification and reunion. In Sachs's book, photographs do some of the same work as identifying marks.

book with the story of a still-grieving man named David, who hopes that a childhood scar on his hand will help him locate his birth family, a scar that for Sachs represents metonymically "the various tragedies of his life" (his "other scars"), implicitly linking physical scars to David's melancholia.[92]

In contrast to the melancholic David, Ballard appears in Sachs's book as the voice of completed mourning; he urbanely urges fellow Babylift adoptees to get over their anger and move on, providing Sachs with her haunting book title by remarking, "This is the life we were given."[93] Yet Sachs also uses his story to exemplify the egregious disregard, by US-run orphanages and adoption agencies, for birth records—and perhaps the enduring effects of this disregard. A US adoptive mother is described physically resisting a doctor who looks for "identifiable marks" on a baby whose documents have obviously been falsified: identified as Vu Tien Do II when he was placed on an airplane at three weeks of age, his papers were blatantly not his own but duplicates of another child's, and the mother fears the birth parents will find him and take him away. The misidentified and presumably unmarked baby Vu Tien Do II grew up, knowing "absolutely nothing about his past," as Robert L. Ballard, whose editorial work in *Pieces of Me* reveals a strong commitment to preserving the birth identities of adoptees and, too, suggests a lingering sense of loss.[94]

The yearning for a bodily mark to establish recognition, belonging, and identity, even for a mark that derives from and preserves pain, is nowhere more vividly represented than in Toni Morrison's *Beloved.* In the deep reservoir of memories the novel excavates, Sethe hardly knew her own mother, a field slave on a rice plantation. Nursed and raised by the one-armed Nan, Sethe could not recognize (and still cannot recall) her mother, "who was pointed out to her . . . as the one among many backs turned away from her, stooping in a watery field."[95] In this situation of unwilling abandonment and virtual adoption, Sethe remembers her naïve yearning for connection. Once, in an inversion of the nurturing connection that mother and daughter ought to but do not share, her mother opened her dress and showed her the brand underneath her breast.

Right on her rib was a circle and a cross burnt right in the skin. She said,

92. Sachs, *Life We Were Given,* xviii.
93. Sachs, *Life We Were Given,* xix.
94. Sachs, *Life We Were Given,* 189.
95. Toni Morrison, *Beloved* (New York: Knopf, 1987), 30 (hereafter cited in the text).

> "This is your ma'am. This," and she pointed. "I am the only one got this mark now. The rest dead. If something happens to me and you can't tell me by my face, you can know me by this mark." (*Beloved,* 61)

Sethe, anxious to say the right thing, says what earns her instead a slap in the face: "'Yes, ma'am,' I said. 'But how will you know me? How will you know me? Mark me, too,' I said. 'Mark the mark on me too.'"

Sethe "chuckle[s]" at the memory of her naïvety, yet this wish for reciprocal marking and mutual recognition between mother and daughter—even in the horrific signage of slavery—comes ironically true in a variety of ways in the novel. Sethe notes that she understood what her mother meant later on, when "I had a mark of my own."[96] Sethe's body, moreover, bears the novel's most extravagant "mark" in the form of the massive scarring on her back that Amy Denver claims looks like a tree. Other reciprocal markings emerge as the ghostly Beloved's identity is revealed. Denver recognizes her by "the tip of the thing she always saw in its entirety when Beloved undressed to sleep" (*Beloved,* 75), the scar or mark made when Sethe cut her baby's throat with the handsaw. As Sethe gradually lets herself believe in Beloved's return, her own mother's words as she pointed to her brand come again into her mind, as if her frustrated yearning for mutual marking and recognition with her mother were being answered by this mutual recognition with Beloved. But Sethe has resisted seeing the marks on Beloved that ought to have identified her right away, marks she made herself in a horrific playing out of her demand to have her mother "mark the mark on me too." Apologizing in an interior address to Beloved for not recognizing her sooner, she notes that she should have "seen my fingernail prints right there on your forehead . . . from when I held your head up, out in the shed" (*Beloved,* 202–3). It seems to take Sethe still longer to see "the scar, the tip of which Denver had been looking at whenever Beloved undressed—the

---

96. Immediately upon narrating this memory and that of later trying to identify her mother's body, Sethe is assaulted by an unbidden rememory, "something privately shameful that had seeped into a slit in her mind right behind the slap on her face and the circled cross." This memory is of Nan, speaking to her in her mother's African tongue (which Sethe no longer recalls), telling her the story of her conception and survival. Raped by white men on the voyage and after, Sethe's mother "threw away" all the babies so conceived; only Sethe, the child of a black man "she put her arms around," she kept and named. Why does this memory assault and "shame" Sethe? Why was it (and not the brand or the pile of corpses) so firmly locked away? Because it forms a still more nightmarish link between mother and daughter: both have killed their own children? See *Beloved,* 61–62.

little curved shadow of a smile in the kootchy-kootchy-coo place under her chin" (239). This ghastly, perverse "smile" appeared as a mark on Sethe's mother as well, in the scarring from the "bit" forced so often into her mouth: "She'd had the bit so many times she smiled. When she wasn't smiling she smiled, and I never saw her own smile" (203). It appears on Sethe too, as a circle of scarring surrounding her neck that Beloved both kisses and attacks. In the violent, inverted genealogy of slavery, grandmother, mother, and daughter are first divided by slavery and then linked and mutually identified by the marks of injury that they bear in common and unintentionally pass on. Incorporating one another's losses in these bodily signs, they form melancholic identities.

These brands and scars are the signs first and foremost of slavery's violence. Yet Sethe attempts to resignify her mother's brand as a sign of mother-daughter connection. Moreover, love motivates Sethe to cut her daughter's throat: Schoolteacher having arrived to recapture them, killing her children is her only way to save them from slavery. Once she has recognized Beloved, Sethe sees the scar as a smile because she believes (mistakenly) that Beloved has understood her loving intent. Denver, too, finds Beloved's scar endearing because it identifies her as her sister, and Beloved attaches both lovingly and violently to her mother's mirroring scar. Jennifer Putzi identifies a nineteenth-century sentimental tradition of resignifying slavery's marks of violent possession. In *Uncle Tom's Cabin,* for example, George Harris manages to turn the "H" his master brands onto his hand (to prevent his escape) into "part of his identity as a free man."[97] And in Lydia Maria Child's *Romance of the Republic* a baby (white but raised as a free black) is tattooed "GF," not to mark him as property but to protect him should he be sold into slavery.[98] But this sentimental tradition derives, Putzi argues, from white abolitionists' habit of displaying and interpreting slaves' damaged bodies while failing to listen to their voices. By sympathizing with yet also scourging Sethe, Morrison almost but not quite interprets Margaret Garner's action and the marks it produces as a sentimental novelist would. The mothers' and daughters' brands and scars, no matter how positively they may be read at certain moments in the novel, never lose the history of violence contained within them. Young Sethe's naïve instinct to treasure and continue the wound and the scar that preserves it—"mark the mark on me too"—is a paradigm of how the wound of loss can be transformed into a mark of

97. Jennifer Putzi, *Identifying Marks: Race, Gender, and the Marked Body in Nineteenth-Century America* (Athens: University of Georgia Press, 2006), 112.

98. Putzi discusses this tattoo in *Identifying Marks,* 123–26.

identity: how identity can form melancholically not despite but because of loss.

This chapter has surveyed several apparently different kinds of marks to which adoptees attribute identity-conferring meanings: the epidermal signs of race, as discussed in the film *Outside Looking In* and by the scholars and their interview subjects in *BirthMarks* and *In Their Own Voices;* marks projected onto the interior of the body, as in the marked blood and bones in *One Small Sacrifice* and in Lifton's and other adoptee rights advocates' claims about blood connection; inherited family, ethnic, and racial features, as in *Coming Apart Together, Lost and Found,* and *The Book of Sarahs;* such random genetic marks as birthmarks, as in "My Birthmark"; and the scars that mark sites of injury, as in *Oedipus the King* or *Beloved.* Although these marks have widely divergent social and historical meanings, I am arguing that because they condense traces of loved, lost objects with marks left by loss itself, they share in common a melancholic affect and ground melancholic identities in the subjects who bear them. Representations of adoption frequently equate these marks with one another and transfer an affect seemingly more appropriate to one onto another. This condensation occurs in Patton's book when she uses the term "birthmark" to name both the emotional pain of all adoptees ("the birthmarks of difference stemming from adoption were only internal, yet deeply felt" [*BirthMarks,* 20]) and the social meanings of racialized appearance. It occurs in *Beloved,* where the brand and other scars and marks of injury are just so many localized intensifications of the historical meanings of the characters' racialized appearance; in the world of *Beloved,* to be dark skinned is to be marked for continuous vulnerability to injury.[99] Another condensation or transfer of affect occurs when McKinley experiences her resemblance to her birth families as being marked "with ferocity" just as when, for the child who misses her mother in *Beloved,* the mark of injury becomes paradoxically a treasured sign of family inheritance, recognition, and solidarity. When the signs of loss, injury, and pain become for adoptees privileged sources of their identity and belonging ("mark the mark on me too"), much as when visual traces of beloved lost objects become freighted with negative affect ("I would look at myself in the mirror and see Estie, and I'd feel angry at my

99. Putzi explains that, in nineteenth-century American representations, scars and brands are interchangeable with the epidermal signs of race, as in the case of the light-skinned George Harris, whose "scars and brands mark [him] as 'black'—and therefore a slave—even if his skin color indicates otherwise" (*Identifying Marks,* 110–11).

image"), the formation and maintaining of identity can become unbearably painful.

Belief in another kind of identity-conferring, injurious mark has circulated since China began its overseas adoption program in the early 1990s: the belief that some Chinese birthmothers mark their babies before leaving them to be found. These marks would memorialize both the lost parents and the moment of rupture itself, and the belief expresses a set of ambivalent thoughts on the part of adoptive parents. On the one hand, Chinese birthmothers must love their children so much, and must be so devastated by parting with them, that they take extreme measures to be able to find them again. In this view, these (presumptively uneducated) mothers superstitiously imagine their bond to be too strong to break. On the other hand, they must be barbaric as well as naïve, inflicting pain on tiny infants, much as even the sympathetic Paul D accuses Sethe of behaving like an animal when she kills her baby daughter to save her. This belief at once pays tribute to and distances Chinese birthmothers; it makes them simultaneously into the good mothers adoptive parents want to invoke to reassure their children that they were loved and into the bad mothers that turn the adoptive parents into rescuers. It thus makes the marks, imagined or real, into melancholy incorporations of loved, reviled objects.

Although serious research scholarship on Chinese adoption pays this belief no heed (neither Kay Johnson nor Sara Dorow mentions it in their authoritative books on adoption from China),[100] claims about birthmothers marking their children abound on the internet, as well as in casual conversation among adoptive parents. In 2008 Brian Stuy's blog Research-China.org considered the evidence for the deliberate marking of children and decided to call this an "urban legend," on the grounds that most if not all small scars could easily be from accidents caused by the unsafe and unsanitary conditions of rural Chinese homes and orphanages (a demystification that nonetheless retains the urban legend's patronizing view of China). Prominent scars resembling cigarette burns on an upper arm are common in China, Stuy reports, the result of infec-

100. Kay Ann Johnson, *Wanting a Daughter, Needing a Son: Abandonment, Adoption, and Orphanage Care in China* (St. Paul: Yeong and Yeong, 2004); Dorow, *Transnational Adoption.* Karin Evans's *The Lost Daughters of China: Abandoned Girls, Their Journey to America, and the Search for a Missing Past* (New York: Penguin Putnam, 2000) echoes the belief figuratively by taking baby Kelly's ready smile to be the mark made by her mother's love (207).

tion at a vaccination site. A foster mother was able to explain that a child with a half-moon scar on her buttocks had sat down accidentally on a can of heating coals. The birthmothers Stuy knows "are revolted by the idea of intentionally hurting their child," and orphanage directors claim no knowledge of the practice.[101]

Nonetheless, among the twenty-two comments posted in the two years after the initial posting, while half confirm that their children's scars resulted from such accidents, the rest describe marks that the writers believe can only have been deliberately made. One child has identical, coin-sized marks in the same location on her two heels; another has a puzzlingly neat scar on her cheek. Yet another has "two round burn marks on the back of her neck." This last comment sheds light on how such stories circulate, the blog itself continuing the process: "Sitting at breakfast one morning in the White Swan Hotel my husband and I overheard another couple discussing these 'love marks' and wondered" about their own child's scars. The White Swan is the hotel in Guanzhou where nearly all adopting US families make their last stop before leaving China. Together with the shops surrounding it on Shamian Island, it is one of the most important sites for the propagation of a US culture of Chinese adoption.[102] Talk circulating at the White Swan reaches a wide and highly communicative audience. Another comment on the blog claims such marks represent "an underground tradition of marking the girls before abandonment, a sign of some kind, perhaps too much to claim that it is a sign of love." Other comments allude to "ancient" traditions of marking children in China. Those who believe their children's scars were deliberately made tend to read the marks as signs of China's otherness, a place where strange acts of violence are routine and parental views of children hard to fathom. In *China Ghosts,* Jeff Gammage discusses at length the horrific "scar" (an open, "ragged, four-inch gouge") on his newly adopted daughter's head; although he never suggests that it was made by her birth parents or for identification, his prolonged effort to interpret its etiology and meaning echoes these discussions of "love marks": possibly the result of neglect (an infected bug bite), the scar may also be evidence of extraordinary care (other marks on her head suggest IV treatment), and for his daughter it may become "an indelible reminder of a missing past."[103]

101. Brian Stuy, research-china.org, Apr. 14, 2008. Stuy conducts commissioned searches for birth parents in China, and his website is a storehouse of information for those conducting their own searches.

102. See e.g. Dorow, *Transnational Adoption,* 152–62.

103. Gammage, *China Ghosts,* 41–45, 71–73, 125–27, 134–36, 235.

The debate on Stuy's blog echoes a pair of articles published in *China Connection* in 1995 and 2008. According to the first, some San Diego parents were told by a pediatrician in China that the small marks on their newly adopted children's abdomens were "marks of love" made "to let the daughter know there is a spiritual connection" and to express regret about having to give her away.[104] The doctor described two traditional methods of making the marks (involving pricking or burning), which the article goes on to associate with "ancient custom" or perhaps traditional medicine, although the authors' other Chinese contacts are unfamiliar with the practice. The second article, "'Marks of Love' Revisited," summarizes the earlier piece and reports that no further evidence has emerged to corroborate the pediatrician's story. Although parents continue to find marks they believe to have been made on their children's bodies as signs, there is no evidence of "a marking practice" of the kind the doctor described. The author speculates that the doctor, "feeling he had to give some explanation . . . may have offered his story as one which would excuse the birth parent (for subjecting the child to the treatment) while also providing comfort to the adoptive parent." In a concluding paragraph, the author offers further speculations, that birth parents might make such marks in order to recognize their children later on and, possibly, "that a parent might have a wish to find the child again at some later time."[105] Thus the second article, while apparently setting out to debunk the pediatrician's story as a kindly fabrication, ends by affirming speculations that have as little grounding in evidence. As in the blog, and as in Gammage's speculations about the meaning of his daughter's scar, China becomes an imaginary space for the playing out of fantasies about foreign cultures of parenthood and care.

When Eng and Cheng discuss racial melancholy, the representation of repudiated Asianness that their subjects incorporate within the psyche is most often that of the mother. Typically it is the mother's unacknowledged loss and grief that the child inherits, internalizes, and forms her melancholy identification around. According to Eng's reading of Rea Tajiri's film about the legacy of the World War II internment camps, *History and Memory,* Tajiri inherits and is haunted by traumatic memories her mother never verbally expressed. Similarly, Cheng reads Maxine Hong

---

104. BB and BC, "Marks of Love," *China Connection: A Newsletter for the Exchange of Information and Ideas among Families with Adopted Children from China* 1, no. 5 (Oct.–Nov. 1995): 1. I am grateful to Jenna Cook for calling my attention to these articles.

105. BC, "'Marks of Love' Revisited," *China Connection: A Newsletter for the Exchange of Information and Ideas among Families with Adopted Children from China* 14, no. 5 (Oct.–Nov. 2008): 3.

Kingston's childhood hypochondria as a symptom of her melancholia, expressing the grief hidden in the stories that her mother, Brave Orchid, tells about others' sufferings even as she herself "never articulated" what she suffered in being displaced from China to America (*Melancholy of Race,* 87). Of "No Name Woman," the devastating story of an aunt driven to kill her newborn and commit suicide, Cheng writes: "The mourner whom the story never names as such and the mourner whom the daughter/narrator is herself mourning is the mother." The "Shaman" chapter, Cheng writes, "introduces the mother as an invincible woman who can exorcise even ghosts. Yet the mother's subsequent losses through the process of immigration must have been tremendous, traumatic, and spectral" (*Melancholy of Race,* 87). Neither Eng and Han's readings of case histories of adoptees nor Eng's reading of *First Person Plural,* however, focuses on the inheritance of unarticulated maternal grief. Instead, focusing on the child's viewpoint, Eng turns, as does Cheng for part of her reading of Kingston (*Melancholy of Race,* 75–76), to Melanie Klein's idea that the child divides the mother into good and bad objects. Eng finds his subjects distribute these roles to adoptive and birth mothers, and he locates racial melancholy in the subject's attributing Asianness (or, sometimes, white racism) to the bad mother and then simultaneously denying and introjecting her. In other words, when reading adoption stories, Eng focuses on the subject's fantasies about the mother (and the melancholic identity formation that results) rather than (as in Cheng's readings and in his own reading of Tajiri) on the mother's own history of trauma.

It would be possible to use Eng's and Cheng's Kleinian matrix to interpret the rumors about Chinese birthmothers who mark their children: the birthmothers are loving or they are violent, in contradistinction to the new parents who are, by contrast, either insufficient or idealized. But another emerging set of representations calls for extending their discussion of the inheritance of maternal loss to adoption stories, works of fiction and nonfiction that focus on the birthmother's point of view and show her experiencing the loss that she not only silently passes on to her child but also experiences simultaneously with her child's. The loss of relinquishment can be both an inherited and a shared wound that marks both mother and child, as when Wozek imagines that he and his birthmother must share identical birthmarks, or when the same marks of violence (scars that look like smiles) circulate among the women in *Beloved.*

Ann Hood's novel *The Red Thread,* discussed in chapter 1 in terms of its investment in "love," rehearses the urban legend of the Chinese birthmother who marks her child. The snobbish Nell Walker-Adams introduces the idea by asking, "Is it true they mark the children?"[106] She has heard that "'they cut them here or here'—she indicated between her fingers, around her ankles. 'Or they burn them with a cigarette.'" On the internet she has read of a "woman whose baby had slashes around both ankles."[107] Like the responsible adoption expert that she is, Maya judiciously if inarticulately downplays the topic ("the marks on babies could be from so many places").

In the novel's italicized accounts of the devastated birthmothers in China, none physically marks her child, although all love their children and suffer from their loss. But they do attempt to mark their babies in other ways. Ni Fan leaves a valuable sweet potato with her baby, hoping whoever finds her will understand how precious she is; when the referrals come in from China, it seems this gesture has been understood (*Red Thread,* 264). Wang Chun has more ambitiously left "clues" in the form of the distinctively woven basket and printed fabric in which her baby is wrapped. Although these are accurately read as identifying the baby's village, Wang Chun intends the quilt, carefully cut and sewn from her own clothing, to point directly to her. Such clues pose risks for the women who leave them, since child abandonment is a crime in China: "*Chun chides herself for her sentimentality. It is a bad idea to leave clues. Her very own neighbor was recently caught leaving an infant daughter in this very city*" (*Red Thread,* 12). The new parents, Emily and Michael, seem unlikely, however, to follow this daring clue or even to recognize it as one. Such marks depend, for their legibility, on an unbroken chain of transmission and on skilled and sympathetic reading (12, 263).[108] Although one section of the novel bears the epigraph, "A child is like a piece of paper on which every person leaves a mark" (111), these marks fade quickly. The birth parents wish their children to bear identifying marks, but only the narrator and the reader share this knowledge; as we saw in chapter 1, for the

106. Ann Hood, *The Red Thread: A Novel* (New York: W. W. Norton, 2010), 98 (hereafter cited in the text).

107. The ankles are also where the red thread is usually said to be tied; see, e.g., Maxine Hong Kingston, *The Woman Warrior: Memoirs of a Girlhood among Ghosts* (New York: Vintage, 1977), 226. Do these two myths together suggest that scarred ankles mean the tearing away of a prior red thread? Oedipus's wound is also on his ankles.

108. By contrast, in Elizabeth Gaskell's sentimental Victorian story "Lizzie Leigh," the grandmother recognizes her granddaughter—the child of her loved but "fallen" daughter Lizzie—by the fabric of her baby clothes, cut from a dress Lizzie and her mother bought together in happier times.

new parents the children are unmarked, bearing no hint of prior identities, nor will there be anything left for the children themselves to read.

The intensely personal narrative journalism of Xinran (the pen name of Xue Xinran) in her *Message from an Unknown Chinese Mother* contains several stories of birthmothers attempting to mark their children in this unreliable and risky way. Xinran was the pioneering radio host from 1989 to 1997 of *Words on the Night Breeze,* China's first radio call-in show for and about women. Her book consists for the most part of found stories about birthmothers psychologically devastated by having had to abandon—or in some cases countenance the killing of—their baby daughters. Newborn girls in these stories are likely to be "done": casually, routinely killed by submersion in a chamber pot (one such occurrence Xinran reports she witnessed) or by strangulation with the umbilical cord.[109] Wounds and injuries mark both children and mothers. Baby girls used to arrive at one orphanage bearing burn scars between their legs, made by midwives holding oil lamps or candles to check the sex of the child as soon as it is delivered. To be born a girl is itself injurious, and the injury of gender extends to the mothers, who suffer for having borne daughters rather than sons.[110] In one of Xinran's stories, a mother who was forced to relinquish two infant girls repeatedly tries to kill herself, and the book ends with an appendix about suicide rates in China, "one of the few countries in the world where the female suicide rate is higher than that for males" (*Message,* 203). Xinran quotes an orphanage worker: "those poor women, carrying their babies in their bellies for nine months, giving them up is like having their own flesh sliced out" (*Message,* 114).

The messages and marks that mothers try to make in Xinran's stories are attempts to overwrite, with meaning and connection, the wounds and scars of gender and of separation and abandonment. For Xinran, the children's blood is marked: "even though these girls have been brought up in a foreign land and a foreign culture, the blood of their Chinese mothers still runs in their veins" (*Message,* 13); but birthmothers also actively mark their children. From Red Mary, an orphanage worker who was herself an orphan, Xinran learns of mothers' efforts to mark or identify their children before leaving them:

109. Xinran, *Message from an Unknown Chinese Mother: Stories of Loss and Love,* trans. Nicky Harman (London: Chatto and Windus, 2010), 33 (hereafter cited in the text).

110. Karin Evans also discusses violence toward women who give birth to daughters (*Lost Daughters,* (116–18).

> Mothers used to leave little keepsakes with their babies. But I don't think any of the places where I worked kept these. Like everything else, they were thrown away. . . . They're evidence about the child's life. But the orphanage administrators just told me that there was no space to keep "rubbish" like this. Sometimes it went straight into the stove as kindling, that very day!
>
> There were all sorts of little tokens! Even words. A few mothers had written long, heart-breaking letters on the baby's clothing. Others had embroidered things, or sewn some little crosses or Xs on the cloth. The poorest would make a fingerprint in blood! Some babies looked as if they'd come with nothing—until you looked closely at a little fingernail and saw there was a cross or an X on it. Perhaps the parents were too unhappy and their circumstances too difficult to do anything else—but didn't they realize the baby's fingernails would grow and be cut? (*Message,* 113)

The bloody fingerprint and the scratched fingernail are as close as Xinran comes to confirming the urban legend of birthmothers physically marking their babies. Neither mark would have injured the child in its making, and neither would endure long enough for the child to see or attempt to interpret it. Yet both kinds of mark render into visible, physical form both connection and loss. In the case of the fingerprint, although the injury is literally to the mother, not the child, still the gesture seems to say, we share one blood, my blood once surrounded you, now we share one wound, my injury is your injury: "mark the mark on me too."

Sometimes a keepsake substitutes for a bodily mark. In the next chapter Xinran tells the story of Na, who leaves her (illegitimate) daughter at an orphanage, believing that she will be adopted in the United States. She then, in hopes of finding her, herself emigrates to the United States, where Xinran interviews her. Na's mother takes the child to the orphanage because Na cannot bear to do it herself, and Na continues the story:

> I'll tell you what really, really hurts: I had wanted us both to have a keepsake, something to know each other by, so I got the top I used to wear when I was breast-feeding her and laid it edge to edge with the garment I was going to put her in, and with an indelible red pen I wrote three big characters, half on one, half on the other: Xinxin [the baby's name]—two heart characters—and the character for "love." I hoped we'd always have this way of identifying each other, if at some time in the future we could match them up again. (*Message,* 129)

But the orphanage tells the grandmother that all such garments are incinerated, and the child goes unmarked. "Hurt" by this unmarking, Na still searches for her daughter and hopes one day "to give her the garment with my half of the three characters, so she would know how very, very much her Chinese mother loved her" (*Message,* 130).[111]

Because the messages and marks the birthmothers make on and for their children are so ephemeral, Xinran presents her book as a more enduring, though less personalized, "message" to accompany Chinese girls as they pass from their first mothers to the orphanages to their new parents. Xinran wants the adopted girls to imagine these marks, to read their traces, and to incorporate them into who they are. Because children ask, "Xinran, do you know why my Chinese mother didn't want me?" (*Message,* 10), her message is that their birthmothers wanted to keep them and that they grieve for them still. And yet Xinran has, of necessity, more information about mothers' efforts at marking than about daughters' interpretations of such marks. (US representations, too, have so far focused on parents' beliefs and wishes, for example, Stuy's blog, the *China Connection* articles, and Hood's novel.) In the penultimate chapter Xinran recounts a haunting pair of stories, from communities along the Yangtze River, about separated mothers and daughters, stories that model how Xinran wants her book to be used. First she meets a peasant mother who lost her infant daughter to kidnappers and who gives Xinran a pebble to give the girl, should she encounter her in her travels downriver. Years later, Xinran meets a girl, stolen as a baby to serve as a forced laborer, who gives Xinran a leaf to give to her mother, should she encounter her in her travels upstream. "I often put the pebble and the leaf together after that," comments Xinran, "feeling somehow that it allowed the mother to embrace her daughter" (161). This, she says, is the logic behind the Mother's Bridge of Love, the charity Xinran founded that helps children in China and Chinese children adopted in the West: "that pebble and that leaf represented those millions of mothers who never saw their daughters again; they were my way of bringing a message and a loving embrace to all those daughters who have never known their

111. Although Xinran does not make the connection, a mother's writing on her daughter's skin or on fabric before parting evokes the tradition of Nushu, the ancient, secret women's language used in part of Hunan province by mothers and daughters and by women friends to exchange messages after marriage separated them; the characters, derived in part from embroidery stitches, were written or embroidered. See Orie Endo, "Nushu: An Endangered System of Women's Writing from Hunan China," paper given at the 1999 Association for Asian Studies Annual Conference, Boston, MA, "World of Nushu," homepage3.nifty.com/nushu/home/htm.

mothers" (162).[112] Although neither the pebble nor the leaf reaches its desired destination or communicates its intended meaning, by holding these objects and unfolding the narratives they contain, Xinran endows them with the force of identifying marks. Like characters written on baby clothes or a bloody fingerprint on a baby's tender skin, the stories in this book constitute Xinran's effort to transmit such marks between mothers and daughters.

Xinran's investment in communicating these signs is deeper than that of the professional journalist or even the charitable activist. Throughout, she locates herself in her narratives as a sympathetic listener and records her occasional interventions. Her foreword to the book attributes her decision to write it to her sorrow at having missed her own mother's love because families were separated during the Cultural Revolution. But in the final chapter she reveals an even stronger personal motivation to pursue her subject: Xinran is herself searching for a child she once tried to adopt, Little Snow, whose forehead bears a dark pink "teardrop birthmark" and who she believes is somewhere in the United States (*Message,* 172). The nurses at the hospital where Little Snow was born in 1990 thought the birthmark was "etched into her skin . . . by a tear the dying mother shed as she held her daughter in her arms" (163). Legally prohibited from adopting her (she has a son already), Xinran arranges to foster Little Snow, but the fostering is not legal either, and, threatened with the loss of her job and those of her coworkers, Xinran relinquishes to the state the child she now considers hers. For a time she attempts to foster the entire impoverished orphanage where Little Snow now lives, visiting frequently and bringing food and supplies, but one day, returning from a business trip, Xinran finds the children gone without a trace. There are no records remaining to connect children who will be adopted to their past selves. "No orphans," she is told, "ever find their mothers" (171). As her professional travels take her to the West, she continues to search for Little Snow. At an adoption event in the United Kingdom in 2005, attended by "more than a hundred little Chinese girls, I could not help myself: Little Snow's features seemed to be stamped on every one of those innocent, happy faces" (172). Two years later, meeting a group of Chinese teenagers in Berkeley, California, "I scrutinized each face carefully, hoping to see the teardrop birthmark on one of those youthful foreheads" (172–73). Calling herself at the end of the book one of the

112. In the book, Xinran tells Na that the website for "The Mother's Bridge of Love" has a place where people searching for birth connections can post descriptions of identifying marks.

"mothers who have lost their daughters," she proclaims herself "lucky" at least to see and embrace other Chinese daughters in her travels, even if she cannot find her own.

Although it was Little Snow's birthmother who initially marked her face with her sorrow, when Xinran imaginatively "stamp[s]" Little Snow's birthmark on the faces of so many children, she marks all adopted Chinese girls—her imagined target audience, the recipients of her book's "message"—as hers. Thus the book not only transmits a message from Chinese birthmothers to adopted daughters in the aggregate, but it also serves to mark those daughters with an identity born of loss: all are potential Little Snows, children not only of their own birthmothers but also of Xinran and of the Mother's Bridge of Love. This loss, specific to relinquishment in adoption, is both inherited and shared by mothers and daughters; experiencing her own loss as theirs, and their loss as her own, Xinran projects onto adopted Chinese girls the identifying sign of grief.

What might such marks and signs mean to adoptees, should they be able to see and read them? What if a girl with a dark pink teardrop on her face born in China in 1990 and adopted in the West were to read her story in Xinran's book? Karin Evans tells the story of a little girl in a Chinese orphanage who wears a precious string bracelet ("My mama gave me this") and will not take it off, even as it presses injuriously into her growing wrist.[113] This story fleetingly captures the intertwining of love, loss, and injury, the traces of lost objects and of loss itself, and the ambivalent, melancholic formation of identity around such marks, in the representations discussed in this chapter. The mother's loving and loved gift may become a source of damage even as it forms a mark to which the child psychologically clings. The yearning on the part of mothers to identify and hold onto their children corresponds to, though it seldom meets, some adoptees' feeling that their bodies contain the marks of their inherited identity: that they can know who they are by reading correctly their bodies, their blood, their skin. Young adoptees who suffer when the "ethnic expectations" aroused by their appearance do not match their sense of who they are express such a wish, too. Yet bodily signs of birth identity can be so closely bound up with the pain of loss that not all can wish to bear them.

Nonetheless, a highly visible piece of popular culture, consumed for years by children adopted from China, supplies a vivid and positive image of identity created by injurious parental marks. The story of Fa Mu

113. Evans, *Lost Daughters,* 153.

Lan was popularized in this country first by *The Woman Warrior* and then by the Disney animated movie *Mulan,* which appeared in 1998 in time for the cohort of girls adopted from China since 1991 to see it as impressionable children. American children from China encounter this story often and in many forms: there are a number of picture-book versions of the story in English, and Shanti Fry (then president of the FCC of New England) mentions "a rousing reading of the Mulan legend" as part of a school celebration of Chinese New Year.[114] As might be expected of any such cultural translation, both the film and Kingston's version diverge significantly from the original Chinese folk ballad, first collected in the thirteenth century.[115]

As Kingston reports her mother's version of this "chant" in the chapter of *The Woman Warrior* titled "White Tigers," the girl leaves her parents when she is seven and is raised and trained as a warrior by an elderly couple until it is time for her to assume her mission, to overthrow the emperor and take revenge on the tyrannical baron who oppresses her family. She returns to her parents, who "carve revenge" into the skin of her back, a lengthy "list of grievances" together with "their names and address [so that she] would come back."[116] The "scarwords" create both pain and beauty—"If an enemy should flay me, the light would shine through my skin like lace" (*Woman Warrior,* 41)—and they confer on her a complete identity, one that unites her interests with those of her birth family. At the head of her army, Fa Mu Lan successfully carries out the revenge her parents had written, helping to defeat the emperor and showing the baron the words on her back moments before slicing off his head. Returning home, she resumes her life as dutiful daughter and daughter-in-law, having married and borne a son along the way. During her journey she has known that "I would be told of in fairy tales" (46), and the "chant" ends in this way: "From the words on my back, and how they were fulfilled, the villagers would make a legend about my perfect filiality" (54). The performative "scarwords" carved by her parents give her life a clear meaning and purpose. That meaning, self-reflexively, is not the particular act of revenge to which the words refer, but, instead,

114. Shanti Fry, "Adoption Goes to Kindergarten: How Stuffed Bears and Rabbits Expand a Child's View," in MacLeod and Macrae, *Adoption Parenting,* 287–89, quotation at 287.

115. For a history of the legend and analysis of its many retellings, see Lan Dong, *Mulan's Legend and Legacy in China and the United States* (Philadelphia: Temple University Press, 2011). For the original ballad, see www.yellowbridge.com/onlinelit/mulan.php.

116. Kingston, *Woman Warrior,* 41, 44 (hereafter cited in the text).

the obedience to which the revenge attests. She embodies the will of her birth family.

Neither Eng nor Cheng comments on this aspect of "White Tigers."[117] Their insights about the inheritance of maternal loss, however, seem highly relevant here. If Cheng is right that Brave Orchid's tales are all obliquely autobiographical (*Melancholy of Race,* 87), this story of parents injuring their child could be an account of immigrant parents passing on their suffering to the next generation. Kingston, taking up the story of what it meant to her to hear this "chant," reflects on her difficulty as a child in assuming the role of Fa Mu Lan, much as she wished to, because the enemy had become so complex and hard to locate. Back in contemporary China, the emperor already overthrown, the peoples' government punished Kingston's relatives as if they were as bad as the baron. At home in California, her enemies were not the same as her parents' enemies; as a girl steeped in traditional Chinese misogyny, hearing family members say that "feeding girls is feeding cowbirds," she "had to get out of hating range" (*Woman Warrior,* 54, 62). Yet despite this inheritance of injury and her separation from her family and community, the chapter ends by her claiming nonetheless:

> The swordswoman and I are not so dissimilar. May my people understand the resemblance soon so that I can return to them. What we have in common are the words at our backs. The ideographs for *revenge* are "report a crime" and "report to five families." The reporting is the vengeance—not the beheading, not the gutting, but the words. And I have so many words . . . that they do not fit on my skin. (*Woman Warrior,* 62–63)

Like the mixed pain and beauty of Fa Mu Lan's "scarwords," Kingston's verbal legacy from her parents is ambivalent, yet with parental words at her back, especially her mother's "talk-story," Kingston sees her task clearly: to write the book the reader is holding in her hand.

Kingston made some notable changes to the traditional story of Fa Mu Lan, including her heroine's leaving home to train as a warrior and the carving of the words on her back, which she borrowed from a completely different Chinese legend.[118] She hybridized the story by borrowing

117. In her reading of the child's melancholically internalized racism in *The Woman Warrior,* Cheng discusses the white thumbprint Maxine makes on her classmate in "A Song for a Barbarian Reed Pipe" but not the marks made on the heroine in "White Tigers," which she discusses in *Melancholy of Race,* 101–2.

118. For the story of Yue Fei, a military officer who had patriotic words engraved in his

from the kung-fu movies of her youth and other Americanizing elements, for which "inauthenticity" she was sharply criticized by Frank Chin. The Disney film *Mulan* returns to the original in some ways: rather than overthrowing established power as in Kingston, Mulan defends the emperor. The film also differs from the original and from Kingston in having Mulan defy rather than fulfill her family's wishes when she runs off to take her father's place in the army, so there is no carving of "scarwords."

Nonetheless the movie quietly retains Kingston's potent image of familial writing on the heroine's body. The movie opens with Mulan writing on her own forearm, making notes with brush and ink to help her remember the Confucian gender rules she is expected to recite to the matchmaker. These inked characters wash off, as if to indicate how little Mulan internalizes their meaning, but later her body appears marked a second time. Her family's shrine to their ancestors is lined with stone tablets carved with old-style Chinese characters. Here her father goes to pray that Mulan will become a dutiful wife, and here Mulan later goes to seek consolation after her failed visit to the matchmaker. In the animation in this scene the tablets become mirrors. As Mulan (the voice of Lea Salonga) sings, "when will my reflection show who I am inside," and as she wipes off her white makeup (the artifice of femininity she has temporarily assumed), she looks straight into the mirrored surface of a tablet so that the written characters appear projected onto her face.[119] "Who I am inside," then, in this visual shorthand, appears to be identified with the ancestors, their names superimposed on her skin. With its reference to the mirror stage, this image shows Mulan composing an illusory wholeness out of disparate parts: not only brown and white and feminine and unfeminine, but also epidermal and graphic.[120] In another scene in the shrine after Mulan has left for the army, the ancestors appear as

---

skin, see Dong, *Mulan's Legend and Legacy,* 104; Dong discusses Kingston's other borrowings, and Chin's attack (104–19).

119. The lyrics, by David Zeppel, as sung in the Disney film: "Look at me / I will never pass for a perfect bride / Or a perfect daughter / Can it be / I'm not meant to play this part? / Now I see / That if I were truly to be myself / I would break my family's heart. / Who is that girl I see / Staring straight / Back at me? / Why is my reflection someone / I don't know? / Somehow I cannot hide / Who I am / Though I've tried. / When will my reflection show / Who I am inside? / When will my reflection show / Who I am inside?" www.fpx.de/fp/Disney/Lyrics/Mulan.html Reflection, July 30, 1998. There is also a longer version, produced as a single.

120. The scene may also allude to, in order to correct, the notorious scene in the film *Flower Drum Song* in which the "whitened" and assimilated Linda Low (Nancy Kwan) gazes unironically at her own beautiful femininity in a mirror; see Cheng, *Melancholy of Race,* 46.

ghosts whooshing out from and embodying these same carved characters. Unlike Mulan's living family, they endorse and assist her plan. Thus the characters earlier projected onto Mulan's body repeat, if painlessly, Kingston's "scarwords": they represent the daughter's understanding that her chosen identity and plan of action fulfill familial intentions, despite her parents' opposition. At least fleetingly, they epidermalize her "inside," her identity, and the meaning of her life.

Why did Kingston add the "scarwords" to the traditional story, and why did Disney retain them in this way, while otherwise rejecting most of Kingston's changes? Kingston's story and Disney's both demonstrate that the meaning and purpose of life might be inherited from parents, reside in and on the surface of the body, and be legible to all. In context, this is a specifically American reflection on the racialization of appearance. As Kingston is the child of Chinese immigrants to California in the mid-twentieth century, immigrants whose experience of racism (as Cheng points out) must have been traumatic, her bearing the mark of a racial minority is part of the "words at [her] back" that shape her destiny. The sentence that closes the "White Tigers" chapter of *The Woman Warrior* reads in full, "And I have so many words—'chink' words and 'gook' words too—that they do not fit on my skin" (63). To bear the epidermal signs of non-white race in twentieth-century California is to be marked out for racial slurs, whether a child's parents have deliberately inscribed those marks or merely passed them on. It is to inherit the parents' own sufferings from racialization. As in *Beloved*'s condensation of brand, scars, and racialized skin tone, the mix of pain and beauty in the "scarwords" that Kingston imagines "at [her] back" represents ambivalence about discovering what her appearance means. No longer *un*marked, as she would be in China and as she was as a small child at home, Kingston as a "marked" child needs her mother's talk-story to project an empowered identity such as that of the swordswoman onto her minoritized racial appearance, even as that talk-story also recognizes and compresses her mother's sufferings under racism. A Disney film can hardly retain the pain, but for an audience acutely attuned to racial signs, it does preserve the potent image of writing on the body. Never overtly acknowledging racialization or racism (indeed practicing it: the evil Huns have darker skins than the heroes), the film nonetheless pays homage to Kingston's reimagining of racialized "marks" as melancholic yet empowering familial "scarwords" that determine identity by founding it upon loss.

Disney's *Mulan* came out in 1998, just as the first cohort of girls adopted from China were turning seven, and each successive wave of adop-

Figure 5. "When will my reflection show who I am inside?" From Disney's *Mulan*.

tees has encountered this film at an impressionable age, including, for example, Jeff Gammage's daughter, who "has taken to watching repeated screenings"; Gammage finds this "Disney princess" version of Mulan "not a bad role model at all" for his girls adopted from China.[121] Its production (like that of its Disney precursor *Pochahontas*) was a response to 1990s multiculturalism and the marketing opportunities it opened up, rather than a response specifically to adoptions from China. Families with children from China represented too small a demographic to have been Disney's target audience. Nonetheless, *Mulan* scholar Lan Dong speculates that "the growing number of Chinese girls adopted by American (mostly Caucasian) families might have contributed to Disney's decision to produce this film in the late 1990s."[122] Disney's Mulan is not an adoptee or foster child as is Kingston's Fa Mu Lan, but she is probably the most visible media representation of a transculturated Chinese girl available to US children adopted from China. And for at least some in this demographic, she serves as a powerful figure of identification.

In *Sofia's Journey*, Sofia (the teen who draws her mother by looking at herself in the mirror) sings Mulan's song for the group of friends and

121. Gammage, *China Ghosts*, 224.
122. Dong, *Mulan's Legend and Legacy*, 220.

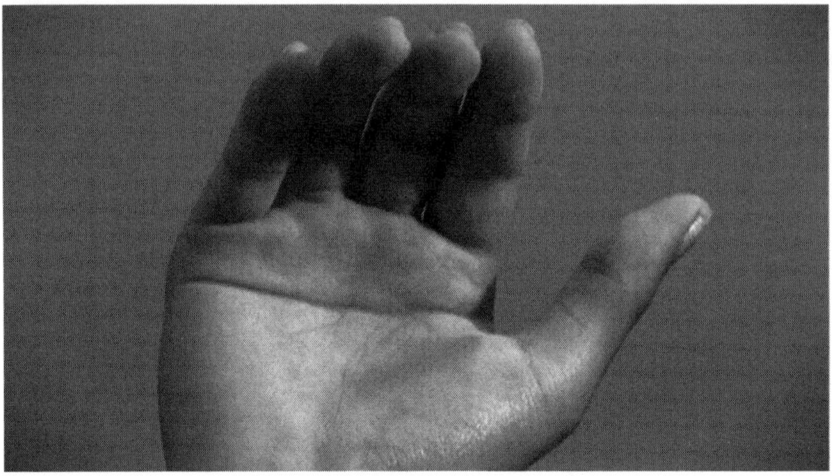

Figure 6. Sofia's "very special mark." From Changfu Chang, *Sofia's Journey*.

family who have gathered to help her. In the scene that immediately follows, repeating in her speaking voice the line "Why is my reflection someone I don't know?", she explains what the words mean to her: "Who are you? . . . Kids back home, they have their birth parents. . . . I don't; you look at yourself in the mirror and you're not able to . . . 'cause you don't know who you came from really." She is searching because, as she puts it, she has "a hole in [her] heart"; she wants, she says, especially to know what her birth parents look like. For Sofia, Mulan's alienation from her artificially feminine appearance speaks for the lack of connection between the adoptee's appearance and her identity. Sofia also possesses "a very special feature," a kind of birthmark that aids her search: a crease straight across her palm where most people have two curving lines. The camera dwells repeatedly, perhaps melancholically, on both the mirror drawing and on Sofia's marked hand. For this audience, the Mulan story invokes the same possibility as the urban legend of the marked Chinese adoptee, that the markings on your body—signs that may condense racialized or familial appearance with signs of grievous loss or injury—might tell you who you are related to, who you are, and what to do with your life.

It is important to notice here that the becoming-legible of such marks is not the same as the complete restoration of the familial, national, and cultural contexts in which they were passed on or made. Finding or creating meaning and identity from such marks does not require returning to or recovering the past. As Eng writes about Tajiri's film, "the daughter's cure . . . does not involve the recovery of a lost narrative or the restoration of a set of causal, referential events."[123] Glimpsing Sofia's drawing of herself and her imagined mother in the film, one wishes Sofia could value her artwork as self-portraiture and for what it reveals about herself in the present, rather than valuing it as a clue in a search that may never reach its goal. Just as Kingston constructs Chinese American community not through racial solidarity or through the (unattainable) "authenticity" Frank Chin excoriated her for eschewing, but "*through* difference, disappointment, and failure" (*Melancholy of Race,* 101), the adoptee's identity resides not in the temporally and geographically distant referent of the mark, but in the mark itself and what she can make of it here and now.

CHOSEN MARKS

In the epilogue to *The Book of Sarahs,* McKinley reveals that as she was reaching the end of her "search for self-definition" (*Book of Sarahs,* 286) in the late 1990s, she moved to West Africa for a year and a half to research indigo, a lifelong passion of hers: "Indigo is the color of the deep, druglike haze of melancholy I once lived in, and of the cloth that became a balm" (286). Traveling to places where traditional indigo dyeing is still practiced and where the cloth retains its ancient spiritual value, she went "in search of blue-stained women's hands, tracing the routes of trade, the stories of women whose once powerful dye economy . . . stretched across half of a continent" (286). Indigo connects her to a female community in Accra where she feels at home, where to "tie your cloth to my cloth" means to join in friendship and solidarity (288).

In the book that resulted from her research, *Indigo: In Search of the Color That Seduced the World,* she recounts historical discoveries and personal revelations about the myriad ways in which indigo is intertwined with human life. Once part of the slave trade, "a length of blue cloth was a common exchange for human life."[124] Yet indigo is connected to life in more affirmative ways, too: the dye process requires exposure to oxygen,

123. Eng, *Feeling of Kinship,* 171.

124. Catherine E. McKinley, *Indigo: In Search of the Color That Seduced the World* (New York: Bloomsbury, 2011), 11 (hereafter cited in the text).

as if the cloth were alive and breathing, and indigo traditionally accompanies significant rituals from birth to burial. It looks like the sky and the sea yet smells like earth, smoke, even urine. A piece of Yoruba-made cloth she receives as a gift while still living in the United States not only "rushed my senses" but literally penetrates her body:

> Each time I handled the cloth, it left ghostlike traces of blue on my hands, beautiful against the skin. They felt like a blessing or protection. . . . I tried to preserve the stains, as if keeping that blue in my eye and on my hands was essential to preserving my balance, but they quickly faded. (*Indigo,* 8)

Indigo dye, rubbed into cut skin, is traditionally used to deepen scarification marks (9, 130), and the designs marked on indigo cloth sometimes resemble scarification patterns. McKinley includes a stunning archival photograph of a Yoruba woman on the last page of the book's color plates to illustrate this continuity between indigo-marked skin and indigo fabric; could this also be a kind of wishful self-image? Her indigo-stained hands are her westerner's equivalent of indigo scarification, and her wish to "preserve the stains" is her affirmative revision of the impulse to cut herself that once afflicted her. She notices admiringly those whose bodies seem to merge with their indigo garments, such as the "deep blue-stained brown face" of a Tuareg man from whom she buys a *taglemust,* or indigo-dyed turban, and she hopes to find dyers' compounds and markets where "indigo once dripped everywhere, bled into everything here" (54, 187). (Synthetic dyes and imported cloth have mostly replaced indigo production even in rural areas.) Yearning to absorb and be absorbed into the starkly beautiful lifeways of the indigo-wearing people she sees on a trip to northern Niger, she buys another *taglemust* and feels "the loose, metallic indigo powder, mixed with goat fat [as it] sifted into my palms. It smelled rich and loamy, of the vat"; watching "a sea of men, most heads wrapped in indigo," kneeling in prayer, "my body welled with longing to enter the depths of that collision of faith, feeling, history, and divine beauty" (197–98). On a crowded bus returning to Ghana, she is squeezed so close to two men (their faces, hands, and clothes stained blue) that the indigo of their *taglemusts* stains her clothing; teased about running off with a man, she reflects, "I simply wanted the ride to go on long enough that I was bathed in indigo" (202).

Although she can trace connections between various parts of her family tree and the cloth trade, McKinley's desire to be marked by indigo expresses her aspiration to create her own African-identified markings to supersede her prior experience of being "mark[ed]" by others "with ferocity" and, too, to redeem the marks she once made on her body in pain. (Ironically, in Africa she is given the identity of rich, white European lady.) But her desire for indigo markings also expresses her identification as a writer. In the white designs and patterns made on indigo fabric through stitching or batik, McKinley sees something "like handwriting," and she links her fascination with indigo with her love of reading and writing (*Indigo,* 8). Hiking one day in Mali, she sees, against a bare rock cliff, a line of Dogon women walking, all dressed in darkest indigo; her host explains that they are "sorceresses" and that "you can read their stories on their wrappers" (9). This vision prompts her yearning to return to Africa to study indigo: "I felt flooded by a strange anxiety at the loss of that beauty, at not being able to read those marks." This wish to read indigo, which means reading bodies as well as fabrics and which mingles with her wish to be marked or written on by indigo, she traces back to her love of reading as a child, which she experienced as a complete bodily practice:

> I loved the print on book pages, newspaper ink, and the dark tattoo of the funny pages—it smelled pungent and rubbed off and stained, as if allowing the stories to live in you. I would chew the corners of the Sunday *Times,* forming small, hard tablets that I would swallow, associating those dyes with the power to speak and write. The Dogon women, wearing blue texts and signs, brought that sense of power and beauty back to me. (*Indigo,* 10)

To surround herself with indigo fabrics and to "bathe in" and become stained with indigo is at once to become marked or legible to others in the language of her choice and to "swallow" the power to write. *Indigo* completes the story of McKinley's recovery from—or, to be more accurate, her repurposing of—melancholy and her search for identity, when she is able to replace compulsory marks of blood with the chosen marks of the bluest of blues.

4 / "THE MOTHER WHO ISN'T ONE"

SILENCE

Birthmothers' stories are hard to come by. Up to this point in this book, birthmothers have appeared mostly in the position of abjection to which fictional and nonfiction adoption narratives normally consign them: disparaged and disappeared, like Molly Farren Cass, the drug addict in *Silas Marner* whose convenient and unmourned death makes possible the narrative of her daughter's adoption; the objects of disappointing or failed searches, such as Lifton's or Prager's, or John Smith's or Jennifer Marcus's; lost, ill, dead, unreachable, like the mothers in memoirs by Trenka, Robinson, or Hopgood; or scarcely glimpsed in postures of excruciating self-sacrifice, like the nameless third world "producers" of babies aggregated by critics of transnational adoption or as in the accounts of Chinese birthmothers by Hood and Xinran. Recreated occasionally in such fleeting images as the pink blanket enfolding Turtle, the stuff of terrifying nightmares for Jadine, or dreamed of by a wistful teenage girl looking at herself in the mirror—and how different *The Love Wife* would be if Lan were really the birthmother and not her somewhat alarming avatar: birthmothers may be desired, disavowed, or reviled, but their own stories are seldom heard. In these instances and others, birthmothers become the silent, static, material ground against which the forward-moving achievements of adoption stories stand out: the muse who inspires adoptees' and adoptive parents' creative imaginings, the object of a search legitimized by the high cultural value placed on questing for origins. This chapter argues for the fruitfully destabilizing potential of the birthmother who—from her position of no position within the adoptive family—speaks out and tells her own story, even if it is only the story of her silence.

In the case of US birthmothers, Ann Fessler has documented the profound secrecy and shame among "the girls who went away," the unmarried, underage women who relinquished their children in the period before *Roe v. Wade.*[1] That shame, together with the "sealed and secret kinship" of the period before open records and open adoption, effectively prevented birthmothers from making their stories known, whether privately or in public.[2] As Maureen Sweeney writes, the "socially and legally constructed role of birth mother"—as a woman with a shameful secret she must wish to hide and as a laborer producing goods for the baby market—"combined with the intensity of a birth mother's grief, makes it very difficult for a birth mother to speak out publicly."[3] Barbara Melosh reports that birth parents have produced by far the fewest accounts of their experiences, in contrast to the outpouring of search narratives by adoptees and writings by adoptive parents.[4] A birthmother may feel strong pressure to conceal her experience: as Jan Waldron writes, "she can lie; it is hoped, often, that she will."[5]

The problem is not simply that birthmothers have been discouraged from sharing their stories. In culturally prevalent views of stranger adoption, the birthmother is not meant to survive, much less to speak. She is not just circumstantially but also constitutively absent. Margaret Moorman writes that she did not even recognize herself as a party to her child's adoption until she read *The Adoption Triangle,* the book that gave a name to who she was:

> It was the first time I had considered myself an integral part of the whole business. I'd felt like persona non grata, the fly in the ointment, the fifth wheel that would tip the otherwise perfectly balanced cart. I was so used to thinking of myself as someone who was no longer supposed to exist.[6]

Adoption typically begins with the writing of a new birth certificate

1. Ann Fessler, *The Girls Who Went Away: The Hidden History of Women Who Surrendered Children for Adoption in the Decades before* Roe v. Wade (New York and London: Penguin Books, 2006) (hereafter cited in the text).
2. Judith S. Modell, *A Sealed and Secret Kinship: The Culture of Policies and Practices in American Adoption* (New York: Berghahn Books, 2002). See also Wayne E. Carp, *Family Matters: Secrecy and Disclosure in the History of Adoption* (Cambridge: Harvard University Press, 1998).
3. Maureen A. Sweeney, "Between Sorrow and Happy Endings: A New Paradigm of Adoption," *Yale Journal of Law and Feminism* 2 (1990): 329–69, quotation at 341.
4. Barbara Melosh, "Adoption Stories: Autobiographical Narrative and the Politics of Identity," in *Adoption in America: Historical Perspectives,* ed. E. Wayne Carp (Ann Arbor: University of Michigan Press, 2002), 218–45.
5. Jan L. Waldron, *Giving Away Simone: A Memoir* (New York: Doubleday, 1995), 135.
6. Margaret Moorman, *Waiting to Forget: A Motherhood Lost and Found* (New York: Norton, 1996), 130 (hereafter cited in the text). She cites Arthur D. Sorosky, Annette Baran, and Reuben Pannor, *The Adoption Triangle* (New York: Anchor Books, 1979).

that retroactively constitutes the adoptive parents as the original parents and erases all traces of the birthmother. In the zero sum game of adoption prior to open adoption and the emergent notion "that a child can have . . . multiple mothers and fathers,"[7] the creation of the new nuclear family requires the erasure, the de-ontologizing, of those with prior claims. If there can be only one mother, the birthmother must be dead to the world, and her nonexistence is confirmed by the lack of any proper terms to name her, as Karen Salyer McElmurray's self-description as "the mother who isn't one" suggests.[8] "For the adoptive mother to become 'real,'" writes Mary Lyndon Shanley, "the birth mother had to become a nonmother."[9] The requirement of her nonexistence, which is at once legal, social, cultural, and narrative, has made it particularly hard for birthmothers to speak or write, much less make their stories known. It is not just that she is ashamed of her story, but that to tell her story means attempting to speak from an untenable, nonspeaking position. In the cultural logic of adoption, the birthmother cannot represent herself, and she is representable by others only as an absence.

The birthmother's erasure has long been, in part, an intensification of cultural attitudes to motherhood generally, so that the difficulty of telling her story is of a piece with the undervaluation and underrepresentation of mothers' stories (as of many aspects of women's lives) more widely. Those who bear children may no longer be burdened by what Patricia Yaeger termed in 1992 "one of our most persistent cultural myths," the "obliterat[ion of] gestation and parturition from the story of . . . birth,"[10] yet aspects of this muting of maternal experience persist.

---

7. Mary Lyndon Shanley, *Making Babies, Making Families: What Matters Most in an Age of Reproductive Technologies, Surrogacy, Adoption, and Same-Sex and Unwed Parents* (Boston: Beacon Press, 2001), 23. This chapter focuses on birthmothers prior to the trend toward open adoptions, but open adoption does not simply solve the difficulty of the birthmother's role. Sheila Ganz's film *Unlocking the Heart of Adoption* includes bitter testimony from a birthmother who expected to sustain a relationship with her birth children (twins) but found the relationship terminated unilaterally by the parents when the children were five. Of the open adoption into which she placed her son, Kate Livingston reports a mixed experience, as part of her son's life but not a member of the family: "Toward a Public Accounting of a Private Legacy: Family, Politics, and the (Feminist) Possibilities of Birthmotherhood," paper delivered at ASAC Conference, MIT, Apr. 30, 2010, and partially summarized in her "Adoption: Experience, Research, and Activism," *ASAC News* (Fall 2010): 4–5.
8. Karen Salyer McElmurray, *Surrendered Child: A Birth Mother's Journey* (Athens: University of Georgia Press, 2004), 174 (hereafter cited in the text).
9. Shanley, *Making Babies, Making Families*, 23.
10. Patricia Yaeger, "The Poetics of Birth," in *Discourses of Sexuality from Aristotle to AIDS*, ed. Domna C. Stanton (Ann Arbor: University of Michigan Press, 1992), 262–96, quotation at 263.

In her book about writing, *Listen to Me,* Lynn Lauber, a writer and writing teacher who is also a birthmother, describes workshops she has run for "older women who have spent a lifetime in relative silence" for whom Lauber's writing assignments make possible "the roaring unleashing of years of held-back rage and truth."[11] Cultural biases have eliminated many women's topics, "mired" as they have tended to be "in the domestic"; times have changed, "but I still find women so bound by these old prohibitions, so drenched in a legacy of anonymity and silence, that they are reluctant to write a word about themselves" (*Listen to Me,* 89–90). Placing her own self-censorship as a birthmother in this gendered context, Lauber reminds both herself and her students to follow Virginia Woolf's example and rid themselves of the Angel in the House, the voice that tells women to be good rather than to tell the truth. A birthmother's story can be at least doubly unspeakable: as that of the illegitimate, rejecting, "bad" mother, and as that the mutely material body, mother in body only.

Birthmothers not only must overcome social taboos to write their stories; they also lack of some of the essential linguistic and literary tools for doing so. It is partially, but not only, a matter of "unleashing" pent-up voices. The available terms and narrative conventions for telling family stories are inadequate to their task, and their harrowing experiences often make it difficult to claim the entitled subjectivity that lets a writer say "I" or claim that her story counts as a human experience. Birthmother Janet Mason Ellerby, looking back to the 1960s, laments her entrapment by "the fairy tales of my childhood and the fiction and music of my adolescence, stories of first love that would ultimately and ineluctably triumph" but that failed her once she became pregnant at sixteen. The "new script of teenage rebellion" only intensified her subjection to unlivable narrative paradigms, her boyfriend's "dreamy adolescent fantasy" merely replacing "happily ever after" with the stormy excitements of *Wuthering Heights.*[12] In *Listen to Me,* Lauber explains her youthful rebellion by critiquing the plot line available to young women of her social location, the plot of "every female story I heard," that of marriage: "I wanted to start another story cycle" (*Listen to Me,* 21, 22). That new story is hard to conceive and live out, and even harder to narrate intelligibly: "A heroine without a maxim, like a rebel without a cause, is destined to

11. Lynn Lauber, *Listen to Me: Writing Life into Meaning* (New York: W. W. Norton, 2004), 40 (hereafter cited in the text).

12. Janet Mason Ellerby, *Following the Tambourine Man: A Birthmother's Memoir* (Syracuse: Syracuse University Press, 2007), 12, 73, 50 (hereafter cited in the text).

be misunderstood," writes feminist literary critic Nancy K. Miller.[13] Young American women who became birthmothers in the years before *Roe v. Wade* were told that if they followed the script prepared for them—the narrative of concealment, relinquishment, and forgetting—they could resume their lives postpartum as if nothing had happened. The adults who constructed these narratives could not conceive of story lines in which sexual desire and motherhood existed outside of the patrifocal family, hence their belief that the experience would drop away from the memories of the young mothers they coerced. This story line failed most of the birthmothers whose stories we know, just as much as the plots of courtship and marriage and of romantic love failed them prior to that, yet no new story line emerged to take its place.

Feminist literary critics have long observed that the available plots of literature, androcentric and heteronormative as they are, have abetted social and legal constraints on women by limiting men's and women's conceptions of their freedom.[14] The plots of "traditional fictional narratives," writes Susan Winnett, with their "dynamics of beginnings, middles, and ends," are structured around "what men want, how they go about trying to get it, and the stories they tell about this pursuit."[15] "Our own education," she continues, places "obstacles . . . in the way both of women's conceiving (of) their own pleasure and of men's conceding that female pleasure might have a different plot."[16] What, she speculates, would a plot look like that put childbirth (as one among several possible distinctive female bodily experiences) not at the remote edges, but at the center of a narrative, and in terms not just of theme, but of form as well?[17] Like Yeager calling for a poetics and a philosophy of birth, Winnett points to the lack of narrative paradigms derived from women's sexual and reproductive experiences, paradigms on the basis of which a birthmother might begin to construct her story. The relinquishment of a birth child makes a story even less easily accommodated within the usual forms of narrative

13. Nancy K. Miller, "Emphasis Added: Plots and Plausibilities in Women's Fiction," *PMLA* 96 (1981): 36–48, quotation at 36.
14. Marianne Novy, too, finds the feminist critique of traditional plots suggestive for reading adoption stories; see *Reading Adoption: Family and Difference in Fiction and Drama* (Ann Arbor: University of Michigan Press, 2005), especially 3, 25–31.
15. Susan Winnett, "Coming Unstrung: Women, Men, Narrative, and Principles of Pleasure," *PMLA* 105 (1990): 505–18, quotation at 506.
16. Winnett, "Coming Unstrung," 507.
17. Winnett, "Coming Unstrung," 509; for other feminist critiques of traditional plots, see Rachel Blau DuPlessis, *Writing Beyond the Ending* (Bloomington: Indiana University Press, 1985); and Joseph Allen Boone, *Tradition Counter Tradition: Love and the Form of Fiction* (Chicago: University of Chicago Press, 1987).

than is childbirth alone. The title of birthmother Meredith Hall's memoir *Without a Map* aptly captures this absence of an available form, as she explains in describing her life with her recovered birth son:

> There are no patterns for how to do this, how to hold each other safely and fully after a lifetime apart. We cannot plot out the future. We are a family. We love each other. We need each other. That is our only map.[18]

Because the available plots of family life have erased her, the birthmother must invent her own plot, as well as a new place from which to speak.

This chapter attempts to uncover some of the cultural biases making birthmothers' stories so hard to tell and to discuss some new ways birthmother-writers have found to overcome their silencing. Beyond the social and legal norms laid bare by Wayne Carp and other historians of adoption that compelled shame, secrecy, and silence during the experience and aftermath of relinquishment, norms whose grip is starting to loosen, conventions of language and of narrative can compound the silence by making these stories difficult to narrate even when secrecy and shame have been overcome. The first section of this chapter examines some recent, highly visible representations of birthmothers that exemplify the cultural norms and literary conventions that birthmothers must struggle to reshape for their own use; in the second and third sections I read against them some remarkable works by and about birthmothers that meet these difficulties, rendering the birthmother's story narratable by telling the story of the difficulty of the telling. This shift of focus from trying to recapture a lost referential past to the act of self-reflexive storytelling in the present aligns these writers with those discussed in chapters 2 and 3 for whom making something new becomes more salutary than continuing to search for meaning in the past. It aligns them, too, with the project to overturn adoption's invidious binary oppositions between figure and ground, culture and nature.

Typical of normative representations is the figure of the birthmother in Mary Gaitskill's short story "Don't Cry." The narrator has come to Ethiopia to help a friend, Katya, adopt; the harrowing events of the adoption (mystifying bureaucratic resistance, gun battles in the streets) serve as catalyst for the narrator's reflections on her marriage, which has just ended with the death of her husband. The story positions the birthmother as an abject body whose plight engages the privileged visitors'

18. Meredith Hall, *Without a Map: A Memoir* (Boston: Beacon Press, 2007), 182.

pity but who is finally in the story to serve their needs. The mother whose baby Katya will eventually adopt left her baby at a hospital six months before, apparently abandoning him; the official is ready to complete the adoption when the mother reappears. This is how the narrator describes the scene at the hospital, where a noisy crowd gathers:

> My eyes went to the only silent one among them: a small beaten-looking woman with long dirty hair and flat breasts hanging way down her body. She was dressed in filthy ragged clothes, and the earrings had been torn from her ears. Her eyes were small and hot and I could not read their expression.[19]

Although the official hands the baby back, the mother indicates that she wants to give the baby to Katya, and the next morning she succeeds in doing so. Katya overcomes her scruples about taking a baby from a victim of imperial oppression, and the story ends affirmatively with the two white women preparing to leave the country. As the narrator holds the baby, "*I thrive,* his body said to mine. *I will thrive.* I put my hand on the back of his head and held it to my shoulder, my cheek against his hair. It was time to go" ("Don't Cry," 111, emphasis in original). The consolation that the baby provides to the sorrowing, backward-looking narrator is made possible by the inarticulate silence of the birthmother, her silence redoubled by the barriers of culture and language, her only intelligible desire the desire to meet the adoptive mother's needs. (Why does she, after returning to reclaim her child despite her poverty, suddenly choose to relinquish him? The story sheds no light.) In conformity with the practices of many adoptive parents (see chapter 2), Katya has already replaced the absent birthmother with a well-intentioned fantasy that further erases her. What if he asks about his mother? "I'll tell him that his mother was a great woman. That she was a fighter, and because she had to fight so hard she gave me her most precious child to keep him safe. Something like that" ("Don't Cry," 111). Katya has already absorbed a key directive from adoption professionals: in the absence of knowledge about the birthmother, together parent and child should "fantasize about her."[20] But here the fantasy is a deliberate erasure of the birthmother's desperate reality.

19. Mary Gaitskill, "Don't Cry," *New Yorker,* June 9 and 16, 2008, 96–111, quotation at 105 (hereafter cited in the text).

20. Susan Tompkins, "The Importance of Loving Your Child's Birthmother," in *A Passage to the Heart: Writings from Families with Children from China,* ed. Amy Klatzkin (St. Paul: Yeong and Yeong, 1999), 313–15, quotation at 315.

These caricatures—the silent, opaque birthmother and the expressive, self-justifying adoptive mother—serve as foils for the more complex figure of the narrator; nonetheless their reiteration in such a context, the story's assumption of their general recognizability, means their continued cultural acceptance. Lorrie Moore similarly, in *A Gate at the Stairs,* relies on a rapid caricature of the abject birthmother to highlight contrastingly her sympathetic psychological portraits of the witty babysitter-narrator and even of the very flawed adoptive mother: "Bonnie was not bonnie. . . . She was heavy, perhaps still from the pregnancy. . . . She looked puffy and medicated. . . . The person who most needed adopting, it seemed to me, was Bonnie."[21] Ann Patchett's 2007 novel *Run* provides a more extended example of the cultural normativity of the figure of the abjected birthmother, and it should be no surprise that in this case as in the Gaitskill story the woman is black.

Run presents the dream of US transracial adoption: that poor black children can seamlessly join well-off white families, to the benefit of the children, the white parents and siblings, and even the racist world they inhabit. In the novel's prehistory, two black brothers (now college age) were successfully adopted by the Boston Irish Doyles; the novel's present-time action dramatizes the adoption of their younger sister Kenya, whose integration into her new family signifies both her own flourishing and an end to the tiresome feuds that have marred the ingrown Doyle clan. For the whites, difference refreshes the literal and metaphorical gene pool; for the blacks, access to white culture means fulfillment. Waking up for the first time in her spacious new home, Kenya notices that "in the light that soaked this room a girl could read the spines of the books on the very top shelf. '*The Double Helix,*' she said aloud. '*A Separate Peace.*'"[22] She notices, too, the contrast between this intense morning light and the remembered "dimness" of her own home (*Run,* 157). John Updike praises this scene's celebration of "the civilized enlightenment whose glories should be available to all"; to Updike it is an unquestionable good that Kenya should gain access to the benefits of white middle-class culture.[23] The two older sons apparently experience no difficulty negotiating their transracial identities in a fictional Boston where the color line

21. Lorrie Moore, *A Gate at the Stairs* (New York: Knopf, 2009), 88, 93.
22. Ann Patchett, *Run* (New York: HarperCollins, 2007), 157 (hereafter cited in the text).
23. John Updike, "A Boston Fable: Ann Patchett's New Novel," *New Yorker,* Oct. 1, 2007, 98–100, quotation at 100. For a contrasting perspective, see, e.g., Pamela Anne Quiroz's skeptical account of transracial adoption "into a white hegemonic system" as being far from "race-neutral, altruistic, [or] advantageous to children of color": *Adoption in a Color-Blind Society* (Lanham MD: Roman and Littlefield, 2007), 19.

is rarely visible. Nor do they suffer any sense of loss from lacking their birthmother, about whom they never wonder while they are growing up.

Balancing this utopian picture of transracial adoption is the fate Patchett creates for the black mother. Like Gaitskill's birthmother, Tennessee and her story are mostly flattened into stereotype. Unbelievably self-sacrificing in the novel's prehistory (having given her infant up for adoption, she soon gave up her eighteen-month-old too, so he could look after his little brother), and again in the episode that precipitates the novel's action, when she throws herself in front of an SUV to prevent the older son from being run over, Tennessee spends the entirety of the novel's present time slowly and almost speechlessly dying, an abject lump of black flesh. Valerie Smith pointed out two decades earlier that black women have served for generations to represent everything that western culture denigrates about embodiment; both "in classic Western philosophy and in nineteenth-century cultural constructions of womanhood . . . women of color [have been associated with] the body and therefore with animal passions and slave labor."[24] Except in some lengthy flashbacks, we do not see Tennessee whole and human; in the present time of the novel, she is always injured, exhausted, bloody, and silenced, dying of blood leaking into her abdomen from an undetected internal injury, clutching her belly, her complaints of stomach pain dismissed because they do not match the official diagnosis of a broken hip.

Why should the three children's transcendence, not to mention the happiness of their white family, depend upon their first mother's immanence and abjection? Tennessee's death is not unmourned, but the novel conspicuously omits what might have been the novel's emotional center: Kenya's discovery of her loss when, to everyone's surprise, her much-loved mother dies after seeming on the road to recovery. To foreground and celebrate the transracial adoptive relationships seems to require the muting and even the violent severing of black family ties, just as Kenya's accession to Eurocentric culture is made to seem worth the price of her mother's death. Indeed, at the end of the novel Kenya imagines that her mother deliberately sacrificed herself to give her daughter the cultural and educational advantages of the Doyles' world. The birthmother is, constitutively, outside the family, a position she herself has seemed to embrace by—we learn in retrospect—following her sons all

24. Valerie Smith, "Black Feminist Theory and the Representation of the 'Other,'" in *Changing Our Own Words: Essays on Criticism, Theory, and Writing by Black Women*, ed. Cheryl A. Wall (New Brunswick: Rutgers University Press, 1989), 38–57, quotation at 44.

over Boston, Kenya in tow, without ever revealing herself. Her narrative function is the same as her familial role, to serve as a resource for others who gains nothing for herself. Her injury not only propels the adoption plot but also prompts the extended Doyle clan to gather and reconcile after years of mutual alienation.

No one in the novel hears Tennessee's story from her. As in Hood's *The Red Thread,* the birthmother's story is a secret shared only between author and readers. Here, the reader learns that Tennessee was not always the near-caricature of the black birthmother that she embodies in the novel's present time. She once aspired to go to college and perhaps to law school, perhaps to enter politics. Her potential to have become a rich and interesting character, always located in the past before she became a mother, is brought out in a highly contrived plot twist that, depending on the reader's viewpoint, either mitigates or intensifies the stereotypicality of the black birthmother's imprisonment in her doomed and silenced body. After some carefully dropped hints, the novel reveals that Tennessee is not the biological mother of Kenya, who was born to Tennessee's best friend, a woman also named Tennessee who died when Kenya was a baby. We learn this when Tennessee, emerging from anesthesia after surgery, hallucinates that her friend is with her, visiting from the dead. To facilitate the adoption, Tennessee assumed her friend's name and identity. As Tennessee puts it, "In my last life I was somebody named Beverly who had two little boys and gave them up. In this life I'm you and I have a daughter" (*Run,* 197).

On the one hand, the story of Kenya's prior adoption complicates the identification of Tennessee with abject maternity. As Kenya's adoptive rather than biological mother, Tennessee lines up on the same side of the dichotomy between the parent-in-culture and parent of the body as other adopters in the novel, the cultured whites. She is an artificer who astutely gamed the system: lacking the resources to adopt legally, and realizing that no one would notice the disappearance of a little black girl, she simply steps into her friend's role and walks off with her baby. On the other hand, the death of yet another black birthmother behind the death of Tennessee in the present underscores the theme of maternal erasure. Invisible as Tennessee has been, she erases her friend's identity along with her own, doubly burying her. It is as if this character were created only to emphasize the disposability of black birthmothers. Moreover, it is when she secretly appropriates her friend's identity and adopts Kenya that she loses both her vocational ambitions and her sense of existing as a self. When the hallucinatory Tennessee suggests that her friend might have married or made friends, Tennessee replies: "How was I going to make friends? I couldn't tell them about my boys or about you or Kenya or even what my name was. I don't know how much there is after you take all that away" (*Run,* 210). While Patchett does imagine a birthmother telling her own story, she places that story in the surreal and private space of hallucination. It is unimaginable within the rest of the novel's frame of urban realism, and neither the plot nor the other characters are ever aware of or affected by it.

Patchett's earlier novel about birthmothers, *The Patron Saint of Liars,* does acknowledge the birthmother's point of view, and yet it too illustrates the silence and avoidance that seems to encircle birthmother subjectivity.[25] The action occurs over two decades (pre– and post–*Roe v. Wade*) at a Catholic home for unwed mothers, and the main characters are embedded in a changing population of pregnant girls, several of whom are individuated as interesting and sympathetic characters and all of whom will leave to deliver and relinquish their babies. The main character at the start of the novel is Rose, a woman who has married young, finds herself pregnant and unhappy, and decides to cut her ties by driving in secrecy to the faraway St. Elizabeth's to bear her child and give it up for adoption. Out-of-wedlock pregnancy, as well as Rose's more unusual situation, inspire a predictable amount of fabrication, as the title suggests: most of the girls have lied to their families and the nuns (each girl tells the mother superior she was married but the husband died in a car crash); Rose conceals her past. Through first-person narration, we watch Rose reinventing herself in the new setting, and during her pregnancy the novel explores Rose's thoughts, troubles, and motivations with a high degree of psychological refinement.

So it comes as something of a shock, though not a surprise, that just before Rose is to give birth, the narrative point of view shifts to that of the man she has suddenly married, the devoted and gentle Son, who is unaware, like everyone else at St. Elizabeth's, of Rose's past. Rose hides this truth in order to keep her baby, inspired by a pregnant girl who goes to heroic lengths to hold her twin babies for a mere five hours before seeing them taken away. Given the rigidity of the system that mandates relinquishment, the understanding already mobilized for Rose, and the pleasure it gives the appealing Son, the reader will likely sympathize with her imposture. Yet the narrative leaves Rose at a point where her lying becomes unsavory, when she insists on a further lie (involving the

---

25. Ann Patchett, *The Patron Saint of Liars* (New York: Houghton Mifflin, 1992).

choice of a name for the baby) that abuses Son's feelings. As Rose ceases to anchor the narrative point of view, she also loses her appeal, as her own traumas cut her off from her second family. She gradually abandons her husband and daughter, devoting herself instead to caring for the nuns and girls at St. Elizabeth's and finally leaving altogether. Son's first-person narrative is followed by that of Cecilia, the now-teenage daughter; the novel, devolving into her coming-of-age story, never returns to Rose's point of view, instead presenting Rose from Cecilia's viewpoint as increasingly opaque, isolated, secretive, and silent. Cecilia's maturation narrative involves her learning to take care of herself, her father, and a beloved friend in the absence of her mother, who thus moves from being the center of subjectivity to serving as the nearly grotesque catalyst for another's. Thus Patchett's initial narrative choice to grant a birthmother a plausible point of view is reversed when Rose acts out the paradigmatic birthmother narrative, abandoning her child just as if she had been compelled to. It is as if the narrative logic of the birthmother story compels a departure from the birthmother's subjectivity; like the birthmothers in *Run* and "Don't Cry," the story, along with the child, is no longer hers.

The birthmothers who speak in Ann Fessler's oral histories and who write of their experiences in the memoirs I will discuss here all struggle with the narrative paradigm Patchett's work presents, in which birthmotherhood is incompatible with speaking subjectivity. Rose's deliberate choice to abandon her child means that we do not see her suffering from the relinquishment, yet those who have read Fessler's *The Girls Who Went Away* or any other testimony from closed adoption birthmothers are aware that relinquishment can lead to such pain and grief that the woman may feel she has lost the grounds on which her personhood stands. Told to behave and feel as if nothing had happened—like gays and lesbians who are dehumanized when the deaths of partners and loved ones are not counted as grievable losses[26]—birthmothers often say that the denial of their status as mothers and of their entitlement to mourn deprives them of identity and humanity. And this is not because nature has made them mother and child, but rather because the identity category "mother" is so strongly marked in US culture, so that to become a mother and simultaneously to be denied as a mother is to feel a radical dissonance in identity. "I was and was not a mother from that birth day on," writes Karen Salyer McElmurray (*Surrendered Child,* 19).

26. This is a problem often addressed by Judith Butler, e.g., in *The Psychic Life of Power: Theories in Subjection* (Stanford: Stanford University Press, 1997); and Butler, *Precarious Life: The Powers of Mourning and Violence* (London and New York: Verso, 2004).

Lorraine Dusky calls her experience "a living death."[27] Again and again the birthmothers in Fessler's book describe the sensation of ceasing to be a recognizable person after relinquishment:

> I wasn't even the same person anymore. . . . I was expected to go back and be this teenager and live under their rules. I was a mom, but I wasn't allowed to be the mom . . . We were not criminals. We're mothers. The difference was I was not an *authenticated* mother. I was an illegal mother. I was a denied mother. (Karen I, *Girls Who Went Away,* 160, 163)[28]

Some women compare the experience of self-eradication to being closeted; others, to battlefield trauma: "they never really get over what they see" (Maggie, *Girls Who Went Away,* 227).

To articulate the experience of becoming a non-person is already to have reconstituted some degree of personhood. Yet birthmothers often speak or write of having gone through a radical loss of language. The dehumanizing of the "denied mother," "the mother who isn't one," is in part the result of an insufficiency in language that reflects and perpetuates the social non-being of the birthmother. Birthmother and political theorist Kate Livingston opens her essay "The Birthmother Dilemma" with a list of ill-fitting terms for what she is—"Mother. Birth Mother. Natural Mother. First Mother. Biological Mother. Life Mother. Real Mother. Not a Mother at All."—and for what she did—"Relinquished. Gave Up. Placed. Gave Away. Abandoned. Lost. Chose."[29] She comments, "Society can literally find no words to define the function of these women and the nature of their relationship to their offspring." Pamela Anne Quiroz reports that efforts, starting in the 1970s and 1980s, to ameliorate the language used about adoption (changing "real parent" to "birth parent" or "surrender" to "choose adoption") were seen by some birthmothers as "a tool of oppression . . . meant to marginalize natural mothers and dehumanize them" while serving the interests of

27. Lorraine Dusky, "Family Reunions," in *The Adoption Reader: Birth Mothers, Adoptive Mothers, and Adopted Daughters Tell Their Stories,* ed. Susan Wadia-Ells (Seattle: Seal Press, 1995), 3–9, quotation at 3.

28. Because Fessler quotes the birthmothers' oral testimonies over their first-name signatures, granting them something like coauthorship as if in an anthology, I follow her practice by citing not just page numbers but the speakers' names as well.

29. Kate Livingston, "The Birthmother Dilemma," paper presented at NWSA Conference, Cincinnati, June 2008.

adoptive parents.[30] Every phase of the birthmother's role in adoption bristles with unsuitable terms: "'What "decision"?' one birthmother demands. 'There was no decision. The word *decision* doesn't apply to relinquishing a child,'" writes Merry Bloch Jones.[31] "Don't tell me I 'surrendered' them. . . . Each time I hear the word used in that way I want to scream."[32] Jan Waldron writes of trying to use the term "birthchild" for her daughter: "But it is understandable why almost no one uses the language of birthrelations: When we do, we are delivering the first line of a tumbling, complicated story" that it can be painful and awkward to explain.[33]

Time and again Ann Fessler's speakers and others record a resulting disorder in self-representation, whereby the birthmother is reduced not only to silence but to nonhuman sounds and bodily symptoms. These women vomit, they stutter, they have migraines, they bleed, they suffer mysterious pains during the birth month—everything but speak the unspeakable truth of what happened. One woman recalls "my voice problem" starting with a "slight hitch" when she entered the maternity home and increasing to a stutter. Asked by a doctor when it started,

> I could not get the words out. It took about five minutes. I'd open my mouth to say . . . it's happening right now, I can't get the words out of my mouth. . . . I cannot say . . . "I had a child out of wedlock. I am an unwed mother." (Sheryl, *Girls Who Went Away,* 224, ellipses in original)

Another woman says she emitted "a wail . . . like a wounded animal" on finally seeing a picture of her daughter (Christine, *Girls Who Went Away,* 269). In the courtroom to confirm that the relinquishment is final, another woman recalls, "They keep asking you to speak up. There is nothing to push your voice out. A scream is starting. Deep inside of you."[34] Similarly, Janet Ellerby, who would later produce a full-length memoir, found telling her secret even to the most sympathetic listener so difficult that "pres-

---

30. Quiroz quotes the group Exiled Mothers Concerned United Birthparents (*Adoption in a Color-Blind Society,* 47, 42).
31. Merry Bloch Jones, *Birthmothers: Women Who Have Relinquished Babies for Adoption Tell Their Stories* (Chicago: Chicago Review Press, 1993), 11.
32. Marian Modelle Howard, "Shadows Burning," in Wadia-Ells, *Adoption Reader,* 60–67, quotation at 64; see also Moorman, *Waiting to Forget,* 187.
33. Waldron, *Giving Away Simone,* 135.
34. Priscilla T. Nagle, "This Is the Day We Give Babies Away," in Wadia-Ells, *Adoption Reader,* 27–31, quotation at 30.

sure built in my chest, a lump formed in my throat, tears welled up in my eyes, and speech became impossible" (*Tambourine Man,* 211). Even after writing her story for publication, "I still cannot speak it without experiencing an instantaneous catch in my throat, serious trouble inhaling, and such a clenching in my chest that I have great difficulty speaking at all."[35]

Even for those who can get the words out, birthmotherhood produces sentences that appear to violate logic—"If Janice is my daughters' mother, what does that make me?"[36]—and questions that cannot be answered. Asked if the child she is bearing at age forty is her first, Margaret Moorman answers yes to one doctor, no to another, and "mmm" to the nurse (*Waiting to Forget,* 115). By the same token, relief and recovery may begin with the use of appropriate words, as when Moorman claims that, by naming her experience, *The Adoption Triangle* enabled her to see herself as an active and entitled participant. A nurse at the hospital where one of Fessler's speakers gave birth referred to her, to her surprise, as "that baby's mother" and thus "gave me the foundation on which to rebuild my sense of self" (Margaret, *Girls Who Went Away,* 192).

The voices audible in Fessler's book testify to the near-incompatibility of birthmotherhood and writing. They are providing oral histories, not written texts, and their stories are sympathetically heard, recorded, and shaped by Fessler, an adoptee who frames their stories within the narrative of searching for her own birthmother. Even the first-person pieces in *The Adoption Reader* appear as brief stories "told" rather than written. Janet Ellerby, by contrast, found that though she could not speak, she could write. Memoirs by birthmothers who became writers before they began narrating their own stories exhibit and thematize the same struggles in ways that start to transform the silencing experience into a source of original literary power.

BIRTHMOTHER SUBJECTIVITY

Lynn Lauber's three books—two works of fiction from the early 1990s and a more recent writing guide—contribute significantly to the literature of the untellable birthmother story, for each gives a version of Lauber's story indirectly and circuitously, without employing the "I" of memoir. Lauber's writing acknowledges (both as a symptom and as a de-

35. Janet Mason Ellerby, *Intimate Reading: The Contemporary Women's Memoir* (Syracuse: Syracuse University Press, 2001), 5 (hereafter cited in the text).

36. Howard, "Shadows Burning," 65.

liberate strategy) that the birthmother's is not a position of first-person subjectivity, yet she makes that impossible position a place to start. As she herself acknowledges, she has been unable to stop writing the story of giving up her child, "circling" the story "over and over" in an effort to get it "right" (*Listen to Me,* 50, 82). Because there is no way to tell her story, there are an infinite number of ways to avoid telling it. (Lauber also wrote a column for the *New York Times* blog about adoption that recounts her typical 1960s story of rebellious behavior, maternity home, relinquishment, trauma, denial, and finally search and reunion. Nowhere in her three published works is Lauber as explicit about her history as she is in the blog.[37])

Lauber's first work of fiction, *White Girls,* comprises linked stories that introduce an autobiographical character called Loretta, who is also the protagonist of Lauber's novel *21 Sugar Street,* published three years later. (Lauber identifies Loretta as "my alter ego" in *Listen to Me* [117].) The final, long story in *White Girls,* "Homecoming," narrates blond Loretta's mixed-race teenage romance with Luther, her pregnancy, and its aftermath, the same material that provides the plot of *21 Sugar Street.* Yet neither work (except for a few scattered paragraphs) turns to Loretta's point of view, and neither does more than glance at her experiences beyond the small-town setting, at the maternity home or later. "Homecoming" focuses on Luther and his family: central characters include his mother, Annie, and his sister, Netty; the story recounts their struggles as wives and mothers and their responses to Luther's taboo-breaking romance with the white girl. Although three or four short sections of this story are written from Loretta's point of view to explain her attraction to Luther, the key moments in her pregnancy story are seen from others' viewpoints. The news that Loretta must give the baby up is reported from Luther's point of view: "'I can't keep it. They're sending me away,' Loretta blubbered into the collar of a knit sweater he had just picked up from the dry cleaners."[38]

For the most part, Loretta's story is strictly disciplined to its narrative function as a catalyst for the stories of Luther and the women in his family. Yet the very last section, comprising two paragraphs written from Loretta's point of view, unexpectedly reveals Loretta's hidden centrality and reveals, too, the hand of the writer whose autobiography is refracted

---

37. Lynn Lauber, "Reunion," in "Relative Choices," *New York Times,* Nov. 20, 2007, Relativechoices.blogs.nytimes.com/2007/11/20/Reunion.
38. Lynn Lauber, *White Girls* (New York: Vintage, 1991), 171 (hereafter cited in the text).

so indirectly in the story. Loretta, walking away from a final meeting with Luther years later, recollects having missed a high school history course because of her pregnancy and recalls her feelings:

> Each night as she'd lain on her cot at the home for unwed mothers, her mind had skipped over all she did not know: Was it a beech or elm or chestnut that stood outside her window; a finch or a sparrow's song? . . . Loretta saw she'd never know any of this, possibly in all her life. This was what she'd regret—more than her mother's face at the doctor's door, or Annie's back as she'd said goodbye, even more than the child still lodged there, south of her heart. (*White Girls,* 187)

While continuing to value the kind of emotional depth that has been emphasized in the rest of the story, this ending reads as the beginning of another story, the story of the birthmother who finally completed her education and became a writer. It is as if Lauber were signing her work as the birthmother who is starting to write her own story, but writing it only by looking steadily at the stories of everyone else first.

Lauber's novel *21 Sugar Street* recounts Loretta's romance and pregnancy again. Like "Homecoming," *21 Sugar Street* almost entirely avoids Loretta's point of view, and it embeds her story in an even wider array of other stories and viewpoints. Yet this focus on others besides Loretta herself paradoxically enables the novel's complex positioning of her as an author figure toward the end.

About halfway, the narrative shifts briefly to Loretta's point of view to describe her harrowing experiences in the maternity home and the long aftereffects of relinquishment. Her dismay and grief are shown having the predictable effect of silencing her: the chapter reads much like the brief birthmother narratives in *The Girls Who Went Away* and in *The Adoption Reader.* While her teachers and caretakers at the maternity home taunt her and try to make her confess her misdemeanors, she cannot say "what she wanted to say to her parents":

> She only cried once before she left, in her parents' bedroom, making her mother take her into her arms—an explosion of snot and tears and incoherence—and that was the closest she came to communicating anything to anyone.[39]

39. Lynn Lauber, *21 Sugar Street* (New York: W. W. Norton, 1993), 111 (hereafter cited in the text).

Later, finding it difficult to form serious romantic relationships but mourning with unwarranted intensity the loss of a decrepit car, "Loretta knew she was grieving for something else" (*21 Sugar Street,* 121). Failing to grieve or even to name her ungrievable loss, Loretta is possessed and silenced by what she cannot represent.

The compensatory function of the novel's multiple centers of interest in articulating Loretta's untellable story emerges fifty pages later. Years have passed in which we hear about other characters but not about Loretta. Now Loretta—in a section that shifts back to her point of view—has, at age twenty-seven, returned to her small hometown, Union, Ohio. Some complex plotting involving her father's illness, the suicide of the birth child's adoptive mother, a stroke suffered by Annie, and the reunion of another set of long-estranged characters places Loretta at the center of a conspicuous web of coincidences and thus gives her the role of the author who weaves characters together and determines their fates. In the novel's final section, narrated from the point of view of Loretta's brother, Loretta has become a professional writer with an exotic life far from Union. A glamorous stranger returning to celebrate her fortieth birthday and to introduce her long-lost child, Loretta is an object of envy and speculation, and the novel inserts a long, philosophical letter from her displaying her skills as a writer. Loretta can become a writing subject who fulfills the promise held out at the end of "Homecoming" only by exiting the narrative as well as leaving town and only by the novel's reassigning to other women characters the silence that was earlier and more predictably linked to Loretta herself as the birthmother. Annie is speechless after her stroke, the adoptive mother is dead, and some conspicuously artificial plotting removes Luther's wife Elaine from the final party scene. Loretta's newfound serenity along with her command as a writer thus depend on the novel's having displaced and redistributed the birthmother's silence. The decentering of the narrative away from the birthmother ultimately and paradoxically serves to enable her transformation into a writing subject: other characters who at first seem to usurp her place as protagonist later shoulder her burden of silence.

Before and during her pregnancy, Loretta is represented as silent only in the realm of judgmental white adults. By contrast, both works of fiction depict Loretta in free and absorbing conversation in Annie's house in the black neighborhood at 21 Sugar Street. The novel repeats from "Homecoming" a scene of Loretta, in the early days of her affair with Luther, visiting Annie's kitchen to talk and listen. In both works, the bond Annie and Loretta create is a deep communion that almost excludes Luther. In *21 Sugar Street* their intimacy includes sharing domestic work and "the tattered maroon photograph album that contained Annie's girlhood and a tin of cornbread, half gone" (*21 Sugar Street,* 92). Two women listening to each other: Annie's love for Loretta and her affirmative wish for Loretta to keep or at least to find her baby suggest an alternative narrative for a pregnant unwed teenager in the early 1960s. Black unwed mothers in the period typically kept their babies;[40] it is Loretta's class and racial culture that keeps her from doing so. In contrast to the oppressive silence surrounding Loretta's pregnancy everywhere else, the easy flow of the two women's conversation anticipates the title of Lauber's third book, *Listen to Me: Writing Life into Meaning.*

This writing guide incorporates yet another retelling of Lauber's birthmother story, a retelling that is of necessity even less direct than the fictional ones. Using herself as an example, Lauber argues for the life-saving power of personal writing. "Something deep in us needs to tell each other stories—and to be listened to in return"; after giving up her child "caused a great break between my heart and body . . . I began to write then as a way of restoring my fractured self. . . . I was joined together, reunited, through words" (*Listen to Me,* 28, 13, 14, 16). Because she is offering her story ostensibly just as an example, she tells it discontinuously and casually, always subordinating it to the advice she is offering to "you," the reader.

Thus recontextualized in the art of teaching and advising, her painful story becomes part of an intimate and rewarding conversation, not unlike the one depicted at the emotional heart of "Homecoming" and *21 Sugar Street.* The title *Listen to Me* refers to the imperative to tell one's story, but it is also a command addressed to the reader of the book itself. The book models, even performatively creates, the kind of community of mutual listening for which Lauber's stories express a yearning. To "listen" to Lauber as sympathetically as Annie and Loretta listen to each other would mean for the reader to hear the personal story embedded and barely audible in her didactic, second-person discourse. Yet the embedding of the first-person story is what makes its telling possible, and her advice reads like a description of her own books. She urges you, the writer, to recast a first-person story in the third person, to write from the point of view of "the people in your life"; "it is chastening and valuable to see ourselves in the stories of others, as secondary, even minor charac-

40. Rickie Solinger, *Wake Up Little Susie: Single Pregnancy and Race before* Roe v. Wade (New York: Routledge, 1992); Laura Briggs, *Somebody's Children: The Politics of Transracial and Transnational Adoption* (Durham: Duke University Press, 2012), 32–37.

ters" (*Listen to Me,* 52, 24). This is exactly the technique Lauber adopted in her published personal fictions, after years (she says) of placing her "heroic" self at the center of first-person stories no one wanted to read (136). Writing as a form of intersubjectivity even informs her metaphors for the writing process itself: "characters in one's writing can sometimes see things far earlier and with greater clarity than you" (92). In one of the writing prompts that follow each chapter, she urges "you" to write in the first person about "a traumatic event from your past" and then to "make the monumental shift and write the same episode using the other person's point of view" (148). Addressing herself to "you," Lauber invites her reader to share her own conversational writing style, which values companionable mutual listening over self-centered telling.

Other narratives by and about birthmothers have made good use of this intersubjective style to address the problem of the radical deontologizing that birthmothers often experience. Ann Fessler's book assembles and frames a multitude of brief, oral first-person birthmother stories so that the whole reads as a decentered communal conversation, as each story echoes and confirms the rest. This technique mimics the effect of Fessler's powerful installation artworks about birthmothers, *Everlasting* (2003) and *Everlasting: New England* (2004), in which recordings of birthmothers' voices telling their stories are projected into a space defined by a circle of empty chairs; the "audio perspective" shifts as the viewer moves from one chair to the next. Jill Deans's meditation on the various meanings of "circling" in Fessler's art recalls Lauber's use of the term to indicate repetition, "avoidance," yet also the community formed by "multiple perspectives."[41] Shamed, silenced, and excluded as individuals, the birthmothers speaking together reconstitute speaking subjectivity. Birthmother and artist Camille Billops's personal documentary film *Finding Christa* likewise uses an intersubjective structure in which birthmother and daughter both speak.[42] Filmmaker and artist Sheila Ganz, instead of telling her first-person birthmother story on its own, produced a documentary film about a broad spectrum of individuals from each side of the adoption triangle, embedding her own story, feelings, and opinions in a conspicuously even-handed account of adoption's varieties (closed and open, domestic and transnational) and of its failures and

41. Jill Deans, "Circling Adoption: The Art of Ann Fessler," *Adoption & Culture* 1 (2007): 205–38, quotations at 207, 229.
42. Camille Billops and James Hatch, prods. and dirs., *Finding Christa,* VHS (New York: Hatch-Billops Inc., 1991).

successes.[43] Ganz's voice telling her story—of rape, pregnancy, struggle to keep the baby, forced relinquishment, traumatic suffering, and efforts to connect with her daughter—frames and punctuates the film, but as in Lauber's fiction hers appears as only one among many points of view. The multiplication of viewpoints dramatizes a feeling of self-fragmentation yet also creates a community in which Ganz's story becomes intelligible.

Whenever Ganz narrates her own story, the camera focuses on Ganz's hands gradually creating a life-sized sculpture out of chicken wire, bamboo, burlap, and plaster that represents "the ten minutes I was allowed to hold her." Ganz's shears cutting the wire and her hands draping plaster-soaked cloth evoke the pain and messiness of childbirth and relinquishment. The artwork that results—the abstract shape of a mother holding a baby on a hospital bed—is both blankly monumental and rough as well as hollow, corresponding, perhaps, to Ganz's not quite resolved feelings in her final voiceover, in which she is still struggling with her daughter's disappointing response to being found. At the very end, the camera circles the finished (yet unfinished-looking) sculpture, a visual equivalent of Fessler's "circling" and of Lauber's idea that as a writer she "circles" the birthmother story that can never be told just right. At the same time, a caption (ironic, given the context of Ganz's difficult reunion) and then the scrolling credits partially conceal the sculpture. Closing the film in this way, Ganz seems at once to celebrate her reconstructed sense of self—her maternal subjectivity reclaimed by creating a community in which she can be named, respected, and heard as a mother—and to acknowledge the fear that this subjectivity is unstable and at risk of becoming fragmented, overlooked, or obscured.

Janet Ellerby, who found she could write but not speak her story, is like Lauber a professional writer and has, also like her, been "circling" her story for years. Like Lauber and Ganz, too, she created a community of voices within which to tell her story gradually without making hers central—until she was ready. By her account, as a PhD candidate in English in the late 1980s, burdened with the secret shame of having given up the baby she bore at age sixteen, she wrote a dissertation that channeled her private preoccupation through literary criticism:

> I was fascinated by first-person narrators who harbored secret traumas that could not be healed unless they could tell the story that would as-

---

43. Sheila Ganz, prod. and dir., *Unlocking the Heart of Adoption*, DVD (San Francisco: Pandora's Box Productions, 2003).

Figure 7. Ganz sculpture of "the ten minutes I was allowed to hold her," partially obscured while the camera circles it. From Sheila Ganz, *Unlocking the Heart of Adoption.*

> suage their pain. It is no wonder that four years of study would eventually lead me to write a dissertation entitled *Repetition and Redemption* where I would focus on narrators obsessed with their pasts and their offenses: confessors, like Rousseau and Augustine, and anguished malcontents like Conrad's Lord Jim, Faulkner's Quentin, and Proust's Marcel. (*Tambourine Man,* 199)

The dissertation distinguished between "creative and compulsive repetitions"; when asked by a prospective publisher to write an "autobiographical introduction" about her own "creative repetition," she felt exposed, as if her own "need for redemption" were on public view, and she never opened the dissertation again (*Tambourine Man,* 204–5). The chapter in which she recounts this history is titled "Repetition without Redemption": she was able to write about her story indirectly, but with limited benefit to herself or anyone else.

Rather than publish her dissertation, a decade later she wrote and published a scholarly book about recent American women's memoirs in which she also narrates, in the opening chapter, "Bearing Sorrow," the story of her secret pregnancy, lonely delivery, unwilling relinquishment, and years of torment that followed (her worst symptom: chronic insomnia and nightmares). Unlike Lauber's practice of telling her story indirectly (from other points of view, in service of teaching others how to write), Ellerby narrates her story in the first person and in detail. (There is also a second personal chapter on a family secret that shaped her family's response to her pregnancy.) But the book is not primarily her memoir: after the first two chapters, she analyzes other memoirs that raise themes and issues visible in her story but also common to many contemporary memoirs (shame, audience, trauma, mental illness, etc.), so that each subsequent chapter puts her story in conversation with others, using her personal insights to illuminate other stories and vice versa. As she describes her motivation and process in the introduction:

> Determined now to tell my secret, I sought other writers who had decided to tell their secrets. I looked for support and inspiration by reading memoirs by women whose experiences struck an intuitive emotional response in me. As I tentatively began the writing process, I relied on fellow memoirists in the same way I have relied on intimate women friends. I sought that corresponding puissant connection and imagined a circle of fellow women memoirists just as I have created my circle of women friends. (*Intimate Reading,* xiii–xiv)

As she moves back and forth between accounts of other memoirs and her own story, Ellerby links them conversationally with the formulation "I, too": for example, "I too have depended," "I too found how difficult," and "we who keep secrets" (95, 120, 121). Like Lauber having Loretta converse with Annie in her fiction and reproducing that warmly reciprocal relationship in *Listen to Me,* Ellerby sees her literary work of "intimate reading" as both scholarship and friendship.

Far more direct a confessor than Lauber, Ellerby sometimes seems overeager to connect her stories to others', yet the overall effect of diffusing her personal reflections across so many chapters primarily devoted to others is to subordinate herself to the community she is creating in prose. She also, like Lauber, revised her narrative to make it less egocentric than it might have been, reporting that she wrote "Bearing Sorrow" first as an outpouring intended only for herself; next as narrative to be shared with husband and friends; and later as a piece for public performance "at a women's retreat, seated in a circle with thirty women," and on a panel at a scholarly conference (*Intimate Reading,* 72). By presenting her story as part of a community of stories, she gains the confidence to share it publicly and also, by saying "we," circumvents the imperative that the birthmother not say "I":

> Memoirists have taught me that we need not be outsiders because of our shame and our secrets. . . . By writing my memoir, I have surrendered the concealment that kept me a stranger; you know me now. But mine is not a unique story; it joins a common narrative, the shared and sorrowful stories that other birth mothers will tell when they can. (*Intimate Reading,* 211–12)

Like Lauber, she includes the reader ("you") in her circle, a category that may include other silenced birthmothers she hopes her story will reach and inspire.

Intimate Reading diffuses the focus on the birthmother's personal story not only by linking it to other memoirs and perhaps to other untold birthmother stories but also by presenting it as a socially useful warning about the consequences of secrecy in adoption and as a cultural critique of middle-class American values in the 1960s. Ellerby's full-length memoir, *Following the Tambourine Man,* is at least her third retelling of her story (not counting the versions of "Bearing Sorrow" she circulated and revised prior to publication); like Lauber, she cannot stop telling it, parts of the book even repeating verbatim passages from "Bearing Sorrow."[44] This volume, although it focuses far more squarely on Ellerby herself than either Lauber's work or *Intimate Reading,* again diffuses its self-centeredness by presenting itself as cultural critique. The title, with its allusion to Bob Dylan, places Ellerby's story in the context of social change in suburban southern California in the 1960s, the kind of change that made teen sex and other forms of rebellion prevalent ("everything forbidden is enticing" [*Tambourine Man,* 16]), even as strait-laced middle-

44. Janet Mason Ellerby's personal writing also extends into her literary and cultural criticism, for example in a critique of Diablo Cody's film *Juno,* in which she uses her own story to dismiss the film as a "sentimental romance" that commits "a sweeping act of historical and cultural repression" by harmfully repeating the lies that were told to birthmothers of the babyscoop era, that relinquishment in closed adoption would lead to a happy ending; see "The Happy-Ending Myth: *Juno* Re-Embroiders the Scarlet A," *Adoption & Culture* 2 (2009): 65–89, quotations at 65, 85.

class families like hers lacked frameworks for tolerating, much less appropriately handling, the consequences. Discovering that she gave birth just a month after Joni Mitchell, who finally went public with her story in 1996, she creates a textual community, as she does in *Intimate Reading*, this time of 1960s birthmothers joined together as "we": "still influenced by the cultural rigidity of the fifties, we had no means to become the loving, responsible, proud, and capable young mothers we might have been" (120). Like Ganz and Fessler as well as Lauber, she again forms a circle within which to tell her story safely.

Ellerby explores the impossible speaking position of the birthmother in another way as well, by naming and tracing the history of the divided subjectivity she inhabited as a person with a secret grief, a person with "tangled, conflicted layers of self, a complicated orchestration that consistently failed me" (*Tambourine Man*, 108–9). One of the most striking features of her narrative is the elaborate plot her parents and other relatives concocted to keep her pregnancy and delivery secret. She stayed with relatives in distant cities, wrote to friends at home about her imaginary life, and even had postcards sent from yet other another location so as to maintain the imposture of enjoying a carefree, interesting school year away while she was instead hiding her pregnancy, giving birth alone and in pain, and suffering from the aftereffects of what she experienced as traumatic loss. In the letters she wrote, "although I was given free rein to invent a counterlife of my own," she

> retreated back to a hodgepodge of fairytale characters that had one thing in common: they were all good, and ironically, as I fabricated shamelessly, they were all innocent of deceit. I constructed myself as a teenage Snow White . . . in her own new enchanted village . . . that was peopled with jolly friends and family, fine-looking horses, soft snowflakes, and my pick of handsome princes. (*Tambourine Man*, 89–90)

Her imposture was so complete that the baby's father refused to believe there had ever been a child, when she eventually told him about Sorrow, and neither her parents nor the relatives who were in on the secret ever spoke with her of her experience or of the baby once she returned home to complete high school.

Required to live duplicitously, Ellerby traces her lifelong personal instability to this year. Losing Sorrow, she reflects, "ignited the implosion of a self I had only tenuously pieced together by sixteen." That tentative self, "the girl I had been, . . . was obliterated that night as I turned into a helpless, unfamiliar, straining body consumed by unimaginable pain." She then "split" into two selves: the "deeply wounded child who emerged from a secret trauma [and] the counterfeit teenager, pretending to be that other, sunny girl" (*Tambourine Man*, 108). As an adult, she "construct[ed] a passable identity," but because it never incorporated her grief at Sorrow's loss, she was doomed to be assaulted by literally repeating memories of the traumatic event, leaving her again and again "discomposed" (109). *Intimate Reading,* with its scholarly aims, articulates this personal "discomposure" with postmodern theories of the subject, which for Ellerby as a thoughtful PhD student in the 1990s posed a new challenge to her already great dismay over never feeling "authentic." Although she knows that any "authentic core" she may believe herself to have achieved is only "a new mirage" and that "finally our identities remain unfinished" (*Intimate Reading,* 44, 93)—she cites Chris Weedon's definition of the postmodern subject as "'precarious, contradictory and in process, constantly being reconstituted in discourse each time we think or speak'"[45]—she nonetheless believes that "the truth telling of the memoir is indispensable for mental health" (153) and strives for "the most genuine subjectivity I can construct" (44). Her feeling of being split into two selves (grieving and hidden, sunny and public) is displaced onto a different division, between the intellectual appeal of postmodern theory, on the one hand, and, on the other, her private yearning to be a unified, self-identical subject. Julia Kristeva, whose theory of maternal subjectivity she does not cite, provides Ellerby with a strong formulation of this division: "'This discovery . . . that I myself at the deepest levels of my wants and desires am unsure, centerless, and divided . . . does not eliminate my capacities for commitment and trust.'"[46] Ellerby does not resolve these tensions between her selves and between her intellectual and her emotional allegiances: the book's voice, like its theory of memoir, remains productively divided.

THE BIRTHMOTHER'S PLOT

The struggle to claim the legitimacy of one's voice in the face of an annihilating experience is one of the main challenges faced by birthmothers

45. Ellerby, *Intimate Reading,* 148, citing Chris Weedon, *Feminist Practice and Poststructuralist Theory* (Oxford: Blackwell, 1987).
46. Ellerby, *Intimate Reading,* 174, citing Julia Kristeva, *In the Beginning Was Love* (New York: Columbia University Press, 1997).

who seek to convey their stories. Another is the lack of usable narrative paradigms. When adoptees narrate the stories of their identity crises and the searches they prompt, the epic quest is close at hand to serve as narrative template, with the adoptee in the attractive role of hero.[47] The hero is lost, spiritually and geographically, strives to find the way home, and eventually reclaims his place of origin, which is also his identity: think of Odysseus returning to Ithaka, or Aeneas voyaging to a land that he is told is his "ancient mother." Whether or not they succeed, as we have seen in chapter 2, adoptees journey to find themselves by searching out their origins, and the plot of the search parallels the plot of growth and development that informs the *bildungsroman* tradition in Britain, Europe, and the United States. But birthmothers' stories do not easily conform to this or any other familiar plot paradigm. Mothers have, in our prevailing cultural myths, been the objects or the points of departure of epic quests, not their subjects. Although both adoptees and birthmothers seek to recover something from the past, the trauma and social stigma the birthmother suffers make her want to reverse or deny the passage of time and keep her from moving forward. While the adoptee typically pursues a distinct goal—however unlikely it is that that goal will be reached or, if reached, will deliver the desired sense of completion—the birthmother's retrospective task is more complex: perhaps to find her child again (although without imagining that the mystery of her own identity will be solved by her discovery of the adult her child has become) but also to revisit her past choices and the damage she incurred when young and vulnerable. There is no obvious or traditional narrative template for undoing the passage of time.

Moreover, in practical terms, birthmothers have historically had fewer opportunities for action, epic or otherwise. Adoptees led the movement to open sealed adoption records, and their need for medical and other identifying information from their birth parents has long seemed more legitimate than birthmothers' merely emotional yearnings. Jean Strauss's films advocating for open records (see the introduction) do so from the point of view of adoptees searching for their original birth certificates; this perspective makes a stronger, simpler case than the more complex searches of birthmothers trying to track their children's subsequent lives, happy though the birthmothers in her films are to be found. For the purposes of appealing to policy makers, the child, it can

47. See Melosh, "Adoption Stories," 228–29; Emily Hipchen and Jill Deans, "Introduction: Adoption Life Writing: Origins and Other Ghosts," *a/b: Auto/Biography Studies* 18 (2003): 163–70, this point at 167; and Novy, *Reading Adoption*, 45.

be said, did not choose to be relinquished; the mother can be expected to be more bound by her decision (never mind how involuntary it may have been) and by her presumed desire for secrecy than is her child. Working up her nerve to begin searching for her son, Margaret Moorman registers with the Soundex Reunion Registry, only to find that her son is not searching, and so her action leads nowhere (*Waiting to Forget,* 143–44). Birthmothers often describe having to wait to be searched for, held back both by their own scruples and by the law; Fessler finds many birthmothers striving only "to make themselves findable."[48] Alarmed by a young acquaintance's hostile response to being found by his birthmother, Ellerby, who had just begun some tentative and "uneasy" searching, felt "stunned" and "even more certain that only Sorrow had the right to make the search that might someday bring us together. . . . I was the bad mother, and by looking for her, I was the intrusive interloper. . . . I could do nothing more but wait and hope" (*Tambourine Man,* 217–18). Narrating the "halting progress" of her attenuated search for her son, Margaret Moorman notes the many turning points at which "again I did nothing" (*Waiting to Forget,* 142, 158). Her story idles—"I could begin and begin and begin again," she writes (101)—and its movement is sporadic, not epic.

Time freezes up and stutters in birthmothers' stories, much as their speech sometimes does. Their claim to the identity "mother" arises from an action lodged in the past rather than from an ongoing practice. They describe a feeling of being stuck in time, as when Lauber admits that she cannot stop writing about Ohio in the 1960s. In her film Sheila Ganz remarks, "contrary to what people say—that it's just a loss, it's in the past—the losses mount up": the loss of her child happens to her again each day that they are apart. "It's like somebody ripping out a piece of me for thirty-two years" (Ruth, *Girls Who Went Away,* 132). Some birthmothers say that they feel they remain the age they were when they gave birth: "the part of me that was his mother remained seventeen," says a woman who took a job in the hospital where she gave birth because "I had to be where my son was" (Margaret, *Girls Who Went Away,* 193, 195). Another birthmother tells her lost and found daughter, "I wish I could put you back in here and start all over again" (Christine, *Girls Who Went Away,* 270). Some birthmothers never have another child, while others, such as Ellerby, keep having or wanting more and more babies in hopes of repeating

48. Fessler, *Girls Who Went Away,* 251; see also Artemis OakGrove, "Full Circle," in Wadia-Ells, *Adoption Reader,* 39–43.

the first pregnancy and finally getting it right. The births of her second and third children failed to "mend me," Ellerby writes; she has a fourth pregnancy against her then-husband's wishes (he leaves), and "I have tried since to become pregnant, driven by that fruitless search for the baby that would supplant the memory. . . . I could ask myself how many babies would it have taken to restore what I lost, but I know the answer" (*Intimate Reading*, 28). These birthmothers try to turn time back on itself.

The birthmother-writer whose work supplies the title of this chapter, Karen Salyer McElmurray, published a memoir in 2004 that vividly captures the difficulty birthmothers can have affirming subjectivity and telling their stories that Lynn Lauber's and Janet Ellerby's work highlights and transforms. McElmurray writes in the first person but in several different voices; her narrator is alienated from her postpartum body, sometimes anorexic and drug addled; and her memory often fails her. McElmurray's memoir also and even more strikingly dramatizes the challenges to plot conventions and to temporal movement that a birthmother's experience can pose. She not only records her experiences but renders them aspects of her memoir's challenging and original form.

The novelistic plotting of McElmurray's *Surrendered Child: A Birth Mother's Journey* is complex and sometimes disorienting. The reader may feel she is experiencing, along with the birthmother-narrator, the kind of stoppage of time and simultaneity of all times that Ganz, Fessler's interviewees, and others describe as a consequence of unchosen relinquishment. Tenses seem to swing wildly in McElmurray's prose, pushing the limits even of postmodern plot conventions, even as time also seems fastened to one spot, the moment of her son's birth and departure. As events zigzag back and forth between the distant past and the more recent past, she turns frequently to formulations that look forward to the future (which is now the recent past) from a point further back in the past. For example, an early paragraph begins, "For twenty-five years, I will have only a few facts," then moves into the past tense to narrate those facts: "My son, relinquished to adoption on the day he was born, was named Brian Keith McElmurray by the Kentucky Department of Social Services" (*Surrendered Child*, 4). The paragraph goes on with a recitation of facts, all prefaced with the words "I know" (as in "I know that he weighed six pounds and something when he slid from my womb"). The next paragraph returns to the future as seen from that point in the past: "By 2000 I will know more than I could imagine and by 2002 I will know more than that, but in 1998 I will be told only what is permissible by Kentucky adoption law" (4). The narrator and the reader seem to be anchored in the events of 1973, looking forward, and yet fleetingly we also pause in 2002, looking back at 1998 as seen from the point of view of 1973. And where in time is the present tense of "I know"? A few pages later she speculates, "*what if there is . . . . no real present, but only an accumulation of memories of the past and wishes for the future?*" (20, emphasis in original). In this and similarly dizzying sequences, the reader can feel unmoored as McElmurray dramatizes what it feels like to suffer the kinds of temporal distortions that she says her loss occasioned. In the description of her experience of childbirth that soon follows, she thematizes what she has just performed: "I heard him crying, and then that was all. It was the last moment there was, and I felt them take him from me. . . . *The truth is that for years after my son's birth, I can't feel a thing*" (17, emphasis in original). Time stops for the narrator and flattens into a continuous present that remains riveted to 1973 ("I can't feel" instead of "I couldn't feel"), even as the narrative also rushes forward ("for years after").

"The last moment there was" suggests that the story and the possibility of forward, questing motion have stopped, and yet the pace of the first chapter is frenetic. The first chapter, "Birth Day," opens in medias res with a pastoral scene in which the narrator is pregnant and happy; the second sentence flashes forward to a near future when she will wear the same dress; the scene shifts forward a month or two to the moment of delivery; forward again to 1998, to her effort to get her records; back to the night she left her boyfriend's home for the hospital; a flashback to the plan they had projected forward for this night; forward again to the chaos, humiliation, and pain of the delivery of a baby who seems to refuse to come out (it has been ten months—perhaps he too is stuck in time); forward again to 1997 to more efforts to obtain records; back in time to her sixth month and her state of denial; forward from there to her seventh and eighth months as a runaway and her return to marry her son's father; forward again "years after" to an excursion with a lover; and finally—on page 22—back to the days after her return from the hospital. The rest of the memoir is structured in roughly this manner, proceeding forward and backward at the same time.

In the opening pastoral scene, the narrator breaks a precious necklace of glass beads, a gift from her absent mother. The first chapter ends with this image: "I wanted to gather them to me, all the lost beads of love and birth and afterbirth, string them new again on a string that would never break" (*Surrendered Child,* 22). The chapter, and the book as a whole, reads like a scattering of beads that the narrator is struggling to restring, as she performs the difficulty of making a sequential plot out of events that for her have no internal coherence, no causal logic. She cannot even determine the date of her son's birth; two official sources disagree, and she was so distant from her own experience that she cannot remember. The narrator makes this struggle explicit when she considers her family history: *"I want to remember it all like a story about family, chapter to chapter, until I reach a happy ending"* (20, emphasis in original). But she can find no story line that conforms to accepted notions of story, in part because when Karen was fifteen her mother's obsession with cleanliness and order drove her back to her own parents' home to resume her life as their child, leaving Karen unparented and establishing a paradigm of temporal reversals that robs her daughter of a clear sense of beginning, progression, and ending. Building up to an episode about a third of the way through the book in which she rebels against her mother, she writes: *"A story, I'm told, should be Aristotelian. It follows a logical pattern from beginning to middle to end. . . . But what, you might wonder, are endings, and what are beginnings?"* (75). The narrator presents the episode as an ending, but at this time in her life the story of the pregnancy has yet to begin (even though its story has already been narrated). McElmurray's plot consists of so many scattered beads, or perhaps, as in Margaret Moorman's phrasing, "the spokes of a wheel," every turn in the story bringing her back to the central catastrophe (*Waiting to Forget,* 172).

Without the forward movement of a linear plot, time compresses. Right after the birth and its stoppage of time, "time was me, standing naked in front of a mirror and seeing every girl I'd ever been. I was ten and my father took me to the junkyard to shoot rats and bottles and cans. I was fourteen and I hadn't lost my virginity yet . . . I was fifteen . . . I was sixteen," and so on (*Surrendered Child,* 152–53, and again on page 245). Moving fast but progressing nowhere, the narrative uncovers a disturbingly oedipal correlate to this temporal problem: a lack of differentiation among generations. The Appalachian setting helps to animate this theme (incidental characters include a boy whose father is also his grandfather), but it appears in many birthmother narratives. For those who cannot progress past the age they were when they gave birth, meeting their sons as handsome young adults can arouse unexpected sexual feelings. Falling in love with her son, Robyn Flatley writes, "I wanted him inside of me and the only way I could have that again was to have this man. . . . I felt torn apart by all the eighteen-year-old desires I thought I had long ago left behind."[49] McElmurray links this temporal disorder

49. Robyn Flatley, "My Son," in Wadia-Ells, *Adoption Reader,* 48–59, quotation at 49; for a

(the indistinctness of generations, the confusion between the desire for a baby and the desire for a man) to the problem of insufficient terms: "I was and was not a mother from that birth day on" (*Surrendered Child,* 19); "*I'm a mother and I'm not a mother*" (133, emphasis in original). The narrator defends her decision to give up her baby by showing how the indifferentiation between generations is also a verbal problem: "*How . . . can I be a child and keep a child and be married to one?*" (20, emphasis in original). Struggling to avoid the collapsing of generations, when her father wants to adopt the baby, the narrator insists that her son must not become part of "the very past [I] had just managed to escape. My son would never be my brother" (139).

Nonetheless the narrator remains erotically vulnerable to the collapse of time and difference. In a chapter titled "Lovers," she describes her attraction to younger men who are wounded and innocent: "*I am the mother who isn't one who wants to take the boy back, take him deep inside herself. . . . They don't know I'm frozen in time, my boy lovers*" (*Surrendered Child,* 174). Later she makes explicit that all are substitutes for her son:

> I glimpsed the faces of so many people I have loved, the faces of boy upon boy. I saw the face of the father of my son. . . . Behind his face was another one, and another, a far-reaching sequence of sad boys' faces, and behind them all was the one face I will never see. My son's. My son, a baby, unformed and unreachable, suspended in light too hot and white to touch. (*Surrendered Child,* 182)

Her son, a baby, becomes the origin or father of all these men, including his own father, as if the baby's priority in her feelings could make him prior in time.

As if to vindicate McElmurray's theory of its impossible time frame and plot structure, the book itself has no proper ending. Completed in the year 2000, the manuscript apparently ended with an epiphany following a car crash in 1998, a shift in consciousness that the narrator hopes will enable her to find "forgiveness" and "to begin" (*Surrendered Child,* 236). She makes a point of saying that the crash broke and scattered her mother's beads, as if to admit that she accepts her memoir's lack of coherent shape. McElmurray in 2000 had not found her son,

similar situation see Fessler, *Girls Who Went Away,* 125. By contrast, Meredith Hall, in *Without a Map,* depicts a favorable confusion of generations in her relationship with her recovered birth son: in his twenties when they meet, he is as much like a father to her two younger sons as he is an older brother.

though she describes many stages in her search, having been frustrated like other birthmothers by the state's refusal to divulge any information (226–27). Thus the plot as originally conceived was not driving teleologically toward anything recognizable as an ending. The book was accepted and advertised for sale in 2001 under the title "Mother of the Disappeared: An Appalachian Birthmother's Journey."

By her account, however, the events of September 11, 2001, delayed publication, and she eventually chose another publisher. At Thanksgiving 2001, the manuscript only by chance still unpublished, she was contacted by a woman who turned out to be her son's girlfriend, who had seen McElmurray's website photo (in connection with her first book, a novel) and noticed a telling similarity. This led to the reunion with her son, now named Andrew, that McElmurray had given up expecting. To her book manuscript McElmurray added an afterword dated 2003 in which she recounts this story and ends with a strong claim for the efficacy of her writing:

> What has been born, I believe, is the power of words. By what coincidence did I name my novel's main character Andrew? . . . There is no separation of the power of words and this thing called a memoir, no separation, in the end, of writing and living. . . . I have birthed this thing called a book, and called to life the lost past I have so wanted. (*Surrendered Child,* 247–48)

Her desire and her writing have, in her view, caused Andrew to reappear. And this is not just magical thinking: Andrew's girlfriend was looking for a good new novel when she came across McElmurray's website. Making the past present, her writing not only depicts lived reality but creates it. The writer, no longer the passive recorder of a life she cannot master, becomes the active author of her own potentially happy tale.

Like Lynn Lauber, whose story and novel close with the optimistic emergence of the birthmother-writer and whose *Listen to Me* celebrates the writer's ability to heal herself through speaking and listening, McElmurray places great faith in the power of the birthmother's writing. Ellerby, too, reveals in both books that she was reunited very happily with her daughter (Merideth, no longer Sorrow) because she shared her essay "Bearing Sorrow" with a network of women expert at searching. "Thankful for the restorative power of disclosure," she can claim her writing generated this turn in her life's own fortunate plot (*Intimate Reading,* 214). Indeed, if there is a telos in these works, it is the self-generation of the birthmother as author, which recalls Maisie's "profitable" self-authoring discussed in chapter 1; the celebrations of present-time storytelling that close the failed quests for authenticity, the past, and origins discussed in chapter 2; and the affirmation of the adoptee's writing on her body that concludes chapter 3.

Nonetheless McElmurray resisted the temptation to give her narrative a conventional happy ending. She might have recast her entire story as a plot leading up to her reunion with her son, as if it were a courtship novel. Margaret Moorman's *Waiting to Forget* does precisely this, leading suspensefully right up to the moment when Moorman establishes contact with her son. Because the formal and thematic challenges that both trouble and animate McElmurray's writing are principally about time and structure (what is the birthmother's plot?) rather than, as for Lauber and Ellerby, about the subject (how can the birthmother speak?), *Surrendered Child* even in its finished form retains its anti-logical time frame. Although it might seem that the narrator has at last achieved every birthmother's goal of finding her child, there is no endpoint to her story, since its origin in her son's birth is also its product: seeing her son's face "for the first time ever" is "the last or the first glass bead on a string of moments I've accumulated till now" (*Surrendered Child,* 245). Endless sorrow is replaced by an endless temporal loop in which, she unsentimentally recognizes, she and her son may never really locate one another in a secure or rewarding relationship. She is confused by an attraction to him that translates her wish to return him to her womb into a wish to be his lover. Moreover, "he is a young man on the threshold of the world and I am a woman who still longs to hold my son on the day he was born" (247). The scattered beads of her life and plot are now restrung, but they still do not form a coherent sequence. This paradoxical looping of time is reflected in her choice to tack on the afterword rather than integrate its content into the memoir: both formally and thematically, the book has no end.

For Ellerby, the temptation to write a perfectly happy ending is greater than for McElmurray. Although she too describes the feeling of being stuck in time that other birthmothers report, her lucid narrative never formally exhibits this quality. Near the conclusion of a far more sequential and orderly plot than McElmurray's, she and her lost daughter meet and create so harmonious a reunion that, when Merideth gives birth to her fourth child, she invites Janet to visit her in the hospital and gives her the hour-old baby to hold:

> I reach and take this baby from my daughter, the daughter I had reached out for so desperately years and years ago.
>
> Silently, I walk with him to the window and am immediately swept back to that frigid, bare morning in Akron with Sorrow wailing just out of my arms' reach. This time I have been given the baby to hold. I bend and kiss his forehead. Finally my arms can cradle the baby. Tears come quickly and my chest tightens in the old familiar way. I glance outside into the thickening twilight. Tiny snowflakes are beginning to fall, and I feel myself falling, falling back into that black pool of sorrow. My Sorrow.
>
> But this baby . . . stops my fall. (*Tambourine Man,* 286)

Warmed by the loving circle of family sharing the moment with her, reassured that she needn't give the baby back till she is ready, "My chest loosens, I breathe again, my tears subside." Since meeting Merideth, Ellerby has wondered if all her sorrows will be repealed and her nightmares of losing a baby will cease: "Had I actually gotten back to the baby that I had left behind again and again in my dreams?" (247). It seems as though a perfect circle has been completed, a neat conclusion reached.

But she soon recognizes that "I will always be drawn back to that shattered girl," herself returning babyless to her room at the Crittenton Home, and that "beyond logic, . . . beyond Merideth's very real presence in my life, still an unappeasable and irrevocable loss lives on, so that even as I write these words, I weep once again for Sorrow" (*Tambourine Man,* 264). Although holding Merideth's new baby seems to promise that "my book can conclude with an ending full of poetic justice" (288), a month after the baby's birth she is still having her nightmare about losing a child. The book ends with her recognition that although she has attempted to "step in the same river twice"—to turn back time by means of the births of new children—she knows she cannot, so that "the circle of my journey closes, but not completely" (289). There is no closure possible as long as she remains two selves: Janet Mason Ellerby, the happy and successful writer, teacher, mother, and wife; and "Jan Mason," her alias at the Crittenton Home, the girl who can't stop grieving. Her divided subjectivity both enables her distinctive narrative voice and keeps open her plot. The book's last word is Sorrow: almost but not quite a happy end.

Lauber, Ellerby, McElmurray, and other birthmothers discussed here refuse to accept the birthmother's normative place in family narratives, that is, her exclusion from the story or her positioning as the silent ground from which someone else's family story takes its point of departure. To return to literary critic Susan Winnett's idea that women's bodily experiences may call for new narrative forms: for their experiences of childbirth, relinquishment, and loss, these writers have created new expressions of subjectivity and have shaped their plots in distinctive ways. Deftly recuperating the birthmother's silencing and nonentity as the foundation for a new kind of narrative subjectivity, refusing the teleological plots of courtship or quest and substituting a stubbornly non-teleological narration of relinquishment and loss that does not drive forward toward a merely happy ending, these writers—drawing on and extending "the power of words"—have devised original forms in which to tell their untellable birthmother stories.

AFTERWORD

"The Imprint of Another Life"

After I thought I had finished this book, Jeanette Winterson published *Why Be Happy When You Could Be Normal?,* the adoption memoir that, I soon realized, would provide this book with its title and the first of its two epigraphs. Offering a brief reading here, I will try to suggest how I think this memoir captures some of this book's major themes and arguments. It is an account of the pain of living with being adopted that is also about the prompting to creativity that can be adoption's gift.

In her first, prize-winning novel, *Oranges Are Not the Only Fruit,* Winterson's autobiographical fiction vividly evokes her working-class childhood among Pentecostals in a suburb of Manchester in the 1960s and 1970s. Her adoption serves as a metaphor for the estrangement she came to feel from her mother's tight-knit community on account of her emerging sexuality and her intellectual aspirations. Her mother frames the adoption strictly within a religious idiom in which a child can be seen as a word: not the child of her body, Jeanette is the Lord's child, "sprung from her head . . . not the jolt beneath the hipbone, but water and the word."[1] In this definition of adoption, the birthmother has no existence: when Jeanette discovers her adoption papers by accident, her mother responds, "You were always mine, I had you from the Lord," and when the birthmother comes to their house, Mum dismisses Jeanette's frantic yearning to see her with the novel's most notorious line: "I'm your mother . . . She was a carrying case" (*Oranges,* 100–101). Jeanette also compares her discovery of her adoption papers to her discovery that her mother "had rewritten the ending" of *Jane Eyre* when she read it aloud.[2] Learning that Jane didn't marry St. John Rivers and go to India

1. Jeanette Winterson, *Oranges Are Not the Only Fruit* (London: Pandora, 1985), 10 (hereafter cited in the text).
2. *Oranges,* 74. Winterson reports on her mother's *Jane Eyre* revision again in *Why Be*

as a missionary, as in her mother's pious version, was like discovering that her mother had falsified her origins. These passages recall Betty Jean Lifton's discovery that her mother had been spinning tales about her birth parents and had required her to live a "fictitious" life, and Winterson denigrates her mother's fabrications just as Lifton does. A coming-of-age story, the novel moves the protagonist away from home and toward the truth.

Nonetheless, just as Lifton's text balances its antagonism toward fiction by celebrating myth and the adoptee's self-creation, Winterson too equivocates. In the analogy between the false ending of *Jane Eyre* and lying about the adoption, it is not some paradigm of bedrock reality but rather the extravagant fiction of *Jane Eyre* that becomes the standard of truth-telling. For her mother to have been truthful about Jeanette's origins would have been like her accurately reporting the ending of a novel. And in *Why Be Happy When You Could Be Normal?* Winterson revisits these themes and finds fresh power and advantage both in the idea of originating in a word or words and in identifying with and as a fictional character. She also reclaims the adoptee's pain as a positive source of her identity.

As we have seen, the memoir opens with Winterson's strong declaration of the importance of language and storytelling to the adopted. "Adopted children are self-invented because we have to be," she writes, and she says she became a writer from her need to "rewrite the hurt." "Part fact part fiction is what life is. . . . I wrote my way out": writing *Oranges* as her "cover story," Winterson fabricated a life that sounded crazy enough to most readers but that, compared to "the other one" that "was too painful," constituted a livable life—Winterson added a kindly older friend, for example (*Why Be Happy*, 5–6). In effect, she claims, she enabled herself to become the other Jeanette, the fictional one she had created. She also weighs the value of breaking silence in families bound by trauma, as she believes hers was at the time when she published *Oranges*. Referencing both Christian and Greek mythology ("the story of Philomel"), she offers a credo about the power not only of words but of literature:

> I believe in fiction and the power of stories because that way we speak

---

Happy When You Could Be Normal? (London: Jonathan Cape, and New York: Grove Press, 2011), 102 (hereafter cited in the text).

> in tongues. We are not silenced. All of us, when in deep trauma, find we hesitate, we stammer; there are long pauses in our speech. . . . We get our language back through the language of others. We can turn to the poem. We can open the book. Somebody has been there for us and deep-dived the words.
>
> I needed words. (*Why Be Happy,* 9)

In the body of the memoir, Winterson credits her Pentecostal upbringing with giving her privileged access to language and for impressing on her the concrete value of imagination. The third chapter, titled "In the Beginning Was the Word," opens, "My mother was in charge of language" (27), and describes her mother's nightly dramatic Bible reading; her favorite part was the Book of Revelation. Raised memorizing the King James Bible's beautiful language and complex stories and believing in her mother's compelling religious fantasies (her belief in "miracle stories" [31], her belief in heaven), she traces a direct line from this early training to her love of reading, inventing, and writing. When her mother accuses her of not telling the truth in *Oranges,* she reflects: "Truth? This was a woman who explained the flash-dash of mice activity in the kitchen as ectoplasm" (6). Thus the cause—her mother's fantastical theory of her unfleshly origin, her belief in her daughter as an avatar of the word—becomes the cure: Winterson's own capacity to invent, to invest in literature, and to "rewrite the hurt," to trace "the imprint of another life."

As a teen, Winterson found the library her refuge and gave herself the task of reading every book in the section labeled "ENGLISH LITERATURE IN PROSE A–Z," an assignment to which she soon added poetry; by sixteen she had reached Marvell (*Why Be Happy,* 39). Although or perhaps because her mother forbade her to read fiction and burned her paperback collection once she uncovered it under Jeanette's mattress, "I began to realize that I had company. Writers are often exiles, outsiders, runaways and castaways. These writers were my friends" (116). Their stories countered the stories that darkened her life: "I read on, . . . past the foundling stories and the Nori brickworks, past the Devil and the wrong crib" (117). Anticipating her choice to write autobiographical fiction, she says she was especially drawn to works that mingle fact and fiction, such as *Orlando* and *The Autobiography of Alice B. Toklas,* because "reading yourself as a fiction as well as a fact is the only way to keep the narrative open" (119). When, after many struggles, she eventually entered Oxford and was snubbed by her male tutor, she formed a reading group with other marginalized students; she insists, looking back, that "books were my birthright too" (143). If works of fiction can contain elements of fact, can indeed stand for "truth" as in the *Jane Eyre* episode from her early childhood, then she can create her own real life on the basis of her reading of English literature. Approaching Oxford she identified apprehensively with Jude the Obscure, and once there, "I felt connected across time to other lives and deeper sympathies. . . . The past is another country, but one that we can visit, and once there we can bring back the things we need" (144). This claim counters one of adoptees' most common laments by substituting, for personal origins that can never be revisited, the common "birthright" of literary history that is available to all.

Having constructed a livable life in and through literature, Winterson treats as a linguistic crisis the overwhelming feeling that arises years later when she confronts her adoption. When she finds again the adoption papers she had glimpsed as a child (her name and that of her birthmother defaced, apparently by her mother's hand) at the same time that she is being left by a lover, she "began to go mad." She had always resisted investigating her past because "It isn't 'my past,' is it? I have written over it. I have recorded on top of it" (*Why Be Happy*, 156). But the discovery of the documents forces her to admit, "There is a past after all, no matter how much I have written over it" (160). Although "the rope was poetry" (the one rope she could hold onto), "often I could not talk. Language left me. I was in the place before I had any language. The abandoned place" (162–63). She regresses, "finding myself on all fours shouting 'Mummy, Mummy'" (162); in the government office where she is applying to see her files, "I stumble on my words, hesitate, slow down and finally fall silent. The lost loss I experience as physical pain is prelanguage. That loss happened before I could speak, and I return to that place, speechless" (191).

Her account of her symptoms and her theory of their cause—maternal abandonment when her birthmother relinquished her at six weeks of age—adheres closely to Nancy Verrier's "primal wound" and related models of adoption trauma discussed briefly in this book's introduction and in chapter 2. According to these models, adoption is inherently traumatic and creates a wound or hole in the subject; denial makes it worse and prompts intrusions into the present; and the only cure is the discovery of the truth about the past and contact with the adoptee's origins. I have tried to suggest how and why such claims may be misleading and what—on the evidence of fiction and memoirs about adoption and searches—might offer more effective help: not an unavailing search for the past but instead self-creation, the invention of a new story about identity in the present. It would be possible to read Winterson here through the critical lens supplied by, among others, Kimberly Leighton, whose critique of "genealogical bewilderment" implies a critique as well of the "primal wound." Winterson's misery, it could be argued, came not from any original maternal abandonment but instead from the social biases against adoption that prevented her adoptive mother from adequately connecting with her. The often repeated phrase "the wrong crib"—emphasizing that her parents made a mistake when they got her from the orphanage—is the summary phrase with which Winterson indicates her mother's insistence on Jeanette's strangeness and her status as stranger in the family. When the teenaged Jeanette falls in love with one girl and then another, the Pentecostal community, along with Mrs W, treats her as if she were the devil incarnate. But whether or not there was a primal wound, Winterson believes there was: "The baby knows it has been abandoned—I am sure of that" (*Why Be Happy*, 180). What is interesting is what she makes of it.

At a climactic moment in her search, a social worker tells her that she was breastfed for six weeks, proving beyond a doubt that she was loved and wanted, and then hands her a piece of paper with her birthmother's and her own original names on it. About the emotional impact of reading these long-sought names she reflects: "The names read like runes. / Written on the body is a secret code only visible in certain lights" (*Why Be Happy*, 185). Winterson implies that though the names are in one sense meaningless ("runes"), in the context of learning she was breastfed—"when she gave you up . . . you were still part of her body" (184)—they also meaningfully translate an identifying mark or "secret code" on her body. Unlike some adoptees whose writings we have surveyed, Winterson never focuses on her appearance or wishes for the company of those she resembles (she yearns instead for love, regardless of physical similarity). Yet here she claims a corporeal tie of the kind discussed in chapter 3: something like the birthmarks and scars that adoptees feel identify them by connecting them to the lost past. Like Gerald Wozek with his birthmark, for example, Winterson describes a mark that recalls simultaneously her bodily connection to her first mother and the wounding loss of that first tie. Like Wozek, like the mothers in Xinran's *Message from an Unknown Chinese Mother*, she shares the wound that is also a "code" with her birthmother: "My mother had to sever some part of herself to let me go. I have felt the wound ever since" (220). Yet the phrase "written on the body" recalls something else, too: it is the title of one of Winterson's novels, a novel in which physical appearance matters a great deal but in which the gender of the first-person protagonist is unknowable.[3] "Written on the body," in the context of Winterson's own literary history, doesn't only suggests the inscrutability of the body's signs; her use of the phrase in this context also defines the "secret code" as her own writing, even though, paradoxically, it was inscribed on her body by her birth parents.

"The imprint of another life": Whose story is it? Who makes an imprint on whom? The phrasing at the opening of Winterson's book implies that the adoptee is written upon; the "imprint" is "the fossil record" of "the missing past." And yet it is up to her to "trace the space where it might have been" and in the process to move from reading to writing: "There are markings here, raised like welts. Read them. Read the hurt. Rewrite them. Rewrite the hurt" (*Why Be Happy*, 5). And this, she says, is "why I am a writer." Written on the body is, in the end, her own writing. There is no story—no "imprint"—unless she writes it.

As Winterson moves through the "process of looking for your other life" (*Why Be Happy*, 179), eventually meeting her birthmother, her half siblings, and a large and accepting family, she contemplates the "forking paths" that could have led to a different life, one in which she might have married and had children instead of becoming a lesbian and a writer. ("What if I hadn't had to fight for a girlfriend, fight for myself?" [215].) "And yet there feels like an inevitability to who I am" (209), she writes, much as Emily Hipchen can't picture the other self she might have become. Although Winterson wants to honor her birthmother's palpable regrets,

> I would rather be this me—the me that I have become—than the me I might have become without books, without education, and without all the things that have happened to me along the way, including Mrs W. (*Why Be Happy*, 228)

In this coda to her memoir, she claims finally, "I think I am lucky."

In a last chapter, titled "The Wound," Winterson reaffirms the "me" she has created on the basis of what she sees as her wound, by identifying it with famous identity-conferring wounds in literary history. Odysseus comes first ("his wife recognizes him by the scar on his thigh" [*Why Be Happy*, 220]), then Chiron and Prometheus; Jesus's wound that enables

3. Jeanette Winterson, *Written on the Body* (London: Jonathan Cape, 1992).

doubting Thomas to know him; the never-healing wound in Gulliver's knee that "is the reminder of another life" (221); Harry Potter; and finally Oedipus, whose story "is an adoption story and a wound story too" (222), as I have argued in chapter 3. Reading these stories, she notices "value here as well as agony" for those "marked out" by their wounds; the wound is always a source of "difference" and of recognizability: "it is a blood-trail" (221–22). Concluding this sequence, she claims for her own wounded condition, "All my life I have worked from the wound. To heal it would mean an end to one identity—the defining identity." Even were she to heal it, "there will always be a scar. I will always be recognisable by my scar" (223). She thus locates herself (her fictional self, which is also her real self) in august fictional company: Jeanette joins Odysseus and Oedipus in bearing a scar that is also a "gift," a scar that marks who she is. As when the writing on her body turns out to be her own writing, the scar she lays claim to is literature's scar, because her person, like her story, is "both real and invented" (186). To recall the discovery she affirmed when she entered Oxford, literature is her "birthright," and not only because she, a working-class northern girl, is entitled to read all the books in the Bodleian; she is also born from books. Jeanette's "heredity" is the rich heritage of English and European literary history, and by creating herself as a character who writes, she writes her own origin and place in literary history, the family lineage that matters most to her.

Each chapter of this book has ended by celebrating a writer or writers who recuperate their struggles with adoption through literary (or in one case, cinematic) self-creation. Chapter 2 argues that an adoptee's actual, much-desired origins cannot be recovered, but that origins can be satisfactorily invented, and it ends with memoirs of disappointing return journeys that nonetheless reaffirm the creative power of the memoirist. Chapter 3 argues that adoptees wishing in vain to "look like what [they] are" may instead form identities based on the visual traces of loss itself, and it ends with Catherine McKinley turning indigo markings into a resource for the writer's self-creation. Even Henry James's unparented Maisie Farange, not literally a writer, takes possession of her story at the novel's end to serve as chapter 1's figure of the artist who "profits" from becoming the narrator of her own life. Finally, chapter 4 analyzes the cultural silencing of birthmothers and celebrates birthmother-writers who have created distinctive literary modes out of the challenges posed to their voices, selves, and stories. By closing with this reading of Winterson, I highlight the creativity that can be prompted by adoption's challenges. I began the research for this book because of a series of negative experiences: my anger at the sanctimonious acquaintance who remarked to me—an adoptive mother—that she (the mother of two biological children) would never pay money for a child; my dismay at what I saw as the harmful "therapeutic" teaching of grief to the youngest adoptees; and my astonishment at the prominent role played by race, racism, and genetic essentialism in adoption. I set out to write the book wanting to warn against needlessly manufactured pain and against illusions that lead to emotional dead ends. I came to appreciate that, however illusory its causes, the pain associated with adoption is real for many adoptees, birthmothers, and those who love them. The writing of this book has ended in the most positive way, with my ever-increasing admiration for the adoptees and birthmothers (and, too, for some creative writers who have sympathetically imagined them) who have written their way through and beyond those struggles to make something very new out of "the imprint of another life."

Index